ROBERT POLLOK. A.M.

Boston, Phillips & Sampson

THOMSON AND POLLOK:

CONTAINING THE

SEASONS,

BY JAMES THOMSON,

AND THE

COURSE OF TIME,

BY ROBERT POLLOK, A.M.

A NEW EDITION.

BOSTON:
PHILLIPS, SAMPSON, AND COMPANY
110 WASHINGTON STREET.
1850.

SPRING.

The subject proposed. Inscribed to the Countess of Hertford. The Season is described as it affects the various parts of Nature, ascending from the lower to the higher; with digressions arising from the subject. Its influence on inanimate Matter, on Vegetables, on brute Animals, and last on Man; concluding with a dissuasive from the wild and irregular passion of Love, opposed to that of a pure and happy kind.

Come, gentle Spring, ethereal Mildness, come,
And from the bosom of yon dropping cloud,
While music wakes around, veil'd in a shower
Of shadowing roses, on our plains descend.
O Hertford, fitted or to shine in courts
With unaffected grace, or walk the plain
With innocence and meditation join'd
In soft assemblage, listen to my song,
Which thy own Season paints; when Nature all
Is blooming and benevolent, like thee.
And see where surly Winter passes off,
Far to the north, and calls his ruffian blasts:
His blasts obey, and quit the howling hill,
The shatter'd forest, and the ravaged vale;
While softer gales succeed, at whose kind touch,
Dissolving snows in livid torrents lost,
The mountains lift their green heads to the sky
As yet the trembling year is unconfirm'd,
And Winter oft at eve resumes the breeze,
Chills the pale morn, and bids his driving sleets
Deform the day delightless: so that scarce
The bittern knows his time, with bill ingulf'd,
To shake the sounding marsh; or from the shore
The plovers when to scatter o'er the heath,
And sing their wild notes to the listening waste.

At last from Aries rolls the bounteous sun,
And the bright Bull receives him. Then no more
The' expansive atmosphere is cramp'd with cold;
But, full of life and vivifying soul,
Lifts the light clouds sublime, and spreads them thin,
Fleecy, and white o'er all surrounding heaven.
Forth fly the tepid airs; and unconfined,
Unbinding earth, the moving softness strays.
Joyous, the' impatient husbandman perceives
Relenting Nature, and his lusty steers
Drives from their stalls, to where the well used plough
Lies in the furrow, loosen'd from the frost.
There unrefusing, to the harness'd yoke,
They lend their shoulder, and begin their toil,
Cheer'd by the simple song and soaring lark.
Meanwhile incumbent o'er the shining share
The master leans, removes the' obstructing clay,
Winds the whole work, and sidelong lays the glebe.
While thro' the neighbouring fields the sower stalks,
With measured step; and liberal throws the grain
Into the faithful bosom of the ground:
The harrow follows harsh, and shuts the scene.
Be gracious, Heaven! for now laborious man
Has done his part. Ye fostering breezes, blow;
Ye softening dews, ye tender showers, descend!
And temper all, thou world-reviving sun,
Into the perfect year! Nor ye who live
In luxury and ease, in pomp and pride,
Think these lost themes, unworthy of your ear:
Such themes as these the rural Maro sung
To wide-imperial Rome, in the full height
Of elegance and taste, by Greece refined.
In ancient times, the sacred plough employ'd
The kings, and awful fathers of mankind:
And some, with whom compared your insect tribes
Are but the beings of a summer's day,
Have held the scale of empire, ruled the storm
Of mighty war; then, with unwearied hand,

Disdaining little delicacies, seized
The plough, and greatly independent lived.
  Ye generous Britons, venerate the plough!
And o'er your hills and long withdrawing vales
Let Autumn spread his treasures to the sun,
Luxuriant and unbounded: as the sea,
Far through his azure turbulent domain,
Your empire owns, and from a thousand shores
Wafts all the pomp of life into your ports;
So with superior boon may your rich soil,
Exuberant, Nature's better blessings pour
O'er every land, the naked nations clothe,
And be the' exhaustless granary of a world!
  Nor only through the lenient air this change,
Delicious, breathes; the penetrative sun,
His force deep darting to the dark retreat
Of vegetation, sets the steaming Power
At large, to wander o'er the verdant earth,
In various hues; but chiefly thee, gay green!
Thou smiling Nature's universal robe!
United light and shade! where the sight dwells
With growing strength and ever new delight.
  From the moist meadow to the wither'd hill,
Led by the breeze, the vivid verdure runs,
And swells and deepens to the cherish'd eye.
The hawthorn whitens; and the juicy groves
Put forth their buds, unfolding by degrees,
Till the whole leafy forest stands display'd,
In full luxuriance, to the sighing gales;
Where the deer rustle through the twining brake,
And the birds sing conceal'd. At once array'd
In all the colours of the flushing year,
By Nature's swift and secret working hand,
The garden flows, and fills the liberal air
With lavish fragrance; while the promised fruit
Lies yet a little embryo, unperceived,
Within its crimson folds. Now from the town,
Buried in smoke and sleep and noisome damps,

Oft let me wander o'er the dewy fields,
Where freshness breathes, and dash the trembling drops
From the bent bush, as through the verdant maze
Of sweetbriar hedges I pursue my walk;
Or taste the smell of dairy; or ascend
Some eminence, Augusta, in thy plains,
And see the country, far diffused around,
One boundless blush, one white-empurpled shower
Of mingled blossoms; where the raptured eye
Hurries from joy to joy, and, hid beneath
The fair profusion, yellow Autumn spies.
If, brush'd from Russian wilds, a cutting gale
Rise not, and scatter from his humid wings
The clammy mildew; or, dry blowing, breathe
Untimely frost; before whose baleful blast
The full blown Spring through all her foliage shrinks
Joyless and dead, a wide dejected waste.
For oft, engender'd by the hazy north,
M,riads on myriads, insect armies waft
Keen in the poison'd breeze; and wasteful eat,
Through buds and bark, into the blacken'd core,
Their eager way. A feeble race! yet oft
The sacred sons of vengeance; on whose course
Corrosive Famine waits, and kills the year.
To check this plague, the skilful farmer chaff
And blazing straw before his orchard burns;
Till, all involved in smoke, the latent foe
From every cranny suffocated falls:
Or scatters o'er the blooms the pungent dust
Of pepper, fatal to the frosty tribe:
Or, when the' envenom'd leaf begins to curl,
With sprinkled water drowns them in their nest:
Nor, while they pick them up with busy bill,
The little trooping birds unwisely scares.
Be patient, swains; these cruel-seeming winds
Blow not in vain. Far hence they keep repress'd
Those deepening clouds on clouds, surcharged with rain,
That o'er the vast Atlantic hither borne,

In endless train, would quench the summer blaze,
And, cheerless, drown the crude unripen'd year.
 The north-east spends his rage; he now shut up
Within his iron cave, the' effusive south
Warms the wide air, and o'er the void of heaven
Breathes the big clouds with vernal showers distent.
As first a dusky wreath they seem to rise,
Scarce staining ether; but, by swift degrees,
In heaps on heaps, the doubling vapour sails
Along the loaded sky, and mingling deep
Sits on the' horizon round a settled gloom:
Not such as wintry storms on mortals shed,
Oppressing life; but lovely, gentle, kind,
And full of every hope and every joy,
The wish of Nature. Gradual sinks the breeze
Into a perfect calm; that not a breath
Is heard to quiver through the closing woods,
Or rustling turn the many-twinkling leaves
Of aspen tall. The' uncurling floods, diffused
In glassy breadth, seem through delusive lapse
Forgetful of their course. 'Tis silence all,
And pleasing expectation. Herds and flocks
Drop the dry sprig, and mute imploring eye
The falling verdure. Hush'd in short suspense,
The plumy people streak their wings with oil,
To throw the lucid moisture trickling off:
And wait the' approaching sign to strike, at once,
Into the general choir. Even mountains, vales,
And forests seem impatient to demand
The promised sweetness. Man superior walks
Amid the glad creation, musing praise,
And looking lively gratitude. At last,
The clouds consign their treasures to the fields;
And, softly shaking on the dimpled pool
Prelusive drops, let all their moisture flow,
In large effusion, o'er the freshen'd world.
The stealing shower is scarce to patter heard,
By such as wander through the forest walks,

Beneath the' umbrageous multitude of leaves.
But who can hold the shade while Heaven descends
In universal bounty, shedding herbs
And fruits and flowers on Nature's ample lap!
Swift Fancy fired anticipates their growth;
And, while the milky nutriment distils,
Beholds the kindling country colour round.
  Thus all day long the full distended clouds
Indulge their genial stores, and well shower'd earth
Is deep enrich'd with vegetable life;
Till, in the western sky, the downward sun
Looks out, effulgent, from amid the flush
Of broken clouds, gay-shifting to his beam.
The rapid radiance instantaneous strikes
The' illumined mountain, through the forest streams,
Shakes on the floods, and in a yellow mist,
Far smoking o'er the' interminable plain,
In twinkling myriads lights the dewy gems.
Moist, bright, and green, the landscape laughs around
Full swell the woods; their very music wakes,
Mix'd in wild concert with the warbling brooks
Increased, the distant bleatings of the hills,
And hollow lows responsive from the vales,
Whence blending, all the sweeten'd zephyr springs.
Meantime, refracted from yon eastern cloud,
Bestriding earth, the grand ethereal bow
Shoots up immense; and every hue unfolds,
In fair proportion running from the red
To where the violet fades into the sky.
Here, awful Newton, the dissolving clouds
Form, fronting on the sun, thy showery prism;
And to the sage-instructed eye unfold
The various twine of light, by thee disclosed
From the white mingling maze. Not so the boy:
He wondering views the bright enchantment bend,
Delightful, o'er the radiant fields, and runs
To catch the falling glory; but amazed
Beholds the' amusive arch before him fly,

Then vanish quite away. Still night succeeds,
A soften'd shade, and saturated earth
Awaits the morning beam, to give to light,
Raised through ten thousand different plastic tubes,
The balmy treasures of the former day.
Then spring the living herbs, profusely wild,
O'er all the deep-green earth, beyond the power
Of botanists to number up their tribes:
Whether he steals along the lonely dale,
In silent search; or through the forest, rank
With what the dull incurious weeds account,
Bursts his blind way; or climbs the mountain rock,
Fired by the nodding verdure of its brow.
With such a liberal hand has Nature flung
Their seeds abroad, blown them about in winds,
Innumerous mix'd them with the nursing mould,
The moistening current, and prolific rain.
But who their virtues can declare? who pierce,
With vision pure, into these secret stores
Of health and life and joy? the food of Man,
While yet he lived in innocence, and told
A length of golden years; unflesh'd in blood,
A stranger to the savage arts of life,
Death, rapine, carnage, surfeit, and disease,
The lord, and not the tyrant, of the world.
The first fresh dawn then waked the gladden'd race
Of uncorrupted Man, nor blush'd to see
The sluggard sleep beneath its sacred beam;
For their light slumbers gently fumed away;
And up they rose as vigorous as the sun,
Or to the culture of the willing glebe
Or to the cheerful tendance of the flock:
Meantime the song went round; and dance and sport,
Wisdom and friendly talk, successive, stole
Their hours away: while in the rosy vale
Love breathed his infant sighs, from anguish free,
And full replete with bliss; save the sweet pain,
That, inly thrilling, but exalts it more

Nor yet injurious act, nor surly deed,
Was known among those happy sons of heaven;
For reason and benevolence were law.
Harmonious Nature too look'd smiling on.
Clear shone the skies, cool'd with eternal gales,
And balmy spirit all. The youthful sun
Shot his best rays, and still the gracious clouds
Dropp'd fatness down; as o'er the swelling mead,
The herds and flocks, commixing, play'd secure.
This when, emergent from the gloomy wood,
The glaring lion saw, his horrid heart
Was meeken'd, and he join'd his sullen joy
For music held the whole in perfect peace:
Soft sigh'd the flute; the tender voice was heard,
Warbling the varied heart; the woodlands round
Applied their choir; and winds and waters flow'd
In consonance. Such were those prime of days.
 But now those white unblemish'd manners, whence
The fabling poets took their golden age,
Are found no more amid these iron times,
These dregs of life! now the distemper'd mind
Has lost that concord of harmonious powers,
Which forms the soul of happiness; and all
Is off the poise within: the passions all
Have burst their bounds; and reason, half extinct,
Or impotent, or else approving, sees
The foul disorder. Senseless, and deform'd,
Convulsive anger storms at large; or, pale
And silent, settles into fell revenge.
Base envy withers at another's joy,
And hates that excellence it cannot reach
Desponding fear, of feeble fancies full,
Weak and unmanly, loosens every power
E'en love itself is bitterness of soul,
A pensive anguish pining at the heart;
Or, sunk to sordid interest, feels no more
That noble wish that never cloy'd desire,
Which, selfish joy disdaining, seeks alone

To bless the dearer object of its flame.
Hope sickens with extravagance ; and grief,
Of life impatient, into madness swells ;
Or in dead silence wastes the weeping hours.
These, and a thousand mix'd emotions more,
From ever changing views of good and ill
Form'd infinitely various, vex the mind
With endless storm ; whence, deeply rankling grows
The partial thought, a listless unconcern,
Cold, and averting from our neighbour's good ;
Then dark disgust, and hatred, winding wiles,
Coward deceit, and ruffian violence :
At last, extinct each social feeling, fell
And joyless inhumanity pervades
And petrifies the heart. Nature disturb'd
Is deem'd, vindictive, to have changed her course.

Hence, in old dusky time, a deluge came :
When the deep-cleft disparting orb, that arch'd
The central waters round, impetuous rush'd,
With universal burst, into the gulf,
And o'er the high-piled hills of fractured earth
Wide dash'd the waves, in undulation vast ;
Till, from the centre to the streaming clouds,
A shoreless ocean tumbled round the globe.

The Seasons since have, with severer sway,
Oppress'd a broken world : the Winter keen
Shook forth his waste of snows : and Summer shot
His pestilential heats. Great Spring, before,
Green'd all the year ; and fruits and blossoms blush'd,
In social sweetness, on the selfsame bough.
Pure was the temperate air ; an even calm
Perpetual reign'd, save what the zephyrs bland
Breathed o'er the blue expanse : for then nor storms
Were taught to blow nor hurricanes to rage ;
Sound slept the waters ; no sulphureous glooms
Swell'd in the sky, and sent the lightning forth ;
While sickly damps, and cold autumnal fogs,
Hung not, relaxing, on the springs of life.

But now, of turbid elements the sport,
From clear to cloudy toss'd, from hot to cold,
And dry to moist, with inward-eating change,
Our drooping days are dwindled down to nought,
Their period finish'd ere 'tis well begun.
  And yet the wholesome herb neglected dies;
Though with the pure exhilarating soul
Of nutriment and health and vital powers,
Beyond the search of art, 'tis copious bless'd.
For, with hot ravine fired, ensanguined Man
Is now become the lion of the plain,
And worse. The wolf, who from the nightly fold
Fierce drags the bleating prey, ne'er drunk her milk,
Nor wore her warming fleece: nor has the steer,
At whose strong chest the deadly tiger hangs,
E'er plough'd for him. They too are temper'd high,
With hunger stung and wild necessity,
Nor lodges pity in their shaggy breast
But Man, whom Nature form'd of milder clay,
With every kind emotion in his heart,
And taught alone to weep; while from her lap
She pours ten thousand delicacies, herbs,
And fruits, as numerous as the drops of rain
Or beams that gave them birth: shall he, fair form!
Who wears sweet smiles, and looks erect on heaven,
E'er stoop to mingle with the prowling herd,
And dip his tongue in gore? the beast of prey,
Blood-stain'd, deserves to bleed; but you, ye flocks,
What have you done; ye peaceful people, what,
To merit death? you, who have given us milk
In luscious streams, and lent us your own coat
Against the Winter's cold? and the plain ox,
That harmless, honest, guileless animal,
In what has he offended? he, whose toil,
Patient, and ever ready, clothes the land
With all the pomp of harvest; shall he bleed,
And struggling groan beneath the cruel hands
Even of the clown he feeds? and that, perhaps,

To swell the riot of the' autumnal feast,
Won by his labour? thus the feeling heart
Would tenderly suggest: but 'tis enough,
In this late age, adventurous, to have touch'd
Light on the numbers of the Samian sage.
High Heaven forbids the bold presumptuous strain,
Whose wisest will has fix'd us in a state
That must not yet to pure perfection rise.
  Now when the first foul torrent of the brooks,
Swell'd with the vernal rains, is ebb'd away,
And, whitening, down their mossy-tinctured stream
Descends the billowy foam: now is the time,
While yet the dark-brown water aids the guile,
To tempt the trout. The well dissembled fly,
The rod fine-tapering with elastic spring,
Snatch'd from the hoary steed the floating line,
And all thy slender watery stores prepare.
But let not on thy hook the tortured worm
Convulsive twist in agonizing folds;
Which, by rapacious hunger swallow'd deep,
Gives, as you tear it from the bleeding breast
Of the weak, helpless, uncomplaining wretch,
Harsh pain and horror to the tender hand.
  When with his lively ray the potent sun
Has pierced the streams, and roused the finny race,
Then, issuing cheerful, to thy sport repair;
Chief should the western breezes curling play,
And light o'er ether bear the shadowy clouds.
High to their fount, this day, amid the hills,
And woodlands warbling round, trace up the brooks,
The next, pursue their rocky-channel'd maze
Down to the river, in whose ample wave
Their little naiads love to sport at large.
Just in the dubious point, where with the pool
Is mix'd the trembling stream, or where it boils
Around the stone, or from the hallow'd bank
Reverted plays in undulating flow,
There throw, nice judging, the delusive fly;

And, as you lead it round in artful curve,
With eye attentive mark the springing game.
Straight as above the surface of the flood
They wanton rise, or urged by hunger leap,
Then fix, with gentle twitch, the barbed hook:
Some lightly tossing to the grassy bank,
And to the shelving shore slow dragging some,
With various hand proportion'd to their force.
If yet too young, and easily deceived,
A worthless prey scarce bends your pliant rod,
Him, piteous of his youth and the short space
He has enjoy'd the vital light of heaven.
Soft disengage, and back into the stream
The speckled captive throw. But should you lure
From his dark haunt, beneath the tangled roots
Of pendent trees, the monarch of the brook,
Behoves you then to ply your finest art.
Long time he, following cautious, scans the fly;
And oft attempts to seize it, but as oft
The dimpled water speaks his jealous fear.
At last, while haply o'er the shaded sun
Passes a cloud, he desperate takes the death,
With sullen plunge. At once he darts along
Deep-struck, and runs out all the lengthen'd line:
Then seeks the furthest ooze, the sheltering weed,
The cavern'd bank, his old secure abode;
And flies aloft, and flounces round the pool,
Indignant of the guile. With yielding hand,
That feels him still, yet to his furious course
Gives way, you, now retiring, following now
Across the stream, exhaust his idle rage:
Till, floating broad upon his breathless side,
And to his fate abandon'd, to the shore
You gaily drag your unresisting prize.
  Thus pass the temperate hours; but when the sun
Shakes from his noonday throne the scattering clouds,
Even shooting listless languor through the deeps;
Then seek the bank where flowering elders crowd,

Where scatter'd wild the lily of the vale
Its balmy essence breathes, where cowslips hang
The dewy head, where purple violets lurk,
With all the lowly children of the shade:
Or lie reclined beneath yon spreading ash,
Hung o'er the steep; whence, borne on liquid wing,
The sounding culver shoots; or where the hawk,
High in the beetling cliff, his eyry builds.
There let the classic page thy fancy lead
Through rural scenes; such as the Mantuan swain
Paints in the matchless harmony of song,
Or catch thyself the landscape, gliding swift
Athwart imagination's vivid eye:
Or by the vocal woods and waters lull'd,
And lost in lonely musing, in the dream,
Confused, of careless solitude, where mix
Ten thousand wandering images of things,
Sooth every gust of passion into peace;
All but the swellings of the soften'd heart,
That weaken, not disturb, the tranquil mind.
Behold yon breathing prospect bids the Muse
Throw all her beauty forth. But who can paint
Like Nature? Can imagination boast,
Amid its gay creation, hues like hers?
Or can it mix them with that matchless skill,
And lose them in each other, as appears
In every bud that blows? If fancy then
Unequal fails beneath the pleasing task,
Ah, what shall language do? Ah, where find words
Tinged with so many colours; and whose power,
To life approaching, may perfume my lays
With that fine oil, those aromatic gales,
That inexhaustive flow continual round?
Yet, though successless, will the toil delight.
Come then, ye virgins and ye youths, whose hearts
Have felt the raptures of refining love;
And thou, Amanda, come, pride of my song!
Form'd by the Graces, loveliness itself!

Come with those downcast eyes, sedate and sweet,
Those looks demure, that deeply pierce the soul,
Where, with the light of thoughtful reason mix'd,
Shines lively fancy and the feeling heart:
Oh, come! and while the rosy-footed May
Steals blushing on, together let us tread
The morning dews, and gather in their prime
Fresh-blooming flowers, to grace thy braided hair,
And thy loved bosom that improves their sweets.
  See, where the winding vale its lavish stores,
Irriguous, spreads. See, how the lily drinks
The latent rill, scarce oozing through the grass,
Of growth luxuriant; or the humid bank,
In fair profusion, decks. Long let us walk,
Where the breeze blows from yon extended field
Of blossom'd beans. Arabia cannot boast
A fuller gale of joy, than, liberal, thence
Breathes through the sense, and takes the ravish'd soul.
Nor is the mead unworthy of thy foot,
Full of fresh verdure and unnumber'd flowers,
The negligence of Nature, wide and wild;
Where, undisguised by mimic Art, she spreads
Unbounded beauty to the roving eye.
Here their delicious task the fervent bees,
In swarming millions, tend: around, athwart,
Through the soft air, the busy nations fly,
Cling to the bud, and, with inserted tube,
Suck its pure essence, its ethereal soul;
And oft, with bolder wing, they soaring dare
The purple heath, or where the wild thyme grows,
And yellow load them with the luscious spoil.
  At length the finish'd garden to the view
Its vistas opens, and its alleys green.
Snatch'd through the verdant maze, the hurried eye
Distracted wanders; now the bowery walk
Of covert close, where scarce a speck of day
Falls on the lengthen'd gloom, protracted sweeps.
Now meets the bending sky; the river now

Dimpling along, the breezy ruffled lake,
The forest darkening round, the glittering spire,
The' ethereal mountain, and the distant main.
But why so far excursive; when at hand,
Along these blushing borders, bright with dew,
And in yon mingled wilderness of flowers,
Fair-handed Spring unbosoms every grace;
Throws out the snowdrop and the crocus first
The daisy, primrose, violet darkly blue,
And polyanthus of unnumber'd dyes;
The yellow wallflower, stain'd with iron brown;
And lavish stock that scents the garden round:
From the soft wing of vernal breezes shed,
Anemones; auriculas, enrich'd
With shining meal o'er all their velvet leaves;
And full ranunculas of glowing red.
Then comes the tulip race, where Beauty plays
Her idle freaks; from family diffused
To family, as flies the father dust,
The varied colours run; and, while they break
On the charm'd eye, the' exulting florist marks,
With secret pride, the wonders of his hand.
No gradual bloom is wanting; from the bud,
Firstborn of Spring, to Summer's musky tribes.
Nor hyacinths, of purest virgin white,
Low-bent, and blushing inward; nor jonquilles,
Of potent fragrance; nor narcissus fair,
As o'er the fabled fountain hanging still;
Nor broad carnations, nor gay spotted pinks;
Nor, shower'd from every bush, the damask rose.
Infinite numbers, delicacies, smells,
With hues on hues expression cannot paint,
The breath of Nature, and her endless bloom.
  Hail, Source of Being! Universal Soul
Of heaven and earth! Essential Presence, hail!
To Thee I bend the knee; to Thee my thoughts,
Continual, climb; who, with a master hand,
Hast the great whole into perfection touch'd.

By Thee the various vegetative tribes,
Wrapp'd in a filmy net and clad with leaves,
Draw the live ether and imbibe the dew;
By Thee disposed into congenial soils,
Stands each attractive plant, and sucks and swells
The juicy tide; a twining mass of tubes.
At Thy command the vernal sun awakes
The torpid sap, detruded to the root
By wintry winds; that now, in fluent dance,
And lively fermentation mounting, spreads
All this innumerous-colour'd scene of things.
  As rising from the vegetable world
My theme ascends, with equal wing ascend,
My panting Muse; and hark, how loud the woods
Invite you forth in all your gayest trim.
Lend me your song, ye nightingales! oh, pour
The mazy-running soul of melody
Into my varied verse! while I deduce,
From the first note the hollow cuckoo sings,
The symphony of Spring, and touch a theme
Unknown to fame,—the Passion of the Groves.
  When first the soul of love is sent abroad,
Warm through the vital air, and on the heart
Harmonious seizes, the gay troops begin,
In gallant thought, to plume the painted wing;
And try again the long forgotten strain,
At first faint warbled. But no sooner grows
The soft infusion prevalent and wide,
Than, all alive, at once their joy o'erflows
In music unconfined. Up springs the lark,
Shrill-voiced and loud, the messenger of morn;
Ere yet the shadows fly, he mounted sings
Amid the dawning clouds, and from their haunts
Calls up the tuneful nations. Every copse
Deep tangled, tree irregular, and bush
Bending with dewy moisture, o'er the heads
Of the coy quiristers that lodge within,
Are prodigal of harmony. The thrush

And woodlark, o'er the kind contending throng
Superior heard, run through the sweetest length
Of notes; when listening Philomela deigns
To let them joy, and purposes, in thought
Elate, to make her night excel their day.
The blackbird whistles from the thorny brake;
The mellow bullfinch answers from the grove:
Nor are the linnets, o'er the flowering furze
Pour'd out profusely, silent. Join'd to these
Innumerous songsters, in the freshening shade
Of new-sprung leaves, their modulations mix
Mellifluous. The jay, the rook, the daw,
And each harsh pipe, discordant heard alone,
Aid the full concert: while the stockdove breathes
A melancholy murmur through the whole.
'Tis love creates their melody, and all
This waste of music is the voice of love;
That even to birds and beasts the tender arts
Of pleasing teaches. Hence the glossy kind
Try every winning way inventive love
Can dictate, and in courtship to their mates
Pour forth their little souls. First, wide around,
With distant awe, in airy rings they rove,
Endeavouring by a thousand tricks to catch
The cunning, conscious, half averted glance
Of the regardless charmer. Should she seem
Softening the least approvance to bestow,
Their colours burnish, and, by hope inspired,
They brisk advance; then, on a sudden struck,
Retire disorder'd; then again approach;
In fond rotation spread the spotted wing,
And shiver every feather with desire.
Connubial leagues agreed, to the deep woods
They haste away, all as their fancy leads,
Pleasure, or food, or secret safety prompts;
That Nature's great command may be obey'd:
Nor all the sweet sensations they perceive
Indulged in vain. Some to the holly hedge

Nestling repair, and to the thicket some;
Some to the rude protection of the thorn
Commit their feeble offspring. The cleft tree
Offers its kind concealment to a few,
Their food its insects, and its moss their nests.
Others apart, far in the grassy dale,
Or roughening waste, their humble texture weave.
But most in woodland solitudes delight,
In unfrequented glooms, or shaggy banks,
Steep, and divided by a babbling brook,
Whose murmurs sooth them all the livelong day,
When by kind duty fix'd. Among the roots
Of hazel, pendent o'er the plaintive stream,
They frame the first foundation of their domes;
Dry sprigs of trees, in artful fabric laid,
And bound with clay together. Now 'tis nought
But restless hurry through the busy air,
Beat by unnumber'd wings. The swallow sweeps
The slimy pool, to build his hanging house
Intent. And often, from the careless back
Of herds and flocks, a thousand tugging bills
Pluck hair and wool; and oft, when unobserved,
Steal from the barn a straw: till, soft and warm,
Clean and complete, their habitation grows.
  As thus the patient dam assiduous sits,
Not to be tempted from her tender task,
Or by sharp hunger or by smooth delight,
Though the whole loosen'd Spring around her blows,
Her sympathizing lover takes his stand
High on the' opponent bank, and ceaseless sings
The tedious time away; or else supplies
Her place a moment, while she sudden flits
To pick the scanty meal. The' appointed time
With pious toil fulfill'd, the callow young,
Warm'd and expanded into perfect life,
Their brittle bondage break, and come to light,
A helpless family, demanding food
With constant clamour: O, what passions then,

What melting sentiments of kindly care,
On the new parents seize! Away they fly
Affectionate, and undesiring bear
The most delicious morsel to their young,
Which equally distributed, again
The search begins. E'en so a gentle pair,
By fortune sunk, but form'd of generous mould,
And charm'd with cares beyond the vulgar breast,
In some lone cot amid the distant woods,
Sustain'd alone by providential Heaven,
Oft, as they weeping eye their infant train,
Check their own appetites, and give them all
 Nor toil alone they scorn; exalting love,
By the great Father of the Spring inspired,
Gives instant courage to the fearful race,
And, to the simple, art. With stealthy wing,
Should some rude foot their woody haunts molest,
Amid a neighbouring bush they silent drop,
And whirring thence, as if alarm'd, deceive
The' unfeeling schoolboy. Hence, around the head
Of wandering swain, the white-wing'd plover wheels
Her sounding flight, and then directly on
In long excursion skims the level lawn
To tempt him from her nest. The wild-duck, hence,
O'er the rough moss, and o'er the trackless waste
The heath-hen flutters, pious fraud. to lead
The hot pursuing spaniel far astray.
 Be not the Muse ashamed here to bemoan
Her brothers of the grove, by tyrant Man
Inhuman caught, and in the narrow cage
From liberty confined and boundless air.
Dull are the pretty slaves, their plumage dull,
Ragged, and all its brightening lustre lost;
Nor is that sprightly wildness in their notes,
Which, clear and vigorous, warbles from the beech.
O then, ye friends of love and love-taught song,
Spare the soft tribes, this barbarous art forbear

If on your bosom innocence can win,
Music engage, or piety persuade.
  But let not chief the nightingale lament
Her ruin'd care, too delicately framed
To brook the harsh confinement of the cage.
Oft when, returning with her loaded bill,
The astonish'd mother finds a vacant nest,
By the hard hands of unrelenting clowns
Robb'd, to the ground the vain provision falls;
Her pinions ruffle, and low-drooping scarce
Can bear the mourner to the poplar shade;
Where, all abandon'd to despair, she sings
Her sorrows through the night; and, on the bough,
Sole-sitting, still at every dying fall
Takes up again her lamentable strain
Of winding woe; till, wide around, the woods
Sigh to her song, and with her wail resound.
  But now the feather'd youth their former bounds,
Ardent, disdain; and, weighing oft their wings,
Demand the free possession of the sky:
This one glad office more, and then dissolves
Parental love at once, now needless grown.
Unlavish Wisdom never works in vain.
'Tis on some evening, sunny, grateful, mild,
When nought but balm is breathing through the woods,
With yellow lustre bright, that the new tribes
Visit the spacious heavens, and look abroad
On Nature's common, far as they can see,
Or wing, their range and pasture. O'er the boughs
Dancing about, still at the giddy verge
Their resolution fails; their pinions still,
In loose libration stretch'd, to trust the void
Trembling refuse: till down before them fly
The parent guides, and chide, exhort, command,
Or push them off. The surging air receives
Its plumy burden; and their self-taught wings
Winnow the waving element. On ground

Alighted, bolder up again they lead,
Farther and farther on, the lengthening flight,
Till vanish'd every fear, and every power
Roused into life and action, light in air
The' acquitted parents see their soaring race,
And once rejoicing never know them more.
  High from the summit of a craggy cliff,
Hung o'er the deep, such as amazing frowns
On utmost Kilda's* shore, whose lonely race
Resign the setting sun to Indian worlds,
The royal eagle draws his vigorous young,
Strong-pounced, and ardent with paternal fire.
Now fit to raise a kingdom of their own,
He drives them from his fort, the towering seat,
For ages, of his empire; which, in peace,
Unstain'd he holds, while many a league to sea
He wings his course, and preys in distant isles.
  Should I my steps turn to the rural seat,
Whose lofty elms and venerable oaks
Invite the rook, who high amid the boughs,
In early Spring, his airy city builds,
And ceaseless caws amusive; there, well pleased,
I might the various polity survey
Of the mix'd household kind. The careful hen
Calls all her chirping family around,
Fed and defended by the fearless cock;
Whose breast with ardour flames, as on he walks,
Graceful, and crows defiance. In the pond,
The finely checker'd duck, before her train,
Rows garrulous. The stately sailing swan
Gives out his snowy plumage to the gale;
And, arching proud his neck, with oary feet
Bears forward fierce, and guards his osier isle,
Protective of his young. The turkey nigh,
Loud threatening, reddens; while the peacock spreads,
His every-colour'd glory to the sun

* The furthest of the western islands of Scotland.

And swims in radiant majesty along
O'er the whole homely scene the cooing dove
Flies thick in amorous chase, and wanton rolls
The glancing eye, and turns the changeful neck.
While thus the gentle tenants of the shade
Indulge their purer loves, the rougher world
Of brutes below rush furious into flame
And fierce desire. Through all his lusty veins
The bull, deep-scorch'd, the raging passion feels.
Of pasture sick, and negligent of food,
Scarce seen, he wades among the yellow broom,
While o'er his ample sides the rambling sprays
Luxuriant shoot; or through the mazy wood
Dejected wanders, nor the' enticing bud
Crops, though it presses on his careless sense.
And oft, in jealous maddening fancy wrapp'd,
He seeks the fight; and, idly butting, feigns
His rival gored in every knotty trunk.
Him should he meet, the bellowing war begins;
Their eyes flash fury; to the hollow'd earth,
Whence the sand flies, they mutter bloody deeds,
And, groaning deep, the' impetuous battle mix:
While the fair heifer, balmy-breathing, near,
Stands kindling up their rage. The trembling steed,
With this hot impulse seized in every nerve,
Nor heeds the rein, nor hears the sounding thong:
Blows are not felt; but, tossing high his head.
And by the well known joy to distant plains
Attracted strong, all wild he bursts away;
O'er rocks and woods and craggy mountains flies:
And, neighing, on the' aerial summit takes
The' exciting gale; then, steep-descending, cleaves
The headlong torrents foaming down the hills,
E'en where the madness of the straiten'd stream
Turns in black eddies round: such is the force
With which his frantic heart and sinews swell.
Nor undelighted by the boundless Spring
Are the broad monsters of the foaming deep

From the deep ooze and gelid cavern roused,
They flounce and tumble in unwieldly joy.
Dire were the strain, and dissonant, to sing
The cruel raptures of the savage kind:
How by this flame their native wrath sublimed,
They roam, amid the fury of their heart,
The far resounding waste in fiercer bands,
And growl their horrid loves. But this the theme
I sing, enraptured, to the British Fair,
Forbids, and leads me to the mountain brow,
Where sits the shepherd on the grassy turf,
Inhaling, healthful, the descending sun.
Around him feeds his many-bleating flock,
Of various cadence; and his sportive lambs,
This way and that convolved, in friskful glee,
Their frolics play. And now the sprightly race
Invites them forth; when swift, the signal given,
They start away, and sweep the massy mound
That runs around the hill; the rampart once
Of iron war, in ancient barbarous times,
When disunited Britain ever bled,
Lost in eternal broil: ere yet she grew
To this deep-laid indissoluble state.
Where Wealth and Commerce lift their golden heads
And o'er our labours Liberty and Law,
Impartial, watch; the wonder of a world!
  What is this mighty breath, ye sages, say,
That, in a powerful language, felt, not heard,
Instructs the fowls of heaven? and through their breast
These arts of love diffuses? What, but God?
Inspiring God! who, boundless Spirit all,
And unremitting Energy, pervades,
Adjusts, sustains, and agitates the whole.
He ceaseless works alone; and yet alone
Seems not to work: with such perfection framed
Is this complex stupendous scheme of things.
But, though conceal'd, to every purer eye
The informing Author in his works appears:

Chief, lovely Spring, in thee, and thy soft scenes,
The Smiling God is seen; while water, earth,
And air attest his bounty; which exalts
The brute creation to this finer thought
And annual melts their undesigning hearts
Profusely thus in tenderness and joy.
Still let my song a nobler note assume,
And sing the' infusive force of Spring on man.
When heaven and earth, as if contending, vie
To raise his being and serene his soul,
Can he forbear to join the general smile
Of Nature? Can fierce passions vex his breast,
While every gale is peace, and every grove
Is melody? hence! from the bounteous walks
Of flowing Spring, ye sordid sons of earth,
Hard, and unfeeling of another's woe,
Or only lavish to yourselves; away!
But come, ye generous minds, in whose wide thought,
Of all his works, creative Bounty burns
With warmest beam; and on your open front
And liberal eye, sits, from his dark retreat
Inviting modest Want. Nor, till invoked,
Can restless goodness wait; your active search
Leaves no cold wintry corner unexplored;
Like silent-working Heaven, surprising oft
The lonely heart with unexpected good.
For you the roving Spirit of the wind
Blows Spring abroad; for you the teeming clouds
Descend in gladsome plenty o'er the world;
And the sun sheds his kindest rays for you,
Ye flower of human race! in these green days,
Reviving Sickness lifts her languid head;
Life flows afresh; and young-eyed Health exalts
The whole creation round. Contentment walks
The sunny glade, and feels an inward bliss
Spring o'er his mind, beyond the power of kings
To purchase. Pure serenity apace
Induces thought and contemplation still

By swift degrees the love of Nature works,
And warms the bosom; till at last, sublimed
To rapture and enthusiastic heat,
We feel the present Deity, and taste
The joy of GOD to see a happy world!
These are the sacred feelings of thy heart,
Thy heart inform'd by reason's purer ray,
O Lyttelton, the friend! thy passions thus
And meditations vary, as at large,
Courting the Muse, through Hagley Park thou stray'st;
Thy British Tempé! there along the dale,
With woods o'erhung, and shagg'd with mossy rocks,
Whence on each hand the gushing waters play,
And down the rough cascade white dashing fall,
Or gleam in lengthen'd vista through the trees,
You silent steal; or sit beneath the shade
Of solemn oaks, that tuft the swelling mounts
Thrown graceful round by nature's careless hand,
And pensive listen to the various voice
Of rural peace: the herds, the flocks, the birds,
The hollow-whispering breeze, the plaint of rills
That, purling down amid the twisted roots
Which creep around, their dewy murmurs shake
On the sooth'd ear. From these abstracted oft,
You wander through the philosophic world;
Where in bright train continual wonders rise,
Or to the curious or the pious eye.
And oft, conducted by historic truth,
You tread the long extent of backward time:
Planning, with warm benevolence of mind
And honest zeal, unwarp'd by party rage,
Britannia's weal; how from the venal gulf
To raise her virtue, and her arts revive.
Or, turning thence thy view, these graver thoughts
The Muses charm: while, with sure taste refined,
You draw the' inspiring breath of ancient song;
Till nobly rises, emulous, thy own.
Perhaps thy loved Lucinda shares thy walk,

With soul to thine attuned. Then Nature all
Wears to the lover's eye a look of love:
And all the tumult of a guilty world,
Toss'd by ungenerous passions, sinks away.
The tender heart is animated peace;
And as it pours its copious treasures forth,
In varied converse, softening every theme,
You, frequent pausing, turn, and from her eyes,
Where meeken'd sense, and amiable grace,
And lively sweetness dwell, enraptured, drink
That nameless spirit of ethereal joy,
Unutterable happiness! which love
Alone bestows, and on a favour'd few.
Meantime you gain the height, from whose fair brow
The bursting prospect spreads immense around:
And snatch'd o'er hill and dale, and wood and lawn,
And verdant field, and darkening heath between,
And villages embosom'd soft in trees,
And spiry towns by surging columns mark'd
Of household smoke, your eye excursive roams:
Wide-stretching from the hall, in whose kind haunt
The Hospitable Genius lingers still,
To where the broken landscape, by degrees
Ascending, roughens into rigid hills;
O'er which the Cambrian mountains, like far clouds
That skirt the blue horizon, dusky rise.
   Flush'd by the spirit of the genial year,
Now from the virgin's cheek a fresher bloom
Shoots, less and less, the live carnation round;
Her lips blush deeper sweets; she breathes of youth;
The shining moisture swells into her eyes,
In brighter flow; her wishing bosom heaves
With palpitations wild; kind tumults seize
Her veins, and all her yielding soul is love.
From the keen gaze her lover turns away,
Full of the dear ecstatic power, and sick
With sighing languishment. Ah then, ye fair!
Be greatly cautious of your sliding hearts

Dare not the' infectious sigh ; the pleading look,
Downcast and low, in meek submission dress'd,
But full of guile. Let not the fervent tongue,
Prompt to deceive, with adulation smooth,
Gain on your purposed will. Nor in the bower,
Where woodbines flaunt, and roses shed a couch,
While Evening draws her crimson curtains round,
Trust your soft minutes with betraying Man.
And let the' aspiring youth beware of love,
Of the smooth glance beware ; for 'tis too late,
When on his heart the torrent softness pours ;
Then wisdom prostrate lies, and fading fame
Dissolves in air away ; while the fond soul,
Wrapp'd in gay visions of unreal bliss,
Still paints the' illusive form ; the kindling grace ;
The' enticing smile ; the modest seeming eye,
Beneath whose beauteous beams, belying heaven,
Lurk searchless cunning, cruelty, and death :
And still, false-warbling in his cheated ear,
Her siren voice, enchanting, draws him on
To guileful shores and meads of fatal joy.
E'en present, in the very lap of love
Inglorious laid ; while music flows around,
Perfumes, and oils, and wine, and wanton hours ;
Amid the roses fierce Repentance rears
Her snaky crest ; a quick returning pang
Shoots through the conscious heart ; where honour still
And great design, against the' oppressive load
Of luxury, by fits, impatient heave.
But absent, what fantastic woes, aroused,
Rage in each thought, by restless musing fed,
Chill the warm cheek, and blast the bloom of life ?
Neglected fortune flies ; and, sliding swift,
Prone into ruin, fall his scorn'd affairs.
Tis nought but gloom around : the darken'd sun
Loses his light. The rosy-bosom'd Spring
To weeping fancy pines ; and yon bright arch,
Contracted, bends into a dusky vault

All Nature fades extinct; and she alone,
Heard, felt, and seen, possesses every thought,
Fills every sense, and pants in every vein.
Books are but formal dulness, tedious friends;
And sad amid the social band he sits,
Lonely, and inattentive. From his tongue
Th' unfinish'd period falls: while, borne away
On swelling thought, his wafted spirit flies
To the vain bosom of his distant fair;
And leaves the semblance of a lover, fix'd
In melancholy site, with head declined,
And love-dejected eyes. Sudden he starts,
Shook from his tender trance, and restless runs
To glimmering shades and sympathetic glooms;
Where the dun umbrage o'er the falling stream,
Romantic, hangs: there through the pensive dusk
Strays, in heart-thrilling meditation lost,
Indulging all to love: or on the bank
Thrown, amid drooping lilies, swells the breeze
With sighs unceasing, and the brook with tears.
Thus in soft anguish he consumes the day,
Nor quits his deep retirement, till the Moon
Peeps through the chambers of the fleecy east,
Enlighten'd by degrees, and in her train
Leads on the gentle Hours; then forth he walks,
Beneath the trembling languish of her beam,
With soften'd soul, and woos the bird of eve
To mingle woes with his: or, while the world
And all the sons of Care lie hush'd in sleep,
Associates with the midnight shadows drear;
And, sighing to the lonely taper, pours
His idly-tortured heart into the page,
Meant for the moving messenger of love;
Where rapture burns on rapture, every line
With rising frenzy fired. But if on bed
Delirious flung, sleep from his pillow flies,
All night he tosses, nor the balmy power
In any posture finds, till the gray Morn

Lifts her pale lustre on the paler wretch,
Exanimate by love ; and then perhaps
Exhausted Nature sinks awhile to rest,
Still interrupted by distracted dreams,
That o'er the sick imagination rise,
And in black colours paint the mimic scene.
Oft with the' enchantress of his soul he talks ;
Sometimes in crowds distress'd ; or if retired
To secret winding flower-enwoven bowers,
Far from the dull impertinence of Man,
Just as he, credulous, his endless cares
Begins to loose in blind oblivious love,
Snatch'd from her yielded hand, he knows not how,
Through forests huge, and long untravel'd heaths
With desolation brown, he wanders waste,
In night and tempest wrapp'd : or shrinks aghast,
Back, from the bending precipice ; or wades
The turbid stream below, and strives to reach
The further shore ; where succourless and sad,
She with extended arms his aid implores ;
But strives in vain ; borne by the' outrageous flood
To distance down, he rides the ridgy wave,
Or whelm'd beneath the boiling eddy sinks.
  These are the charming agonies of love,
Whose misery delights. But through the heart
Should jealousy its venom once diffuse,
'Tis then delightful misery no more,
But agony unmix'd, incessant gall,
Corroding every thought, and blasting all
Love's paradise. Ye fairy prospects, then,
Ye beds of roses, and ye bowers of joy,
Farewell ! ye gleamings of departed peace,
Shine out your last ! the yellow-tinging plague
Internal vision taints, and in a night
Of livid gloom imagination wraps.
Ah, then ! instead of love-enliven'd cheeks,
Of sunny features, and of ardent eyes
With flowing rapture bright, dark looks succeed,

Suffused and glaring with untender fire,
A clouded aspect, and a burning cheek,
Where the whole poison'd soul, malignant, sits,
And frightens love away. Ten thousand fears
Invented wild, ten thousand frantic views
Of horrid rivals, hanging on the charms
For which he melts in fondness, eat him up
With fervent anguish and consuming rage.
In vain reproaches lend their idle aid,
Deceitful pride, and resolution frail,
Giving false peace a moment. Fancy pours,
Afresh, her beauties on his busy thought,
Her first endearments twining round the soul,
With all the witchcraft of ensnaring love.
Straight the fierce storm involves his mind anew,
Flames through the nerves, and boils along the veins;
While anxious doubt distracts the tortured heart ·
For e'en the sad assurance of his fears
Were ease to what he feels. Thus the warm youth,
Whom love deludes into his thorny wilds,
Through flowery-tempting paths, or leads a life
Of fever'd rapture or of cruel care;
His brightest aims extinguish'd all, and all
His lively moments running down to waste.
But happy they! the happiest of their kind!
Whom gentler stars unite, and in one fate
Their hearts, their fortunes, and their beings blend.
'Tis not the coarser tie of human laws,
Unnatural oft and foreign to the mind,
That binds their peace, but harmony itself,
Attuning all their passions into love;
Where friendship full exerts her softest power,
Perfect esteem enlivened by desire
Ineffable, and sympathy of soul;
Thought meeting thought, and will preventing will,
With boundless confidence: for nought but love
Can answer love, and render bliss secure.
Let him, ungenerous, who, alone intent

To bless himself, from sordid parents buys
The loathing virgin, in eternal care,
Well merited, consume his nights and days
Let barbarous nations, whose inhuman love
Is wild desire, fierce as the suns they feel;
Let eastern tyrants from the light of heaven
Seclude their bosom-slaves, meanly possess'd
Of a mere lifeless, violated form;
While those whom love cements in holy faith,
And equal transport, free as Nature live,
Disdaining fear. What is the world to them,
Its pomp, its pleasure, and its nonsense all!
Who in each other clasp whatever fair
High fancy forms, and lavish hearts can wish;
Something than beauty dearer, should they look
Or on the mind, or mind-illumined face;
Truth, goodness, honour, harmony, and love,
The richest bounty of indulgent Heaven.
Meantime a smiling offspring rises round,
And mingles both their graces. By degrees,
The human blossom blows; and every day,
Soft as it rolls along, shows some new charm,
The father's lustre, and the mother's bloom.
Then infant reason grows apace, and calls
For the kind hand of an assiduous care.
Delightful task! to rear the tender thought,
To teach the young idea how to shoot,
To pour the fresh instruction o'er the mind,
To breathe the' enlivening spirit, and to fix
The generous purpose in the glowing breast.
Oh, speak the joy! ye, whom the sudden tear
Surprises often, while you look around,
And nothing strikes your eye but sights of bliss,
All various Nature pressing on the heart:
An elegant sufficiency, content,
Retirement, rural quiet, friendship, books,
Ease and alternate labour, useful life,
Progressive virtue, and approving Heaven!

These are the matchless joys of virtuous love;
And thus their moments fly. The Seasons thus,
As ceaseless round a jarring world they roll,
Still find them happy; and consenting SPRING
Sheds her own rosy garland on their heads:
Till evening comes at last, serene and mild;
When after the long vernal day of life,
Enamour'd more, as more remembrance swells
With many a proof of recollected love,
Together down they sink in social sleep;
Together freed, their gentle spirits fly
To scenes where love and bliss immortal reign.

SUMMER

The subject proposed. Invocation. Address to Mr. Dodington An introductory reflection on the motion of the heavenly bodies; whence the succession of the seasons. As the face of Nature in this season is almost uniform, the progress of the poem is a description of a summer's day. The dawn. Sun-rising. Hymn to the sun. Forenoon. Summer insects described. Haymaking. Sheepshearing. Noonday. A woodland retreat. Group of herds and flocks. A solemn grove: how it affects a contemplative mind. A cataract, and rude scene. View of Summer in the torrid zone. Storm of thunder and lightning. A tale. The storm over, a serene afternoon. Bathing. Hour of walking. Transition to the prospect of a rich well cultivated country; which introduces a panegyric on Great Britain. Sun-set. Evening. Night. Summer meteors. A comet. The whole concluding with the praise of philosophy.

From brightening fields of ether fair disclosed,
Child of the Sun, refulgent Summer comes,
In pride of youth, and felt through Nature's depth
He comes attended by the sultry Hours,
And ever fanning breezes, on his way;
While, from his ardent look, the turning Spring
Averts her blushful face; and earth, and skies,
All smiling, to his hot dominion leaves.
Hence, let me haste into the midwood shade,
Where scarce a sunbeam wanders through the gloom;
And on the dark-green grass, beside the brink
Of haunted stream, that by the roots of oak
Rolls o'er the rocky channel, lie at large,
And sing the glories of the circling year.
Come, Inspiration! from thy hermit-seat,
By mortal seldom found: may Fancy dare,
From thy fix'd serious eye, and raptured glance
Shot on surrounding heaven, to steal one look
Creative of the Poet, every power
Exalting to an ecstasy of soul.

And thou, my youthful Muse's early friend,
In whom the human graces all unite:
Pure light of mind, and tenderness of heart:
Genius, and wisdom; the gay social sense,
By decency chastised; goodness and wit,
In seldom-meeting harmony combined;
Unblemish'd honour, and an active zeal
For Britain's glory, Liberty, and Man;
O Dodington! attend my rural song,
Stoop to my theme, inspirit every line,
And teach me to deserve thy just applause.
With what an awful world-revolving power
Were first the unwieldly planets launch'd along
The' illimitable void! thus to remain,
Amid the flux of many thousand years,
That oft has swept the toiling race of men
And all their labour'd monuments away,
Firm, unremitting, matchless, in their course;
To the kind-temper'd change of night and day,
And of the seasons ever stealing round,
Minutely faithful: such the' All-perfect Hand!
That poised, impels, and rules the steady whole.
When now no more the' alternate Twins are fired,
And Cancer reddens with the solar blaze,
Short is the doubtful empire of the night;
And soon, observant of approaching day,
The meek-eyed Morn appears, mother of dews,
At first faint-gleaming in the dappled east:
Till far o'er ether spreads the widening glow;
And, from before the lustre of her face,
White break the clouds away. With quicken'd step,
Brown Night retires: young Day pours in apace,
And opens all the lawny prospect wide.
The dripping rock, the mountain's misty top
Swell on the sight, and brighten with the dawn.
Blue, through the dusk, the smoking currents shine,
And from the bladed field the fearful hare
Limps, awkward; while along the forest glade

The wild deer trip, and often turning gaze
At early passenger. Music awakes
The native voice of undissembled joy;
And thick around the woodland hymns arise.
Roused by the cock, the soon-clad shepherd leaves
His mossy cottage, where with Peace he dwells;
And from the crowded fold, in order, drives
His flock, to taste the verdure of the morn.
  Falsely luxurious! will not Man awake;
And, springing from the bed of sloth, enjoy
The cool, the fragrant, and the silent hour,
To meditation due and sacred song?
For is there ought in sleep can charm the wise?
To lie in dead oblivion, losing half
The fleeting moments of too short a life;
Total extinction of the' enlighten'd soul!
Or else, to feverish vanity alive,
Wilder'd, and tossing through distemper'd dreams?
Who would in such a gloomy state remain
Longer than Nature craves; when every Muse
And every blooming pleasure wait without,
To bless the wildly devious morning walk?
  But yonder comes the powerful King of Day,
Rejoicing in the east. The lessening cloud,
The kindling azure, and the mountain's brow
Illumed with fluid gold, his near approach
Betoken glad. Lo! now, apparent all,
Aslant the dew-bright earth, and colour'd air,
He looks in boundless majesty abroad;
And sheds the shining day, that burnish'd plays
On rocks and hills and towers and wandering streams,
High gleaming from afar. Prime cheerer, Light!
Of all material beings first and best!
Efflux divine! Nature's resplendent robe!
Without whose vesting beauty all were wrapp'd
In unessential gloom! and thou, O Sun!
Soul of surrounding worlds! in whom best seen
Shines out thy Maker! may I sing of thee?

'Tis by thy secret, strong, attractive force,
As with a chain indissoluble bound,
Thy system rolls entire: from the far bourn
Of utmost Saturn, wheeling wide his round
Of thirty years, to Mercury, whose disk
Can scarce be caught by philosophic eye,
Lost in the near effulgence of thy blaze.
Informer of the planetary train!
Without whose quickening glance their cumbrous orbs
Were brute unlovely mass, inert and dead,
And not, as now, the green abodes of life!
How many forms of being wait on thee!
Inhaling spirit; from the' unfetter'd mind,
By thee sublimed, down to the daily race,
The mixing myriads of thy setting beam.
The vegetable world is also thine,
Parent of Seasons! who the pomp precede
That waits thy throne, as through thy vast domain,
Annual, along the bright ecliptic road,
In world-rejoicing state, it moves sublime.
Meantime the' expecting nations, circled gay
With all the various tribes of foodful earth,
Implore thy bounty, or send grateful up
A common hymn: while, round thy beaming car,
High seen, the Seasons lead, in sprightly dance
Harmonious knit, the rosy-finger'd Hours,
The Zephyrs floating loose, the timely Rains,
Of bloom ethereal the light footed Dews,
And soften'd into joy the surly Storms.
These, in successive turn, with lavish hand,
Shower every beauty every fragrance shower,
Herbs, flowers, and fruits, and, kindling at thy touch,
From land to land is flush'd the vernal year
Nor to the surface of enliven'd earth,
Graceful with hills and dales, and leafy woods,
Her liberal tresses, is thy force confined:
But, to the bowel'd cavern darting deep,
The mineral kinds confess thy mighty power

Effulgent, hence the veiny marble shines;
Hence Labour draws his tools; hence burnish'd War
Gleams on the day! the nobler works of Peace
Hence bless mankind, and generous Commerce binds
The round of nations in a golden chain.
The' unfruitful rock itself, impregn'd by thee,
In dark retirement forms the lucid stone.
The lively diamond drinks thy purest rays,
Collected light, compact; that, polish'd bright,
And all its native lustre let abroad,
Dares, as it sparkles on the fair one's breast,
With vain ambition emulate her eyes.
At thee the ruby lights its deepening glow,
And with a waving radiance inward flames.
From thee the sapphire, solid ether, takes
Its hue cerulean; and, of evening tinct,
The purple-streaming amethyst is thine.
With thy own smile the yellow topaz burns.
Nor deeper verdure dyes the robe of Spring,
When first she gives it to the southern gale,
Than the green emerald shows. But, all combined,
Thick through the whitening opal play thy beams;
Or, flying several from its surface, form
A trembling variance of revolving hues,
As the site varies in the gazer's hand.
The very dead creation, from thy touch,
Assumes a mimic life. By thee refined,
In brighter mazes the relucent stream
Plays o'er the mead. The precipice abrupt,
Projecting horror on the blacken'd flood,
Softens at thy return. The desert joys,
Wildly, through all his melancholy bounds.
Rude ruins glitter; and the briny deep,
Seen from some pointed promontory's top,
Far to the blue horizon's utmost verge,
Restless, reflects a floating gleam. But this,
And all the much transported Muse can sing,

Are to thy beauty, dignity, and use,
Unequal far, great delegated source
Of light, and life, and grace, and joy below!
  How shall I then attempt to sing of HIM!
Who, Light Himself, in uncreated light
Invested deep, dwells awfully retired
From mortal eye or angel's purer ken;
Whose single smile has, from the first of time,
Fill'd, overflowing, all those lamps of heaven
That beam for ever through the boundless sky:
But, should he hide his face, the' astonish'd sun
And all the' extinguish'd stars would loosening reel
Wide from their spheres, and Chaos come again.
  And yet was every faltering tongue of Man,
ALMIGHTY FATHER! silent in thy praise;
Thy Works themselves would raise a general voice,
E'en in the depth of solitary woods
By human foot untrod; proclaim thy power,
And to the choir celestial THEE resound,
The' eternal cause, support, and end of all!
  To me be Nature's volume broad display'd;
And to peruse its all instructing page,
Or, haply catching inspiration thence,
Some easy passage raptured to translate,
My sole delight; as through the falling glooms
Pensive I stray, or with the rising dawn
On Fancy's eagle wing excursive soar.
  Now, flaming up the heavens, the potent sun
Melts into limpid air the high-raised clouds,
And morning fogs, that hover'd round the hills
In party-colour'd bands; till wide unveil'd
The face of Nature shines, from where earth seems,
Far stretch'd around, to meet the bending sphere.
  Half in a blush of clustering roses lost,
Dew-dropping Coolness to the shade retires;
There, on the verdant turf, or flowery bed,
By gelid founts and careless rills to muse

While tyrant Heat, dispreading through the sky,
With rapid sway, his burning influence darts
On man and beast and herb and tepid stream.
Who can unpitying see the flowery race,
Shed by the morn, their new-flush'd bloom resign,
Before the parching beam ? so fade the fair,
When fevers revel through their azure veins.
But one, the lofty follower of the sun,
Sad when he sets, shuts up her yellow leaves,
Drooping all night ; and, when he warm returns,
Points her enamour'd bosom to his ray.
Home, from his morning task, the swain retreats ;
His flock before him stepping to the fold :
While the full-udder'd mother lows around
The cheerful cottage, then expecting food,
The food of innocence and health ! the daw,
The rook, and magpie, to the gray grown oaks
That the calm village in their verdant arms,
Sheltering, embrace, direct their lazy flight :
Where on the mingling boughs they sit embower'd,
All the hot noon, till cooler hours arise.
Faint, underneath, the household fowls convene ;
And, in a corner of the buzzing shade,
The housedog with the vacant greyhound lies,
Outstretch'd and sleepy. In his slumbers one
Attacks the nightly thief, and one exults
O'er hill and dale ; till, waken'd by the wasp,
They starting snap. Nor shall the Muse disdain
To let the little noisy summer race
Live in her lay, and flutter through her song,
Not mean though simple ; to the sun allied,
From him they draw their animating fire.
Waked by his warmer ray, the reptile young
Come wing'd abroad ; by the light air upborne,
Lighter, and full of soul. From every chink,
And secret corner, where they slept away
The wintry storms ; or, rising from their tombs,

To higher life; by myriads, forth at once,
Swarming they pour; of all the varied hues
Their beauty-beaming parent can disclose,
Ten thousand forms, ten thousand different tribes
People the blaze. To sunny waters some
By fatal instinct fly; where on the pool
They sportive wheel: or, sailing down the stream,
Are snatch'd immediate by the quick-eyed trout,
Or darting salmon. Through the greenwood glade
Some love to stray; there lodged, amused, and fed,
In the fresh leaf. Luxurious, others make
The meads their choice, and visit every flower
And every latent herb: for the sweet task,
To propagate their kinds, and where to wrap,
In what soft beds, their young yet undisclosed,
Employs their tender care. Some to the house,
The fold, and dairy, hungry, bend their flight;
Sip round the pail, or taste the curdling cheese;
Oft, inadvertent, from the milky stream
They meet their fate; or, weltering in the bowl,
With powerless wings around them wrapp'd, expire.
But chief to heedless flies the window proves
A constant death; where, gloomily retired,
The villain spider lives, cunning and fierce,
Mixture abhorr'd! amid a mangled heap
Of carcasses, in eager watch he sits,
O'erlooking all his waving snares around.
Near the dire cell the dreadless wanderer oft
Passes, as oft the ruffian shows his front,
The prey at last ensnared, he dreadful darts,
With rapid glide, along the leaning line;
And, fixing in the wretch his cruel fangs,
Strikes backward grimly pleased; the fluttering wing
And shriller sound declare extreme distress,
And ask the helping hospitable hand.
Resounds the living surface of the ground
Nor undelightful is the ceaseless hum

To him who muses through the woods at noon;
Or drowsy shepherd, as he lies reclined,
With half-shut eyes, beneath the floating shade
Of willows gray, close crowding o'er the brook.
  Gradual, from these what numerous kinds descend,
Evading e'en the microscopic eye!
Full Nature swarms with life; one wondrous mass
Of animals, or atoms organized,
Waiting the vital breath, when parent Heaven
Shall bid his spirit blow. The hoary fen,
In putrid steams, emits the living cloud
Of pestilence. Through subterranean cells,
Where searching sunbeams scarce can find a way,
Earth animated heaves. The flowery leaf
Wants not its soft inhabitants. Secure,
Within its winding citadel, the stone
Holds multitudes. But chief the forest boughs,
That dance unnumber'd to the playful breeze,
The downy orchard, and the melting pulp
Of mellow fruit the nameless nations feed
Of evanescent insects. Where the pool
Stands mantled o'er with green, invisible,
Amid the floating verdure millions stray.
Each liquid too, whether it pierces, sooths,
Inflames, refreshes, or exalts the taste,
With various forms abounds. Nor is the stream
Of purest crystal, nor the lucid air,
Though one transparent vacancy it seems,
Void of their unseen people. These, conceal'd
By the kind art of forming Heaven, escape
The grosser eye of man: for, if the worlds
In worlds enclosed should on his senses burst,
From cates* ambrosial, and the nectar'd bowl
He would abhorrent turn: and in dead night,
When silence sleeps o'er all, be stunn'd with noise
  Let no presuming impious railer tax
CREATIVE WISDOM, as if aught was form'd
In vain, or not for admirable ends.

Snall little haughty Ignorance pronounce
His works unwise, of which the smallest part
Exceeds the narrow vision of her mind?
As if upon a full proportion'd dome,
On swelling columns heaved, the pride of art!
A critic-fly, whose feeble ray scarce spreads
An inch around, with blind presumption bold,
Should dare to tax the structure of the whole.
And lives the Man, whose universal eye
Has swept at once the' unbounded scheme of things;
Mark'd their dependance so, and firm accord,
As with unfaltering accent to conclude
That this availeth nought? Has any seen
The mighty chain of beings, lessening down
From Infinite Perfection to the brink
Of dreary nothing, desolate abyss!
From which astonish'd thought, recoiling, turns?
Till then alone let zealous praise ascend,
And hymns of holy wonder to that Power
Whose wisdom shines as lovely on our minds
As on our smiling eyes his servant sun.
  Thick in yon stream of light, a thousand ways,
Upward and downward, thwarting and convolved,
The quivering nations sport; till, tempest-wing'd,
Fierce Winter sweeps them from the face of day.
E'en so luxurious men, unheeding, pass
An idle summer life in fortune's shine,
A season's glitter; thus they flutter on
From toy to toy, from vanity to vice;
Till, blown away by death, oblivion comes
Behind, and strikes them from the book of life.
  Now swarms the village o'er the jovial mead;
The rustic youth, brown with meridian toil,
Healthful and strong; full as the summer rose
Blown by prevailing suns, the ruddy maid,
Half naked, swelling on the sight, and all
Her kindled graces burning o'er her cheek.
E'en stooping age is here; and infant hands

Trail the long rake, or, with the fragrant load
O'ercharged, amid the kind oppression roll.
Wide flies the tedded grain; all in a row
Advancing broad, or wheeling round the field,
They spread the breathing harvest to the sun,
That throws refreshful round a rural smell:
Or, as they rake the green-appearing ground,
And drive the dusky wave along the mead,
The russet haycock rises thick behind,
In order gay. While heard from dale to dale,
Waking the breeze, resounds the blended voice
Of happy labour, love, and social glee.
  Or rushing thence, in one diffusive band,
They drive the troubled flocks, by many a dog
Compell'd, to where the mazy-running brook
Forms a deep pool; this bank abrupt and high,
And that fair-spreading in a pebbled shore.
Urged to the giddy brink, much is the toil,
The clamour much, of men and boys and dogs,
Ere the soft fearful people of the flood
Commit their woolly sides. And oft the swain,
On some impatient seizing, hurls them in;
Embolden'd then, nor hesitating more,
Fast, fast they plunge amid the flashing wave,
And, panting, labour to the farthest shore.
Repeated this, till deep the well wash'd fleece
Has drunk the flood, and from his lively haunt
The trout is banish'd by the sordid stream;
Heavy and dripping, to the breezy brow
Slow move the harmless race: where, as they spread
Their swelling treasures to the sunny ray,
Inly disturb'd and wondering what this wild
Outrageous tumult means, their loud complaints
The country fill; and, toss'd from rock to rock,
Incessant bleatings run around the hills.
At last, of snowy white, the gather'd flocks
Are in the wattled pen innumerous press'd,
Head above head: and ranged in lusty rows

The shepherds sit, and whet the sounding shears.
The housewife waits to roll her fleecy stores,
With all her gay-dress'd maids attending round.
One, chief, in gracious dignity enthroned,
Shines o'er the rest, the pastoral queen, and rays
Her smiles, sweet beaming on her shepherd king;
While the glad circle round them yield their souls
To festive mirth, and wit that knows no gall.
Meantime, their joyous task goes on apace;
Some mingling stir the melted tar, and some,
Deep on the new-shorn vagrant's heaving side,
To stamp the master's cipher ready stand;
Others the' unwilling wether drag along;
And, glorying in his might, the sturdy boy
Holds by the twisted horns the' indignant ram.
Behold where bound, and of its robe bereft,
By needy Man, that all-depending lord,
How meek, how patient, the mild creature lies!
What softness in its melancholy face,
What dumb complaining innocence appears!
Fear not, ye gentle tribes, 'tis not the knife
Of horrid slaughter that is o'er you waved;
No, 'tis the tender swain's well guided shears,
Who having now, to pay his annual care,
Borrow'd your fleece, to you a cumbrous load,
Will send you bounding to your hills again.
A simple scene! yet hence Britannia sees
Her solid grandeur rise: hence she commands
The' exalted stores of every brighter clime,
The treasures of the Sun without his rage:
Hence, fervent all, with culture, toil, and arts,
Wide glows her land: her dreadful thunder hence
Rides o'er the waves sublime, and now, e'en now,
Impending hangs o'er Gallia's humbled coast;
Hence rules the circling deep, and awes the world.
'Tis raging noon; and, vertical, the sun
Darts on the head direct his forceful rays.
O'er heaven and earth, far as the ranging eye

Can sweep, a dazzling deluge reigns, and all
From pole to pole is undistinguish'd blaze.
In vain the sight, dejected, to the ground
Stoops for relief; thence hot ascending steams
And keen reflection pain. Deep to the root
Of vegetation parch'd, the cleaving fields
And slippery lawn an arid hue disclose,
Blast Fancy's bloom, and wither e'en the soul.
Echo no more returns the cheerful sound
Of sharpening scythe: the mower sinking heaps
O'er him the humid hay, with flowers perfumed;
And scarce a chirping grasshopper is heard
Through the dumb mead. Distressful Nature pants.
The very streams look languid from afar:
Or, through the' unshelter'd glade, impatient, seem
To hurl into the covert of the grove.
  All-conquering Heat, oh, intermit thy wrath!
And on my throbbing temples potent thus
Beam not so fierce! incessant still you flow,
And still another fervent flood succeeds,
Pour'd on the head profuse. In vain I sigh,
And restless turn, and look around for night;
Night is far off; and hotter hours approach.
Thrice happy he! who on the sunless side
Of a romantic mountain, forest-crown'd,
Beneath the whole collected shade reclines:
Or in the gelid caverns, woodbine-wrought,
And fresh bedew'd with ever spouting streams,
Sits coolly calm; while all the world without,
Unsatisfied, and sick, tosses in noon.
Emblem instructive of the virtuous man,
Who keeps his temper'd mind serene and pure,
And every passion aptly harmonized,
Amid a jarring world with vice inflamed.
  Welcome, ye shades! ye bowery thickets, hail!
Ye lofty pines! ye venerable oaks!
Ye ashes wild, resounding o'er the steep!
Delicious is your shelter to the soul,

As to the hunted hart the sallying spring,
Or stream full flowing, that his swelling sides
Laves, as he floats along the herbaged brink.
Cool, through the nerves, your pleasing comfort glides;
The heart beats glad; the fresh-expanded eye
And ear resume their watch; the sinews knit;
And life shoots swift through all the lighten'd limbs
Around the' adjoining brook, that purls along
The vocal grove, now fretting o'er a rock,
Now scarcely moving through a reedy pool,
Now starting to a sudden stream, and now
Gently diffused into a limpid plain;
A various group the herds and flocks compose,
Rural confusion! on the grassy bank
Some ruminating lie; while others stand
Half in the flood, and often bending sip
The circling surface. In the middle droops
The strong laborious ox, of honest front,
Which incomposed he shakes; and from his sides
The troublous insects lashes with his tail,
Returning still. Amid his subjects safe,
Slumbers the monarch swain: his careless arm
Thrown round his head, on downy moss sustain'd;
Here laid his scrip, with wholesome viands fill'd;
There, listening every noise, his watchful dog.
Light fly his slumbers, if perchance a flight
Of angry gadflies fasten on the herd;
That startling scatters from the shallow brook,
In search of lavish stream. Tossing the foam,
They scorn the keeper's voice, and scour the plain,
Through all the bright severity of noon;
While, from their labouring breasts, a hollow moan,
Proceeding, runs low-bellowing round the hills.
Oft in this season too the horse, provoked,
While his big sinews full of spirits swell,
Trembling with vigour, in the heat of blood,
Springs the high fence; and, o'er the field effused,
Darts on the gloomy flood, with steadfast eye,

And heart estranged to fear: his nervous chest,
Luxuriant, and erect, the seat of strength!
Bears down the' opposing stream: quenchless his thirst,
He takes the river at redoubled draughts;
And with wide nostril, snorting, skims the wave.
Still let me pierce into the midnight depth
Of yonder grove, of wildest largest growth:
That, forming high in air a woodland choir,
Nods o'er the mount beneath. At every step,
Solemn and slow, the shadows blacker fall,
And all is awful listening gloom around.
These are the haunts of Meditation, these
The scenes where ancient bards the' inspiring breath,
Ecstatic, felt; and, from this world retired,
Conversed with angels and immortal forms,
On gracious errands bent: to save the fall
Of virtue struggling on the brink of vice;
In waking whispers, and repeated dreams,
To hint pure thought, and warn the favour'd soul
For future trials fated to prepare;
To prompt the poet, who devoted gives
His muse to better themes; to sooth the pangs
Of dying worth, and from the patriot s breast
(Backward to mingle in detested war,
But foremost when engaged) to turn the death;
And numberless such offices of love,
Daily and nightly, zealous to perform.
Shook sudden from the bosom of the sky,
A thousand shapes or glide athwart the dusk,
Or stalk majestic on. Deep roused, I feel
A sacred terror, a severe delight
Creep through my mortal frame; and thus, methinks,
A voice, than human more, the' abstracted ear
Of fancy strikes:—" Be not of us afraid,
Poor kindred man! thy fellow-creatures, we
From the same Parent Power our beings drew,
The same our Lord and laws and great pursuit,
Once some of us, like thee, through stormy life

Toil'd, tempest-beaten, ere we could attain
This holy calm, this harmony of mind,
Where purity and peace immingle charms.
Then fear not us ; but with responsive song,
Amid these dim recesses, undisturb'd
By noisy folly and discordant vice,
Of Nature sing with us, and Nature's God.
Here frequent, at the visionary hour,
When musing midnight reigns or silent noon,
Angelic harps are in full concert heard,
And voices chanting from the wood-crown'd hill,
The deepening dale, or inmost silvan glade :
A privilege bestow'd by us, alone,
On Contemplation, or the hallow'd ear
Of poet, swelling to seraphic strain."
And art thou, Stanley,* of that sacred band,
Alas, for us too soon ! though raised above
The reach of human pain, above the flight
Of human joy ; yet, with a mingled ray
Of sadly pleased remembrance, must thou feel
A mother's love, a mother's tender woe :
Who seeks thee still in many a former scene ;
Seeks thy fair form, thy lovely beaming eyes,
Thy pleasing converse, by gay lively sense
Inspired : where mortal wisdom mildly shone,
Without the toil of art ; and virtue glow'd,
In all her smiles, without forbidding pride.
But, O thou best of parents ! wipe thy tears ;
Or rather to Parental Nature pay
The tears of grateful joy, who for awhile
Lent thee this younger self, this opening bloom
Of thy enlightened mind and gentle worth.
Believe the Muse : the wintry blast of death
Kills not the buds of virtue ; no, they spread,
Beneath the heavenly beam of brighter suns,
Through endless ages, into higher powers.

* A young lady, who died at the age of eighteen, in the year 1738, upon whom Thompson wrote an epitaph.

Thus up the mount, in airy vision wrapp'd,
I stray, regardless whither; till the sound
Of a near fall of water every sense
Wakes from the charm of thought: swift shrinking back,
I check my steps, and view the broken scene.
Smooth to the shelving brink a copious flood
Rolls fair and placid; where, collected all
In one impetuous torrent, down the steep
It thundering shoots, and shakes the country round.
At first an azure sheet, it rushes broad;
Then whitening by degrees, as prone it falls,
And from the loud-resounding rocks below
Dash'd in a cloud of foam, it sends aloft
A hoary mist, and forms a ceaseless shower.
Nor can the tortured wave here find repose:
But, raging still amid the shaggy rocks,
Now flashes o'er the scatter'd fragments, now
Aslant the hollow channel rapid darts;
And, falling fast from gradual slope to slope,
With wild infracted course and lessen'd roar,
It gains a safer bed, and steals, at last,
Along the mazes of the quiet vale.
Invited from the cliff, to whose dark brow
He clings, the steep-ascending eagle soars,
With upward pinions, through the flood of day·
And, giving full his bosom to the blaze,
Gains on the sun; while all the tuneful race,
Smit by afflictive noon, disorder'd droop,
Deep in the thicket; or, from bower to bower
Responsive, force an interrupted strain.
The stockdove only through the forest coos,
Mournfully hoarse; oft ceasing from his plaint,
Short interval of weary woe! again
The sad idea of his murder'd mate,
Struck from his side by savage fowler's guile,
Across his fancy comes; and then resounds
A louder song of sorrow through the grove
Beside the dewy border let me sit,

All in the freshness of the humid air:
There in that hollow'd rock, grotesque and wild,
An ample chair moss-lined, and over head
By flowering umbrage shaded; where the bee
Strays diligent, and with the' extracted balm
Of fragrant woodbine loads his little thigh.
Now, while I taste the sweetness of the shade,
While Nature lies around deep lull'd in noon
Now come, bold Fancy, spread a daring flight,
And view the wonders of the torrid zone:
Climes unrelenting! with whose rage compared,
Yon blaze is feeble, and yon skies are cool.
See, how at once the bright effulgent sun,
Rising direct, swift chases from the sky
The short-lived twilight: and with ardent blaze
Looks gaily fierce through all the dazzling air:
He mounts his throne; but kind before him sends,
Issuing from out the portals of the morn,
The general breeze,* to mitigate his fire,
And breathe refreshment on a fainting world.
Great are the scenes, with dreadful beauty crown'd
And barbarous wealth, that see, each circling year,
Returning suns and double seasons† pass:
Rocks rich in gems, and mountains big with mines,
That on the high equator ridgy rise,
Whence many a bursting stream auriferous plays:
Majestic woods, of every vigorous green,
Stage above stage, high waving o'er the hills;
Or, to the far horizon wide diffused,
A boundless deep immensity of shade.
Here lofty trees, to ancient song unknown,
The noble sons of potent heat and floods,

* Which blows constantly between the tropics from the east, or the collateral points, the north-east and south-east: caused by the pressure of the rarefied air on that before it, according to the diurnal motion of the sun from east to west.

† In all climates between the tropics, the sun, as he passes and repasses in his annual motion, is twice a year vertical, which produces this effect.

Prone-rushing from the clouds, rear high to heaven
Their thorny stems, and broad around them throw
Meridian gloom. Here, in eternal prime,
Unnumber'd fruits, of keen delicious taste
And vital spirit, drink amid the cliffs,
And burning sands that bank the shrubby vales,
Redoubled day, yet in their rugged coats
A friendly juice to cool its rage contain.
Bear me, Pomona! to thy citron groves;
To where the lemon and the piercing lime,
With the deep orange, glowing through the green,
Their lighter glories blend. Lay me reclined
Beneath the spreading tamarind that shakes,
Fann'd by the breeze, its fever cooling fruit.
Deep in the night the massy locust sheds,
Quench my hot limbs; or lead me through the maze,
Embowering endless, of the Indian fig;
Or, thrown at gayer ease, on some fair brow,
Let me behold, by breezy murmurs cool'd,
Broad o'er my head the verdant cedar wave,
And high palmetos lift their graceful shade.
Or, stretch'd amid these orchards of the sun,
Give me to drain the cocoa's milky bowl,
And from the palm to draw its freshening wine!
More bounteous far than all the frantic juice
Which Bacchus pours. Nor, on its slender twigs
Low bending, be the full pomegranate scorn'd;
Nor, creeping through the woods, the gelid race
Of berries. Oft in humble station dwells
Unboastful worth, above fastidious pomp.
Witness, thou best Anana, thou the pride
Of vegetable life, beyond whate'er
The poets imaged in the golden age:
Quick let me strip thee of thy tufty coat,
Spread thy ambrosial stores, and feast with Jove!
From these the prospect varies. Plains immense
Lie stretch'd below, interminable meads,
And vast savannahs, where the wandering eye,

Unfix'd, is in a verdant ocean lost.
Another Flora there, of bolder hues,
And richer sweets, beyond our garden's pride,
Plays o'er the fields, and showers with sudden hand
Exuberant spring : for oft these valleys shift
Their green-embroider'd robe to fiery brown,
And swift to green again, as scorching suns,
Or streaming dews and torrent rains, prevail.
  Along these lonely regions, where, retired
From little scenes of art, great Nature dwells
In awful solitude, and nought is seen
But the wild herds that own no master s stall,
Prodigious rivers roll their fattening seas :
On whose luxuriant herbage, half conceal'd,
Like a fallen cedar, far diffused his train,
Cased in green scales, the crocodile extends.
The flood disparts : behold ! in plaited mail,
Behemoth* rears his head. Glanced from his side,
The darted steel in idle shivers flies :
He fearless walks the plain, or seeks the hills ;
Where, as he crops his varied fare, the herds,
In widening circle round, forget their food,
And at the harmless stranger wondering gaze.
  Peaceful beneath primeval trees, that cast
Their ample shade o'er Niger's yellow stream,
And where the Ganges rolls his sacred wave ;
Or. mid the central depth of blackening woods,
High raised in solemn theatre around,
Leans the huge elephant : wisest of brutes !
O truly wise ! with gentle might endow'd,
Though powerful, not destructive ! here he sees
Revolving ages sweep the changeful earth,
And empires rise and fall ; regardless he
Of what the never resting race of men
Project : thrice happy ! could he scape their guile,
Who mine, from cruel avarice, his steps ;
Or with his towery grandeur swell their state,

* The Hippopotamus, or river-horse

The pride of kings! or else his strength pervert,
And bid him rage amid the mortal fray,
Astonish'd at the madness of mankind.
  Wide o'er the winding umbrage of the floods,
Like vivid blossoms glowing from afar,
Thick swarm the brighter birds. For Nature's hand,
That with a sportive vanity has deck'd
The plumy nations, there her gayest hues
Profusely pours.* But if she bids them shine
Array'd in all the beauteous beams of day,
Yet frugal still, she humbles them in song.
Nor envy we the gaudy robes they lent
Proud Montezuma's realm, whose legions cast
A boundless radiance waving on the sun,
While Philomel is ours; while in our shades,
Through the soft silence of the listening night,
The sober-suited songstress trills her lay.
  But come, my Muse, the desert-barrier burst,
A wild expanse of lifeless sand and sky:
And, swifter than the toiling caravan,
Shoot o'er the vale of Sennar; ardent climb
The Nubian mountains, and the secret bounds
Of jealous Abyssinia boldly pierce.
Thou art no ruffian, who beneath the mask
Of social commerce comest to rob their wealth;
No holy fury thou blaspheming Heaven,
With consecrated steel to stab their peace,
And through the land, yet red from civil wounds,
To spread the purple tyranny of Rome.
Thou, like the harmless bee, mayst freely range
From mead to mead bright with exalted flowers,
From jasmine grove to grove mayst wander gay
Through palmy shades and aromatic woods,
That grace the plains, invest the peopled hills,
And up the more than Alpine mountains wave

* In all the regions of the torrid zone, the birds, though more beautiful in their plumage, are observed to be less melodious than ours.

There on the breezy summit, spreading fair,
For many a league ; or on stupendous rocks,
That from the sun-redoubling valley lift,
Cool to the middle air, their lawny tops ;
Where palaces and fanes and villas rise ;
And gardens smile around, and cultured fields ;
And fountains gush ; and careless herds and flocks
Securely stray ; a world within itself,
Disdaining all assault : there let me draw
Ethereal soul, there drink reviving gales,
Profusely breathing from the spicy groves
And vales of fragrance ; there at distance hear
The roaring floods, and cataracts, that sweep
From disembowel'd earth the virgin gold ;
And o'er the varied landscape, restless, rove,
Fervent with life of every fairer kind :
A land of wonders ! which the sun still eyes
With ray direct, as of the lovely realm
Enamour'd, and delighting there to dwell.
  How changed the scene ! in blazing height of noon,
The sun, oppress'd, is plunged in thickest gloom.
Still horror reigns, a dreary twilight round,
Of struggling night and day malignant mix'd.
For to the hot equator crowding fast,
Where, highly rarefied, the yielding air
Admits their stream, incessant vapours roll,
Amazing clouds on clouds continual heap'd ;
Or whirl'd tempestuous by the gusty wind,
Or silent borne along, heavy, and slow,
With the big stores of steaming oceans charged
Meantime, amid these upper seas, condensed
Around the cold aerial mountain's brow,
And by conflicting winds together dash'd,
The Thunder holds his black tremendous throne ;
From cloud to cloud the rending lightnings rage ;
Till, in the furious elemental war
Dissolved, the whole precipitated mass
Unbroken floods and solid torrents pours.

The treasures these, hid from the bounded search
Of ancient knowledge; whence, with annual pomp,
Rich king of floods! o'erflows the swelling Nile.
From his two springs, in Gojam s sunny realm,
Pure-welling out, he through the lucid lake
Of fair Dambea rolls his infant stream.
There, by the naiads nursed, he sports away
His playful youth amid the fragrant isles,
That with unfading verdure smile around
Ambitious thence the manly river breaks;
And, gathering many a flood, and copious fed
With all the mellow'd treasures of the sky,
Winds in progressive majesty along:
Through splendid kingdoms now devolves his maze,
Now wanders wild o'er solitary tracts
Of life-deserted sand; till, glad to quit
The joyless desert, down the Nubian rocks,
From thundering steep to steep, he pours his urn,
And Egypt joys beneath the spreading wave.
His brother Niger too, and all the floods
In which the full form'd maids of Afric lave
Their jetty limbs; and all that from the tract
Of woody mountains stretch'd through gorgeous Ind
Fall on Cormandel's coast, or Malabar;
From Menam's* orient stream, that nightly shines
With insect lamps, to where Aurora sheds
On Indus' smiling banks the rosy shower:
All, at this bounteous season, ope their urns,
And pour untoiling harvest o'er the land.
Nor less thy world, Columbus, drinks, refresh'd,
The lavish moisture of the melting year.
Wide o'er his isles the branching Oronoque
Rolls a brown deluge; and the native drives
To dwell aloft on life-sufficing trees,
At once his dome, his robe, his food, and arms

* The river that runs through Siam; on whose banks a vast multitude of those insects called Fire Flies make a beautiful appearance in the night.

Swell'd by a thousand streams, impetuous hurl'd
From all the roaring Andes, huge descends
The mighty Orellana.* Scarce the muse
Dares stretch her wing o'er this enormous mass
Of rushing water; scarce she dares attempt
The sealike Plata; to whose dread expanse,
Continuous depth, and wondrous length of course
Our floods are rills. With unabated force,
In silent dignity they sweep along,
And traverse realms unknown, and blooming wilds,
And fruitful deserts, worlds of solitude,
Where the sun smiles and seasons teem in vain,
Unseen and unenjoy'd. Forsaking these,
O'er peopled plains they fair diffusive flow,
And many a nation feed, and circle safe,
In their soft bosom, many a happy isle;
The seat of blameless Pan, yet undisturb'd
By Christian crimes and Europe's cruel sons.
Thus pouring on they proudly seek the deep,
Whose vanquish'd tide, recoiling from the shock,
Yields to the liquid weight of half the globe;
And Ocean trembles for his green domain.
But what avails this wondrous waste of wealth?
This gay profusion of luxurious bliss?
This pomp of Nature? what their balmy meads,
Their powerful herbs, and Ceres void of pain?
By vagrant birds dispersed, and wafting winds,
What their unplanted fruits? what the cool draughts,
The' ambrosial food, rich gums, and spicy health
Their forests yield? their toiling insects what,
Their silky pride, and vegetable robes?
Ah! what avail their fatal treasures hid
Deep in the bowels of the pitying earth,
Golconda's gems, and sad Potosi's mines;
Where dwelt the gentlest children of the sun!
What all that Afric's golden rivers roll,
Her odorous woods, and shining ivory stores?

* The river of the Amazons.

Ill fated race! the softening arts of Peace,
Whate'er the humanizing Muses teach;
The godlike wisdom of the temper'd breast;
Progressive truth, the patient force of thought;
Investigation calm, whose silent powers
Command the world; the light that leads to heaven;
Kind equal rule, the government of laws,
And all-protecting Freedom, which alone
Sustains the name and dignity of man:
These are not theirs. The parent sun himself
Seems o'er this world of slaves to tyrannise;
And, with oppressive ray, the roseate bloom
Of beauty blasting, gives the gloomy hue,
And feature gross: or worse, to ruthless deeds,
Mad jealousy, blind rage, and fell revenge,
Their fervid spirit fires. Love dwells not there,
The soft regards, the tenderness of life,
The heart-shed tear, the' ineffable delight
Of sweet humanity: these court the beam
Of milder climes; in selfish fierce desire,
And the wild fury of voluptuous sense,
There lost. The very brute creation there
This rage partakes, and burns with horrid fire.
Lo! the green serpent, from his dark abode,
Which even Imagination fears to tread,
At noon forth issuing, gathers up his train
In orbs immense, then, darting out anew,
Seeks the refreshing fount; by which diffused,
He throws his folds: and while, with threatening tongue,
And deathful jaws erect, the monster curls
His flaming crest, all other thirst appall'd,
Or shivering flies, or check'd at distance stands,
Nor dares approach. But still more direful he,
The small close-lurking minister of fate,
Whose high-concocted venom through the veins
A rapid lightning darts, arresting swift
The vital current. Form'd to humble man,
This child of vengeful nature! there, sublimed

To fearless lust of blood, the savage race
Roam, licensed by the shading hour of guilt,
And foul misdeed, when the pure day has shut
His sacred eye. The tiger darting fierce
Impetuous on the prey his glance has doom'd:
The lively shining leopard, speckled o'er
With many a spot, the beauty of the waste;
And, scorning all the taming arts of man,
The keen hyena, fellest of the fell.
These, rushing from the' inhospitable woods
Of Mauritania, or the tufted isles
That verdant rise amid the Libyan wild,
Innumerous glare around their shaggy king,
Majestic, stalking o'er the printed sand;
And, with imperious and repeated roars,
Demand their fated food. The fearful flocks
Crowd near the guardian swain; the nobler herds,
Where round their lordly bull, in rural ease
They ruminating lie, with horror hear
The coming rage. The' awaken'd village starts;
And to her fluttering breast the mother strains
Her thoughtless infant. From the pirate's den,
Or stern Morocca's tyrant fang escaped,
The wretch half wishes for his bonds again:
While, uproar all, the wilderness resounds,
From Atlas eastward to the frighted Nile.
Unhappy he! who from the first of joys,
Society, cut off, is left alone
Amid this world of death. Day after day,
Sad on the jutting eminence he sits,
And views the main that ever toils below;
Still fondly forming in the farthest verge,
Where the round ether mixes with the wave,
Ships, dim-discover'd, dropping from the clouds;
At evening, to the setting sun he turns
A mournful eye, and down his dying heart
Sinks helpless; while the wonted roar is up,
And hiss continual through the tedious night.

Yet here, e'en here, into these black abodes
Of monsters, unappall'd, from stooping Rome,
And guilty Cæsar, Liberty retired,
Her Cato following through Numidian wilds:
Disdainful of Campania's gentle plains,
And all the green delights Ausonia pours;
When for them she must bend the servile knee,
And fawning take the splendid robber's boon.
Nor stop the terrors of these regions here.
Commission'd demons oft, angels of wrath,
Let loose the raging elements. Breathed hot
From all the boundless furnace of the sky,
And the wide glittering waste of burning sand,
A suffocating wind the pilgrim smites
With instant death. Patient of thirst and toil,
Son of the desert! even the camel feels,
Shot through his wither'd heart, the fiery blast.
Or from the black-red ether, bursting broad,
Sallies the sudden whirlwind. Straight the sands,
Commoved around, in gathering eddies play:
Nearer and nearer still they darkening come;
Till, with the general all-involving storm
Swept up, the whole continuous wilds arise;
And by their noonday fount dejected thrown,
Or sunk at night in sad disastrous sleep,
Beneath descending hills, the caravan
Is buried deep. In Cairo's crowded streets
The' impatient merchant, wondering, waits in vain,
And Mecca saddens at the long delay.
But chief at sea, whose every flexile wave
Obeys the blast, the' aerial tumult swells.
In the dread ocean, undulating wide,
Beneath the radiant line that girts the globe,
The circling Typhon* whirl'd from point to point,
Exhausting all the rage of all the sky,
And dire Ecnephia* reign. Amid the heavens,

* Typhon and Ecnephia, names of particular storms or hurricanes, known only between the tropics.

Falsely serene, deep in a cloudy speck*
Compress'd, the mighty tempest brooding dwells·
Of no regard, save to the skilful eye,
Fiery and foul, the small prognostic hangs
Aloft, or on the promontory's brow
Musters its force. A faint deceitful calm,
A fluttering gale, the demon sends before,
To tempt the spreading sail. Then down at once,
Precipitant, descends a mingled mass
Of roaring winds and flame and rushing floods.
In wild amazement fix'd the sailor stands.
Art is too slow: by rapid fate oppress'd,
His broad-wing'd vessel drinks the whelming tide,
Hid in the bosom of the black abyss.
With such mad seas the daring Gama† fought,
For many a day, and many a dreadful night,
Incessant, labouring round the stormy Cape;
By bold ambition led, and bolder thirst
Of gold. For then from ancient gloom emerged
The rising world of trade: the Genius, then,
Of navigation, that, in hopeless sloth,
Had slumber'd on the vast Atlantic deep,
For idle ages, starting, heard at last
The Lusitanian Prince;‡ who, Heaven-inspired,
To love of useful glory roused mankind,
And in unbounded commerce mix'd the world.
  Increasing still the terrors of these storms,
His jaws horrific arm'd with threefold fate,
Here dwells the direful shark. Lured by the scent
Of steaming crowds, of rank disease, and death,
Behold! he rushing cuts the briny flood,

* Called by sailors the Ox-eye, being in appearance at first no bigger.

† Vasco de Gama, the first who sailed round Africa by the Cape of Good Hope, to the East Indies.

‡ Don Henry, third son to John the First, King of Portugal. His strong genius to the discovery of new countries was the chief source of all the modern improvements of navigation.

Swift as the gale can bear the ship along,
And, from the partners of that cruel trade
Which spoils unhappy Guinea of her sons,
Demands his share of prey; demands themselves.
The stormy fates descend: one death involves
Tyrants and slaves; when straight, their mangled limbs
Crashing at once, he dyes the purple seas
With gore, and riots in the vengeful meal.
  When o'er this world, by equinoctial rains
Flooded immense, looks out the joyless sun,
And draws the copious steam; from swampy fens,
Where putrefaction into life ferments,
And breathes destructive myriads: or from woods,
Impenetrable shades, recesses foul,
In vapours rank and blue corruption wrapp'd,
Whose gloomy horrors yet no desperate foot
Has ever dared to pierce; then, wasteful, forth
Walks the dire Power of pestilent disease.
A thousand hideous fiends her course attend,
Sick Nature blasting, and to heartless woe,
And feeble desolation, casting down
The towering hopes and all the pride of Man.
Such as, of late, at Carthagena quench'd
The British fire. You, gallant Vernon, saw
The miserable scene; you, pitying, saw
To infant weakness sunk the warrior's arm;
Saw the deep-racking pang, the ghastly form,
The lip pale-quivering, and the beamless eye
No more with ardour bright: you heard the groans
Of agonizing ships from shore to shore;
Heard, nightly plunged amid the sullen waves,
The frequent corse: while on each other fix'd,
In sad presage, the blank assistants seem'd,
Silent, to ask, whom Fate would next demand.
  What need I mention those inclement skies,
Where, frequent o'er the sickening city, Plague,
The fiercest child of Nemesis divine,
Descends? From Ethiopia's poison'd woods,

From stifled Cairo's filth, and fetid fields
With locust armies putrefying heap'd,
This great destroyer sprung. Her awful rage
The brutes escape: Man is her destined prey,
Intemperate Man! and, o'er his guilty domes,
She draws a close incumbent cloud of death;
Uninterrupted by the living winds,
Forbid to blow a wholesome breeze; and stain'd
With many a mixture by the sun, suffused,
Of angry aspect. Princely wisdom, then,
Dejects his watchful eye; and from the hand
Of feeble justice, ineffectual, drop
The sword and balance: mute the voice of joy,
And hush'd the clamour of the busy world.
Empty the streets, with uncouth verdure clad;
Into the worst of deserts sudden turn'd
The cheerful haunt of men; unless escaped
From the doom'd house, where matchless horror reigns,
Shut up by barbarous fear, the smitten wretch,
With frenzy wild, breaks loose; and, loud to Heaven
Screaming, the dreadful policy arraigns,
Inhuman, and unwise. The sullen door,
Yet uninfected, on its cautious hinge
Fearing to turn, abhors society:
Dependants, friends, relations, Love himself,
Savaged by woe, forget the tender tie,
The sweet engagement of the feeling heart.
But vain their selfish care: the circling sky,
The wide enlivening air is full of fate;
And, struck by turns, in solitary pangs
They fall, unbless'd, untended, and unmourn'd.
Thus o'er the prostrate city black Despair
Extends her raven wing; while, to complete
The scene of desolation, stretch'd around,
The grim guards stand, denying all retreat,
And give the flying wretch a better death.
  Much yet remains unsung: the rage intense
Of brazen-vaulted skies, of iron fields,

Where drought and famine starve the blasted year
Fired by the torch of noon to tenfold rage,
The' infuriate hill that shoots the pillar'd flame;
And, roused within the subterranean world,
The' expanding earthquake, that resistless shakes
Aspiring cities from their solid base,
And buries mountains in the flaming gulf.
But 'tis enough; return, my vagrant Muse:
A nearer scene of horror calls thee home.
  Behold, slow-settling o'er the lurid grove
Unusual darkness broods; and growing gains
The full possession of the sky, surcharged
With wrathful vapour, from the secret beds,
Where sleep the mineral generations, drawn.
Thence nitre, sulphur, and the fiery spume
Of fat bitumen, steaming on the day,
With various tinctured trains of latent flame,
Pollute the sky, and in yon baleful cloud,
A reddening gloom, a magazine of fate
Ferment; till, by the touch ethereal roused,
The dash of clouds, or irritating war
Of fighting winds, while all is calm below,
They furious spring. A boding silence reigns,
Dread through the dun expanse; save the dull sound
That from the mountain, previous to the storm,
Rolls o'er the muttering earth, disturbs the flood,
And shakes the forest-leaf without a breath.
Prone, to the lowest vale, the aerial tribes
Descend: the tempest-loving raven scarce
Dares wing the dubious dusk. In rueful gaze
The cattle stand, and on the scowling heavens
Cast a deploring eye; by man forsook,
Who to the crowded cottage hies him fast,
Or seeks the shelter of the downward cave.
  'Tis listening fear, and dumb amazement all:
When to the startled eye the sudden glance
Appears far south, eruptive through the cloud;
And, following slower, in explosion vast,

The Thunder raises his tremendous voice.
At first, heard solemn o'er the verge of heaven,
The tempest growls; but as it nearer comes,
And rolls its awful burden on the wind,
The lightnings flash a larger curve, and more
The noise astounds: till over head a sheet
Of livid flame discloses wide; then shuts,
And opens wider; shuts and opens still
Expansive, wrapping ether in a blaze.
Follows the loosen'd aggravated roar,
Enlarging, deepening, mingling; peal on peal
Crush'd horrible, convulsing heaven and earth.
  Down comes a deluge of sonorous hail,
Or prone-descending rain. Wide-rent, the clouds
Pour a whole flood; and yet, its flame unquench'd,
The' unconquerable lightning struggles through,
Ragged and fierce, or in red whirling balls,
And fires the mountains with redoubled rage.
Black from the stroke, above, the smouldering pine
Stands a sad shatter'd trunk; and, stretch'd below,
A lifeless group the blasted cattle lie:
Here the soft flocks, with that same harmless look
They wore alive, and ruminating still
In fancy's eye; and there the frowning bull,
And ox half-raised. Struck on the castled cliff,
The venerable tower and spiry fane
Resign their aged pride. The gloomy woods
Start at the flash, and from their deep recess,
Wide-flaming out, their trembling inmates shake.
Amid Carnarvon's mountains rages loud
The repercussive roar: with mighty crush,
Into the flashing deep, from the rude rocks
Of Penmanmaur heap'd hideous to the sky,
Tumble the smitten cliffs: and Snowden's peak,
Dissolving, instant yields his wintry load.
Far seen, the heights of heathy Cheviot blaze,
And Thulè bellows through her utmost isles.
  Guilt hears appall'd, with deeply troubled thought

And yet not always on the guilty head
Descends the fated flash. Young Celadon
And his Amelia were a matchless pair;
With equal virtue form'd, and equal grace,
The same, distinguished by their sex alone
Hers the mild lustre of the blooming morn,
And his the radiance of the risen day.
  They loved: but such the guileless passion was,
As in the dawn of time inform'd the heart
Of innocence, and undissembling truth.
'Twas friendship heighten'd by the mutual wish;
The' enchanting hope and sympathetic glow
Beam'd from the mutual eye. Devoting all
To love, each was to each a dearer self;
Supremely happy in the' awaken'd power
Of giving joy. Alone, amid the shades,
Still in harmonious intercourse they lived
The rural day, and talk'd the flowing heart,
Or sigh'd and look'd unutterable things.
  So pass'd their life, a clear united stream,
By care unruffled; till, in evil hour,
The tempest caught them on the tender walk,
Heedless how far and where its mazes stray'd,
While, with each other bless'd, creative love
Still bade eternal Eden smile around.
Presaging instant fate her bosom heaved
Unwonted sighs, and, stealing oft a look
Of the big gloom, on Celadon her eye
Fell tearful, wetting her disorder'd cheek.
In vain, assuring love and confidence
In Heaven repress'd her fear; it grew, and shook
Her frame near dissolution. He perceived
The' unequal conflict; and as angels look
On dying saints, his eyes compassion shed,
With love illumined high. "Fear not," he said,
"Sweet innocence! thou stranger to offence,
And inward storm! He, who yon skies involves
In frowns of darkness, ever smiles on thee

With kind regard. O'er thee the secret shaft
That wastes at midnight, or the' undreaded hour
Of noon, flies harmless : and that very voice,
Which thunders terror through the guilty heart,
With tongues of seraphs whispers peace to thine
Tis safety to be near thee sure, and thus
To clasp perfection !" From his void embrace,
(Mysterious Heaven !) that moment, to the ground,
A blacken'd corse, was struck the beauteous maid.
But who can paint the lover, as he stood,
Pierced by severe amazement, hating life,
Speechless, and fix'd in all the death of woe !
So, faint resemblance ! on the marble tomb,
The well desembled mourner stooping stands,
For ever silent and for ever sad.
  As from the face of heaven the shatter'd clouds
Tumultuous rove, the' interminable sky
Sublimer swells, and o'er the world expands
A purer azure. Through the lighten'd air
A higher lustre and a clearer calm,
Diffusive, tremble ; while, as if in sign
Of danger past, a glittering robe of joy,
Set off abundant by the yellow ray,
Invests the fields ; and nature smiles revived.
  'Tis beauty all, and grateful song around,
Join'd to the low of kine, and numerous bleat
Of flocks thick-nibbling through the clover'd vale.
And shall the hymn be marr'd by thankless Man,
Most favour'd ! who with voice articulate
Should lead the chorus of this lower world ;
Shall he, so soon forgetful of the Hand
That hush'd the thunder, and serenes the sky,
Extinguish'd feel that spark the tempest waked,
That sense of powers exceeding far his own,
Ere yet his feeble heart has lost its fears ?
  Cheer'd by the milder beam, the sprightly youth
Speeds to the well known pool, whose crystal depth
A sandy bottom shows. Awhile he stands

Gazing the' inverted landscape, half afraid
To meditate the blue profound below;
Then plunges headlong down the circling flood.
His ebon tresses and his rosy cheek
Instant emerge; and, through the' obedient wave,
At each short breathing by his lip repell'd,
With arms and legs according well, he makes.
As humour leads, an easy-winding path;
While, from his polish'd sides, a dewy light
Effuses on the pleased spectators round.

This is the purest exercise of health,
The kind refresher of the summer heats;
Nor when cold Winter keens the brightening flood,
Would I weak-shivering linger on the brink.
Thus life redoubles, and is oft preserved,
By the bold swimmer, in the swift elapse
Of accident disastrous. Hence the limbs
Knit into force; and the same Roman arm,
That rose victorious o'er the conquer'd earth,
First learn'd, while tender, to subdue the wave.
Even from the body's purity, the mind
Receives a secret sympathetic aid.

Close in the covert of a hazel copse,
Where winded into pleasing solitudes
Runs out the rambling dale, young Damon sat,
Pensive, and pierced with love's delightful pangs.
There to the stream that down the distant rocks
Hoarse-murmuring fell, and plaintive breeze that play'd
Among the bending willows, falsely he
Of Musidora's cruelty complain'd.
She felt his flame; but deep within her breast
In bashful coyness, or in maiden pride,
The soft return conceal'd; save when it stole
In sidelong glances from her downcast eye,
Or from her swelling soul in stifled sighs.
Touch'd by the scene, no stranger to his vows,
He framed a melting lay, to try her heart;
And, if an infant passion struggled there,

To call that passion forth. Thrice happy swain!
A lucky chance, that oft decides the fate
Of mighty monarchs, then decided thine.
For lo! conducted by the laughing Loves,
This cool retreat his Musidora sought:
Warm in her cheek the sultry season glow'd;
And, robed in loose array, she came to bathe
Her fervent limbs in the refreshing stream.
What shall he do? In sweet confusion lost,
And dubious flutterings, he awhile remain'd:
A pure ingenuous elegance of soul,
A delicate refinement, known to few,
Perplex'd his breast, and urged him to retire:
But love forbade. Ye prudes in virtue, say,
Say, ye severest, what would you have done?
Meantime, this fairer nymph than ever bless'd
Arcadian stream, with timid eye around
The banks surveying, stripp'd her beauteous limbs,
To taste the lucid coolness of the flood.
Ah then! not Paris on the piny top
Of Ida panted stronger, when aside
The rival-goddesses the veil divine
Cast unconfined, and gave him all their charms,
Than, Damon, thou; as from the snowy leg,
And slender foot, the' inverted silk she drew;
As the soft touch dissolved the virgin zone;
And, through the parting robe, the' alternate breast,
With youth wild-throbbing, on thy lawless gaze
In full luxuriance rose. But, desperate youth,
How durst thou risk the soul-distracting view;
As from her naked limbs of glowing white,
Harmonious swell'd by Nature's finest hand,
In folds loose-floating fell the fainter lawn;
And fair-exposed she stood, shrunk from herself,
With fancy blushing, at the doubtful breeze
Alarm'd, and starting like the fearful fawn?
Then to the flood she rush'd; the parted flood
Its lovely guest with closing waves received;

And every beauty softening, every grace
Flushing anew, a mellow lustre shed:
As shines the lily through the crystal mild;
Or as the rose amid the morning dew,
Fresh from Aurora's hand, more sweetly glows.
While thus she wanton'd, now beneath the wave
But ill concealed; and now with streaming locks,
That half-embraced her in a humid veil,
Rising again, the latent Damon drew
Such maddening draughts of beauty to the soul
As for awhile o'erwhelm'd his raptured thought
With luxury too daring. Check'd, at last,
By love's respectful modesty, he deem'd
The theft profane, if aught profane to love
Can e'er be deem'd; and, struggling from the shade,
With headlong hurry fled: but first these lines,
Traced by his ready pencil, on the bank
With trembling hand he threw:—"Bathe on, my fair,
Yet unbeheld save by the sacred eye
Of faithful love: I go to guard thy haunt,
To keep from thy recess each vagrant foot,
And each licentious eye." With wild surprise,
As if to marble struck, devoid of sense,
A stupid moment motionless she stood:
So stands the statue* that enchants the world,
So bending tries to veil the matchless boast,
The mingled beauties of exulting Greece.
Recovering, swift she flew to find those robes
Which blissful Eden knew not; and, array'd
In careless haste, the' alarming paper snatch'd.
But, when her Damon's well known hand she saw,
Her terrors vanish'd, and a softer train
Of mix'd emotions, hard to be described,
Her sudden bosom seized: shame void of guilt,
The charming blush of innocence, esteem,
And admiration of her lover's flame,
By modesty exalted: even a sense

* The Venus of Medici.

Of self-approving beauty stole across
Her busy thought. At length, a tender calm
Hush'd by degrees the tumult of her soul;
And on the spreading beech, that o'er the stream
Incumbent hung, she with the silvan pen
Of rural lovers this confession carved,
Which soon her Damon kiss'd with weeping joy:
"Dear youth! sole judge of what these verses mean,
By fortune too much favour'd, but by love,
Alas! not favour'd less, be still as now
Discreet; the time may come you need not fly."
The sun has lost his rage: his downward orb
Shoots nothing now but animating warmth,
And vital lustre; that, with various ray,
Lights up the clouds, those beauteous robes of heaven,
Incessant roll'd into romantic shapes,
The dream of waking fancy! broad below
Cover'd with ripening fruits, and swelling fast
Into the perfect year, the pregnant earth
And all her tribes rejoice. Now the soft hour
Of walking comes: for him who lonely loves
To seek the distant hills, and there converse
With Nature; there to harmonize his heart,
And in pathetic song to breathe around
The harmony to others. Social friends,
Attuned to happy unison of soul;
To whose exalting eye a fairer world,
Of which the vulgar never had a glimpse,
Displays its charms; whose minds are richly fraught
With philosophic stores, superior light;
And in whose breast, enthusiastic, burns
Virtue, the sons of interest deem romance;
Now call'd abroad enjoy the falling day:
Now to the verdant Portico of woods,
To Nature's vast Lyceum, forth they walk;
By that kind School where no proud master reigns,
The full free converse of the friendly heart,
Improving and improved. Now from the world,

Sacred to sweet retirement, lovers steal,
And pour their souls in transport, which the Sire
Of love approving hears, and calls it good.
Which way, Amanda, shall we bend our course?
The choice perplexes. Wherefore should we choose?
All is the same with thee. Say, shall we wind
Along the streams? or walk the smiling mead?
Or court the forest glades? or wander wild
Among the waving harvest? or ascend,
While radiant Summer opens all its pride,
Thy hill, delightful Shene?* Here let us sweep
The boundless landscape: now the raptured eye,
Exulting swift, to huge Augusta send;
Now to the Sister Hills† that skirt her plain,
To lofty Harrow now, and now to where
Majestic Windsor lifts his princely brow.
In lovely contrast to this glorious view
Calmly magnificent, then will we turn
To where the silver Thames first rural grows
There let the feasted eye unwearied stray:
Luxurious, there, rove through the pendent woods
That nodding hang o'er Harrington's retreat;
And, stooping thence to Ham's embowering walks,
Beneath whose shades, in spotless peace retired,
With Her the pleasing partner of his heart,
The worthy Queensberry yet laments his Gay,
And polish'd Cornbury woos the willing Muse.
Slow let us trace the matchless Vale of Thames;
Fair-winding up to where the Muses haunt
In Twit'nam's bowers, and for their Pope implore
The healing God;‡ to royal Hampton's pile,
To Clermont's terraced height, and Esher's groves,
Where in the sweetest solitude, embraced
By the soft windings of the silent Mole,
From courts and senates Pelham finds repose.

* The old name of Richmond, signifying, in Saxon, Shining or Splendour.

† Highgate and Hampstead. ‡ In his last sickness.

Enchanting vale! beyond whate'er the Muse
Has of Achaia or Hesperia sung!
O vale of bliss! O softly swelling hills!
On which the Power of Cultivation lies,
And joys to see the wonders of his toil.
 Heavens! what a goodly prospect spreads around,
Of hills, and dales, and woods, and lawns, and spires,
And glittering towns, and gilded streams, till all
The stretching landscape into smoke decays!
Happy Britannia! where the Queen of Arts,
Inspiring vigour, Liberty abroad
Walks, unconfined, even to thy furthest cots,
And scatters plenty with unsparing hand.
 Rich is thy soil, and merciful thy clime;
Thy streams unfailing in the Summer's drought;
Unmatch'd thy guardian oaks; thy valleys float
With golden waves: and on thy mountains flocks
Bleat numberless! while, roving round the sides,
Bellow the blackening herds in lusty droves.
Beneath, thy meadows glow, and rise unquell'd
Against the mower's scythe. On every hand
Thy villas shine. Thy country teems with wealth,
And property assures it to the swain,
Pleased and unwearied, in his guarded toil.
 Full are thy cities with the sons of Art;
And trade and joy, in every busy street,
Mingling are heard: e'en Drudgery himself,
As at the car he sweats, or dusty hews
The palace stone, looks gay. Thy crowded ports,
Where rising masts an endless prospect yield,
With labour burn, and echo to the shouts
Of hurried sailor, as he hearty waves
His last adieu, and, loosening every sheet,
Resigns the spreading vessel to the wind.
 Bold, firm, and graceful are thy generous youth,
By hardship sinew'd, and by danger fired,
Scattering the nations where they go; and first
Or on the lisped plain, or stormy seas.

Mild are thy glories too, as o'er the plans
Of thriving peace thy thoughtful sires preside;
In genius and substantial learning high;
For every virtue, every worth, renown'd;
Sincere, plain-hearted, hospitable, kind;
Yet like the mustering thunder when provoked,
The dread of tyrants, and the sole resource
Of those that under grim oppression groan.
Thy sons of Glory many! Alfred thine,
In whom the splendour of heroic war,
And more heroic peace, when govern'd well,
Combine; whose hallow'd name the Virtues saint,
And his own Muses love; the best of Kings!
With him thy Edwards and thy Henries shine,
Names dear to fame; the first who deep impress'd
On haughty Gaul the terror of thy arms,
That awes her genius still. In statesman thou,
And patriots, fertile. Thine a steady More,
Who, with a generous though mistaken zeal,
Withstood a brutal tyrant's useful rage,
Like Cato firm, like Aristides just,
Like rigid Cincinnatus nobly poor,
A dauntless soul erect, who smiled on death.
Frugal and wise, a Walsingham is thine;
A Drake, who made thee mistress of the deep,
And bore thy name in thunder round the world.
Then flamed thy spirit high: but who can speak
The numerous worthies of the Maiden Reign?
In Raleigh mark their every glory mix'd;
Raleigh, the scourge of Spain! whose breast with all
The sage, the patriot, and the hero burn'd.
Nor sunk his vigour, when a coward reign
The warrior fetter'd, and at last resign'd,
To glut the vengeance of a vanquish'd foe.
Then, active still and unrestrain'd, his mind
Explored the vast extent of ages past,
And with his prison-hours enrich'd the world;
Yet found no times, in all the long research,

So glorious or so base as those he proved,
In which he conquer'd, and in which he bled.
Nor can the Muse the gallant Sidney pass,
The plume of war! with early laurels crown'd,
The lover's myrtle, and the poet's bay.
A Hampden too is thine, illustrious land,
Wise, strenuous, firm, of unsubmitting soul,
Who stemm'd the torrent of a downward age
To slavery prone, and bade thee rise again,
In all thy native pomp of freedom bold.
Bright, at his call, thy Age of Men effulged,
Of Men on whom late time a kindling eye
Shall turn, and tyrants tremble while they read.
Bring every sweetest flower, and let me strew
The grave where Russel lies; whose temper'd blood
With calmest cheerfulness for thee resign'd,
Stain'd the sad annals of a giddy reign;
Aiming at lawless power, though meanly sunk
In loose inglorious luxury. With him
His friend, the British Cassius,* fearless bled:
Of high determin'd spirit, roughly brave,
By ancient learning to the' enlighten'd love
Of ancient freedom warm'd. Fair thy renown
In awful sages and in noble bards;
Soon as the light of dawning Science spread
Her orient ray, and waked the Muses' song:
Thine is a Bacon; hapless in his choice,
Unfit to stand the civil storm of state,
And through the smooth barbarity of courts,
With firm but pliant virtue, forward still
To urge his course: him for the studious shade
Kind Nature form'd, deep, comprehensive, clear,
Exact, and elegant: in one rich soul,
Plato, the Stagyrite, and Tully join'd.
The great deliverer he! who from the gloom
Of cloister'd monks, and jargon-teaching schools,
Led forth the true Philosophy, there long

* Algernon Sidney.

Held in the magic chain of words and forms,
And definitions void: he led her forth,
Daughter of Heaven! that slow ascending still,
Investigating sure the chain of things,
With radiant finger points to heaven again.
The generous Ashley* thine, the friend of man;
Who scann'd his nature with a brother's eye,
His weakness prompt to shade, to raise his aim,
To touch the finer movements of the mind,
And with the moral beauty charm the heart.
Why need I name thy Boyle, whose pious search,
Amid the dark recesses of his works,
The great Creator sought? And why thy Locke,
Who made the whole internal world his own?
Let Newton, pure intelligence, whom God
To mortals lent, to trace his boundless works
From laws sublimely simple, speak thy fame
In all philosophy. For lofty sense,
Creative fancy, and inspection keen
Through the deep windings of the human heart,
Is not wild Shakspeare thine and Nature's boast?
Is not each great, each amiable Muse
Of classic ages in thy Milton met?
A genius universal as his theme;
Astonishing as chaos, as the bloom
Of blowing Eden fair, as heaven sublime!
Nor shall my verse that elder bard forget,
The gentle Spenser, Fancy's pleasing son;
Who, like a copious river, pour'd his song
O'er all the mazes of enchanted ground:
Nor thee, his ancient master, laughing sage,
Chaucer, whose native manners-painting verse,
Well moralized, shines through the gothic cloud
Of time and language o'er thy genius thrown.
May my song soften, as thy daughters I,
Britannia, hail! for beauty is their own,
The feeling heart, simplicity of life,

* Anthony Ashley Cooper, Earl of Shaftesbury.

And elegance, and taste: the faultless form,
Shaped by the hand of harmony; the cheek,
Where the live crimson, through the native white
Soft-shooting, o'er the face diffuses bloom,
And every nameless grace; the parted lip
Like the red rosebud moist with morning dew
Breathing delight; and, under flowing jet,
Or sunny ringlets, or of circling brown,
The neck slight-shaded, and the swelling breast:
The look resistless, piercing to the soul,
And by the soul inform'd, when dress'd in love
She sits high smiling in the conscious eye.
  Island of bliss! amid the subject seas,
That thunder round thy rocky coasts, set up,
At once the wonder, terror, and delight
Of distant nations; whose remotest shores
Can soon be shaken by thy naval arm;
Not to be shook thyself, but all assaults
Baffling, as thy hoar cliffs the loud sea-wave.
  O thou! by whose Almighty nod the scale
Of empire rises, or alternate falls,
Send forth the saving Virtues round the land,
In bright patrol: white Peace, and social Love;
The tender-looking Charity, intent
On gentle deeds, and shedding tears through smiles;
Undaunted Truth, and dignity of mind;
Courage composed and keen; sound Temperance,
Healthful in heart and looks; clear Chastity,
With blushes reddening as she moves along,
Disorder'd at the deep regard she draws;
Rough Industry; Activity untired,
With copious life informed, and all awake:
While in the radiant front, superior shines
That first paternal virtue, Public Zeal,
Who throws o'er all an equal wide survey,
And, ever musing on the commonweal,
Still labours glorious with some great design.
  Low walks the sun, and broadens by degrees,

Just o'er the verge of day. The shifting clouds
Assembled gay, a richly gorgeous train,
In all their pomp attend his setting throne.
Air, earth, and ocean smile immense. And now,
As if his weary chariot sought the bowers
Of Amphitritè and her tending nymphs,
(So Grecian fable sung,) he dips his orb;
Now half-immersed; and now a golden curve
Gives one bright glance, then total disappears.
  For ever running and enchanted round,
Passes the day, deceitful, vain, and void;
As fleets the vision o'er the formful brain,
This moment hurrying wild the' impassion'd soul,
The next in nothing lost. 'Tis so to him,
The dreamer of this earth, an idle blank:
A sight of horror to the cruel wretch,
Who all day long in sordid pleasure roll'd,
Himself a useless load, has squander'd vile,
Upon his scoundrel train, what might have cheer'd
A drooping family of modest worth.
But to the generous still-improving mind,
That gives the hopeless heart to sing for joy,
Diffusing kind beneficence around,
Boastless as now descends the silent dew;
To him the long review of order'd life
Is inward rapture, only to be felt.
  Confess'd from yonder slow-extinguished clouds,
All ether softening, sober evening takes
Her wonted station in the middle air;
A thousand shadows at her beck. First this
She sends on earth; then that of deeper dye
Steals soft behind; and then a deeper still,
In circle following circle, gathers round,
To close the face of things. A fresher gale
Begins to wave the wood, and stir the stream,
Sweeping with shadowy gust the fields of corn;
While the quail clamours for his running mate.
Wide o'er the thistly lawn, as swells the breeze,

A whitening shower of vegetable down
Amusive floats. The kind impartial care
Of Nature nought disdains: thoughtful to feed
Her lowest sons, and clothe the coming year,
From field to field the feather'd seed she wings.
His folded flock secure, the shepherd home
Hies merry-hearted: and by turns relieves
The ruddy milkmaid of her brimming pail;
The beauty whom perhaps his witless heart,
Unknowing what the joy-mix'd anguish means,
Sincerely loves, by that best language shown
Of cordial glances and obliging deeds.
Onward they pass, o'er many a panting height,
And valley sunk, and unfrequented; where
At fall of eve the fairy people throng,
In various game, and revelry, to pass
The summer night, as village stories tell.
But far about they wander from the grave
Of him, whom his ungentle fortune urged
Against his own sad breast to lift the hand
Of impious violence. The lonely tower
Is also shunn'd; whose mournful chambers hold,
So night-struck fancy dreams, the yelling ghost.
Among the crooked lanes, on every hedge,
The glowworm lights his gem; and through the dark
A moving radiance twinkles. Evening yields
The world to Night; not in her winter robe
Of massy stygian woof, but loose array'd
In mantle dun. A faint erroneous ray,
Glanced from the' imperfect surfaces of things,
Flings half an image on the straining eye;
While wavering woods, and villages, and streams,
And rocks, and mountain tops, that long retain'd
The' ascending gleam, are all one swimming scene,
Uncertain if beheld. Sudden to heaven
Thence weary vision turns; where, leading soft
The silent hours of love, with purest ray
Sweet Venus shines; and from her genial rise,

When daylight sickens till it springs afresh,
Unrival'd reigns, the fairest lamp of Night.
As thus the' effulgence tremulous I drink,
With cherish'd gaze, the lambent lightnings shoot
Across the sky, or horizontal dart
In wondrous shapes: by fearful murmuring crowds
Portentous deem'd. Amid the radiant orbs,
That more than deck, that animate the sky,
The life-infusing suns of other worlds;
Lo! from the dread immensity of space
Returning, with accelerated course,
The rushing comet to the sun descends;
And, as he sinks below the shading earth,
With awful train projected o'er the heavens,
The guilty nations tremble But, above
Those superstitious horrors that enslave
The fond sequacious herd, to mystic faith
And blind amazement prone, the' enlighten'd few
Whose godlike minds Philosophy exalts,
The glorious stranger hail. They feel a joy
Divinely great; they in their powers exult,
That wondrous force of thought, which mounting spurns
This dusky spot, and measures all the sky;
While, from his far excursion through the wilds
Of barren ether, faithful to his time,
They see the blazing wonder rise anew,
In seeming terror clad, but kindly bent
To work the will of all-sustaining Love;
From his huge vapoury train perhaps to shake
Reviving moisture on the numerous orbs,
Through which his long ellipsis winds; perhaps
To lend new fuel to declining suns,
To light up worlds, and feed the' eternal fire.
With thee, serene Philosophy, with thee,
And thy bright garland, let me crown my song!
Effusive source of evidence and truth!
A lustre shedding o'er the' ennobled mind,
Stronger than summer noon; and pure as that,

Whose mild vibrations sooth the parted soul,
New to the dawning of celestial day.
Hence through her nourish'd powers, enlarged by thee,
She springs aloft with elevated pride ;
Above the tangling mass of low desires,
That bind the fluttering crowd ; and, angel-wing'd,
The heights of science and of virtue gains,
Where all is calm and clear ; with Nature round,
Or in the starry regions, or the' abyss,
To Reason's and to Fancy's eye display'd :
The First up tracing, from the dreary void,
The chain of causes and effects to Him,
The world-producing Essence, who alone
Possesses being ; while the Last receives
The whole magnificence of heaven and earth,
And every beauty, delicate or bold,
Obvious or more remote, with livelier sense,
Diffusive painted on the rapid mind.
  Tutor'd by thee, hence Poetry exalts
Her voice to ages; and informs the page
With music, image, sentiment, and thought,
Never to die ! the treasure of mankind !
Their highest honour, and their truest joy !
  Without thee what were unenlighten'd Man ?
A savage roaming through the woods and wilds,
In quest of prey : and with the' unfashion'd fur
Rough clad ; devoid of every finer art
And elegance of life. Nor happiness
Domestic, mix'd of tenderness and care,
Nor moral excellence, nor social bliss,
Nor guardian law were his ; nor various skill
To turn the furrow, or to guide the tool
Mechanic ; nor the heaven-conducted prow
Of navigation bold, that fearless braves
The burning line or dares the wintry pole ;
Mother severe of infinite delights !
Nothing, save rapine, indolence, and guile,
And woes on woes, a still revolving train !

Whose horrid circle had made human life
Than nonexistence worse: but, taught by thee,
Ours are the plans of policy and peace;
To live like brothers, and conjunctive all
Embellish life. While thus laborious crowds
Ply the tough oar, Philosophy directs
The ruling helm; or like the liberal breath
Of potent heaven, invisible, the sail
Swells out, and bears the' inferior world along.
Nor to this evanescent speck of earth
Poorly confined, the radiant tracts on high
Are her exalted range; intent to gaze
Creation through; and, from tnat full complex
Of never ending wonders, to conceive
Of the SOLE BEING right, who spoke the Word,
And Nature moved complete. With inward view,
Thence on the' ideal kingdom swift she turns
Her eye; and instant, at her powerful glance,
The' obedient phantoms vanish or appear;
Compound, divide, and into order shift,
Each to his rank, from plain perception up
To the fair forms of Fancy's fleeting train:
To reason then, deducing truth from truth;
And notion quite abstract; where first begins
The world of spirits, action all, and life
Unfetter'd and unmix'd. But here the cloud
(So wills Eternal Providence) sits deep,
Enough for us to know that this dark state,
In wayward passions lost and vain pursuits,
This Infancy of Being cannot prove
The final issue of the works of GOD,
By boundless Love and perfect Wisdom form'd,
And ever rising with the rising mind.

AUTUMN.

The subject proposed. Addressed to Mr. Onslow. A prospect of the fields ready for harvest. Reflections in praise of Industry raised by that view. Reaping. A tale relative to it. A harvest storm. Shooting and hunting, their barbarity. A ludicrous account of fox-hunting. A view of an orchard. Wall-fruit. A vineyard. A description of fogs, frequent in the latter part of Autumn: whence a digression, inquiring into the rise of fountains and rivers. Birds of season considered, that now shift their habitation. The prodigious number of them that cover the northern and western isl s of Scotland. Hence a view of the country. A prospect of the discoloured, fading woods. After a gentle dusky day, moonlight. Autumnal meteors. Morning: to which succeeds a calm, pure, sunshiny day, such as usually shuts up the season. The harvest being gathered in, the country dissolved in joy. The whole concludes with a panegyric on a philosophical country life.

Crown'd with the sickle and the wheaten sheaf,
While Autumn, nodding o'er the yellow plain,
Comes jovial on; the Doric reed once more,
Well pleased, I tune. Whate'er the wintry frost
Nitrous prepared; the various blossom'd Spring
Put in white promise forth; and Summer suns
Concocted strong, rush boundless now to view
Full, perfect all, and swell my glorious theme
 Onslow! the Muse, ambitious of thy name,
To grace, inspire, and dignify her song,
Would from the public voice thy gentle ear
A while engage. Thy noble care she knows,
The patriot virtues that distend thy thought,
Spread on thy front, and in thy bosom glow;
While listening senates hang upon thy tongue,
Devolving through the maze of eloquence
A roll of periods sweeter than her song.
But she too pants for public virtue, she,
Though weak of power, yet strong in ardent will,
Whene'er her country rushes on her heart,

Assumes a bolder note, and fondly tries
To mix the patriot's with the poet's flame.
When the bright Virgin gives the beauteous days.
And Libra weighs in equal scales the year;
From heaven's high cope the fierce effulgence shook
Of parting Summer, a serener blue,
With golden light enliven'd, wide invests
The happy world. Attemper'd suns arise,
Sweet-beam'd, and shedding oft through lucid clouds
A pleasing calm; while broad, and brown, below
Extensive harvests hang the heavy head.
Rich, silent, deep, they stand; for not a gale
Rolls its light billows o'er the bending plain·
A calm of plenty! till the ruffled air
Falls from its poise, and gives the breeze to blow.
Rent is the fleecy mantle of the sky;
The clouds fly different; and the sudden sun
By fits effulgent gilds the' illumined field,
And black by fits the shadows sweep along.
A gaily chequer'd heart-expanding view,
Far as the circling eye can shoot around,
Unbounded tossing in a flood of corn.
These are thy blessings, Industry! rough power!
Whom labour still attends, and sweat, and pain,
Yet the kind source of every gentle art,
And all the soft civility of life:
Raiser of humankind! by Nature cast,
Naked, and helpless, out amid the woods
And wilds, to rude inclement elements;
With various seeds of art deep in the mind
Implanted, and profusely pour'd around
Materials infinite; but idle all.
Still unexerted, in the' unconscious breast,
Slept the lethargic powers; Corruption still,
Voracious, swallow'd what the liberal hand
Of bounty scatter'd o'er the savage year:
And still the sad barbarian, roving, mix'd
With beasts of prey; or for his acorn-meal

Fought the fierce tusky boar; a shivering wretch,
Aghast and comfortless, when the bleak north,
With Winter charged, let the mix'd tempest fly,
Hail, rain, and snow, and bitter-breathing frost:
Then to the shelter of the hut he fled;
And the wild season, sordid, pined away.
For home he had not; home is the resort
Of love, of joy, of peace and plenty, where,
Supporting and supported, polish'd friends
And dear relations mingle into bliss.
But this the rugged savage never felt,
E'en desolate in crowds; and thus his days
Roll'd heavy, dark, and unenjoy'd along:
A waste of time! till Industry approach'd,
And roused him from his miserable sloth;
His faculties unfolded; pointed out
Where lavish Nature the directing hand
Of Art demanded; show'd him how to raise
His feeble force by the mechanic powers,
To dig the mineral from the vaulted earth;
On what to turn the piercing rage of fire;
On what the torrent, and the gather'd blast;
Gave the tall ancient forest to his axe;
Taught him to chip the wood, and hew the stone
Till by degrees the finish'd fabric rose;
Tore from his limbs the blood-polluted fur,
And wrapp'd them in the woolly vestment warm,
Or bright in glossy silk and flowing lawn;
With wholesome viands fill'd his table; pour'd
The generous glass around, inspired to wake
The life-refining soul of decent wit:
Nor stopp'd at barren bare necessity;
But still advancing bolder, led him on
To pomp, to pleasure, elegance, and grace;
And, breathing high ambition through his soul,
Set science, wisdom, glory, in his view,
And bade him be the Lord of all below.
  Then gathering men their natural powers combined,

And form'd a Public: to the general good
Submitting, aiming, and conducting all.
For this the Patriot-Council met, the full,
The free, and fairly represented Whole;
For this they plann'd the holy guardian laws,
Distinguish'd orders, animated arts,
And with joint force Oppression chaining, set
Imperial Justice at the helm; yet still
To them accountable: nor, slavish, dream'd
That toiling millions must resign their weal,
And all the honey of their search, to such
As for themselves alone themselves have raised.
Hence every form of cultivated life
In order set, protected, and inspired,
Into perfection wrought. Uniting all,
Society grew numerous, high, polite,
And happy. Nurse of art! the city rear'd
In beauteous pride her tower-encircled head;
And, stretching street on street, by thousands drew,
From twining woody haunts, or the tough yew
To bows strong-straining, her aspiring sons.
Then commerce brought into the public walk
The busy merchant; the big warehouse built;
Raised the strong crane; choked up the loaded street
With foreign plenty; and thy stream, O Thames,
Large, gentle, deep, majestic, king of floods!
Chose for his grand resort On either hand,
Like a long wintry forest, groves of masts
Shot up their spires; the bellying sheet between
Possess'd the breezy void: the sooty hulk
Steer'd sluggish on; the splendid barge along
Row'd, regular, to harmony; around,
The boat, light-skimming, stretch'd its oary wings,
While deep the various voice of fervent toil
From bank to bank increased; whence ribb'd with oak,
To bear the British thunder, black and bold,
The roaring vessel rush'd into the main.
Then too the pillar'd dome, magnific, heaved

Its ample roof; and Luxury within
Pour'd out her glittering stores: the canvass smooth,
With glowing life protuberant, to the view
Embodied rose; the statue seem'd to breathe.
And soften into flesh, beneath the touch
Of forming art, imagination flush'd.
All is the gift of Industry; whate'er
Exalts, embellishes, and renders life
Delightful. Pensive Winter cheer'd by him
Sits at the social fire, and happy hears
The' excluded tempest idly rave along;
His harden'd fingers deck the gaudy Spring;
Without him Summer were an arid waste;
Nor to the' Autumnal months could thus transmit
Those full, mature, immeasurable stores,
That, waving round, recal my wandering song.
Soon as the morning trembles o'er the sky,
And, unperceived, unfolds the spreading day;
Before the ripen'd field the reapers stand,
In fair array; each by the lass he loves,
To bear the rougher part, and mitigate
By nameless gentle offices her toil.
At once they stoop and swell the lusty sheaves;
While through their cheerful band the rural talk,
The rural scandal, and the rural jest,
Fly harmless, to deceive the tedious time,
And steal unfelt the sultry hours away.
Behind the master walks, builds up the shocks;
And, conscious, glancing oft on every side
His sated eye, feels his heart heave with joy.
The gleaners spread around, and here and there,
Spike after spike, their scanty harvest pick.
Be not too narrow, husbandmen! but fling
From the full sheaf, with charitable stealth,
The liberable handful. Think, oh grateful think!
How good the God of Harvest is to you;
Who pours abundance o'er your flowing fields;
While these unhappy partners of your kind

Wide-hover round you, like the fowls of heaven,
And ask their humble dole. The various turns
Of fortune ponder; that your sons may want
What now, with hard reluctance, faint ye give.
The lovely young Lavinia once had friends;
And Fortune smiled, deceitful, on her birth.
For, in her helpless years deprived of all,
Of every stay, save Innocence and Heaven,
She, with her widow'd mother, feeble, old,
And poor, lived in a cottage, far retired
Among the windings of a woody vale;
By solitude and deep surrounding shades,
But more by bashful modesty, conceal'd.
Together thus they shunn'd the cruel scorn
Which virtue, sunk to poverty, would meet
From giddy passion and low-minded pride:
Almost on Nature's common bounty fed;
Like the gay birds that sung them to repose,
Content, and careless of to-morrow's fare.
Her form was fresher than the morning rose
When the dew wets its leaves; unstain'd and pure,
As is the lily or the mountain-snow.
The modest virtues mingled in her eyes,
Still on the ground dejected, darting all
Their humid beams into the blooming flowers:
Or when the mournful tale her mother told,
Of what her faithless fortune promised once,
Thrill'd in her thought, they, like the dewy star
Of evening, shone in tears. A native grace
Sat fair-proportion'd on her polish'd limbs,
Veil'd in a simple robe, their best attire,
Beyond the pomp of dress; for loveliness
Needs not the foreign aid of ornament,
But is, when unadorn'd, adorn'd the most.
Thoughtless of beauty, she was Beauty's self,
Recluse amid the close-embowering woods.
As in the hollow breast of Apennine,
Beneath the shelter of encircling hills,

A myrtle rises, far from human eye,
And breathes its balmy fragrance o'er the wild;
So flourish'd blooming, and unseen by all,
The sweet Lavinia; till, at length, compell'd
By strong Necessity's supreme command,
With smiling patience in her looks, she went
To glean Palemon's fields. The pride of swains
Palemon was, the generous and the rich;
Who led the rural life in all its joy
And elegance, such as Arcadian song
Transmits from ancient uncorrupted times;
When tyrant custom had not shackled man,
But free to follow Nature was the mode.
He then, his fancy with autumnal scenes
Amusing, chanced beside his reaper-train
To walk, when poor Lavinia drew his eye;
Unconscious of her power, and turning quick
With unaffected blushes from his gaze:
He saw her charming, but he saw not half
The charms her downcast modesty conceal'd.
That very moment love and chaste desire
Sprung in his bosom, to himself unknown;
For still the world prevail'd, and its dread laugh,
Which scarce the firm philosopher can scorn,
Should his heart own a gleaner in the field;
And thus in secret to his soul he sigh'd:—
"What pity! that so delicate a form,
By beauty kindled, where enlivening sense
And more than vulgar goodness seem to dwell,
Should be devoted to the rude embrace
Of some indecent clown; she looks, methinks,
Of old Acasto's line; and to my mind
Recals that patron of my happy life,
From whom my liberal fortune took its rise;
Now to the dust gone down; his houses, lands,
And once fair-spreading family, dissolved.
'Tis said, that in some lone obscure retreat,
Urged by remembrance sad, and decent pride,

Far from those scenes which knew their better days,
His aged widow and his daughter live,
Whom yet my fruitless search could never find.
Romantic wish! would this the daughter were!"
When, strict inquiring, from herself he found
She was the same, the daughter of his friend,
Of bountiful Acasto; who can speak
The mingled passions that surprised his heart,
And through his nerves in shivering transport ran?
Then blazed his smother'd flame, avow'd, and bold;
And as he view'd her, ardent, o'er and o'er,
Love, gratitude, and pity wept at once.
Confused, and frighten'd at his sudden tears,
Her rising beauties flush'd a higher bloom,
As thus Palemon, passionate and just,
Pour'd out the pious rapture of his soul:
"And art thou then Acasto's dear remains?
She, whom my restless gratitude has sought,
So long in vain? O heavens! the very same,
The soften'd image of my noble friend,
Alive his every look, his every feature,
More elegantly touch'd. Sweeter than Spring!
Thou sole surviving blossom from the root
That nourish'd up my fortune! say, ah where,
In what sequester'd desert, hast thou drawn
The kindest aspect of delighted heaven?
Into such beauty spread, and blown so fair;
Though Poverty's cold wind and crushing rain
Beat keen and heavy on thy tender years?
O, let me now into a richer soil
Transplant thee safe! where vernal suns and showers
Diffuse their warmest, largest influence;
And of my garden be the pride and joy!
Ill it befits thee, oh, it ill befits
Acasto's daughter, his, whose open stores,
Though vast, were little to his ampler heart,
The father of a country, thus to pick
The very refuse of those harvest-fields

Which from his bounteous friendship I enjoy.
Then throw that shameful pittance from thy hand,
But ill apply'd to such a rugged task;
The fields, the master, all, my fair, are thine:
If to the various blessings which thy house
Has on me lavish'd, thou wilt add that bliss,
That dearest bliss, the power of blessing thee!"
Here ceased the youth: yet still his speaking eye
Express'd the sacred triumph of his soul,
With conscious virtue, gratitude, and love,
Above the vulgar joy divinely raised.
Nor waited he reply. Won by the charm
Of goodness irresistible, and all
In sweet disorder lost, she blush'd consent.
The news immediate to her mother brought,
While, pierced with anxious thought, she pined away
The lonely moments for Lavinia's fate:
Amazed, and scarce believing what she heard,
Joy seized her wither'd veins, and one bright gleam
Of setting life shone on her evening hours:
Not less enraptured than the happy pair;
Who flourish'd long in tender bliss, and rear'd
A numerous offspring, lovely like themselves,
And good, the grace of all the country round.
Defeating oft the labours of the year,
The sultry south collects a potent blast.
At first, the groves are scarcely seen to stir
Their trembling tops; and a still murmur runs
Along the soft-inclining fields of corn.
But as the aerial tempest fuller swells,
And in one mighty stream, invisible,
Immense, the whole excited atmosphere
Impetuous rushes o'er the sounding world;
Strain'd to the root, the stooping forest pours
A rustling shower of yet untimely leaves.
High-beat, the circling mountains eddy in,
From the bare wild, the dissipated storm,
And send it in a torrent down the vale.

Exposed, and naked to its utmost rage,
Through all the sea of harvest rolling round,
The billowy plain floats wide; nor can evade,
Though pliant to the blast, its seizing force,
Or whirl'd in air, or into vacant chaff
Shook waste. And sometimes too a burst of rain
Swept from the black horizon, broad, descends
In one continuous flood. Still overhead
The mingling tempest weaves its gloom, and still
The deluge deepens; till the fields around
Lie sunk and flatted in the sordid wave.
Sudden, the ditches swell; the meadows swim.
Red, from the hills, innumerable streams
Tumultuous roar; and high above its banks
The river lift; before whose rushing tide,
Herds, flocks, and harvests, cottages, and swains,
Roll mingled down; all that the winds had spared
In one wild moment ruin'd; the big hopes
And well earn'd treasures of the painful year.
Fled to some eminence, the husbandman
Helpless beholds the miserable wreck
Driving along; his drowning ox at once
Descending, with his labours scatter'd round,
He sees; and instant o'er his shivering thought
Comes Winter unprovided, and a train
Of claimant children dear. Ye masters, then,
Be mindful of the rough laborious hand
That sinks you soft in elegance and ease;
Be mindful of those limbs in russet clad,
Whose toil to yours is warmth and grateful pride,
And, oh! be mindful of that sparing board,
Which covers yours with luxury profuse,
Makes your glass sparkle, and your sense rejoice!
Nor cruelly demand what the deep rains
And all involving winds have swept away.
 Here the rude clamour of the sportsman's joy,
The gun fast thundering, and the winded horn,
Would tempt the Muse to sing the rural game:

How in his mid career the spaniel struck,
Stiff, by the tainted gale, with open nose,
Outstretch'd, and finely sensible, draws full,
Fearful, and cautious, on the latent prey;
As in the sun the circling covey bask
Their varied plumes, and, watchful every way,
Through the rough stubble turn the secret eye.
Caught in the meshy snare, in vain they beat
Their idle wings, entangled more and more:
Nor on the surges of the boundless air,
Though borne triumphant, are they safe; the gun,
Glanced just and sudden from the fowler's eye,
O'ertakes their sounding pinions: and again,
Immediate, brings them, from the towering wing,
Dead to the ground; or drives them wide-dispersed,
Wounded, and wheeling various, down the wind.
  These are not subjects for the peaceful Muse,
Nor will she stain with such her spotless song:
Then most delighted, when she social sees
The whole mix'd animal creation round
Alive and happy. 'Tis not joy to her,
This falsely cheerful barbarous game of death,
This rage of pleasure, which the restless youth
Awakes, impatient, with the gleaming morn·
When beasts of prey retire, that all night long,
Urged by necessity, had ranged the dark,
As if their conscious ravage shunn'd the light,
Ashamed. Not so the steady tyrant Man,
Who, with the thoughtless insolence of power
Inflamed, beyond the most infuriate wrath
Of the worst monster that e'er roam'd the waste,
For sport alone pursues the cruel chase,
Amid the beamings of the gentle days.
Upbraid, ye ravening tribes, our wanton rage,
For hunger kindles you, and lawless want;
But lavish fed, in Nature's bounty roll'd,
To joy at anguish, and delight in blood,
Is what your horrid bosoms never knew.

Poor is the triumph o'er the timid hare!
Scared from the corn, and now to some lone seat
Retired: the rushy fen; the ragged furze,
Stretch'd o'er the stony heath; the stubble chapt,
The thistly lawn; the thick entangled broom;
Of the same friendly hue, the wither'd fern;
The fallow ground laid open to the sun,
Concoctive; and the nodding sandy bank,
Hung o'er the mazes of the mountain brook.
Vain is her best precaution; though she sits
Conceal'd, with folded ears; unsleeping eyes,
By Nature raised to take the' horizon in;
And head couch'd close betwixt her hairy feet,
In act to spring away. The scented dew
Betrays her early labyrinth; and deep,
In scatter'd sullen openings, far behind,
With every breeze she hears the coming storm.
But nearer, and more frequent, as it loads
The sighing gale, she springs amazed, and all
The savage soul of game is up at once:
The pack full-opening, various; the shrill horn,
Resounded from the hills; the neighing steed,
Wild for the chase; and the loud hunters shout;
O'er a weak, harmless, flying creature, all
Mix'd in mad tumult and discordant joy.
The stag, too, singled from the herd, where long
He ranged the branching monarch of the shades,
Before the tempest drives. At first, in speed
He, sprightly, puts his faith; and, roused by fear,
Gives all his swift aerial soul to flight:
Against the breeze he darts, that way the more
To leave the lessening murderous cry behind.
Deception short! though fleeter than the winds
Blown o'er the keen-air'd mountain by the north,
He bursts the thickets, glances through the glades,
And plunges deep into the wildest wood;
If slow, yet sure, adhesive to the track
Hot-steaming, up behind him come again

The' inhuman rout, and from the shady depth
Expel him, circling through his every shift,
He sweeps the forest oft; and sobbing sees
The glades, mild opening to the golden day;
Where, in kind contest, with his butting friends
He wont to struggle, or his loves enjoy.
Oft in the full-descending flood he tries
To lose the scent, and lave his burning sides:
Oft seeks the herd; the watchful herd, alarm'd,
With selfish care avoid a brother's woe.
What shall he do? His once so vivid nerves,
So full of buoyant spirit, now no more
Inspire the course; but fainting breathless toil,
Sick, seizes on his heart: he stands at bay;
And puts his last weak refuge in despair.
The big round tears run down his dappled face;
He groans in anguish: while the growling pack,
Blood-happy, hang at his fair jutting chest,
And mark his beauteous checquer'd sides with gore.
Of this enough. But if the silvan youth,
Whose fervent blood boils into violence,
Must have the chase; behold, despising flight,
The roused-up lion resolute and slow,
Advancing full on the protended spear
And coward-band, that circling wheel aloof.
Slunk from the cavern and the troubled wood,
See the grim wolf; on him his shaggy foe
Vindictive fix, and let the ruffian die:
Or, growling horrid, as the brindled boar
Grins fell destruction, to the monster's heart
Let the dart lighten from the nervous arm.
These Britain knows not; give, ye Britons, then
Your sportive fury, pitiless, to pour
Loose on the nightly robber of the fold;
Him, from his craggy winding haunts unearth'd,
Let all the thunder of the chase pursue.
Throw the broad ditch behind you; o'er the hedge
High-bound, resistless; nor the deep morass

Refuse, but through the shaking wilderness
Pick your nice way; into the perilous flood
Bear fearless, of the raging instinct full;
And as you ride the torrent, to the banks
Your triumph sound sonorous, running round
From rock to rock, in circling echoes toss'd;
Then scale the mountains to their woody tops;
Rush down the dangerous steep; and o'er the lawn,
In fancy swallowing up the space between,
Pour all your speed into the rapid game.
For happy he! who tops the wheeling chase;
Has every maze evolved, and every guile
Disclosed; who knows the merits of the pack;
Who saw the villain seized, and dying hard,
Without complaint, though by a hundred mouths
Relentless torn: O glorious he, beyond
His daring peers! when the retreating horn
Calls them to ghostly halls of gray renown,
With woodland honours graced; the fox's fur,
Depending decent from the roof; and spread
Round the drear walls, with antic figures fierce,
The stag's large front: he then is loudest heard,
When the night staggers with severer toils,
With feats Thessalian Centaurs never knew,
And their repeated wonders shake the dome.
But first the fuel'd chimney blazes wide;
The tankards foam; and the strong table groans
Beneath the smoking sirloin, stretch'd immense
From side to side; in which, with desperate knife,
They deep incision make, and talk the while
Of England's glory, ne'er to be defaced
While hence they borrow vigour: or amain
Into the pasty plunged, at intervals,
If stomach keen can intervals allow,
Relating all the glories of the chase.
Then sated Hunger bids his brother Thirst
Produce the mighty bowl; the mighty bowl,
Swell'd high with fiery juice, steams liberal round

A potent gale, dolicious as the breath
Of Maia to the lovesick shepherdess,
On violets diffused, while soft she hears
Her panting shepherd stealing to her arms.
Nor wanting is the brown October, drawn,
Mature and perfect, from his dark retreat
Of thirty years ; and now his honest front
Flames in the light refulgent, not afraid
E'en with the vineyard's best produce to vie.
To cheat the thirsty moments, Whist awhile
Walks his dull round, beneath a cloud of smoke,
Wreathed, fragrant, from the pipe ; or the quick dice,
In thunder leaping from the box, awake
The sounding gammon : while romp-loving miss
Is haul'd about in gallantry robust.
  At last these puling idlenesses laid
Aside, frequent and full, the dry divan
Close in firm circle ; and set, ardent, in
For serious drinking. Nor evasion sly
Nor sober shift is to the puking wretch
Indulged apart ; but earnest, brimming bowls
Lave every soul, the table floating round,
And pavement, faithless to the fuddled foot.
Thus as they swim in mutual swill, the talk,
Vociferous at once from twenty tongues,
Reels fast from theme to theme ; from horses, hounds,
To church or mistress, politics or ghost,
In endless mazes, intricate, perplex'd.
Meantime, with sudden interruption, loud,
The' impatient catch bursts from the joyous heart ;
That moment touch'd is every kindred soul ;
And, opening in a full-mouth'd cry of joy,
The laugh, the slap, the jocund curse go round ;
While, from their slumbers shook, the kennel'd hounds
Mix in the music of the day again.
As when the tempest, that has vex'd the deep
The dark night long, with fainter murmurs falls ;
So gradual sinks their mirth. Their feeble tongues

Unable to take up the cumbrous word,
Lie quite dissolved. Before their maudlin eyes,
Seen dim and blue, the double tapers dance,
Like the sun wading through the misty sky.
Then, sliding soft, they drop. Confused above,
Glasses and bottles, pipes and gazetteers,
As if the table e'en itself was drunk,
Lie a wet broken scene ; and wide, below,
Is heap'd the social slaughter : where astride
The lubber Power in filthy triumph sits,
Slumberous, inclining still from side to side,
And steeps them drench'd in potent sleep till morn
Perhaps some doctor, of tremendous paunch,
Awful and deep, a black abyss of drink,
Outlives them all ; and from his buried flock
Retiring, full of rumination sad,
Laments the weakness of these latter times.
But if the rougher sex by this fierce sport
Is hurried wild, let not such horrid joy
E'er stain the bosom of the British Fair.
Far be the spirit of the chase from them !
Uncomely courage, unbeseeming skill ;
To spring the fence, to rein the prancing steed,
The cap, the whip, the masculine attire ;
In which they roughen to the sense, and all
The winning softness of their sex is lost.
In them 'tis graceful to dissolve at woe ;
With every motion, every word, to wave
Quick o'er the kindling cheek the ready blush ;
And from the smallest violence to shrink
Unequal, then the loveliest in their fears ;
And by this silent adulation, soft,
To their protection more engaging Man.
O may their eyes no miserable sight,
Save weeping lovers, see ! a nobler game,
Through love's enchanting wiles pursued, yet fled,
In chase ambiguous. May their tender limbs
Float in the loose simplicity of dress !

And, fashion'd all to harmony, alone
Know they to seize the captivated soul,
In rapture warbled from love-breathing lips;
To teach the lute to languish; with smooth step,
Disclosing motion in its every charm,
To swim along, and swell the mazy dance;
To train the foliage o'er the snowy lawn;
To guide the pencil, turn the tuneful page;
To lend new flavour to the fruitful year,
And heighten Nature's dainties: in their race
To rear their graces into second life;
To give society its highest taste;
Well order'd home man's best delight to make;
And by submissive wisdom, modest skill,
With every gentle care-eluding art,
To raise the virtues, animate the bliss,
And sweeten all the toils of human life:
This be the female dignity and praise.
  Ye swains, now hasten to the hazel-bank;
Where, down yon dale, the wildly winding brook
Falls hoarse from steep to steep. In close array,
Fit for the thickets and the tangling shrub,
Ye virgins, come. For you their latest song
The woodlands raise; the clustering nuts for you
The lover finds amid the secret shade;
And, where they burnish on the topmost bough,
With active vigour crushes down the tree;
Or shakes them ripe from the resigning husk,
A glossy shower, and of an ardent brown,
As are the ringlets of Melinda's hair:
Melinda! form'd with every grace complete.
Yet these neglecting, above beauty wise,
And far transcending such a vulgar praise.
  Hence from the busy joy-resounding fields,
In cheerful error, let us tread the maze
Of Autumn unconfined; and taste, revived,
The breath of orchard big with bending fruit.
Obedient to the breeze and beating ray,

From the deep-loaded bough a mellow shower
Incessant melts away. The juicy pear
Lies in a soft profusion scatter'd round.
A various sweetness swells the gentle race;
By Nature's all refining hand prepared;
Of temper'd sun, and water, earth, and air,
In ever changing composition mix'd.
Such, falling frequent through the chiller night,
The fragrant stores, the wide-projected heaps
Of apples, which the lusty-handed Year,
Innumerous, o'er the blushing orchard shakes.
A various spirit, fresh, delicious, keen,
Dwells in their gelid pores; and, active, points
The piercing cider for the thirsty tongue:
Thy native theme, and boon inspirer too,
Philips, Pomona's bard, the second thou
Who nobly durst, in rhyme-unfetter'd verse,
With British freedom sing the British song:
How, from Silurian vats, high-sparkling wines
Foam in transparent floods; some strong, to cheer
The wintry revels of the labouring hind;
And tasteful some, to cool the summer hours.
  In this glad season, while his sweetest beams
The sun sheds equal o'er the meeken'd day;
Oh, lose me in the green delightful walks
Of, Doddington, thy seat, serene and plain,
Where simple Nature reigns; and every view,
Diffusive, spreads the pure Dorsetian downs,
In boundless prospect; yonder shagg'd with wood,
Here rich with harvest, and there white with flocks!
Meantime the grandeur of thy lofty dome,
Far splendid, seizes on the ravish'd eye.
New beauties rise with each revolving day;
New columns swell; and still the fresh Spring finds
New plants to quicken, and new groves to green,
Full of thy genius all! the Muses' seat;
Where, in the secret bower and winding walk,
For virtuous Young and thee they twine the bay.

Here wandering oft, fired with the restless thirst
Of thy applause, I solitary court
The' inspiring breeze: and meditate the book
Of Nature ever open; aiming thence,
Warm from the heart, to learn the moral song.
Here, as I steal along the sunny wall,
Where Autumn basks, with fruit empurpled deep,
My pleasing theme continual prompts my thought:
Presents the downy peach; the shining plum;
The ruddy, fragrant nectarine; and dark,
Beneath his ample leaf, the luscious fig.
The vine too here her curling tendrils shoots;
Hangs out her clusters, glowing to the south;
And scarcely wishes for a warmer sky.
   Turn we a moment Fancy's rapid flight
To vigorous soils and climes of fair extent;
Where, by the potent sun elated high,
The vineyard swells refulgent on the day;
Spreads o'er the vale; or up the mountain climbs,
Profuse; and drinks amid the sunny rocks,
From cliff to cliff increased, the heighten'd blaze.
Low bend the weighty boughs. The clusters clear,
Half through the foliage seen, or ardent flame,
Or shine transparent; while perfection breathes
White o'er the turgent film the living dew.
As thus they brighten with exalted juice,
Touch'd into flavour by the mingling ray;
The rural youth and virgins o'er the field,
Each fond for each to cull the' autumnal prime,
Exulting rove, and speak the vintage nigh.
Then comes the crushing swain; the country floats,
And foams unbounded with the mashy flood;
That, by degrees fermented and refined,
Round the raised nations pours the cup of joy:
The claret smooth, red as the lip we press
In sparkling fancy, while we drain the bowl;
The mellow-tasted burgundy; and, quick
As is the wit it gives, the gay champagne.

Now, by the cool declining year condensed,
Descend the copious exhalations, check'd
As up the middle sky unseen they stole,
And roll the doubling fogs around the hill.
No more the mountain, horrid, vast, sublime,
Who pours a sweep of rivers from his sides,
And high between contending kingdoms rears
The rocky long division, fills the view
With great variety; but in a night
Of gathering vapour, from the baffled sense
Sinks dark and dreary. Thence expanding far,
The huge dusk, gradual, swallows up the plain
Vanish the woods: the dim-seen river seems
Sullen, and slow, to roll the misty wave.
E'en in the height of noon oppress'd, the sun
Sheds weak and blunt his wide-refracted ray;
Whence glaring oft, with many a broaden'd orb,
He frights the nations. Indistinct on earth,
Seen through the turbid air, beyond the life
Objects appear; and, wilder'd, o'er the waste
The shepherd stalks gigantic. Till at last
Wreathed dun around, in deeper circles still
Successive closing, sits the general fog
Unbounded o'er the world; and, mingling thick,
A formless gray confusion covers all.
As when of old (so sung the Hebrew Bard)
Light, uncollected, through the chaos urged
Its infant way; nor Order yet had drawn
His lovely train from out the dubious gloom.
These roving mists, that constant now begin
To smoke along the hilly country, these,
With weighty rains, and melted Alpine snows,
The mountain cisterns fill, those ample stores
Of water, scoop'd among the hollow rocks;
Whence gush the streams, the ceaseless fountains play,
And their unfailing wealth the rivers draw.
Some sages say, that, where the numerous wave
For ever lashes the resounding shore,

Drill'd through the sandy stratum, every way,
The waters with the sandy stratum rise;
Amid whose angles infinitely strain'd,
They joyful leave their jaggy salts behind,
And clear and sweeten as they soak along.
Nor stops the restless fluid, mounting still,
Though oft amidst the' irriguous vale it springs;
But to the mountain courted by the sand,
That leads it darkling on in faithful maze,
Far from the parent main, it boils again
Fresh into day; and all the glittering hill
Is bright with spouting rills. But hence this vain
Amusive dream! why should the waters love
To take so far a journey to the hills,
When the sweet valleys offer to their toil
Inviting quiet and a nearer bed?
Or if, by blind ambition led astray,
They must aspire; why should they sudden stop
Among the broken mountain's rushy dells,
And, ere they gain its highest peak, desert
The' attractive sand that charm'd their course so long?
Besides, the hard agglomerating salts,
The spoil of ages, would impervious choke
Their secret channels; or, by slow degrees,
High as the hills protrude the swelling vales:
Old Ocean too, suck'd through the porous globe,
Had long ere now forsook his horrid bed,
And brought Deucalion's watery times again.
Say then, where lurk the vast eternal springs,
That, like creating Nature lie conceal'd
From mortal eye, yet with their lavish stores
Refresh the globe and all its joyous tribes!
O thou pervading Genius, given to man,
To trace the secrets of the dark abyss,
O, lay the mountains bare! and wide display
Their hidden structure to the' astonish'd view!
Strip from the branching Alps their piny load;
The huge incumbrance of horrific woods

From Asian Taurus, from Imaus stretch'd
Athwart the roving Tartar's sullen bounds!
Give opening Hemus to my searching eye,
And high Olympus pouring many a stream!
O, from the sounding summits of the north,
The Dorfrine hills, through Scandinavia roll'd
To farthest Lapland and the frozen main;
From lofty Caucasus far seen by those
Who in the Caspian and black Euxine toil;
From cold Riphean rocks, which the wild Russ
Believes the stony girdle* of the world:
And all the dreadful mountains, wrapp'd in storm,
Whence wide Siberia draws her lonely floods;
O, sweep the' eternal snows! Hung o'er the deep,
That ever works beneath his sounding base,
Bid Atlas, propping Heaven, as poets feign,
His subterranean wonders spread! unveil
The miny caverns, blazing on the day,
Of Abyssinia's cloud-compelling cliffs,
And of the bending Mountains† of the Moon!
O'ertopping all these giant sons of earth,
Let the dire Andes, from the radiant line
Stretch'd to the stormy seas that thunder round
The southern pole, their hideous deeps unfold!
Amazing scene! behold! the glooms disclose,
I see the rivers in their infant beds!
Deep, deep I hear them labouring to get free,
I see the leaning strata, artful ranged;
The gaping fissures to receive the rains,
The melting snows, and ever dripping fogs.
Strow'd bibulous above I see the sands,
The pebbly gravel next, the layers then
Of mingled moulds, of more retentive earths,
The gutter'd rocks and mazy-running clefts;

* The Muscovites call the Riphean Mountains *Weliki Camenypoys*; that is, *the great stony Girdle*: because they suppose them to encompass the whole earth.

† A range of mountains in Africa, that surround almost all Monomotapa.

That, while the stealing moisture they transmit,
Retard its motion and forbid its waste.
Beneath the' incessant weeping of these drains,
I see the rocky siphons stretch'd immense,
The mighty reservoirs, of harden'd chalk,
Or stiff compacted clay, capacious form'd·
O'erflowing thence, the congregated stores,
The crystal treasures of the liquid world,
Through the stirr'd sands a bubbling passage burst,
And, welling out, around the middle steep,
Or from the bottoms of the bosom'd hills,
In pure effusion flow. United, thus,
The' exhaling sun, the vapour-burden'd air,
The gelid mountains, that to rain condensed
These vapours in continual current draw,
And send them, o'er the fair-divided earth,
In bounteous rivers to the deep again,
A social commerce hold, and firm support
The full adjusted harmony of things.
When Autumn scatters his departing gleams,
Warn'd of approaching Winter, gather'd, play
The swallow-people; and, toss'd wide around,
O'er the calm sky, in convolution swift,
The feather'd eddy floats: rejoicing once,
Ere to their wintry slumbers they retire;
In clusters clung, beneath the mouldering bank,
And where, unpierced by frost, the cavern sweats.
Or rather into warmer climes convey'd,
With other kindred birds of season, there
They twitter cheerful, till the vernal months
Invite them welcome back: for, thronging, now
Innumerous wings are in commotion all.
Where the Rhine loses his majestic force
In Belgian plains, won from the raging deep,
By diligence amazing and the strong
Unconquerable hand of Liberty;
The stork-assembly meets; for many a day,
Consulting deep, and various, ere they take

Their arduous voyage through the liquid sky.
And now their route design'd, their leaders chose,
Their tribes adjusted, clean'd their vigorous wings;
And many a circle, many a short essay,
Wheel'd round and round, in congregation full
The figured flight ascends; and, riding high
The' aerial billows, mixes with the clouds.
Or where the Northern ocean, in vast whirls,
Boils round the naked melancholy isles
Of furthest Thulè, and the' Atlantic surge
Pours in among the stormy Hebrides;
Who can recount what transmigrations there
Are annual made? what nations come and go?
And how the living clouds on clouds arise?
Infinite wings! till all the plume-dark air,
And rude resounding shore are one wild cry.
Here the plain harmless native his small flock,
And herd diminutive of many hues,
Tends on the little island's verdant swell,
The shepherd's seagirt reign; or, to the rocks
Dire-clinging, gathers his ovarious food;
Or sweeps the fishy shore! or treasures up
The plumage, rising full, to form the bed
Of luxury. And here awhile the muse,
High hovering o'er the broad cerulean scene,
Sees Caledonia, in romantic view:
Her airy mountains, from the waving main,
Invested with a keen diffusive sky,
Breathing the soul acute; her forests huge,
Incult, robust, and tall, by Nature's hand
Planted of old; her azure lakes between,
Pour'd out extensive, and of watery wealth
Full; winding deep, and green, her fertile vales;
With many a cool translucent brimming flood
Wash'd lovely, from the Tweed (pure parent stream,
Whose pastoral banks first heard my Doric reed,
With, silvan Jed, thy tributary brook)
To where the north-inflated tempest foams

O'er Orca's or Betubium's highest peak.
Nurse of a people, in Misfortune's school
Train'd up to hardy deeds; soon visited
By Learning, when before the gothic rage
She took her western flight. A manly race
Of unsubmitting spirit, wise, and brave;
Who still through bleeding ages struggled hard,
(As well unhappy Wallace can attest,
Great patriot hero! ill requited chief!)
To hold a generous undiminish'd state;
Too much in vain! Hence of unequal bounds
Impatient, and by tempting glory borne
O'er every land, for every land their life
Has flow'd profuse, their piercing genius plann'd,
And swell'd the pomp of peace their faithful toil,
As from their own clear north, in radiant streams,
Bright over Europe bursts the boreal morn.
  Oh! is there not some patriot, in whose power
That best, that godlike luxury is placed,
Of blessing thousands, thousands yet unborn,
Through late posterity? some, large of soul,
To cheer dejected industry? to give
A double harvest to the pining swain?
And teach the labouring hand the sweets of toil?
How, by the finest art, the native robe
To weave; how, white as hyperborean snow,
To form the lucid lawn; with venturous oar
How to dash wide the billow; nor look on,
Shamefully passive, while Batavian fleets
Defraud us of the glittering finny swarms,
That heave our friths and crowd upon our shores;
How all-enlivening trade to rouse, and wing
The prosperous sail, from every growing port,
Uninjured, round the sea-encircled globe;
And thus, in soul united as in name,
Bid Britain reign the mistress of the deep?
  Yes, there are such. And full on thee, Argyle
Her hope, her stay, her darling, and her boast,

From her first patriots and her heroes sprung,
Thy fond imploring country turns her eye;
In thee, with all a mother's triumph, sees
Her every virtue, every grace combined,
Her genius, wisdom, her engaging turn,
Her pride of honour, and her courage tried,
Calm, and intrepid, in the very throat
Of sulphurous war, on Tenier's dreadful field.
Nor less the palm of peace inwreathes thy brow:
For, powerful as thy sword, from thy rich tongue
Persuasion flows, and wins the high debate;
While mix'd in thee combine the charm of youth,
The force of manhood, and the depth of age.
Thee, Forbes, too, whom every worth attends,
As truth sincere, as weeping friendship kind,
Thee, truly generous, and in silence great,
Thy country feels through her reviving arts,
Plann'd by thy wisdom, by thy soul inform'd;
And seldom has she known a friend like thee.

But see the fading many colour'd woods,
Shade deepening over shade, the country round
Imbrown; a crowded umbrage, dusk, and dun,
Of every hue, from wan declining green
To sooty dark. These now the lonesome Muse,
Low whispering, lead into their leaf-strown walks,
And give the Season in its latest view.

Meantime, light-shadowing all, a sober calm
Fleeces unbounded ether: whose least wave
Stands tremulous, uncertain where to turn
The gentle current: while illumined wide,
The dewy-skirted clouds imbibe the sun,
And through their lucid veil his soften'd force
Shed o'er the peaceful world. Then is the time,
For those whom Wisdom and whom Nature charm,
To steal themselves from the degenerate crowd,
And soar above this little scene of things:
To tread low-thoughted Vice beneath their feet:

To sooth the throbbing passions into peace;
And woo lone Quiet in her silent walks.
  Thus solitary, and in pensive guise,
Oft let me wander o'er the russet mead,
And through the sadden'd grove, where scarce is heard
One dying strain, to cheer the woodman's toil.
Haply some widow'd songster pours his plaint,
Far, in faint warblings, through the tawny copse·
While congregated thrushes, linnets, larks,
And each wild throat, whose artless strains so late
Swell'd all the music of the swarming shades,
Robb'd of their tuneful souls, now shivering sit
On the dead tree, a dull despondent flock;
With not a brightness waving o'er their plumes,
And nought save chattering discord in their note.
O, let not, aim'd from some inhuman eye,
The gun the music of the coming year
Destroy; and harmless, unsuspecting harm,
Lay the weak tribes a miserable prey,
In mingled murder, fluttering on the ground!
  The pale-descending year, yet pleasing still,
A gentler mood inspires; for now the leaf
Incessant rustles from the mournful grove;
Oft startling such as, studious, walk below,
And slowly circles through the waving air.
But should a quicker breeze amid the boughs
Sob, o'er the sky the leafy deluge streams;
Till, choked and matted with the dreary shower,
The forest-walks, at every rising gale,
Roll wide the wither'd waste, and whistle bleak.
Fled is the blasted verdure of the fields;
And, shrunk into their beds, the flowery race
Their sunny robes resign. E'en what remain'd
Of stronger fruits falls from the naked tree;
And woods, fields, gardens, orchards, all around
The desolated prospect thrills the soul.
  He comes! he comes! in every breeze the Power

Of philosophic Melancholy comes!
His near approach the sudden-starting tear,
The glowing cheek, the mild dejected air,
The soften'd feature, and the beating heart,
Pierced deep with many a virtuous pang, declare.
O'er all the soul his sacred influence breathes.
Inflames imagination; through the breast
Infuses every tenderness; and far
Beyond dim earth exalts the swelling thought.
Ten thousand thousand fleet ideas, such
As never mingled with the vulgar dream,
Crowd fast into the mind's creative eye.
As fast the correspondent passions rise,
As varied, and as high: Devotion raised
To rapture and divine astonishment;
The love of Nature, unconfined, and, chief,
Of human race; the large ambitious wish,
To make them bless'd; the sigh for suffering worth
Lost in obscurity; the noble scorn
Of tyrant pride; the fearless great resolve;
The wonder which the dying patriot draws,
Inspiring glory through remotest time;
The' awaken'd throb for virtue and for fame;
The sympathies of love and friendship dear·
With all the social offspring of the heart.
 Oh! bear me then to vast embowering shades,
To twilight groves, and visionary vales;
To weeping grottoes, and prophetic glooms;
Where angel forms athwart the solemn dusk
Tremendous sweep, or seem to sweep along;
And voices more than human, through the void
Deep sounding, seize the' enthusiastic ear!
 Or is this gloom too much? Then lead, ye powers,
That o'er the garden and the rural seat
Preside, which shining through the cheerful land
In countless numbers bless'd Britannia sees;
O, lead me to the wide extended walks,

The fair majestic paradise of Stowe !*
Not Persian Cyrus on Ionia's shore
E'er saw such silvan scenes ; such various art
By genius fired, such ardent genius tamed
By cool judicious art ; that, in the strife
All-beauteous Nature fears to be undone
And there, O Pitt, thy country's early boast,
There let me sit beneath the shelter'd slopes,
Or in that Temple† where, in future times,
Thou well shalt merit a distinguish'd name ;
And, with thy converse bless'd, catch the last smiles
Of Autumn beaming o'er the yellow woods.
While there with thee the' enchanted round I walk,
The regulated wild, gay Fancy then
Will tread in thought the groves of attic land ;
Will from thy standard taste refine her own,
Correct her pencil to the purest truth
Of Nature, or, the unimpassion'd shades
Forsaking, raise it to the human mind.
Or if hereafter she, with juster hand,
Shall draw the tragic scene, instruct her, thou,
To mark the varied movements of the heart,
What every decent character requires,
And every passion speaks : O, through her strain
Breathe thy pathetic eloquence ! that moulds
The' attentive senate, charms, persuades, exalts,
Of honest Zeal the' indignant lightning throws,
And shakes Corruption on her venal throne.
While thus we talk, and through Elysian vales
Delighted rove, perhaps a sigh escapes
What pity, Cobham, thou thy verdant files
Of order'd trees shouldst here inglorious range,
Instead of squadrons flaming o'er the field,
And long embattled hosts ! when the proud foe,
The faithless vain disturber of mankind,

* The seat of Lord Cobham.

† The Temple of Virtue in Stowe Gardens.

Insulting Gaul, has roused the world to war;
When keen, once more, within their bounds to press
Those polish'd robbers, those ambitious slaves,
The British youth would hail thy wise command,
Thy temper'd ardour, and thy veteran skill.
  The western sun withdraws the shorten'd day;
And humid Evening, gliding o'er the sky,
In her chill progress, to the ground condensed
The vapours throws. Where creeping waters ooze,
Where marshes stagnate, and where rivers wind,
Cluster the rolling fogs, and swim along
The dusky mantled lawn. Meanwhile the Moon
Full-orb'd, and breaking through the scatter'd clouds,
Shows her broad visage in the crimson east.
Turn'd to the sun direct, her spotted disk,
Where mountains rise, umbrageous dales descend,
And caverns deep, as optic tube descries,
A smaller earth, gives us his blaze again,
Void of its flame, and sheds a softer day.
Now through the passing cloud she seems to stoop,
Now up the pure cerulean rides sublime.
Wide the pale deluge floats, and streaming mild
O'er the skied mountain to the shadowy vale,
While rocks and floods reflect the quivering gleam,
The whole air whitens with a boundless tide
Of silver radiance, trembling round the world.
  But when, half blotted from the sky, her light,
Fainting, permits the starry fires to burn
With keener lustre through the depth of heaven;
Or near extinct her deaden'd orb appears,
And scarce appears, of sickly beamless white;
Oft in this season, silent from the north
A blaze of meteors shoots; ensweeping first
The lower skies, they all at once converge
High to the crown of heaven, and all at once
Relapsing quick, as quickly reascend,
And mix and thwart, extinguish and renew,
All ether coursing in a maze of light.

From look to look, contagious through the crowd,
The panic runs, and into wondrous shapes
The' appearance throws: armies in meet array,
Throng'd with aerial spears and steeds of fire,
Till the long lines of full extended war
In bleeding fight commix'd, the sanguine flood
Rolls a broad slaughter o'er the plains of heaven.
As thus they scan the visionary scene,
On all sides swells the superstitious din,
Incontinent; and busy frenzy talks
Of blood and battle; citiesoverturn'd,
And late at night in swallowing earthquake sunk,
Or hideous wrapp'd in fierce ascending flame;
Of sallow famine, inundation, storm:
Of pestilence, and every great distress;
Empires subversed, when ruling fate has struck
The' unalterable hour: e'en Nature's self
Is deem'd to totter on the brink of time.
Not so the man of philosophic eye,
And inspect sage; the waving brightness he
Curious surveys, inquisitive to know
The causes and materials, yet unfix'd,
Of this appearance beautiful and new.
Now black and deep the night begins to fall,
A shade immense. Sunk in the quenching gloom,
Magnificent and vast, are heaven and earth.
Order confounded lies; all beauty void;
Distinction lost; and gay variety
One universal blot: such the fair power
Of light, to kindle and create the whole.
Drear is the state of the benighted wretch,
Who then, bewilder'd, wanders through the dark,
Full of pale fancies and chimeras huge;
Nor visited by one directive ray,
From cottage streaming or from airy hall.
Perhaps impatient as he stumbles on,
Struck from the root of slimy rushes, blue,
The wildfire scatters round, or gather'd trails

A length of flame deceitful o'er the moss:
Whither decoy'd by the fantastic blaze,
Now lost and now renew'd, he sinks absorb'd,
Rider and horse, amid the miry gulf:
While still, from day to day, his pining wife
And plaintive children his return await,
In wild conjecture lost. At other times,
Sent by the better genius of the night,
Innoxious, gleaming on the horse's mane,
The meteor sits; and shows the narrow path,
That winding leads through pits of death, or else
Instructs him how to take the dangerous ford.
The lengthen'd night elapsed, the Morning shines
Serene, in all her dewy beauty bright,
Unfolding fair the last autumnal day.
And now the mounting sun dispels the fog;
The rigid hoar-frost melts before his beam;
And hung on every spray, on every blade
Of grass, the myriad dew-drops twinkle round.
Ah, see where, robb'd and murder'd, in that pit
Lies the still heaving hive! at evening snatch'd,
Beneath the cloud of guilt-concealing night,
And fix'd o'er sulphur: while, not dreaming ill,
The happy people, in their waxen cells,
Sat tending public cares, and planning schemes
Of temperance, for Winter poor; rejoiced
To mark, full flowing round, their copious stores.
Sudden the dark oppressive steam ascends;
And, used to milder scents, the tender race,
By thousands, tumble from their honied domes,
Convolved, and agonizing in the dust.
And was it then for this you roam'd the Spring,
Intent from flower to flower? for this you toil'd
Ceaseless the burning Summer heats away?
For this in Autumn search'd the blooming waste,
Nor lost one sunny gleam? for this sad fate?
O Man! tyrannic lord! how long, how long
Shall prostrate Nature groan beneath your rage,

Awaiting renovation? when obliged,
Must you destroy? of their ambrosial food
Can you not borrow; and, in just return
Afford them shelter from the wintry winds;
Or, as the sharp year pinches, with their own
Again regale them on some smiling day?
See where the stony bottom of their town
Looks desolate and wild; with here and there
A helpless number, who the ruin'd state
Survive, lamenting weak, cast out to death.
Thus a proud city, populous and rich,
Full of the works of peace, and high in joy,
At theatre or feast, or sunk in sleep,
(As late, Palermo, was thy fate) is seized
By some dread earthquake, and convulsive hurl'd
Sheer from the black foundation, stench-involved,
Into a gulf of blue sulphureous flame.
Hence every harsher sight! for now the day,
O'er heaven and earth diffused, grows warm and high,
Infinite splendour! wide investing all.
How still the breeze! save what the filmy threads
Of dew evaporate brushes from the plain.
How clear the cloudless sky! how deeply tinged
With a peculiar blue! the' etherial arch
How swell'd immense! amid whose azure throned
The radiant sun how gay! how calm below
The gilded earth! the harvest treasures all
Now gather'd in, beyond the rage of storms,
Sure to the swain; the circling fence shut up;
And instant Winter's utmost rage defied.
While, loose to festive joy, the country round
Laughs with the loud sincerity of mirth,
Shook to the wind their cares. The toil-strung youth,
By the quick sense of music taught alone,
Leaps wildly graceful in the lively dance.
Her every charm abroad, the village-toast,
Young, buxom, warm, in native beauty rich,
Darts not unmeaning looks; and where her eye

Points an approving smile, with double force,
The cudgel rattles, and the wrestler twines.
Age too shines out; and, garrulous, recounts
The feats of youth. Thus they rejoice; nor think
That, with to-morrow's sun, their annual toil
Begins again the never ceasing round.
Oh, knew he but his happiness, of men
The happiest he! who far from public rage,
Deep in the vale, with a choice few retired,
Drinks the pure pleasures of the Rural Life.
What though the dome be wanting, whose proud gate,
Each morning, vomits out the sneaking crowd
Of flatterers false, and in their turn abused?
Vile intercourse! what though the glittering robe
Of every hue reflected light can give,
Or floating loose, or stiff with mazy gold,
The pride and gaze of fools! oppress him not?
What though, from utmost land and sea purvey'd,
For him each rarer tributary life
Bleeds not, and his insatiate table heaps
With luxury, and death? What though his bowl
Flames not with costly juice; nor sunk in beds,
Oft of gay care, he tosses out the night,
Or melts the thoughtless hours in idle state?
What though he knows not those fantastic joys
That still amuse the wanton, still deceive;
A face of pleasure, but a heart of pain;
Their hollow moments undelighted all?
Sure peace is his; a solid life, estranged
To disappointment, and fallacious hope:
Rich in content, in Nature's bounty rich,
In herbs and fruits; whatever greens the Spring,
When heaven descends in showers; or bends the bough
When Summer reddens, and when Autumn beams;
Or in the wintry glebe whatever lies
Conceal'd, and fattens with the richest sap:
These are not wanting; nor the milky drove,
Luxuriant, spread o'er all the lowing vale;

Nor bleating mountains ; nor the chide of streams,
And hum of bees, inviting sleep sincere
Into the guiltless breast, beneath the shade,
Or thrown at large amid the fragrant hay ;
Nor aught besides of prospect, grove, or song,
Dim grottoes, gleaming lakes, and fountain clear.
Here too dwells simple Truth ; plain Innocence ;
Unsullied Beauty ; sound unbroken Youth,
Patient of labour, with a little pleased ;
Health ever blooming ; unambitious Toil ,
Calm Contemplation, and poetic Ease.
Let others brave the flood in quest of gain,
And beat, for joyless months, the gloomy wave
Let such as deem it glory to destroy,
Rush into blood, the sack of cities seek ;
Unpierced, exulting in the widow's wail,
The virgin's shriek, and infant's trembling cry.
Let some, far distant from their native soil,
Urged or by want or harden'd avarice,
Find other lands beneath another sun.
Let this through cities work his eager way,
By legal outrage and establish'd guile,
The social sense extinct ; and that ferment
Mad into tumult the seditious herd,
Or melt them down to slavery. Let these
Insnare the wretched in the toils of law,
Fomenting discord, and perplexing right,
An iron race ! and those of fairer front,
But equal inhumanity, in courts,
Delusive pomp and dark cabals, delight ;
Wreathe the deep bow, diffuse the lying smile,
And tread the weary labyrinth of state.
While he, from all the stormy passions free
That restless men involve, hears, and but hears,
At distance safe, the human tempest roar,
Wrapp'd close in conscious peace. The fall of kings,
The rage of nations, and the crush of states
Move not the man who, from the world escaped,

In still retreats, and flowery solitudes,
To Nature's voice attends, from month to month
And day to day, through the revolving year:
Admiring, sees her in her every shape;
Feels all her sweet emotions at his heart;
Takes what she liberal gives, nor thinks of more.
He, when young Spring protrudes the bursting gems,
Marks the first bud, and sucks the healthful gale
Into his freshen'd soul; her genial hours
He full enjoys; and not a beauty blows,
And not an opening blossom breathes in vain,
In Summer he, beneath the living shade,
Such as o'er frigid Tempè wont to wave,
Or Hemus cool, reads what the Muse, of these,
Perhaps, is in immortal numbers sung;
Or what she dictates writes: and, oft an eye
Shot round, rejoices in the vigorous year.
When Autumn's yellow lustre gilds the world,
And tempts the sickled swain into the field,
Seized by the general joy, his heart distends
With gentle throes; and, through the tepid gleams
Deep musing, then he best exerts his song.
E'en Winter wild to him is full of bliss.
The mighty tempest, and the hoary waste,
Abrupt, and deep, stretch'd o'er the buried earth,
Awake to solemn thought. At night the skies,
Disclosed, and kindled, by refining frost,
Pour every lustre on the' exalted eye.
A friend, a book, the stealing hours secure,
And mark them down for wisdom. With swift wing
O'er land and sea imagination roams;
Or truth, divinely breaking on his mind,
Elates his being, and unfolds his powers;
Or in his breast heroic virtue burns.
The touch of kindred too and love he feels;
The modest eye, whose beams on his alone
Ecstatic shine; the little strong embrace
Of prattling children, twined around his neck,

And emulous to please him, calling forth
The fond parental soul. Nor purpose gay,
Amusement, dance, or song, he sternly scorns;
For happiness and true philosophy
Are of the social, still, and smiling kind.
This is the life which those who fret in guilt,
And guilty cities, never knew; the life,
Led by primeval ages, uncorrupt,
When Angels dwelt, and God himself with Man!
  Oh Nature! all sufficient! over all!
Enrich me with the knowledge of thy works!
Snatch me to heaven; thy rolling wonders there
World beyond world, in infinite extent,
Profusely scatter'd o'er the blue immense,
Show me; their motions, periods, and their laws,
Give me to scan; through the disclosing deep
Light my blind way; the mineral strata there;
Thrust, blooming, thence the vegetable world;
O'er that the rising system, more complex,
Of animals; and higher still, the mind,
The varied scene of quick-compounded thought,
And where the mixing passions endless shift;
These ever open to my ravish'd eye;
A scearch, the flight of time can ne'er exhaust!
But if to that unequal; if the blood,
In sluggish streams about my heart, forbid
That best ambition; under closing shades,
Inglorious, lay me by the lowly brook,
And whisper to my dreams. From Thee begin,
Dwell all on Thee, with Thee conclude my song,
And let me never, never stray from Thee!

WINTER.

The subject proposed. Address to the Earl of Wilmington. First approach of Winter. According to the natural course of the season, various storms described. Rain. Wind. Snow. The driving of the snows; a man perishing among them; whence reflections on the wants and miseries of human life. The wolves descending from the Alps and Apennines. A winter-evening described; as spent by philosophers; by the country people; in the city. Frost. A view of Winter within the polar circle. A thaw. The whole concluding with moral reflections on a future state.

See, Winter comes, to rule the varied year,
Sullen and sad, with all his rising train;
Vapours, and Clouds, and Storms. Be these my theme,
These! that exalt the soul to solemn thought,
And heavenly musing. Welcome, kindred glooms,
Congenial horrors, hail! with frequent foot,
Pleased have I, in my cheerful morn of life,
When nursed by careless Solitude I lived,
And sung of Nature with unceasing joy,
Pleased have I wander'd through your rough domain;
Trod the pure virgin-snows, myself as pure;
Heard the winds roar, and the big torrent burst;
Or seen the deep-fermenting tempest brew'd,
In the grim evening sky. Thus pass'd the time,
Till through the lucid chambers of the south
Look'd out the joyous Spring, look'd out, and smiled.
  To thee, the patron of her first essay,
The Muse, O Wilmington! renews her song.
Since has she rounded the revolving year:
Skimm'd the gay Spring; on eagle pinions borne.
Attempted through the summer blaze to rise;
Then swept o'er Autumn with the shadowy gale;
And now among the wintry clouds again,

Roll'd in the doubling storm, she tries to soar,
To swell her note with all the rushing winds,
To suit her sounding cadence to the floods,
As is her theme, her numbers wildly great:
Thrice happy could she fill thy judging ear
With bold description and with manly thought
Nor art thou skill'd in awful schemes alone,
And how to make a mighty people thrive:
But equal goodness, sound integrity,
A firm unshaken uncorrupted soul
Amid a sliding age, and burning strong,
Not vainly blazing, for thy country's weal,
A steady spirit regularly free;
These, each exalting each, the statesman light
Into the patriot; these, the public hope
And eye to thee converting, bid the Muse
Record what envy dares not flattery call.
Now when the cheerless empire of the sky
To Capricorn the Centaur Archer yields,
And fierce Aquarius stains the' inverted year,
Hung o'er the furthest verge of heaven, the sun
Scarce spreads through ether the dejected day.
Faint are his gleams, and ineffectual shoot
His struggling rays, in horizontal lines,
Through the thick air; as clothed in cloudy storm,
Weak, wan, and broad, he skirts the southern sky;
And, soon descending, to the long dark night,
Wide-shading all, the prostrate world resigns.
Nor is the night unwish'd; while vital heat,
Light, life, and joy the dubious day forsake.
Meantime, in sable cincture, shadows vast,
Deep-tinged and damp, and congregated clouds,
And all the vapoury turbulence of heaven,
Involve the face of things. Thus Winter falls,
A heavy gloom oppressive o'er the world,
Through Nature shedding influence malign,
And rouses up the seeds of dark disease.
The soul of man dies in him, loathing life,

And black with more than melancholy views.
The cattle droop; and o'er the furrow'd land,
Fresh from the plough, the dun discolour'd flocks,
Untended spreading, crop the wholesome root.
Along the woods, along the moorish fens,
Sighs the sad Genius of the coming storm:
And up among the loose disjointed cliffs,
And fractured mountains wild, the brawling brook
And cave, presageful, send a hollow moan,
Resounding long in listening Fancy's ear.
Then comes the father of the tempest forth,
Wrapp'd in black glooms. First joyless rains obscure
Drive through the mingling skies with vapour foul;
Dash on the mountain's brow, and shake the woods,
That grumbling wave below. The' unsightly plain
Lies a brown deluge; as the low-bent clouds
Pour flood on flood, yet unexhausted still
Combine, and deepening into night shut up
The day's fair face. The wanderers of heaven,
Each to his home, retire; save those that love
To take their pastime in the troubled air,
Or skimming flutter round the dimply pool.
The cattle from the' untasted fields return,
And ask, with meaning lowe, their wanted stalls,
Or ruminate in the contiguous shade.
Thither the household feathery people crowd,
The crested cock, with all his female train,
Pensive, and dripping; while the cottage-hind
Hangs o'er the' enlivening blaze, and taleful there
Recounts his simple frolic: much he talks,
And much he laughs, nor recks the storm that blows
Without, and rattles on his humble roof.
Wide o'er the brim, with many a torrent swell'd,
And the mix'd ruin of its banks o'erspread,
At last the roused-up river pours along:
Resistless, roaring, dreadful, down it comes,
From the rude mountain, and the mossy wild,
Tumbling through rocks abrupt, and sounding far;

Then o'er the sanded valley floating spreads,
Calm, sluggish, silent; till again, constrain'd
Between two meeting hills, it bursts away,
Where rocks and woods o'erhang the turbid stream;
Their gathering triple force, rapid, and deep,
It boils and wheels and foams and thunders through.
  Nature! great parent! whose unceasing hand
Rolls round the Seasons of the changeful year,
How mighty, how majestic are thy works!
With what a pleasing dread they swell the soul!
That sees astonish'd! and astonish'd sings!
Ye too, ye winds! that now begin to blow
With boisterous sweep, I raise my voice to you.
Where are your stores, ye powerful beings! say,
Where your aerial magazines reserved,
To swell the brooding terrors of the storm?
In what far distant region of the sky,
Hush'd in deep silence, sleep ye when 'tis calm?
  When from the pallid sky the sun descends,
With many a spot, that o'er his glaring orb
Uncertain wanders, stain'd; red fiery streaks
Begin to flush around. The reeling clouds
Stagger with dizzy poise, as doubting yet
Which master to obey: while rising slow,
Blank, in the leaden-colour'd east, the moon
Wears a wan circle round her blunted horns.
Seen through the turbid fluctuating air,
The stars obtuse emit a shiver'd ray;
Or frequent seem to shoot athwart the gloom,
And long behind them trail the whitening blaze.
Snatch'd in short eddies, plays the wither'd leaf;
And on the flood the dancing feather floats.
With broaden'd nostrils to the sky upturn'd,
The conscious heifer snuffs the stormy gale.
E'en as the matron, at her nightly task,
With pensive labour draws the flaxen thread,
The wasted taper and the crackling flame
Foretel the blast. But chief the plumy race,

The tenants of the sky, its changes speak.
Retiring from the downs, where all day long
They pick'd their scanty fare, a blackening train
Of clamorous rooks thick urge their weary flight.
And seek the closing shelter of the grove;
Assiduous, in his bower, the wailing owl
Plies his sad song. The cormorant on high
Wheels from the deep, and screams along the land.
Loud shrieks the soaring hern; and with wild wing
The circling seafowl cleave the flaky clouds.
Ocean, unequal press'd, with broken tide
And blind commotion heaves; while from the shore,
Eat into caverns by the restless wave,
And forest-rustling mountain, comes a voice,
That solemn sounding bids the world prepare.
Then issues forth the storm with sudden burst,
And hurls the whole precipitated air
Down, in a torrent. On the passive main
Descends the' etherial force, and with strong gust
Turns from its bottom the discolour'd deep.
Through the black night that sits immense around,
Lash'd into foam, the fierce conflicting brine
Seems o'er a thousand raging waves to burn:
Meantime the mountain billows, to the clouds
In dreadful tumult swell'd, surge above surge,
Burst into chaos with tremendous roar,
And anchor'd navies from their stations drive,
Wild as the winds across the howling waste
Of mighty waters: now the' inflated wave
Straining they scale, and now impetuous shoot
Into the secret chambers of the deep,
The wintry Baltic thundering o'er their head.
Emerging thence again, before the breath
Of full-exerted heaven they wing their course,
And dart on distant coasts; if some sharp rock
Or shoal insidious break not their career,
And in loose fragments fling them floating round.
Nor less at hand the loosen'd tempest reigns.

The mountain thunders ; and its sturdy sons
Stoop to the bottom of the rocks they shade.
Lone on the midnight steep, and all aghast,
The dark wayfaring stranger breathless toils,
And, often falling, climbs against the blast.
Low waves the rooted forest, vex'd, and sheds
What of its tarnish'd honours yet remain ;
Dash'd down, and scatter'd, by the tearing wind's
Assiduous fury, its gigantic limbs.
Thus struggling through the dissipated grove,
The whirling tempest raves along the plain ;
And on the cottage thatch'd, or lordly roof,
Keen-fastening, shakes them to the solid base.
Sleep frighted flies ; and round the rocking dome,
For entrance eager, howls the savage blast.
Then too, they say, through all the burden'd air,
Long groans are heard, shrill sounds, and distant sighs,
That, utter'd by the Demon of the night,
Warn the devoted wretch of woe and death.
 Huge uproar lords it wide. The clouds commix'd
With stars swift gliding sweep along the sky.
All Nature reels. Till Nature's King, who oft
Amid tempestuous darkness dwells alone,
And on the wings of the careering wind
Walks dreadfully serene, commands a calm ;
Then, straight, air, sea, and earth are hush'd at once.
 As yet 'tis midnight deep. The weary clouds,
Slow-meeting, mingle into solid gloom.
Now, while the drowsy world lies lost in sleep,
Let me associate with the serious Night,
And Contemplation, her sedate compeer ;
Let me shake off the' intrusive cares of day,
And lay the meddling senses all aside.
 Where now, ye lying vanities of life !
Ye ever tempting ever cheating train !
Where are you now ? and what is your amount ?
Vexation, disappointment, and remorse :
Sad, sickening thought ! and yet, deluded man,

A scene of crude disjointed visions past,
And broken slumbers, rises still resolved,
With new-flush'd hopes, to run the giddy round.
Father of light and life! thou Good Supreme!
O, teach me what is good! teach me Thyself!
Save me from folly, vanity, and vice,
From every low pursuit! and feed my soul
With knowledge, conscious peace, and virtue pure;
Sacred, substantial, never fading bliss!
The keener tempests rise: and fuming dun
From all the livid east, or piercing north,
Thick clouds ascend; in whose capacious womb
A vapoury deluge lies, to snow congeal'd.
Heavy they roll their fleecy world along;
And the sky saddens with the gather'd storm.
Through the hush'd air the whitening shower descends,
At first thin wavering; till at last the flakes
Fall broad and wide and fast, dimming the day
With a continual flow. The cherish'd fields
Put on their winter robe of purest white.
'Tis brightness all; save where the new snow melts
Along the mazy current. Low the woods
Bow their hoar head; and ere the languid sun
Faint from the west emits his evening ray,
Earth's universal face, deep hid, and chill,
Is one wild dazzling waste, that buries wide
The works of man. Drooping, the labourer-ox
Stands cover'd o'er with snow, and then demands
The fruit of all his toil. The fowls of heaven,
Tamed by the cruel season, crowd around
The winnowing store, and claim the little boon
Which Providence assigns them. One alone,
The red-breast, sacred to the household gods,
Wisely regardful of the' embroiling sky,
In joyless fields and thorny thickets, leaves
His shivering mates, and pays to trusted man
His annual visit. Half afraid, he first
Against the window beats; then, brisk, alights

On the warm hearth; then, hopping o'er the floor,
Eyes all the smiling family askance,
And pecks, and starts, and wonders where he is;
Till, more familiar grown, the table-crumbs
Attract his slender feet. The foodless wilds
Pour forth their brown inhabitants. The hare,
Though timorous of heart, and hard beset
By death in various forms, dark snares, and dogs,
And more unpitying men, the garden seeks,
Urged on by fearless want. The bleating kind
Eye the bleak heaven, and next the glistening earth,
With looks of dumb despair; then, sad-dispersed,
Dig for the wither'd herb through heaps of snow.
Now, shepherds, to your helpless charge be kind,
Baffle the raging year, and fill their pens
With food at will; lodge them below the storm,
And watch them strict: for from the bellowing east,
In this dire season, oft the whirlwind's wing
Sweeps up the burden of whole wintry plains
At one wide waft, and o'er the hapless flocks,
Hid in the hollow of two neighbouring hills,
The billowy tempest whelms; till, upward urged,
The valley to a shining mountain swells,
Tipp'd with a wreath high-curling in the sky.
As thus the snows arise; and foul, and fierce,
All Winter drives along the darken'd air;
In his own loose revolving fields, the swain
Disaster'd stands; sees other hills ascend,
Of unknown joyless brow; and other scenes,
Of horrid prospect, shag the trackless plain:
Nor finds the river, nor the forest, hid
Beneath the formless wild; but wanders on
From hill to dale, still more and more astray;
Impatient flouncing through the drifted heaps,
Stung with the thoughts of home; the thoughts of home
Rush on his nerves, and call their vigour forth
In many a vain attempt. How sinks his soul!
What black despair, what horror fills his heart!

When for the dusky spot, which fancy feign'd
His tufted cottage rising through the snow,
He meets the roughness of the middle waste,
Far from the track and bless'd abode of man!
While round him night resistless closes fast,
And every tempest, howling o'er his head,
Renders the savage wilderness more wild.
Then throng the busy shapes into his mind
Of cover'd pits, unfathomably deep,
A dire descent! beyond the power of frost!
Of faithless bogs; of precipices huge,
Smooth'd up with snow; and, what is land, unknown,
What water, of the still unfrozen spring,
In the loose marsh or solitary lake,
Where the fresh fountain from the bottom boils.
These check his fearful steps; and down he sinks
Beneath the shelter of the shapeless drift.
Thinking o'er all the bitterness of death,
Mix'd with the tender anguish Nature shoots
Through the wrung bosom of the dying man,
His wife, his children, and his friends unseen.
In vain for him the' officious wife prepares
The fire fair-blazing, and the vestment warm;
In vain his little children, peeping out
Into the mingling storm, demand their sire,
With tears of artless innocence. Alas!
Nor wife, nor children, more shall he behold,
Nor friends, nor sacred home. On every nerve
The deadly Winter seizes; shuts up sense;
And, o'er his inmost vitals creeping cold,
Lays him along the snows, a stiffen'd corse,
Stretch'd out, and bleaching in the northern blast.
  Ah! little think the gay licentious proud,
Whom pleasure, power, and affluence surround;
They who their thoughtless hours in giddy mirth,
And wanton, often cruel, riot waste;
Ah! little think they, while they dance along,
How many feel, this very moment, death,

And all the sad variety of pain.
How many sink in the devouring flood,
Or more devouring flame. How many bleed,
By shameful variance betwixt man and man.
How many pine in want, and dungeon glooms;
Shut from the common air, and common use
Of their own limbs. How many drink the cup
Of baleful grief, or eat the bitter bread
Of misery. Sore pierced by wintry winds,
How many shrink into the sordid hut
Of cheerless poverty. How many shake
With all the fiercer tortures of the mind,
Unbounded passion, madness, guilt, remorse;
Whence tumbled headlong from the height of life,
They furnish matter for the tragic Muse.
E'en in the vale, where Wisdom loves to dwell,
With friendship, peace, and contemplation join'd,
How many, rack'd with honest passions, droop
In deep retired distress How many stand
Around the death-bed of their dearest friends,
And point the parting anguish. Thought fond Man
Of these, and all the thousand nameless ills,
That one incessant struggle render life,
One scene of toil, of suffering, and of fate,
Vice in his high career would stand appall'd,
And heedless rambling Impulse learn to think;
The conscious heart of Charity would warm,
And her wide wish Benevolence dilate;
The social tear would rise, the social sigh:
And into clear perfection, gradual bliss,
Refining still, the social passions work.
  And here can I forget the generous band,*
Who, touch'd with human woe, redressive search'd
Into the horrors of the gloomy jail?
Unpitied, and unheard, where misery moans;
Where sickness pines; where thirst and hunger burn,
And poor misfortune feels the lash of vice.

* The Jail Committee, in the year 1729.

While in the land of Liberty, the land
Whose every street and public meeting glow
With open freedom, little tyrants raged;
Snatch'd the lean morsel from the starving mouth:
Tore from cold wintry limbs the tatter'd weed;
E'en robb'd them of the last of comforts, sleep;
The freeborn Briton to the dungeon chain'd,
Or, as the lust of cruelty prevail'd,
At pleasure mark'd him with inglorious stripes;
And crush'd out lives, by secret barbarous ways,
That for their country would have toil'd or bled.
O great design! if executed well,
With patient care, and wisdom-temper'd zeal.
Ye sons of Mercy! yet resume the search;
Drag forth the regal monsters into light,
Wrench from their hands Oppression's iron rod,
And bid the cruel feel the pains they give.
Much still untouch'd remains; in this rank age,
Much is the patriot's weeding hand required.
The toils of law (what dark insidious men
Have cumbrous added to perplex the truth,
And lengthen simple justice into trade,)
How glorious were the day! that saw these broke
And every man within the reach of right.
  By wintry famine roused, from all the tract
Of horrid mountains which the shining Alps,
And wavy Apennine, and Pyrenees,
Branch out stupendous into distant lands;
Cruel as death, and hungry as the grave!
Burning for blood! bony and gaunt and grim!
Assembling wolves in raging troops descend;
And, pouring o'er the country, bear along
Keen as the north-wind sweeps the glossy snow.
All is their prize. They fasten on the steed,
Press him to earth, and pierce his mighty heart.
Nor can the bull his awful front defend,
Or shake the murdering savages away.
Rapacious, at the mother's throat they fly,

And tear the screaming infant from her breast.
The godlike face of man avails him nought.
E'en beauty, force divine! at whose bright glance
The generous lion stands in soften'd gaze,
Here bleeds, a hapless undistinguish'd prey.
But if, apprised of the severe attack,
The country be shut up, lured by the scent,
On church-yards drear (inhuman to relate!)
The disappointed prowlers fall, and dig
The shrouded body from the grave; o'er which,
Mix'd with foul shades and frighted ghosts, they howl.
Among those hilly regions, where embraced
In peaceful vales the happy Grisons dwell;
Oft, rushing sudden from the loaded cliffs,
Mountains of snow their gathering terrors roll,
From steep to steep, loud-thundering down they come,
A wintry waste in dire commotion all;
And herds, and flocks, and travellers, and swains,
And sometimes whole brigades of marching troops
Or hamlets sleeping in the dead of night,
Are deep beneath the smothering ruin whelm'd.
Now, all amid the rigours of the year,
In the wild depth of Winter, while without
The ceaseless winds blow ice, be my retreat,
Between the groaning forest and the shore
Beat by the boundless multitude of waves,
A rural, shelter'd, solitary scene;
Where ruddy fire and beaming tapers join,
To cheer the gloom. There studious let me sit,
And hold high converse with the mighty Dead;
Sages of ancient time, as gods revered,
As gods beneficent, who bless'd mankind
With arts, with arms, and humanized a world.
Roused at the' inspiring thought, I throw aside
The longlived volume; and, deep-musing, hail
The sacred shades, that slowly rising pass
Before my wondering eyes. First Socrates,
Who, firmly good in a corrupted state,

Against the rage of tyrants single stood,
Invincible! calm Reason's holy law,
That Voice of God within the' attentive mind,
Obeying, fearless, or in life or death:
Great moral teacher! Wisest of mankind!
Solon the next, who built his commonweal
On equity's wide base; by tender laws
A lively people curbing, yet undamp'd
Preserving still that quick peculiar fire,
Whence in the laurel'd field of finer arts,
And of bold freedom, they unequal'd shone,
The pride of smiling Greece and humankind.
Lycurgus then, who bow'd beneath the force
Of strictest discipline, severely wise,
All human passions. Following him, I see,
As at Thermopylæ he glorious fell,
The firm devoted Chief,* who proved by deeds
The hardest lesson which the other taught.
Then Aristides lifts his honest front;
Spotless of heart, to whom the' unflattering voice
Of freedom gave the noblest name of Just;
In pure majestic poverty revered;
Who, e'en his glory to his country's weal
Submitting, swell'd a haughty Rival's† fame.
Rear'd by his care, of softer ray appears
Cimon sweet-soul'd; whose genius, rising strong,
Shook off the load of young debauch; abroad
The scourge of Persian pride, at home the friend
Of every worth and every splendid art;
Modest and simple in the pomp of wealth.
Then the last worthies of declining Greece,
Late call'd to glory, in unequal times,
Pensive appear. The fair Corinthian boast,
Timoleon, happy temper! mild and firm,
Who wept the brother while the tyrant bled.
And, equal to the best, the Theban Pair‡

* Leonidas. † Themistocles.

‡ Pelopidas and Epaminondas.

Whose virtues, in heroic concord join'd,
Their country raised to freedom, empire, fame.
He too, with whom Athenian honour sunk,
And left a mass of sordid lees behind,
Phocion the Good; in public life severe,
To virtue still inexorably firm;
But when, beneath his low illustrious roof,
Sweet peace and happy wisdom smooth'd his brow,
Not friendship softer was, nor love more kind.
And he, the last of old Lycurgus' sons,
The generous victim to that vain attempt,
To save a rotten state, Agis, who saw
E'en Sparta's self to servile avarice sunk.
The two Achaian heroes close the train:
Aratus, who awhile relumed the soul
Of fondly lingering liberty in Greece;
And he her darling as her latest hope,
The gallant Philopœmen; who to arms
Turn'd the luxurious pomp he could not cure;
Or toiling in his farm, a simple swain;
Or, bold and skilful, thundering in the field
  Of rougher front, a mighty people come!
A race of heroes! in those virtuous times
Which knew no stain, save that with partial flame
Their dearest country they too fondly loved:
Her better Founder first, the light of Rome,
Numa, who soften'd her rapacious sons:
Servius the king, who laid the solid base
On which o'er earth the vast republic spread.
Then the great consuls venerable rise.
The public Father* who the private quell'd,
As on the dread tribunal sternly sad.
He, whom his thankless country could not lose,
Camillus, only vengeful to her foes.
Fabricius, scorner of all conquering gold;
And Cincinnatus, awful from the plough.
Thy willing victim,† Carthage, bursting loose

* Marcus Junius Brutus † Regulus.

From all that pleading Nature could oppose,
From a whole city's tears, by rigid faith
Imperious call'd, and honour's dire command.
Scipio, the gentle chief, humanely brave,
Who soon the race of spotless glory ran,
And, warm in youth, to the poetic shade
With Friendship and Philosophy retired.
Tully, whose powerful eloquence awhile
Restrain'd the rapid fate of rushing Rome.
Unconquer'd Cato, virtuous in extreme:
And, thou, unhappy Brutus, kind of heart,
Whose steady arm, by awful virtue urged,
Lifted the Roman steel against thy friend.
Thousands besides the tribute of a verse
Demand; but who can count the stars of heaven?
Who sing their influence on this lower world?
  Behold, who yonder comes! in sober state,
Fair, mild, and strong, as is a vernal sun:
'Tis Phœbus' self, or else the Mantuan Swain!
Great Homer too appears, of daring wing,
Parent of song! and equal, by his side,
The British Muse: join'd hand in hand they walk,
Darkling, full up the middle steep to fame,
Nor absent are those shades, whose skilful touch
Pathetic drew the' impassion'd heart, and charm'd
Transported Athens with the moral scene;
Nor those who, tuneful, waked the' enchanting lyre.
  First of your kind! society divine!
Still visit thus my nights, for you reserved,
And mount my soaring soul to thoughts like yours.
Silence, thou lonely power! the door be thine;
See on the hallow'd hour that none intrude,
Save a few chosen friends, who sometimes deign
To bless my humble roof, with sense refined,
Learning digested well, exalted faith,
Unstudied wit, and humour ever gay.
Or from the Muses' hill with Pope descend,
To raise the sacred hour, to bid it smile,

And with the social spirit warm the heart?
For though not sweet his own Homer sings,
Yet is his life the more endearing song.
  Where art thou, Hammond? thou, the darling pride,
The friend and lover of the tuneful throng!
Ah, why, dear youth, in all the blooming prime
Of vernal genius, where disclosing fast
Each active worth, each manly virtue lay,
Why wert thou ravish'd from our hope so soon?
What now avails that noble thirst of fame,
Which stung thy fervent breast? that treasured store
Of knowledge, early gain'd? that eager zeal
To serve thy country, glowing in the band
Of youthful patriots, who sustain her name;
What now, alas! that life-diffusing charm
Of sprightly wit? that rapture for the Muse,
That heart of friendship, and that soul of joy,
Which bade with softest light thy virtues smile?
Ah! only show'd, to check our fond pursuits,
And teach our humble hopes that life is vain!
  Thus in some deep retirement would I pass
The winter glooms, with friends of pliant soul,
Or blithe, or solemn, as the theme inspired:
With them would search, if Nature's boundless frame
Was call'd, late-rising from the void of night,
Or sprung eternal from the' Eternal Mind;
Its life, its laws, its progress, and its end.
Hence larger prospects of the beauteous whole
Would, gradual, open on our opening minds;
And each diffusive harmony unite
In full perfection, to the' astonish'd eye.
Then would we try to scan the mortal world,
Which, though to us it seems embroil'd, moves on
In higher order; fitted and impell'd
By Wisdom's finest hand, and issuing all
In general good. The sage historic Muse
Should next conduct us through the deeps of time:
Show us how empire grew, declined, and fell,

In scatter'd states; what makes the nations smile,
Improves their soil, and gives them double suns;
And why they pine beneath the brightest skies,
In Nature's richest lap. As thus we talk'd,
Our hearts would burn within us, would inhale
That portion of divinity, that ray
Of purest heaven, which lights the public soul
Of patriots and of heroes. But if doom'd,
In powerless humble fortune, to repress
These ardent risings of the kindling soul;
Then, even superior to ambition, we
Would learn the private virtues; how to glide
Through shades and plains, along the smoothest stream
Of rural life: or, snatch'd away by hope,
Through the dim spaces of futurity,
With earnest eye anticipate those scenes
Of happiness and wonder; where the mind,
In endless growth and infinite ascent,
Rises from state to state, and world to world.
But when with these the serious thought is foil'd,
We, shifting for relief, would play the shapes
Of frolic fancy; and incessant form
Those rapid pictures, that assembled train
Of fleet ideas, never join'd before,
Whence lively Wit excites to gay surprise;
Or folly-painting Humour, grave himself,
Calls Laughter forth, deep shaking every nerve.
Meantime the village rouses up the fire;
While well attested, and as well believed,
Heard solemn, goes the goblin story round;
Till superstitious horror creeps o'er all.
Or, frequent in the sounding hall, they wake
The rural gambol. Rustic mirth goes round;
The simple joke that takes the shepherd's heart,
Easily pleased; the long loud laugh, sincere;
The kiss, snatch'd hasty from the sidelong maid,
On purpose guardless or pretending sleep:
The leap, the slap, the haul; and, shook to notes

Of native music, the respondent dance
Thus jocund fleets with them the winter night.
The city swarms intense. The public haunt,
Full of each theme, and warm with mix'd discourse,
Hums indistinct. The sons of riot flow
Down the loose stream of false enchanted joy,
To swift destruction. On the rankled soul
The gaming fury falls; and in one gulf
Of total ruin, honour, virtue, peace,
Friends, families, and fortune headlong sink.
Up springs the dance along the lighted dome,
Mix'd and evolved a thousand sprightly ways.
The glittering court effuses every pomp;
The circle deepens: beam'd from gaudy robes,
Tapers, and sparkling gems, and radiant eyes,
A soft effulgence o'er the palace waves:
While, a gay insect in his summer shine,
The fop, light fluttering, spreads his mealy wings.
Dread o'er the scene the ghost of Hamlet stalks;
Othello rages; poor Monimia mourns;
And Belvidera pours her soul in love.
Terror alarms the breast; the comely tear
Steals o'er the cheek: or else the Comic Muse
Holds to the world a picture of itself,
And raises sly the fair impartial laugh.
Sometimes she lifts her strain, and paints the scenes
Of beauteous life; whate'er can deck mankind,
Or charm the heart, in generous Bevil* show'd.
O Thou, whose wisdom, solid yet refined,
Whose patriot virtues, and consummate skill
To touch the finer springs that move the world,
Join'd to whate'er the Graces can bestow,
And all Apollo's animating fire,
Give thee, with pleasing dignity, to shine
At once the guardian, ornament, and joy
Of polish'd life; permit the rural Muse,

* A character in The Conscious Lovers, written by Sir R. Steele.

O Chesterfield, to grace with thee her song!
Ere to the shades again she humbly flies,
Indulge her fond ambition, in thy train
(For every Muse has in thy train a place,)
To mark thy various full-accomplish'd mind:
To mark that spirit which, with British scorn,
Rejects the' allurements of corrupted power;
That elegant politeness, which excels,
E'en in the judgment of presumptuous France,
The boasted manners of her shining court;
That wit, the vivid energy of sense,
The truth of Nature, which, with Attic point
And kind well temper'd satire, smoothly keen,
Steals through the soul, and without pain corrects.
Or rising thence with yet a brighter flame,
O, let me hail thee on some glorious day,
When to the listening senate, ardent, crowd
Britannia's sons to hear her pleaded cause.
Then dress'd by thee, more amiably fair,
Truth the soft robe of mild persuasion wears:
Thou to assenting reason givest again
Her own enlighten'd thoughts; call'd from the heart,
The' obedient passions on thy voice attend;
And e'en reluctant party feels awhile
Thy gracious power; as through the varied maze
Of eloquence, now smooth, now quick, now strong,
Profound, and clear, you roll the copious flood.
To thy loved haunt return, my happy Muse·
For now, behold, the joyous winter days,
Frosty, succeed; and through the blue serene,
For sight too fine, the' etherial nitre flies;
Killing infectious damps, and the spent air
Storing afresh with elemental life.
Close crowds the shining atmosphere; and binds
Our strengthen'd bodies in its cold embrace,
Constringent; feeds and animates our blood;
Refines our spirits, through the new-strung nerves
In swifter sallies darting to the brain;

Where sits the soul, intense, collected, cool,
Bright as the skies, and as the season keen
All Nature feels the renovating force
Of Winter, only to the thoughtless eye
In ruin seen. The frost-concocted glebe
Draws in abundant vegetable soul,
And gathers vigour for the coming year.
A stronger glow sits on the lively cheek
Of ruddy fire: and luculent along
The purer rivers flow; their sullen deeps,
Transparent, open to the shepherd's gaze,
And murmur hoarser at the fixing frost.
What art thou, frost? and whence are thy keen stores
Derived, thou secret all-invading power,
Whom e'en the' illusive fluid cannot fly?
Is not thy potent energy, unseen,
Myriads of little salts, or hook'd, or shaped
Like double wedges, and diffused immense
Through water, earth, and ether? hence at eve,
Steam'd eager from the red horizon round,
With the fierce rage of Winter deep suffused,
An icy gale, oft shifting, o'er the pool
Breathes a blue film, and in its mid career
Arrests the bickering stream. The loosen'd ice,
Let down the flood, and half dissolved by day,
Rustles no more; but to the sedgy bank
Fast grows, or gathers round the pointed stone,
A crystal pavement, by the breath of heaven
Cemented firm; till, seized from shore to shore,
The whole imprison'd river growls below.
Loud rings the frozen earth, and hard reflects
A double noise; while, at his evening watch,
The village dog deters the nightly thief;
The heifer lows; the distant waterfall
Swells in the breeze; and, with the hasty tread
Of traveller, the hollow-sounding plain
Shakes from afar. The full etherial round,
Infinite worlds disclosing to the view,

Shines out intensely keen ; and, all one cope
Of starry glitter, glows from pole to pole.
From pole to pole the rigid influence falls,
Through the still night, incessant, heavy, strong,
And seizes Nature fast. It freezes on ;
Till Morn, late rising o'er the drooping world,
Lifts her pale eye unjoyous. Then appears
The various labour of the silent night :
Prone from the dripping eave, and dumb cascade,
Whose idle torrents only seem to roar,
The pendent icicle ; the frost-work fair,
Where transient hues and fancied figures rise ;
Wide-spouted o'er the hill, the frozen brook,
A livid tract, cold-gleaming on the morn ;
The forest bent beneath the plumy wave ;
And by the frost refined the whiter snow,
Incrusted hard, and sounding to the tread
Of early shepherd, as he pensive seeks
His pining flock, or from the mountain top,
Pleased with the slippery surface, swift descends.
On blithesome frolics bent, the youthful swains,
While every work of man is laid at rest,
Fond o'er the river crowd, in various sport
And revelry dissolved ; where mixing glad,
Happiest of all the train ! the raptured boy
Lashes the whirling top. Or, where the Rhine
Branch'd out in many a long canal extends,
From every province swarming, void of care,
Batavia rushes forth ; and as they sweep,
On sounding skates, a thousand different ways,
In circling poise, swift as the winds, along,
The then gay land is madden'd all to joy.
Nor less the northern courts, wide o'er the snow
Pour a new pomp. Eager, on rapid sleds,
Their vigorous youth in bold contention wheel
The long-resounding course. Meantime to raise
The manly strife, with highly blooming charms,

Flush'd by the season, Scandinavia's dames,
Or Russia's buxom daughters, glow around.
  Pure, quick, and sportful is the wholesome day;
But soon elapsed. The horizontal sun,
Broad o'er the south, hangs at his utmost noon:
And, ineffectual, strikes the gelid cliff:
His azure gloss the mountain still maintains,
Nor feels the feeble touch. Perhaps the vale
Relents awhile to the reflected ray:
Or from the forest falls the cluster'd snow,
Myriads of gems, that in the waving gleam
Gay-twinkle as they scatter. Thick around
Thunders the sport of those, who with the gun,
And dog impatient bounding at the shot,
Worse than the Season, desolate the fields;
And, adding to the ruins of the year,
Distress the footed or the feather'd game.
  But what is this? our infant Winter sinks
Divested of his grandeur, should our eye
Astonish'd shoot into the frigid zone;
Where, for relentless months, continual Night
Holds o'er the glittering waste her starry reign.
  There, through the prison of unbounded wilds,
Barr'd by the hand of Nature from escape,
Wide roams the Russian exile. Nought around
Strikes his sad eye but deserts lost in snow;
And heavy-loaded groves; and solid floods,
That stretch, athwart the solitary vast,
Their icy horrors to the frozen main;
And cheerless towns far distant, never bless'd,
Save when its annual course the caravan
Bends to the golden coast of rich Cathay,*
With news of humankind. Yet there life glows;
Yet cherish'd there, beneath the shining waste,
The furry nations harbour: tipp'd with jet,
Fair ermines, spotless as the snows they press;

* The old name for China.

Sables, of glossy black; and dark-embrown'd,
Or beauteous freak'd with many a mingled hue,
Thousands besides, the costly pride of courts.
There, warm together press'd, the trooping deer
Sleep on the new-fallen snows; and, scarce his head
Raised o'er the heapy wreath, the branching elk
Lies slumbering sullen in the white abyss.
The ruthless hunter wants nor dogs nor toils,
Nor with the dread of sounding bows he drives
The fearful flying race; with ponderous clubs,
As weak against the mountain heaps they push
Their beating breast in vain, and piteous bray,
He lays them quivering on the' ensanguined snows,
And with loud shouts rejoicing bears them home.
There through the piny forest half-absorb'd,
Rough tenant of these shades, the shapeless bear,
With dangling ice all horrid, stalks forlorn;
Slow-paced, and sourer as the storms increase,
He makes his bed beneath the' inclement drift,
And, with stern patience, scorning weak complaint,
Hardens his heart against assailing want.
  Wide o'er the spacious regions of the north,
That see Boötes urge his tardy wain,
A boisterous race, by frosty Caurus* pierced,
Who little pleasure know and fear no pain,
Prolific swarm. They once relumed the flame
Of lost mankind in polish'd slavery sunk,
Drove martial horde on horde,† with dreadful sweep
Resistless rushing o'er the' enfeebled south,
And gave the vanquish'd world another form.
Not such the sons of Lapland: wisely they
Despise the' insensate barbarous trade of war,
They ask no more than simple Nature gives,
They love their mountains, and enjoy their storms
No false desires, no pride-created wants,
Disturb the peaceful current of their time;

* The North-west wind.

† The wandering Scythian clans.

And through the restless ever tortured maze
Of pleasure or ambition bid it rage.
Their reindeer form their riches. These their tents,
Their robes, their beds, and all their homely wealth
Supply, their wholesome fare and cheerful cups.
Obsequious at their call, the docile tribe
Yield to the sled their necks, and whirl them swift
O'er hill and dale, heap'd into one expanse
Of marbled snow, as far as eye can sweep,
With a blue crust of ice unbounded glazed.
By dancing meteors then, that ceaseless shake
A waving blaze refracted o'er the heavens,
And vivid moons, and stars that keener play
With doubled lustre from the glossy waste,
E'en in the depth of polar night, they find
A wondrous day: enough to light the chase,
Or guide their daring steps to Finland fairs.
Wish'd Spring returns; and from the hazy south,
While dim Aurora slowly moves before,
The welcome sun, just verging up at first,
By small degrees extends the swelling curve!
Till seen at last for gay rejoicing months,
Still round and round his spiral course he winds,
And as he nearly dips his flaming orb,
Wheels up again, and reascends the sky.
In that glad season, from the lakes and floods,
Where pure Niemi's* fairy mountains rise,
And fringed with roses Tenglio† rolls his stream,

* M. de Maupertius, in his book on the Figure of the Earth, after having described the beautiful lake and mountain of Niemi, in Lapland, says, "From this height we had opportunity several times to see those vapours rise from the lake, which the people of the country call Haltios, and which they deem to be the guardian spirits of the mountains. We had been frighted with stories of bears that haunted this place, but saw none. It seemed rather a place of resort for fairies and genii than bears."

† The same author observes, "I was surprised to see upon the banks of this river (the Tenglio) roses of as lively a red as any that are in our gardens."

They draw the copious fry. With these, at eve,
They cheerful loaded to their tents repair;
Where, all day long in useful cares employ'd,
Their kind unblemish'd wives the fire prepare.
Thrice happy race! by poverty secured
From legal plunder and rapacious power:
In whom fell interest never yet has sown
The seeds of vice: whose spotless swains ne'er knew
Injurious deed, nor, blasted by the breath
Of faithless love, their blooming daughters woe.
  Still pressing on, beyond Tornea's lake,
And Hecla flaming through a waste of snow,
And furthest Greenland, to the pole itself,
Where, failing gradual, life at length goes out,
The Muse expands her solitary flight;
And, hovering o'er the wild stupendous scene,
Beholds new seas beneath another sky.*
Throned in his palace of cerulean ice,
Here Winter holds his unrejoicing court;
And through his airy hall the loud misrule
Of driving tempest is for ever heard:
Here the grim tyrant meditates his wrath;
Here arms his winds with all-subduing frost;
Moulds his fierce hail, and treasures up his snows,
With which he now oppresses half the globe.
  Thence, winding eastward to the Tartar's coast,
She sweeps the howling margin of the main;
Where undissolving, from the first of time,
Snows swell on snows amazing to the sky;
And icy mountains high on mountains piled,
Seem to the shivering sailor from afar,
Shapeless and white, an atmosphere of clouds.
Projected huge and horrid o'er the surge,
Alps frown on Alps; or, rushing hideous down,
As if old Chaos was again return'd,
Wide rend the deep, and shake the solid pole.

* The other hemisphere.

Ocean itself no longer can resist
The binding fury: but, in all its rage
Of tempest taken by the boundless frost,
Is many a fathom to the bottom chain'd,
And bid to roar no more: a bleak expanse,
Shagg'd o'er with wavy rocks, cheerless, and void
Of every life, that from the dreary months
Flies conscious southward. Miserable they!
Who, here entangled in the gathering ice,
Take their last look of the descending sun;
While, full of death and fierce with tenfold frost,
The long long night, incumbent o'er their heads,
Falls horrible. Such was the Briton's* fate,
As with first prow (what have not Britons dared?)
He for the passage sought, attempted since
So much in vain, and seeming to be shut
By jealous nature with eternal bars.
In these fell regions, in Arzina caught,
And to the stony deep his idle ship
Immediate seal'd, he with his hapless crew,
Each full exerted at his several task,
Froze into statues; to the cordage glued
The sailor, and the pilot to the helm.
  Hard by these shores, where scarce his freezing stream
Rolls the wild Oby, live the last of men;
And, half enliven'd by the distant sun,
That rears and ripens man as well as plants,
Here human Nature wears its rudest form.
Deep from the piercing season sunk in caves,
Here by dull fires, and with unjoyous cheer,
They waste the tedious gloom. Immersed in furs,
Doze the gross race. Nor sprightly jest, nor song,
Nor tenderness they know: nor aught of life
Beyond the kindred bears that stalk without,
Till morn at length, her roses drooping all,

* Sir Hugh Willoughby, sent by Queen Elizabeth to discover the north-east passage.

Sheds a long twilight brightening o'er their fields,
And calls the quiver'd savage to the chase.
What cannot active government perform,
New-moulding man? Wide-stretching from these shores,
A people savage from remotest time,
A huge neglected empire, one vast mind,
By Heaven inspired, from gothic darkness call'd.
Immortal Peter! first of monarchs! he
His stubborn country tamed, her rocks, her fens,
Her floods, her seas, her ill submitting sons;
And while the fierce barbarian he subdued,
To more exalted soul he raised the man.
Ye shades of ancient heroes, ye who toil'd
Through long successive ages to build up
A labouring plan of state, behold at once
The wonder done! behold the matchless prince!
Who left his native throne, where reign'd till then
A mighty shadow of unreal power;
Who greatly spurn'd the slothful pomp of courts;
And roaming every land, in every port
His sceptre laid aside, with glorious hand
Unwearied plying the mechanic tool,
Gather'd the seeds of trade, of useful arts,
Of civil wisdom, and of martial skill.
Charged with the stores of Europe, home he goes!
Then cities rise amid tho' illumined waste;
O'er joyless deserts smiles the rural reign;
Far distant flood to flood is social join'd;
The' astonish'd Euxine hears the Baltic roar;
Proud navies ride on seas that never foam'd
With daring keel before; and armies stretch
Each way their dazzling files, repressing here
The frantic Alexander of the north,
And awing there stern Othman's shrinking sons.
Sloth flies the land, and Ignorance, and Vice,
Of old dishonour proud: it glows around,
Taught by the Royal Hand that roused the whole,

One scene of arts, of arms, of rising trade:
For what his wisdom plann'd, and power enforced,
More potent still, his great example show'd.
 Muttering, the winds at eve, with blunted point,
Blow hollow-blustering from the south. Subdued,
The frost resolves into a trickling thaw.
Spotted the mountains shine; loose sleet descends,
And floods the country round. The rivers swell,
Of bonds impatient. Sudden from the hills,
O'er rocks and woods, in broad brown cataracts,
A thousand snow-fed torrents shoot at once;
And, where they rush, the wide-resounding plain
Is left one slimy waste. Those sullen seas,
That wash'd the' ungenial pole, will rest no more
Beneath the shackles of the mighty north;
But, rousing all their waves, resistless heave.
And hark! the lengthening roar continuous runs
Athwart the rifted deep: at once it bursts,
And piles a thousand mountains to the clouds.
Ill fares the bark, with trembling wretches charged,
That, toss'd amid the floating fragments, moors
Beneath the shelter of an icy isle,
While night o'erwhelms the sea, and horror looks
More horrible. Can human force endure
The' assembled mischiefs that besiege them round?
Heart-gnawing hunger, fainting weariness,
The roar of winds and waves, the crush of ice,
Now ceasing, now renew'd with louder rage,
And in dire echoes bellowing round the main.
More to embroil the deep, Leviathan,
And his unwieldy train, in dreadful sport,
Tempest the loosen'd brine, while through the gloom,
Far from the bleak inhospitable shore
Loading the winds, is heard the hungry howl
Of famish'd monsters, there awaiting wrecks.
Yet Providence, that ever waking eye,
Looks down with pity on the feeble toil

Of mortals lost to hope, and lights them safe,
Through all this dreary labyrinth of fate.
'Tis done! dread Winter spreads his latest glooms,
And reigns tremendous o'er the conquer'd year.
How dead the vegetable kingdom lies!
How dumb the tuneful! horror wide extends
His desolate domain. Behold, fond man!
See here thy pictured life; pass some few years,
Thy flowering Spring, thy Summer's ardent strength,
Thy sober Autumn fading into age,
And pale concluding Winter comes at last,
And shuts the scene. Ah! whither now are fled
Those dreams of greatness? those unsolid hopes
Of happiness? those longings after fame?
Those restless cares? those busy bustling days?
Those gay-spent, festive nights? those veering thoughts,
Lost between good and ill, that shared thy life?
All now are vanish'd! Virtue sole survives,
Immortal never failing friend of Man,
His guide to happiness on high. And see!
'Tis come, the glorious morn! the second birth
Of heaven and earth! awakening Nature hears
The new-creating word, and starts to life,
In every heighten'd form, from pain and death
For ever free. The great eternal scheme,
Involving all, and in a perfect whole
Uniting, as the prospect wider spreads,
To reason's eye refined clears up apace.
Ye vainly wise! ye blind presumptuous! now,
Confounded in the dust, adore that Power
And Wisdom oft arraign'd: see now the cause,
Why unassuming worth in secret lived,
And died neglected: why the good man's share
In life was gall and bitterness of soul:
Why the lone widow and her orphans pined
In starving solitude; while Luxury,
In palaces, lay straining her low thought,

To form unreal wants: why heaven-born truth,
And moderation fair, wore the red marks
Of superstition's scourge: why licensed pain,
That cruel spoiler, that embosom'd foe,
Embitter'd all our bliss. Ye good distress'd!
Ye noble few! who here unbending stand
Beneath life's pressure, yet bear up awhile,
And what your bounded view, which only saw
A little part, deem'd evil is no more:
The storms of Wintry Time will quickly pass,
And one unbounded Spring encircle all.

HYMN.

THESE, as they change, ALMIGHTY FATHER, these
Are but the varied GOD. The rolling year
Is full of THEE. Forth in the pleasing Spring
THY beauty walks, THY tenderness, and love.
Wide flush the fields; the softening air is balm;
Echo the mountains round: the forest smiles;
And every sense, and every heart is joy.
Then comes THY glory in the Summer months,
With light and heart refulgent. Then THY sun
Shoots full perfection through the swelling year:
And oft THY VOICE in dreadful thunder speaks:
And oft at dawn, deep noon, or falling eve,
By brooks and groves, in hollow-whispering gales
THY bounty shines in Autumn unconfined,
And spreads a common feast for all that lives.
In Winter awful THOU! with clouds and storms
Around THEE thrown, tempest o'er tempest roll'd.
Majestic darkness! on the whirlwind's wing,
Riding sublime, THOU bidst the world adore,
And humblest Nature with THY northern blast.
Mysterious round! what skill, what force divine,
Deep felt, in these appear! a simple train,
Yet so delightful mix'd, with such kind art,
Such beauty and beneficence combined;
Shade, unperceived, so softening into shade;
And all so forming an harmonious whole;
That, as they still succeed, they ravish still.
But wandering oft, with brute unconscious gaze,
Man marks not THEE, marks not the mighty hand,
That, ever busy, wheels the silent sphere;

Works in the secret deep; shoots, steaming, thence
The fair profusion that o'erspreads the Spring:
Flings from the sun direct the flaming day;
Feeds every creature; hurls the tempest forth;
And, as on earth this grateful change revolves,
With transport touches all the springs of life
  Nature, attend! join, every living soul
Beneath the spacious temple of the sky,
In adoration join; and, ardent, raise
One general song! To HIM, ye vocal gales,
Breathe soft, whose spirit in your freshness breathes:
Oh, talk of HIM in solitary glooms!
Where, o'er the rock, the scarcely waving pine
Fills the brown shade with a religious awe.
And ye, whose bolder note is heard afar,
Who shake the' astonish'd world, lift high to heaven
The' impetuous song, and say from whom you rage.
HIS praise, ye brooks, attune, ye trembling rills;
And let me catch it as I muse along.
Ye headlong torrents, rapid and profound;
Ye softer floods, that lead the humid maze
Along the vale; and thou, majestic main,
A secret world of wonders in thyself,
Sound HIS stupendous praise: whose greater voice
Or bids you roar or bids your roarings fall.
Soft roll your incense, herbs, and fruits, and flowers,
In mingled clouds to HIM; whose sun exalts,
Whose breath perfumes you, and whose pencil paints.
Ye forests, bend; ye harvests, wave to HIM;
Breathe your still song into the reaper's heart,
As home he goes beneath the joyous moon.
Ye that keep watch in heaven, as earth asleep
Unconscious lies, effuse your mildest beams,
Ye constellations, while your angels strike,
Amid the spangled sky, the silver lyre.
Great source of day! best image here below
Of thy CREATOR, ever pouring wide,
From world to world, the vital ocean round,

On Nature write with every beam His praise.
The thunder rolls: be hush'd the prostrate world,
While cloud to cloud returns the solemn hymn.
Bleat out afresh, ye hills: ye mossy rocks,
Retain the sound: the broad responsive lowe,
Ye valleys, raise; for the Great Shepherd reigns,
And his unsuffering kingdom yet will come.
Ye woodlands all, awake: a boundless song
Burst from the groves! and when the restless day,
Expiring, lays the warbling world asleep,
Sweetest of birds! sweet Philomela, charm
The listening shades, and teach the night His praise.
Ye chief, for whom the whole creation smiles,
At once the head, the heart, and tongue of all,
Crown the great hymn; in swarming cities vast,
Assembled men, to the deep organ join
The long resounding voice, oft breaking clear,
At solemn pauses, through the swelling base;
And, as each mingling flame increases each,
In one united ardour rise to heaven.
Or if you rather choose the rural shade,
And find a fane in every sacred grove;
There let the shepherd's flute, the virgin's lay,
The prompting seraph, and the poet's lyre,
Still sing the God of Seasons as they roll!--
For me, when I forget the darling theme,
Whether the blossom blows, the summer ray
Russets the plain, inspiring Autumn gleams,
Or Winter rises in the blackening east;
Be my tongue mute, my fancy paint no more,
And, dead to joy, forget my heart to beat!
Should fate command me to the furthest verge
Of the green earth, to distant barbarous climes,
Rivers unknown to song; where first the sun
Gilds Indian mountains, or his setting beam
Flames on the' Atlantic isles; 'tis nought to me:
Since God is ever present, ever felt,
In the void waste as in the city full:

And where HE vital breathes there must be joy
When even at last the solemn hour shall come,
And wing my mystic flight to future worlds,
I cheerful will obey; there, with new powers,
Will rising wonders sing: I cannot go
Where Universal Love not smiles around,
Sustaining all yon orbs, and all their suns;
From seeming Evil still educing Good,
And better thence again, and better still
In infinite progression. But I lose
Myself in HIM, in Light ineffable!
Come then expressive Silence, muse His praise.

THE

COURSE OF TIME,

A POEM.

BY ROBERT POLLOK, A.M.

A NEW EDITION.

BOSTON:
PHILLIPS, SAMPSON, AND COMPANY
110 WASHINGTON STREET.
1850.

THE

COURSE OF TIME.

BOOK I.

ANALYSIS OF BOOK I.

Invocation is made to the Eternal Spirit of Truth, and the subject of the Poem is stated.

Long after Time had ceased, and Eternity had rolled on its ages, two youthful sons of Paradise walk on the hills of immortality, enjoying holy converse. A stranger spirit from another world arrives, and is welcomed by them to the abodes of bliss. The stranger desires them to explain the wonderful things he had noticed in his flight from his native world to heaven. Having sailed through empty, nameless regions, where utter nothing dwelt, he suddenly came to a mountainous wall of fiery adamant, on which were horrid figures, traced in fire, imitating life. He entered within, and saw a wide lake of burning fire, and saw most miserable beings walking in the flames, burning continually, yet unconsumed. Filled with horror, he hastened from the dismal prison to the world of light, and now desired to understand this wondrous wretchedness. The Two, unable to explain it, and having their curiosity awakened, propose to visit an "ancient Bard of Earth," who often had sung on this subject to the admiring youth of heaven.

They find the Bard alone, in holy musing, and state to him their desire. He informs them that the prison described is Hell, and promises more fully to meet their curiosity by relating to them the History of Man.

THE

COURSE OF TIME.

BOOK I.

Eternal Spirit! God of truth! to whom
All things seem as they are; Thou, who of old
The prophet's eye unscaled, that nightly saw,
While heavy sleep fell down on other men,
In holy vision tranced, the future pass
Before him, and to Judah's harp attuned
Burdens which made the pagan mountains shake,
And Zion's cedars bow,—inspire my song;
My eye unscale; me what is substance teach,
And shadow what, while I of things to come,
As past, rehearsing, sing the Course of Time,
The second birth, and final doom of man.

The muse, that soft and sickly wooes the ear
Of love, or, chanting loud in windy rhyme
Of fabled hero, raves through gaudy tale
Not overfraught with sense, I ask not: such
A strain befits not argument so high.
Me thought, and phrase severely sifting out
The whole idea, grant; uttering—as 'tis
The essential truth—time gone, the righteous saved,
The wicked damned, and providence approved.

Hold my right hand, Almighty! and me teach
To strike the lyre, but seldom struck, to notes

Harmonious with the morning stars, and pure
As those by sainted bards and angels sung,
Which wake the echoes of Eternity;
That fools may hear and tremble, and the wise,
Instructed, listen, of ages yet to come.

Long was the day, so long expected, past
Of the eternal doom, that gave to each
Of all the human race his due reward.
The sun, earth's sun, and moon, and stars, had ceased
To number seasons, days, and months, and years
To mortal man. Hope was forgotten, and fear:
And time, with all its chance, and change, and smiles,
And frequent tears, and deeds of villany,
Or righteousness, once talked of much, as things
Of great renown, was now but ill remembered;
In dim and shadowy vision of the past
Seen far remote, as country, which has left
The traveller's speedy step, retiring back
From morn till even; and long Eternity
Had rolled his mighty years, and with his years
Men had grown old. The saints, all home returned
From pilgrimage, and war, and weeping, long
Had rested in the bowers of peace, that skirt
The stream of life; and long—alas! how long
To them it seemed!—the wicked, who refused
To be redeemed, had wandered in the dark
Of hell's despair, and drunk the burning cup
Their sins had filled with everlasting wo.

Thus far the years had rolled, which none but God
Doth number, when two sons, two youthful sons
Of Paradise, in conversation sweet,—
For thus the heavenly muse instructs me, wooed
At midnight hour, with offering sincere
Of all the heart, poured out in holy prayer,

High on the hills of immortality,
Whence goodliest prospect looks beyond the walls
Of heaven, walked, casting oft their eye far through
The pure serene, observant if, returned
From errand duly finished, any came,
Or any, first in virtue now complete,
From other worlds arrived, confirmed in good.

Thus viewing, one they saw, on hasty wing
Directing towards heaven his course; and now,
His flight ascending near the battlements
And lofty hills on which they walked, approached.
For round and round, in spacious circuit wide,
Mountains of tallest stature circumscribe
The plains of Paradise, whose tops, arrayed
In uncreated radiance, seemed so pure,
That naught but angel's foot, or saint's, elect
Of God, may venture there to walk. Here oft
The sons of bliss take morn or evening pastime,
Delighted to behold ten thousand worlds
Around their suns revolving in the vast
External space, or listen the harmonies
That each to other in its motion sings.
And hence, in middle heaven remote, is seen
The mount of God in awful glory bright.
Within, no orb create of moon, or star,
Or sun, gives light; for God's own countenance,
Beaming eternally, gives light to all.
But farther than these sacred hills, his will
Forbids its flow, too bright for eyes beyond.
This is the last ascent of Virtue; here
All trial ends, and hope; here perfect joy,
With perfect righteousness, which to these heights
Alone can rise, begins, above all fall.

And now, on wing of holy ardor strong,
Hither ascends the stranger borne upright.—

For stranger he did seem, with curious eye
Of nice inspection round surveying all,—
And at the feet alights of those that stood
His coming, who the hand of welcome gave,
And the embrace sincere of holy love;
And thus with comely greeting kind, began:

Hail, brother! hail, thou son of happiness,
Thou son beloved of God! welcome to heaven,
To bliss that never fades! thy day is past
Of trial and of fear to fall. Well done,
Thou good and faithful servant; enter now
Into the joy eternal of thy Lord.
Come with us, and behold far higher sight
Than e'er thy heart desired, or hope conceived.
See, yonder is the glorious hill of God,
'Bove angel's gaze in brightness rising high.
Come, join our wing, and we will guide thy flight
To mysteries of everlasting bliss—
The tree, and fount of life, the eternal throne,
And presence chamber of the King of kings.
But what concern hangs on thy countenance,
Unwont within this place? Perhaps thou deemst
Thyself unworthy to be brought before
The always Ancient One. So are we, too,
Unworthy; but our God is all in all,
And gives us boldness to approach his throne.

Sons of the Highest! citizens of heaven!
Began the new-arrived, right have ye judged:
Unworthy, most unworthy is your servant,
To stand in presence of the King, or hold
Most distant and most humble place in this
Abode of excellent glory unrevealed.
But God Almighty be for ever praised,
Who of his fullness, fills me with all grace

And ornament, to make me in his sight
Well pleasing, and accepted in his court.
But, if your leisure waits, short narrative
Will tell, why strange concern thus overhangs
My face, ill seeming here; and haply, too,
Your elder knowledge can instruct my youth,
Of what seems dark and doubtful, unexplained.

Our leisure waits thee. Speak; and what we can,
Delighted most to give delight, we will;
Though much of mystery yet to us remains.

Virtue, I need not tell, when proved and full
Matured, inclines us up to God and heaven,
By law of sweet compulsion strong and sure;
As gravitation to the larger orb
The less attracts, through matter's whole domain.
Virtue in me was ripe. I speak not this
In boast; for what I am to God I owe,
Entirely owe, and of myself am naught.
Equipped and bent for heaven, I left yon world,
My native seat, which scarce your eye can reach,
Rolling around her central sun, far out,
On utmost verge of light. But first, to see
What lay beyond the visible creation,
Strong curiosity my flight impelled.
Long was my way, and strange. I passed the bounds
Which God doth set to light, and life, and love;
Where darkness meets with day, where order meets
Disorder, dreadful, waste, and wild; and down
The dark, eternal, uncreated night
Ventured alone. Long, long on rapid wing,
I sailed through empty, nameless regions vast,
Where utter nothing dwells, unformed and void.
There neither eye, nor ear, nor any sense
Of being most acute, finds object; there

For aught external still you search in vain.
Try touch, or sight, or smell; try what you will,
You strangely find naught but yourself alone.
But why should I in words attempt to tell
What that is like, which is, and yet is not?
This past, my path, descending, led me still
O'er unclaimed continents of desert gloom
Immense, where gravitation shifting turns
The other way; and to some dread, unknown,
Infernal centre downward weighs: and now,—
Far travelled from the edge of darkness, far
As from that glorious mount of God to light's
Remotest limb,—dire sights I saw, dire sounds
I heard; and suddenly before my eye
A wall of fiery adamant sprung up,
Wall mountainous, tremendous, flaming high
Above all flight of hope. I paused, and looked;
And saw, where'er I looked upon that mound,
Sad figures traced in fire, not motionless,
But imitating life. One I remarked
Attentively; but how shall I describe
What naught resembles else my eye hath seen?
Of worm or serpent kind it something looked,
But monstrous, with a thousand snaky heads,
Eyed each with double orbs of glaring wrath;
And with as many tails, that twisted out
In horrid revolution, tipped with stings;
And all its mouths, that wide and darkly gaped,
And breathed most poisonous breath, had each a sting,
Forked, and long, and venemous, and sharp;
And, in its writhings infinite, it grasped
Malignantly what seemed a heart, swollen, black,
And quivering with torture most intense;
And still the heart, with anguish throbbing high,
Made effort to escape, but could not; for,
Howe'er it turned—and oft it vainly turned—

These complicated foldings held it fast.
And still the monstrous beast with sting of head
Or tail transpierced it, bleeding evermore.
What this could image, much I searched to know;
And while I stood, and gazed, and wondered long,
A voice—from whence I knew not, for no one
I saw—distinctly whispered in my ear
These words: This is the Worm that never dies.

Fast by the side of this unsightly thing
Another was portrayed, more hideous still:
Who sees it once shall wish to see't no more.
For ever undescribed let it remain!
Only this much I may or can unfold.
Far out it thrust a dart that might have made
The knees of Terror quake, and on it hung,
Within the triple barbs, a being pierced
Through soul and body both. Of heavenly make
Original the being seemed, but fallen,
And worn and wasted with enormous wo.
And still, around the everlasting lance,
It writhed, convulsed, and uttered mimic groans;
And tried and wished, and ever tried and wished
To die; but could not die. Oh, horrid sight!
I trembling gazed, and listened, and heard this voice
Approach my ear: This is Eternal Death.

Nor these alone. Upon that burning wall,
In horrible emblazonry, were limned
All shapes, all forms, all modes of wretchedness,
And agony, and grief, and desperate wo.
And prominent in characters of fire,
Where'er the eye could light, these words you read:
"Who comes this way, behold, and fear to sin!"
Amazed I stood; and thought such imagery
Foretokened, within, a dangerous abode.

But yet to see the worst a wish arose.
For virtue, by the holy seal of God
Accredited and stamped, immortal all,
And all invulnerable, fears no hurt.
As easy as my wish, as rapidly,
I through the horrid rampart passed, unscathed
And unopposed; and, poised on steady wing,
I hovering gazed. Eternal Justice! sons
Of God! tell me, if ye can tell, what then
I saw, what then I heard. Wide was the place,
And deep as wide, and ruinous as deep.
Beneath, I saw a lake of burning fire,
With tempest tost perpetually, and still
The waves of fiery darkness 'gainst the rocks
Of dark damnation broke, and music made
Of melancholy sort; and over head,
And all around, wind warred with wind, storm howled
To storm, and lightning forked lightning crossed,
And thunder answered thunder, muttering sounds
Of sullen wrath; and far as sight could pierce,
Or down descend in caves of hopeless depth,
Through all that dungeon of unfading fire,
I saw most miserable beings walk,
Burning continually, yet unconsumed;
For ever wasting, yet enduring still;
Dying perpetually, yet never dead.
Some wandered lonely in the desert flames,
And some in fell encounter fiercely met,
With curses loud, and blasphemies, that made
The cheek of Darkness pale; and as they fought,
And cursed, and gnashed their teeth, and wished to die,
Their hollow eyes did utter streams of wo.
And there were groans that ended not, and sighs
That always sighed, and tears that ever wept
And ever fell, but not in Mercy's sight.
And Sorrow, and Repentance, and Despair,

Among them walked, and to their thirsty lips
Presented frequent cups of burning gall.
And as I listened, I heard these beings curse
Almighty God, and curse the Lamb, and curse
The earth, the resurrection morn, and seek,
And ever vainly seek, for utter death.
And to their everlasting anguish still,
The thunders from above responding spoke
These words, which, through the caverns of perdition
Forlornly echoing, fell on every ear:
"Ye knew your duty, but ye did it not."
And back again recoiled a deeper groan.
A deeper groan! Oh, what a groan was that!
I waited not, but swift on speediest wing,
With unaccustomed thoughts conversing, back
Retraced my venturous path from dark to light.
Then up ascending, long ascending up,
I hasted on; though whiles the chiming spheres,
By God's own finger touched to harmony,
Held me delaying, till I here arrived,
Drawn upward by the eternal love of God,
Of wonder full and strange astonishment,
At what in yonder den of darkness dwells,
Which now your higher knowledge will unfold.

They answering said: To ask and to bestow
Knowledge, is much of heaven's delight; and now
Most joyfully what thou requirst we would;
For much of new and unaccountable
Thou bringst. Something indeed we heard before,
In passing conversation slightly touched,
Of such a place; yet, rather to be taught,
Than teaching, answer, what thy marvel asks,
We need; for we ourselves, though here, are but
Of yesterday, creation's younger sons.
But there is one, an ancient bard of Earth,

Who, by tne stream of life, sitting in bliss,
Has oft beheld the eternal years complete
The mighty circle round the throne of God;
Great in all learning, in all wisdom great,
And great in song; whose harp in lofty strain
Tells frequently of what thy wonder craves,
While round him, gathering, stand the youth of heaven,
With truth and melody delighted both.
To him this path directs, an easy path,
And easy flight will bring us to his seat.

So saying, they linked hand in hand, spread out
Their golden wings, by living breezes fanned,
And over heaven's broad champaign sailed serene.
O'er hill and valley, clothed with verdure green,
That never fades; and tree, and herb, and flower,
That never fades; and many a river, rich
With nectar, winding pleasantly, they passed
And mansion of celestial mould, and work
Divine. And oft delicious music, sung
By saint and angel bands that walked the vales,
Or mountain tops, and harped upon their harps,
Their ear inclined, and held by sweet constraint
Their wing; not long, for strong desire awaked
Of knowledge that to holy use might turn,
Still pressed them on to leave what rather seemed
Pleasure, due only when all duty's done.

And now beneath them lay the wished-for spot,
The sacred bower of that renowned bard;
That ancient bard, ancient in days and song;
But in immortal vigor young, and young
In rosy health; to pensive solitude
Retiring oft, as was his wont on earth.

Fit was the place, most fit, for holy musing.
Upon a little mount, that gently rose,

He sat, clothed in white robes; and o'er his head
A laurel tree, of lustiest, eldest growth,
Stately and tall, and shadowing far and wide,—
Not fruitless, as on earth, but bloomed and rich
With frequent clusters, ripe to heavenly taste,—
Spread its eternal boughs, and in its arms
A myrtle of unfading leaf embraced—
The rose and lily, fresh with fragrant dew,
And every flower of fairest cheek, around
Him, smiling flocked. Beneath his feet, fast by,
And round his sacred hill, a streamlet walked,
Warbling the holy melodies of heaven;
The hallowed zephyrs brought him incense sweet;
And out before him opened, in prospect long,
The river of life, in many a winding maze
Descending from the lofty throne of God,
That with excessive glory closed the scene.

Of Adam's race he was, and lonely sat,
By chance that day, in meditation deep,
Reflecting much of time, and earth, and man.
And now to pensive, now to cheerful notes,
He touched a harp of wondrous melody.
A golden harp it was, a precious gift,
Which, at the day of judgment, with the crown
Of life, he had received from God's own hand,
Reward due to his service done on earth.

He sees their coming, and with greeting kind,
And welcome, not of hollow forged smiles,
And ceremonious compliment of phrase,
But of the heart sincere, into his bower
Invites. Like greeting they returned. Not bent
In low obeisancy, from creature most
Unfit to creature; but with manly form
Upright they entered in; though high his rank,

His wisdom high, and mighty his renown.
And thus, deferring all apology,
The two their new companion introduced.

Ancient in knowledge! bard of Adam's race!
We bring thee one, of us inquiring what
We need to learn, and with him wish to learn.
His asking will direct thy answer best.

Most ancient bard! began the new-arrived,
Few words will set my wonder forth, and guide
Thy wisdom's light to what in me is dark.

Equipped for heaven, I left my native place.
But first beyond the realms of light I bent
My course; and there, in utter darkness, far
Remote, I beings saw forlorn in wo,
Burning continually, yet unconsumed.
And there were groans that ended not, and sighs
That always sighed, and tears that ever wept
And ever fell, but not in Mercy's sight.
And still I heard these wretched beings curse
Almighty God, and curse the Lamb, and curse
The earth, the resurrection morn, and seek,
And ever vainly seek, for utter death.
And from above the thunders answered still,
"Ye knew your duty, but ye did it not."
And everywhere, throughout that horrid den,
I saw a form of excellence, a form
Of beauty without spot, that naught could see
And not admire, admire and not adore.
And from its own essential beams it gave
Light to itself, that made the gloom more dark.
And every eye in that infernal pit
Beheld it still; and from its face—how fair!
Oh, how exceeding fair!—for ever sought,

But ever vainly sought, to turn away.
That image, as I guess, was Virtue; for
Naught else hath God given countenance so fair.
But why in such a place it should abide?
What place it is? What beings there lament?
Whence came they? and for what their endless groan?
Why curse they God? why seek they utter death?
And chief, what means the resurrection morn?
My youth expects thy reverend age to tell.

Thou rightly deemst, fair youth, began the bard.
The form thou sawst was Virtue, ever fair.
Virtue, like God, whose excellent majesty,
Whose glory virtue is, is omnipresent.
No being, once created rational,
Accountable, endowed with moral sense,
With sapience of right and wrong endowed,
And charged, however fallen, debased, destroyed;
However lost forlorn, and miserable;
In guilt's dark shrouding wrapped however thick;
However drunk, delirious, and mad,
With sin's full cup; and with whatever damned,
Unnatural diligence it work and toil,—
Can banish Virtue from its sight, or once
Forget that she is fair. Hides it in night,
In central night; takes it the lightning's wing,
And flies for ever on, beyond the bounds
Of all; drinks it the maddest cup of sin;
Dives it beneath the ocean of despair;
It dives, it drinks, it flies, it hides in vain.
For still the eternal beauty, image fair,
Once stamped upon the soul, before the eye
All lovely stands, nor will depart; so God
Ordains; and lovely to the worst she seems,
And ever seems; and as they look, and still
Must ever look, upon her loveliness,

Remembrance dire of what they were, of what
They might have been, and bitter sense of what
They are, polluted, ruined, hopeless, lost,
With most repenting torment rend their hearts.
So God ordains, their punishment severe,
Eternally inflicted by themselves.
'Tis this, this Virtue, hovering evermore
Before the vision of the damned, and, in
Upon their monstrous moral nakedness
Casting unwelcome light, that makes their wo,
That makes the essence of the endless flame.
Where this is, there is hell, darker than aught
That he, the bard three-visioned, darkest saw.

The place thou sawst was hell; the groans thou heardst
The wailings of the damned, of those who would
Not be redeemed, and at the judgment day,
Long past, for unrepented sins were damned.
The seven loud thunders which thou heardst, declare
The eternal wrath of the Almighty God.
But whence, or why they came to dwell in wo,
Why they curse God, what means the glorious morn
Of resurrection, these a longer tale
Demand, and lead the mournful lyre far back
Through memory of sin and mortal man.
Yet haply not rewardless we shall trace
The dark disastrous years of finished Time.
Sorrows remembered sweeten present joy.
Nor yet shall all be sad; for God gave peace,
Much peace on earth, to all who feared his name.

But first it needs to say, that other style
And other language than thy ear is wont,
Thou must expect to hear—the dialect
Of man. For each in heaven a relish holds

Of former speech, that points to whence he came.
But whether I of person speak, or place,
Event or action, moral or divine;
Or things unknown compare to things unknown;
Allude, imply, suggest, apostrophize;
Or touch, when wandering through the past, on moods
Of mind thou never feltst;—the meaning still,
With easy apprehension, thou shalt take.
So perfect here is knowledge, and the strings
Of sympathy so tuned, that every word
That each to other speaks, though never heard
Before, at once is fully understood,
And every feeling uttered, fully felt.

So shalt thou find, as from my various song,
That backward rolls o'er many a tide of years,
Directly or inferred, thy asking, thou,
And wondering doubt, shalt learn to answer, while
I sketch in brief the history of man.

THE

COURSE OF TIME

BOOK II.

ANALYSIS OF BOOK II.

The "ancient Bard" begins his story. He relates briefly the creation of the Earth, and of Man; the Apostacy; and the provision for Man's recovery through the Incarnation and Death of the Son of God. The inquiring spirit breaks out in rapturous admiration of Redeeming Love, expressing the supposition that the whole race of Adam must have availed themselves of its benefits. The Bard proceeds, correcting this mistake, and stating further the efforts on the part of God to secure the salvation of men, and the unwillingness of multitudes to receive mercy. The Bible, proceeding from God himself, was sent to them, containing a full exhibition of God's character and law; of man's character, condition, duty, and destiny; of the nature and tendency of sin, and of the method of final pardon; but many refused to regard this voice from heaven; many perverted its testimony; many, after extinguishing the light of revelation, yielded to impious idolatry Some of the influences which operate to counteract the Bible are noticed; particularly the criminal abuse of office and authority, the admiration of philosophy and science, the love of pleasure and indolence. In conclusion, the "primal cause" and "fountain head" of all the opposition manifested to God and to his revealed word, is found in the Pride of the human heart.

THE

COURSE OF TIME.

BOOK II.

THIS said, he waked the golden harp, and thus,
While on him inspiration breathed, began:

As from yon everlasting hills that gird
Heaven northward, I thy course espied, I judge
Thou from the arctic regions came! Perhaps
Thou noticed on thy way a little orb,
Attended by one moon, her lamp by night,
With her fair sisterhood of planets seven,
Revolving round their central sun; she third
In place, in magnitude the fourth. That orb,
New made, new named, inhabited anew,—
Though whiles we sons of Adam visit still,
Our native place, not changed so far but we
Can trace our ancient walks, the scenery
Of childhood, youth, and prime, and hoary age,
But scenery most of suffering and wo,—
That little orb, in days remote of old,
When angels yet were young, was made for man,
And titled Earth, her primal virgin name;—
Created first so lovely, so adorned
With hill, and dale, and lawn, and winding vale,
Woodland, and stream, and lake, and rolling seas,
Green mead, and fruitful tree, and fertile grain,
And herb and flower; so lovely, so adorned

With numerous beasts of every kind, with fowl
Of every wing and every tuneful note,
And with all fish that in the multitude
Of waters swam; so lovely so adorned,
So fit a dwelling place for man, that, as
She rose, complete, at the creating word,
The morning stars, the sons of God, aloud
Shouted for joy; and God, beholding, saw
The fair design, that from eternity
His mind conceived, accomplished, and, well pleased,
His six days finished work most good pronounced,
And man declared the sovereign prince of all.

All else was prone, irrational, and mute,
And unaccountable, by instinct led.
But man He made of angel form erect,
To hold communion with the heavens above;
And on his soul impressed his image fair,
His own similitude of holiness,
Of virtue, truth, and love; with reason high
To balance right and wrong, and consience quick
To choose or to reject; with knowledge great,
Prudence and wisdom, vigilance and strength,
To guard all force or guile; and, last of all,
The highest gift of God's abundant grace,
With perfect, free, unbiased will. Thus man
Was made upright, immortal made, and crowned
The king of all; to eat, to drink, to do
Freely and sovereignly his will entire;—
By one command alone restrained, to prove,
As was most just, his filial love sincere,
His loyalty, obedience due, and faith.
And thus the prohibition ran, expressed,
As God is wont, in terms of plainest truth.

Of every tree that in the garden grows
Thou mayest freely eat; but of the tree

That knowledge hath of good and ill, eat not,
Nor touch; for in the day thou eatest, thou
Shalt die. Go and this one command obey,
Adam, live and be happy, and with thy Eve,
Fit consort, multiply and fill the earth.

Thus they, the representatives of men,
Were placed in Eden, choicest spot of earth.
With royal honor and with glory crowned,
Adam, the Lord of all, majestic walked,
With godlike countenance sublime, and form
Of lofty towering strength; and by his side
Eve, fair as morning star, with modesty
Arrayed, with virtue, grace, and perfect love
In holy marriage wed, and eloquent
Of thought and comely words, to worship God
And sing his praise, the Giver of all good:
Glad, in each other glad, and glad in hope;
Rejoicing in their future happy race.

O lovely, happy, blest, immortal pair!
Pleased with the present, full of glorious hope.
But short, alas! the song that sings their bliss!
Henceforth the history of man grows dark!
Shade after shade of deepening gloom descends;
And Innocence laments her robes defiled.
Who farther sings, must change the pleasant lyre
To heavy notes of wo. Why! dost thou ask,
Surprised? The answer will surprise thee more.
Man sinned; tempted, he ate the guarded tree;—
Tempted of whom thou afterwards shall hear;—
Audacious, unbelieving, proud, ungrateful,
He ate the interdicted fruit, and fell;
And in his fall, his universal race;
For they in him by delegation were,
In him to stand or fall, to live or die.

Man most ingrate! so full of grace, to sin,
Here interposed the new-arrived, so full
Of bliss, to sin against the Gracious One!
The holy, just, and good! the Eternal Love!
Unseen, unheard, unthought of wickedness!
Why slumbered vengeance? No, it slumbered not.
The ever just and righteous God would let
His fury loose, and satisfy his threat.

That had been just, replied the reverend bard;
But done, fair youth, thou ne'er hadst met me here,
I ne'er had seen yon glorious throne in peace.

Thy powers are great, originally great,
And purified even at the fount of light.
Exert them now, call all their vigor out;
Take room, think vastly, meditate intensely,
Reason profoundly; send conjecture forth;
Let fancy fly, stoop down, ascend; all length,
All breadth explore, all moral, all divine;
Ask prudence, justice, mercy ask, and might;
Weigh good with evil, balance right with wrong;
With virtue vice compare, hatred with love;
God's holiness, God's justice, and God's truth,
Deliberately and cautiously compare
With sinful, wicked, vile, rebellious man;—
And see if thou canst punish sin, and let
Mankind go free. Thou failst; be not surprised;
I bade thee search in vain. Eternal love,—
Harp, lift thy voice on high!—eternal love,
Eternal, sovereign love, and sovereign grace,
Wisdom, and power, and mercy infinite,
The Father, Son, and Holy Spirit, God,
Devised the wondrous plan, devised, achieved,
And in achieving made the marvel more.
Attend, ye heavens! ye heaven of heavens, attend!

Attend and wonder, wonder evermore!
When man had fallen, rebelled, insulted God;
Was most polluted, yet most madly proud;
Indebted infinitely, yet most poor;
Captive to sin, yet willing to be bound;
To God's incensed justice and hot wrath
Exposed, due victim of eternal death
And utter wo—Harp, lift thy voice on high!
Ye everlasting hills! ye angels! bow;
Bow, ye redeemed of men!—God was made flesh,
And dwelt with man on earth! The Son of God,
Only begotten and well beloved, between
Men and his Father's justice interposed;
Put human nature on; His wrath sustained;
And in their name suffered, obeyed, and died,
Making his soul an offering for sin;
Just for unjust, and innocence for guilt,
By doing, suffering, dying unconstrained,
Save by omnipotence of boundless grace,
Complete atonement made to God appeased,
Made honorable his insulted law,
Turning the wrath aside from pardoned man.
Thus Truth with Mercy met, and Righteousness,
Stooping from highest heaven, embraced fair Peace,
That walked the earth in fellowship with Love.

O love divine! O mercy infinite!
The audience here in glowing rapture broke;
O love, all height above, all depth below,
Surpassing far all knowledge, all desire,
All thought! The Holy One for sinners dies!
The Lord of life for guilty rebels bleeds,
Quenches eternal fire with blood divine!
Abundant mercy! overflowing grace!
There, whence I came, I something heard of men;
Their name had reached us, and report did speak

Of some abominable horrid thing,
Of desperate offence they had committed.
And something too of wondrous grace we heard.
And oft of our celestial visitants
What man, what God had done, inquired; but they,
Forbid, our asking never met directly,
Exhorting still to persevere upright,
And we should hear in heaven, though greatly blest
Ourselves, new wonders of God's wondrous love.
This hinting, keener appetite to know
Awaked; and as we talked, and much admired
What new we there should learn, we hasted each
To nourish virtue to perfection up,
That we might have our wondering resolved,
And leave of louder praise to greater deeds
Of loving kindness due. Mysterious love!
God was made flesh, and dwelt with men on earth;
Blood holy, blood divine for sinners shed!
My asking ends, but makes my wonder more.
Saviour of men! henceforth be thou my theme;
Redeeming love, my study day and night.
Mankind were lost, all lost, and all redeemed!

Thou errst again, but innocently errst,
Not knowing sin's depravity, nor man's
Sincere and persevering wickdness.
All were redeemed? Not all, or thou hadst heard
No human voice in hell. Many refused,
Although beseeched, refused to be redeemed,
Redeemed from death to life, from wo to bliss!

Canst thou believe my song when thus I sing?
When man had fallen, was ruined, hopeless, lost—
Ye choral harps! ye angels that excel
In strength! and loudest, ye redeemed of men!
To God, to Him that sits upon the throne

On high, and to the Lamb, sing honor, sing
Dominion, glory, blessing sing, and praise!—
When man had fallen, was ruined, hopeless, lost,
Messiah, Prince of Peace, Eternal King,
Died, that the dead might live, the lost be saved.
Wonder, O heavens! and be astonished, earth!
Thou ancient, thou forgotten earth! ye worlds, admire!
Admire and be confounded! and thou hell,
Deepen thy eternal groan!—men would not be
Redeemed,—I speak of many, not of all,—
Would not be saved for lost, have life for death!

Mysterious song! the new-arrived exclaimed,
Mysterious mercy! most mysterious hate!
To disobey was mad, this madder far,
Incurable insanity of will!
What now but wrath could guilty men expect?
What more could love, what more could mercy do?

No more, resumed the bard, no more they could.
Thou hast seen hell. The wicked there lament!
And why? for love and mercy twice despised.
The husbandman, who sluggishly forgot
In spring to plough and sow, could censure none,
Though winter clamored round his empty barns.
But he who, having thus neglected, did
Refuse, when autumn came, and famine threatened,
To reap the golden field that charity
Bestowed; nay, more obdurate, proud, and blind,
And stupid still, refused, though much beseeched,
And long entreated, even with Mercy's tears,
To eat what to his very lips was held,
Cooked temptingly,—he certainly, at least,
Deserved to die of hunger, unbemoaned.
So did the wicked spurn the grace of God;

And so were punished with the second death.
The first, no doubt, punition less severe
Intended; death, belike, of all entire.
But this incurred, by God discharged, and life
Freely presented, and again despised,
Despised, though bought with Mercy's proper blood:
'Twas this dug hell, and kindled all its bounds
With wrath and unextinguishable fire.

Free was the offer, free to all, of life
And of salvation; but the proud of heart,
Because 'twas free, would not accept; and still
To merit wished; and choosing, thus unshipped,
Uncompassed, unprovisioned, and bestormed,
To swim a sea of breadth immeasurable,
They scorned the goodly bark, whose wings the breath
Of God's eternal Spirit filled for heaven,
That stopped to take them in,—and so were lost!

What wonders dost thou tell! to merit how!
Of creature meriting in sight of God,
As right of service done, I never heard
Till now. We never fell; in virtue stood
Upright, and persevered in holiness;
But stood by grace, by grace we persevered.
Ourselves, our deeds, our holiest, highest deeds,
Unworthy aught; grace worthy endless praise.
If we fly swift, obedient to his will,
He gives us wings to fly; if we resist
Temptation, and ne'er fall, it is his shield
Omnipotent that wards it off; if we,
With love unquenchable, before him burn,
'Tis he that lights and keeps alive the flame.
Men surely lost their reason in their fall,
And did not understand the offer made.

They might have understood, the bard replied;
They had the Bible. Hast thou ever heard
Of such a book? The author, God himself;
The subject, God and man, salvation, life
And death—eternal life, eternal death—
Dread words! whose meaning has no end, no bounds—
Most wondrous book! bright candle of the Lord!
Star of eternity! the only star
By which the bark of man could navigate
The sea of life, and gain the coast of bliss
Securely! only star which rose on Time,
And on its dark and troubled billows, still,
As generation, drifting swiftly by,
Succeeded generation, threw a ray
Of heaven's own light, and to the hills of God,
The eternal hills, pointed the sinner's eye.
By prophets, seers, and priests, and sacred bards,
Evangelists, apostles, men inspired,
And by the Holy Ghost anointed, set
Apart and consecrated to declare
To Earth the counsels of the Eternal One,
This book, this holiest, this sublimest book
Was sent. Heaven's will, Heaven's code of laws entire,
To man, this book contained; defined the bounds
Of vice and virtue, and of life and death;
And what was shadow, what was substance taught.
Much it revealed; important all; the least
Worth more than what else seemed of highest worth,
But this of plainest, most essential truth:
That God is one, eternal, holy, just,
Omnipotent, omniscient, infinite;
Most wise, most good, most merciful and true;
In all perfection most unchangeable:
That man, that every man of every clime
And hue, of every age and every rank,
Was bad, by nature and by practice bad;

In understanding blind, in will perverse,
In heart corrupt; in every thought, and word,
Imagination, passion, and desire,
Most utterly depraved throughout, and ill,
In sight of Heaven, though less in sight of man;
At enmity with God his maker born,
And by his very life an heir of death:
That man, that every man was, farther, most
Unable to redeem himself, or pay
One mite of his vast debt to God; nay, more,
Was most reluctant and averse to be
Redeemed, and sin's most voluntary slave:
That Jesus, Son of God, of Mary born
In Bethlehem, and by Pilate crucified
On Calvary, for man, thus fallen and lost,
Died; and, by Death, life and salvation bought,
And perfect righteousness, for all who should
In his great name believe: That He, the third
In the eternal essence, to the prayer
Sincere should come, should come as soon as asked,
Proceeding from the Father and the Son,
To give faith and repentance, such as God
Accepts; to open the intellectual eyes,
Blinded by sin; to bend the stubborn will,
Perversely to the side of wrong inclined,
To God and his commandments, just and good;
The wild, rebellious passions to subdue,
And bring them back to harmony with Heaven;
To purify the conscience, and to lead
The mind into all truth, and to adorn
With every holy ornament of grace,
And sanctify the whole renewed soul,
Which henceforth might no more fall totally,
But persevere, though erring oft, amidst
The mists of Time, in piety to God,
And sacred works of charity to men:

That he who thus believed, and practised thus,
Should have his sins forgiven, however vile;
Should be sustained at mid-day, morn, and even,
By God's omnipotent, eternal grace;
And in the evil hour of sore disease,
Temptation, persecution, war, and death,—
For temporal death, although unstinged, remained,—
Beneath the shadow of the Almighty's wings
Should sit unhurt, and at the judgment day,
Should share the resurrection of the just,
And reign with Christ in bliss for evermore:
That all, however named, however great,
Who would not thus believe, nor practise thus,
But in their sins impenitent remained,
Should in perpetual fear and terror live;
Should die unpardoned, unredeemed, unsaved;
And, at the hour of doom, should be cast out
To utter darkness in the night of hell,
By mercy and by God abandoned, there
To reap the harvests of eternal wo.

This did that book declare in obvious phrase,
In most sincere and honest words, by God
Himself selected and arranged, so clear,
So plain, so perfectly distinct, that none
Who read with humble wish to understand,
And asked the Spirit, given to all who asked,
Could miss their meaning, blazed in heavenly light.

This book, this holy book, on every line
Marked with the seal of high divinity,
On every leaf bedewed with drops of love
Divine, and with the eternal heraldry
And signature of God Almighty stamped
From first to last, this ray of sacred light,
This lamp, from off the everlasting throne,

Mercy took down, and, in the night of Time
Stood, casting on the dark her gracious bow;
And evermore beseeching men, with tears
And earnest sighs, to read, believe, and live.
And many to her voice gave ear, and read,
Believed, obeyed; and now, as the Amen,
True, Faithful Witness swore, with snowy robes
And branchy palms, surround the fount of life,
And drink the streams of immortality,
For ever happy, and for ever young.

Many believed; but more the truth of God
Turned to a lie, deceiving and deceived;
Each with the accursed sorcery of sin,
To his own wish and vile propensity
Transforming still the meaning of the text.

Hear, while I briefly tell what mortals proved,
By effort vast of ingenuity,
Most wondrous, though perverse and damnable,
Proved from the Bible, which, as thou hast heard,
So plainly spoke that all could understand.
First, and not least in number, argued some,
From out this book itself, it was a lie,
A fable, framed by crafty men, to cheat
The simple herd, and make them bow the knee
To kings and priests. These, in their wisdom, left
The light revealed, and turned to fancies wild;
Maintaining loud, that ruined, helpless man,
Needed no Saviour. Others proved that men
Might live and die in sin, and yet be saved,
For so it was decreed; binding the will,
By God left free, to unconditional,
Unreasonable fate. Others believed
That he who was most criminal, debased,
Condemned, and dead, unaided might ascend

The heights of virtue; to a perfect law
Giving a lame, half-way obedience, which
By useless effort only served to show
The impotence of him who vainly strove
With finite arm to measure infinite;
Most useless effort, when to justify
In sight of God it meant, as proof of faith
Most acceptable and worthy of all praise.
Another held, and from the Bible held,
He was infallible, most fallen by such
Pretence; that none the Scriptures, open to all,
And most to humble-hearted, ought to read,
But priests; that all who ventured to disclaim
His forged authority, incurred the wrath
Of Heaven; and he who, in the blood of such,
Though father, mother, daughter, wife, or son,
Imbrued his hands, did most religious work,
Well pleasing to the heart of the Most High.
Others in outward rite devotion placed,
In meats, in drinks, in robe of certain shape,
In bodily abasements, bended knees;
Days, numbers, places, vestments, words, and names;
Absurdly in their hearts imagining,
That God, like men, was pleased with outward show.
Another, stranger and more wicked still,
With dark and dolorous labor, ill applied,
With many a gripe of consience, and with most
Unhealthy and abortive reasoning,
That brought his sanity to serious doubt,
'Mong wise and honest men, maintained that He,
First Wisdom, Great Messiah, Prince of Peace,
The second of the uncreated Three,
Was naught but man, of earthly origin:
Thus making void the sacrifice divine,
And leaving guilty men, God's holy law
Still unatoned, to work them endless death.

These are a part; but to relate thee all
The monstrous, unbaptized fantasies,
Imaginations fearfully absurd,
Hobgoblin rites, and moon-struck reveries,
Distracted creeds, and visionary dreams,
More bodiless and hideously misshapen
Than ever fancy, at the noon of night,
Playing at will, framed in the madman's brain,
That from this book of simple truth were proved,
Were proved, as foolish men were wont to prove,
Would bring my word in doubt, and thy belief
Stagger, though here I sit and sing, within
The pale of truth, where falsehood never came.

The rest, who lost the heavenly light revealed,
Not wishing to retain God in their minds,
In darkness wandered on. Yet could they not,
Though moral night around them drew her pall
Of blackness, rest in utter unbelief.
The voice within, the voice of God, that naught
Could bribe to sleep, though steeped in sorceries
Of hell, and much abused by whisperings
Of evil spirits in the dark, announced
A day of judgment and a Judge, a day
Of misery or bliss: and, being ill
At ease, for gods they chose them stocks and stones,
Reptiles, and weeds, and beasts, and creeping things,
And spirits accursed, ten thousand deities!
Imagined worse than he who craved their peace;
And, bowing, worshipped these, as best beseemed,
With midnight revelry obscene and loud,
With dark, infernal, devilish ceremonies,
And horrid sacrifice of human flesh,
That made the fair heavens blush. So bad was sin;
So lost, so ruined, so depraved was man,
Created first in God's own image fair.

Oh, cursed, cursed Sin! traitor to God,
And ruiner of man! mother of Wo,
And Death, and Hell! wretched, yet seeking worse;
Polluted most, yet wallowing in the mire;
Most mad, yet drinking Frenzy's giddy cup;
Depth ever deepening, darkness darkening still;
Folly for wisdom, guilt for innocence;
Anguish for rapture, and for hope despair;
Destroyed, destroying; in tormenting, pained;
Unawed by wrath, by mercy unreclaimed;
Thing most unsightly, most forlorn, most sad,
Thy time on earth is passed, thy war with God
And holiness. But who, oh, who shall tell,
Thy unrepentable and ruinous thoughts!
Thy sighs, thy groans! who reckon thy burning tears,
And damned looks of everlasting grief,
Where now, with those who took their part with thee,
Thou sittest in hell, gnawed by the eternal Worm,
To hurt no more, on all the holy hills!

That those, deserting once the lamp of truth,
Should wander ever on, from worse to worse
Erroneously, thy wonder needs not ask;
But that enlightened, reasonable men,
Knowing themselves accountable, to whom
God spoke from heaven, and by his servants warned,
Both day and night, with earnest, pleading voice,
Of retribution equal to their works,
Should persevere in evil, and be lost,—
This strangeness, this unpardonable guilt,
Demands an answer, which my song unfolds,
In part, directly; but, hereafter, more,
To satisfy thy wonder, thou shalt learn,
Inferring much from what is yet to sing.

Know, then, of men who sat in highest place,
Exalted, and for sin by others done

Were chargeable, the king and priests were chief.
Many were faithful, holy, just, upright,
Faithful to God and man, reigning renowned
In righteousness, and, to the people, loud
And fearless, speaking all the words of life.
These, at the judgment-day, as thou shalt hear,
Abundant harvest reaped. But many, too,
Alas, how many! famous now in hell,
Were wicked, cruel, tyrannous, and vile;
Ambitious of themselves, abandoned, mad;
And still from servants hasting to be gods,
Such gods as now they serve in Erebus.
I pass their lewd example by, that led
So many wrong, for courtly fashion lost,
And prove them guilty of one crime alone.
Of every wicked ruler, prince supreme,
Or magistrate below, the one intent,
Purpose, desire, and struggle, day and night,
Was evermore to wrest the crown from off
Messiah's head, and put it on his own;
And in His place give spiritual laws to men;
To bind religion, free by birth, by God
And nature free, and made accountable
To none but God, behind the wheels of state;
To make the holy altar, where the Prince
Of life, incarnate, bled to ransom man,
A footstool to the throne. For this they met,
Assembled, counselled, meditated, planned;
Devised in open and secret; and for this
Enacted creeds of wondrous texture, creeds
The Bible never owned, unsanctioned too,
And reprobate in heaven; but, by the power
That made,—exerted now in gentler form,
Monopolizing rights and privileges,
Equal to all, and waving now the sword
Of persecution fierce, tempered in hell,—

Forced on the conscience of inferior men:
The conscience, that sole monarchy in man,
Owing allegiance to no earthly prince;
Made by the edict of creation free;
Made sacred, made above all human laws;
Holding of heaven alone; of most divine
And indefeasible authority;
An individual sovereignty, that none
Created might, unpunished, bind or touch;
Unbound, save by the eternal laws of God,
And unamenable to all below.

Thus did the uncircumcised potentates
Of earth debase religion in the sight
Of those they ruled, who, looking up, beheld
The fair celestial gift despised, enslaved,
And, mimicking the folly of the great,
With prompt docility despised her too.

The prince or magistrate, however named
Or praised, who, knowing better, acted thus,
Was wicked, and received, as he deserved,
Damnation. But the unfaithful priest, what tongue
Enough shall execrate? His doctrine may
Be passed, though mixed with most unhallowed leaven,
That proved, to those who foolishly partook,
Eternal bitterness. But this was still
His sin, beneath what cloak soever veiled,
His ever growing and perpetual sin,
First, last, and middle thought, whence every wish,
Whence every action rose, and ended both:
To mount to place, and power of worldly sort;
To ape the gaudy pomp and equipage
Of earthly state, and on his mitred brow
To place a royal crown. For this he sold
The sacred truth to him who most would give

Of titles, benefices, honors, names;
For this betrayed his Master; and for this
Made merchandise of the immortal souls
Committed to his care. This was his sin.

Of all who office held unfairly, none
Could plead excuse; he least and last of all.
By solemn, awful ceremony, he
Was set apart to speak the truth entire,
By action and by word; and round him stood
The people, from his lips expecting knowledge.
One day in seven, the Holy Sabbath termed,
They stood; for he had sworn, in face of God
And man, to deal sincerely with their souls;
To preach the gospel for the gospel's sake;
Had sworn to hate and put away all pride,
All vanity, all love of earthly pomp;
To seek all mercy, meekness, truth, and grace:
And being so endowed himself, and taught,
In them like works of holiness to move;
Dividing faithfully the word of life.
And oft indeed the word of life he taught;
But practising as thou hast heard, who could
Believe! Thus was Religion wounded sore
At her own altars, and among her friends.
The people went away, and, like the priest,
Fulfilling what the prophet spoke before,
For honor strove, and wealth, and place, as if
The preacher had rehearsed an idle tale.
The enemies of God rejoiced, and loud
The unbeliever laughed, boasting a life
Of fairer character than his who owned,
For king and guide, the undefiled One.

Most guilty, villainous, dishonest man!
Wolf in the clothing of the gentle lamb!

Dark traitor in Messiah's holy camp!
Leper in saintly garb! assassin masked
In Virtue's robe! vile hypocrite accursed!
I strive in vain to set his evil forth!
The words that should sufficiently accurse
And execrate such reprobate, had need
Come glowing from the lips of eldest hell.
Among the saddest in the den of wo,
Thou sawst him saddest, 'mong the damned most damned.

But why should I with indignation burn,
Not well beseeming here, and long forgot?
Or why one censure for another's sin?
Each had his conscience, each his reason, will,
And understanding, for himself to search,
To choose, reject, believe, consider, act.
And God proclaimed from heaven, and by an oath
Confirmed, that each should answer for himself:
And as his own peculiar work should be,
Done by his proper self, should live or die.
But sin, deceitful and deceiving still,
Had gained the heart, and reason led astray.

A strange belief, that leaned its idiot back
On folly's topmost twig,—belief that God,
Most wise, had made a world, had creatures made
Beneath his care to govern and protect,—
Devoured its thousands. Reason, not the true,
Learned, deep, sober, comprehensive, sound;
But bigoted, one-eyed, short-sighted Reason,
Most zealous, and sometimes, no doubt, sincere,
Devoured its thousands. Vanity to be
Renowned for creed eccentrical, devoured
Its thousands; but a lazy, corpulent,
And over-credulous faith, that leaned on all

It met, nor asked if 'twas a reed or oak;
Stepped on, but never earnestly inquired
Whether to heaven or hell the journey led,
Devoured its tens of thousands, and its hands
Made reddest in the precious blood of souls.

In Time's pursuits men ran till out of breath.
The astronomer soared up, and counted stars,
And gazed, and gazed upon the heaven's bright face,
Till he dropped down dim-eyed into the grave.
The numerist, in calculations deep,
Grew gray. The merchant at his desk expired.
The statesman hunted for another place,
Till death o'ertook him, and made him his prey.
The miser spent his eldest energy
In grasping for another mite. The scribe
Rubbed pensively his old and withered brow,
Devising new impediments to hold
In doubt the suit that threatened to end too soon.
The priest collected tithes, and pleaded rights
Of decimation to the very last.
In science, learning, all philosophy,
Men labored all their days, and labored hard,
And, dying, sighed how little they had done.
But in religion, they at once grew wise.
A creed in print, though never understood;
A theologic system on the shelf,
Was spiritual lore enough, and served their turn;
But served it ill. They sinned, and never knew.
For what the Bible said of good and bad,
Of holiness and sin, they never asked.

Absurd, prodigiously absurd, to think
That man's minute and feeble faculties,
Even in the very childhood of his being,
With mortal shadows dimmed and wrapped around,

Could comprehend at once the mighty scheme,
Where rolled the ocean of eternal love;
Where wisdom infinite its master-stroke
Displayed; and where omnipotence, oppressed,
Did travail in the greatness of its strength;
And everlasting Justice lifted up
The sword to smite the guiltless Son of God;
And Mercy smiling bade the sinner go!
Redemption is the science and the song
Of all eternity. Archangels, day
And night, into its glories look. The saints,
The elders round the Throne, old in the years
Of heaven, examine it perpetually;
And, every hour, get clearer, ampler views
Of right and wrong; see virtue's beauty more;
See vice more utterly depraved and vile;
And this, with a more perfect hatred, hate;
That daily love with a more perfect love.

But whether I for man's perdition blame
Office administered amiss, pursuit
Of pleasure false, perverted reason blind,
Or indolence that ne'er inquired; I blame
Effect and consequence, the branch, the leaf.
Who finds the fount and bitter root, the first
And guiltiest cause whence sprung this endless wo,
Must deep descend into the human heart,
And find it there. Dread passion! making men
On earth, and even in hell, if Mercy yet
Would stoop so low, unwilling to be saved,
If saved by grace of God. Hear, then, in brief,
What peopled hell, what holds its prisoners there.

Pride, self-adoring pride, was primal cause
Of all sin passed, all pain, all wo to come.
Unconquerable pride! first, eldest sin,

Great fountain-head of evil! highest source,
Whence flowed rebellion 'gainst the Omnipotent,
Whence hate of man to man, and all else ill.
Pride at the bottom of the human heart
Lay, and gave root and nourishment to all
That grew above. Great ancestor of vice!
Hate, unbelief, and blasphemy of God;
Envy and slander, malice and revenge;
And murder, and deceit, and every birth
Of damned sort, was progeny of pride.
It was the ever-moving, acting force,
The constant aim, and the most thirsty wish
Of every sinner unrenewed, to be
A god; in purple or in rags, to have
Himself adored. Whatever shape or form
His actions took, whatever phrase he threw
About his thoughts, or mantle o'er his life,
To be the highest, was the inward cause
Of all; the purpose of the heart to be
Set up, admired, obeyed. But who would bow
The knee to one who served and was dependent?
Hence man's perpetual struggle, night and day,
To prove he was his own proprietor,
And independent of his God; that what
He had might be esteemed his own, and praised
As such. He labored still, and tried to stand
Alone, unpropped, to be obliged to none;
And in the madness of his pride, he bade
His God farewell, and turned away to be
A god himself; resolving to rely,
Whatever came, upon his own right hand.

O desperate frenzy! madness of the will!
And drunkenness of the heart! that naught could
quench,

But floods of wo, poured from the sea of wrath,
Behind which mercy set. To think to turn
The back on life original, and live!
The creature to set up a rival throne
In the Creator's realm! to deify
A worm! and in the sight of God be proud
To lift an arm of flesh against the shafts
Of the Omnipresent, and, midst his wrath,
To seek for happiness!—insanity
Most mad! guilt most complete! Seest thou those worlds
That roll at various distance round the throne
Of God, innumerous, and fill the calm
Of heaven with sweetest harmony, when saints
And angels sleep? As one of these, from love
Centripetal withdrawing, and from light,
And heat, and nourishment cut off, should rush
Abandoned o'er the line that runs between
Create and increate, from ruin driven
To ruin still, through the abortive waste;
So pride from God drew off the bad; and so,
Forsaken of him, he lets them ever try
Their single arm against the second death;
Amidst vindictive thunders lets them try
The stoutness of their hearts, and lets them try
To quench their thirst amidst the unfading fire;
And to reap joy where he has sown despair;
To walk alone, unguided, unbemoaned,
Where Evil dwells, and Death, and moral Night;
In utter emptiness to find enough;
In utter dark find light; and find repose,
Where God with tempest plagues for evermore.
For so they wished it, so did pride desire.

Such was the cause that turned so many off
Rebelliously from God, and led them on

From vain to vainer still, in endless chase.
And such the cause that made so many cheeks
Pale, and so many knees to shake, when men
Rose from the grave; as thou shalt hear anon.

THE

COURSE OF TIME.

BOOK III.

ANALYSIS OF BOOK III.

The Bard proceeds to a more full description of the "ways of Time," "the fond pursuits and vanities of men." Desire of happiness was universal in every age; but the star of God shining upon the only path to it was not heeded. The Bible taught that happiness was indissolubly connected with virtue; that it was a fruit to be gathered only from the tree of holiness, uprooted by the apostacy, but planted again by the Son of God, and nourished by the dewy influences of the Spirit. But, disregarding this, men pursued happiness in ten thousand mistaken routes, grasping at lying shades until the grave received them. Many "sweat and bled for GOLD;" most for the luxuries it bought, but some with the miser's craving avarice. Blinded votaries also chased the Shadow PLEASURE; who, with her thousand changing forms and varying robes, allured to her thousand fatal haunts; to the hall of giddy dance, the scene of thoughtless revel, the harlot's treacherous bed. Another Phantom fleeting in the mist of time was EARTHLY FAME, whose voice of empty breath oft deceived the men of science, and the poet, the reverend divine, the simple artisan, the vain fair one, the haughty warrior, the proud usurper. Even the Drunkard's bowl and the Skeptic's helmless bark were tried in the wild pursuit of happiness. This was done, too, notwithstanding the warning voice of wisdom speaking to man loudly in the Seasons, the Day, the Night, the Grave, the Word of God; notwithstanding all the pangs of Remorse, and all the sorrows of Disappointment. Against these, reckless men closed their ears and their hearts, until Death revealed to each his folly, and too late convinced him of the grand lesson of the Bible, "Eternity is all."

In the description of Disappointment the Author is happily introduced, and mention made of interesting circumstances in his history.

THE

COURSE OF TIME.

BOOK III.

Beholdst thou yonder, on the crystal sea,
Beneath the throne of God, an image fair,
And in its hand a mirror large and bright?
'Tis truth, immutable, eternal truth,
In figure emblematical expressed.
Before it Virtue stands, and smiling sees,
Well pleased, in her reflected soul, no spot.
The sons of heaven, archangel, seraph, saint,
There daily read their own essential worth;
And, as they read, take place among the just;
Or high, or low, each as his value seems.
There each his certain interest learns, his true
Capacity; and, going thence, pursues,
Unerringly, through all the tracts of thought,
As God ordains, best ends by wisest means.

The Bible held this mirror's place on earth.
But, few would read, or, reading, saw themselves.
The chase was after shadows, phantoms strange,
That in the twilight walked of Time, and mocked
The eager hunt, escaping evermore;
Yet with so many promises and looks
Of gentle sort, that he whose arms returned
Empty a thousand times, still stretched them out,
And, grasping, brought them back again unfilled.

In rapid outline thou hast heard of man,
His death, his offered life, that life by most
Despised, the Star of God, the Bible, scorned,
That else to happiness and heaven had led,
And saved my lyre from narrative of wo.
Hear now more largely of the ways of Time,
The fond pursuits and vanities of men.

"Love God, love truth, love virtue, and be happy;"
These were the words first uttered in the ear
Of every being rational made, and made
For thought, or word, or deed accountable.
Most men the first forgot, the second none.
Whatever path they took, by hill or vale,
By night or day, the universal wish,
The aim, and sole intent, was happiness.
But, erring from the heaven-appointed path,
Strange tracks indeed they took through barren wastes,
And up the sandy mountain climbing toiled,
Which pining lay beneath the curse of God,
And naught produced. Yet did the traveller look
And point his eye before him greedily,
As if he saw some verdant spot, where grew
The heavenly flower, where sprung the well of life,
Where undisturbed felicity reposed;
Though Wisdom's eye no vestige could discern,
That Happiness had ever passed that way.

Wisdom was right, for still the terms remained
Unchanged, unchangeable, the terms on which
True peace was given to man, unchanged as God,
Who, in his own essential nature, binds
Eternally to virtue happiness,
Nor lets them part through all his universe.

Philosophy, as thou shalt hear, when she
Shall have her praise, her praise and censure too,

Did much, refining and exalting man;
But could not nurse a single plant that bore
True happiness. From age to age she toiled.
Shed from her eyes the mist that dimmed them still,
Looked forth on man, explored the wild and tame,
The savage and polite, the sea and land,
And starry heavens; and then retired far back
To meditation's silent, shady seat;
And there sat pale, and thoughtfully, and weighed
With wary, most exact, and scrupulous care
Man's nature, passions, hopes, propensities,
Relations, and pursuits, in reason's scale;
And searched and weighed, and weighed and searched again,
And many a fair and goodly volume wrote,
That seemed well worded too, wherein were found
Uncountable receipts, pretending each,
If carefully attended to, to cure
Mankind of folly, to root out the briers,
And thorns, and weeds, that choked the growth of joy;
And showing too, in plain and decent phrase,
Which sounded much like Wisdom's, how to plant,
To shelter, water, culture, prune, and rear
The tree of happiness; and oft their plans
Were tried; but still the fruit was green and sour.

Of all the trees that in Earth's vineyard grew,
And with their clusters tempted man to pull
And eat, one tree, one tree alone, the true
Celestial manna bore, which filled the soul,
The tree of holiness, of heavenly seed,
A native of the skies; though stunted much
And dwarfed, by Time's cold, damp, ungenial soil,
And chilling winds, yet yielding fruit so pure,
So nourishing and sweet, as, on his way,
Refreshed the pilgrim; and begot desire

Unquenchable to climb the arduous path
To where her sister plants, in their own clime
Around the fount, and by the stream of life,
Blooming beneath the Sun that never sets,
Bear fruit of perfect relish fully ripe.

To plant this tree, uprooted by the fall,
To earth the Son of God descended, shed
His precious blood; and on it evermore,
From off his living wings, the Spirit shook
The dews of heaven, to nurse and hasten its growth
Nor was this care, this infinite expense,
Not needed to secure the holy plant.
To root it out, and wither it from earth,
Hell strove with all its strength, and blew with all
Its blasts! and Sin, with cold, consumptive breath,
Involved it still in clouds of mortal damp.
Yet did it grow, thus kept, protected thus;
And bear the only fruit of true delight;
The only fruit worth plucking under heaven.

But few, alas! the holy plant could see,
For heavy mists that Sin around it threw
Perpetually; and few the sacrifice
Would make, by which alone its clusters stooped,
And came within the reach of mortal man.
For this, of him who would approach and eat,
Was rigorously exacted to the full:
To tread and bruise beneath the foot the world
Entire; its prides, ambitions, hopes, desires;
Its gold and all its 'broidered equipage;
To loose its loves and friendships from the heart,
And cast them off; to shut the ear against
Its praise, and all its flatteries abhor;
And, having thus behind him thrown what seemed
So good and fair, then must he lowly kneel,

And with sincerity, in which the Eye
That slumbers not, nor sleeps, could see no lack,
This prayer pray: "Lord, God! thy will be done,
Thy holy will, howe'er it cross my own."
Hard labor this for flesh and blood! too hard
For most it seemed. So, turning, they the tree
Derided as mere bramble, that could bear
No fruit of special taste; and so set out
Upon ten thousand different routes to seek
What they had left behind, to seek what they
Had lost. For still as something once possessed
And lost, true happiness appeared. All thought
They once were happy; and even while they smoked
And panted in the chase, believed themselves
More miserable to-day than yesterday,
To-morrow than to-day. When youth complained,
The ancient sinner shook his hoary head,
As if he meant to say, Stop till you come
My length, and then you may have cause to sigh.
At twenty, cried the boy, who now had seen
Some blemish in his joys, How happily
Plays yonder child that busks the mimic babe,
And gathers gentle flowers, and never sighs!
At forty, in the fervor of pursuit,
Far on in disappointment's dreary vale,
The grave and sage-like man looked back upon
The stripling youth of plump unseared hope,
Who galloped gay and briskly up behind,
And, moaning, wished himself eighteen again.
And he of threescore years and ten, in whose
Chilled eye, fatigued with gaping after hope,
Earth's freshest verdure seemed but blasted leaves,
Praised childhood, youth, and manhood; and denounced
Old age alone as barren of all joy.
Decisive proof that men had left behind

The happiness they sought, and taken a most
Erroneous path; since every step they took
Was deeper mire. Yet did they onward run,
Pursuing Hope that danced before them still,
And beckoned them to proceed; and with their hands,
That shook and trembled piteously with age,
Grasped at the lying Shade, even till the earth
Beneath them broke, and wrapped them in the grave,

Sometimes indeed, when Wisdom in their ear
Whispered, and with its disenchanting wand,
Effectually touched the sorcery of their eyes,
Directly pointing to the holy tree,
Where grew the food they sought, they turned, surprised,
That they had missed so long what now they found,
As one upon whose mind some new and rare
Idea glances, and retires as quick,
Ere memory has time to write it down;
Stung with the loss, into a thoughtful cast
He throws his face, and rubs his vexed brow;
Searches each nook and corner of his soul
With frequent care; reflects, and re-reflects,
And tries to touch relations that may start
The fugitive again; and oft is foiled;
Till something like a seeming chance, or flight
Of random fancy, when expected least,
Calls back the wandered thought, long sought in vain;
Then does uncommon joy fill all his mind;
And still he wonders, as he holds it fast,
What lay so near he could not sooner find:
So did the man rejoice, when from his eye
The film of folly fell, and what he, day
And night, and far and near, had idly searched,
Sprung up before him suddenly displayed;
So wondered why he missed the tree so long.

But, few returned from Folly's giddy chase,
Few heard the voice of Wisdom, or obeyed.
Keen was the search, and various and wide,
Without, within, along the flowery vale,
And up the rugged cliff, and on the top
Of mountains high, and on the ocean wave.
Keen was the search, and various, and wide,
And ever and anon a shout was heard:
"Ho! here's the tree of life! come, eat, and live!"
And round the new discoverer quick they flocked
In multitudes, and plucked, and with great haste
Devoured; and sometimes in the lips 'twas sweet,
And promised well; but in the belly gall.
Yet after him that cried again, "Ho! here's
The tree of life!" again they ran, and pulled,
And chewed again, and found it bitter still.
From disappointment on to disappointment,
Year after year, age after age, pursued,
The child, the youth, the hoary-headed man,
Alike pursued, and ne'er grew wise. For it
Was folly's most peculiar attribute,
And native act, to make experience void.

But hastily, as pleasures tasted, turned
To loathing and disgust, they needed not
Even such experiment to prove them vain
In hope or in possession, Fear, alike,
Boding disaster, stood. Over the flower
Of fairest sort, that bloomed beneath the sun,
Protected most, and sheltered from the storm,
The Spectre, like a dark and thunderous cloud,
Hung dismally, and threatened, before the hand
Of him that wished could pull it, to descend,
And o'er the desert drive its withered leaves;
Or, being pulled, to blast it unenjoyed.

While yet he gazed upon its loveliness,
And just began to drink its fragrance up.

Gold many hunted, sweat and bled for gold:
Waked all the night, and labored all the day.
And what was this allurement, dost thou ask?
A dust dug from the bowels of the earth,
Which, being cast into the fire, came out
A shining thing that fools admired, and called
A god; and in devout and humble plight
Before it kneeled, the greater to the less;
And on its altar sacrificed ease, peace,
Truth, faith, integrity; good conscience, friends,
Love, charity, benevolence, and all
The sweet and tender sympathies of life;
And, to complete the horrid murderous rite,
And signalize their folly, offered up
Their souls and an eternity of bliss,
To gain them—what?—an hour of dreaming joy,
A feverish hour, that hasted to be done,
And ended in the bitterness of wo.

Most, for the luxuries it bought, the pomp,
The praise, the glitter, fashion, and renown,
This yellow phantom followed and adored.
But there was one in folly farther gone,
With eye awry, incurable, and wild,
The laughing-stock of devils and of men,
And by his guardian angel quite given up,—
The miser, who with dust inanimate
Held wedded intercourse. Ill guided wretch!
Thou mightst have seen him at the midnight hour,
When good men slept, and in light winged dreams
Ascended up to God,—in wasteful hall,
With vigilance and fasting worn to skin
And bone, and wrapped in most debasing rags,—

Thou mightst have seen him bending o'er his heaps,
And holding strange communion with his gold;
And, as his thievish fancy seemed to hear
The night-man's foot approach, starting alarmed,
And in his old, decrepit, withered hand,
That palsy shook, grasping the yellow earth
To make it sure. Of all God made upright,
And in their nostrils breathed a living soul,
Most fallen, most prone, most earthy, most debased;
Of all that sold Eternity for Time,
None bargained on so easy terms with Death.
Illustrious fool! nay, most inhuman wretch!
He sat among his bags, and, with a look
Which hell might be ashamed of, drove the poor
Away unalmsed, and midst abundance died,
Sorest of evils! died of utter want.

Before this Shadow, in the vales of earth,
Fools saw another glide, which seemed of more
Intrinsic worth. Pleasure her name; good name,
Though ill applied. A thousand forms she took,
A thousand garbs she wore; in every age
And clime, changing, as in her votaries changed
Desire; but, inwardly, the same in all.
Her most essential lineaments we trace;
Her general features everywhere alike.

Of comely form she was, and fair of face:
And underneath her eyelids sat a kind
Of witching sorcery that nearer drew
Whoever, with unguarded look, beheld:
A dress of gaudy hue loosely attired
Her loveliness; her air and manner frank,
And seeming free of all disguise; her song
Enchanting; and her words, which sweetly dropped,
As honey from the comb, most large of promise,

Still prophesying days of new delight,
And rapturous nights of undecaying joy;
And in her hand, where'er she went, she held
A radiant cup that seemed of nectar full;
And by her side, danced fair, delusive Hope.
The fool pursued, enamored; and the wise,
Experienced man, who reasoned much and thought,
Was sometimes seen laying his wisdom down,
And vying with the stripling in the chase.

Nor wonder thou, for she was really fair,
Decked to the very taste of flesh and blood,
And many thought her sound within, and gay
And healthy at the heart: but thought amiss.
For she was full of all disease: her bones
Were rotten; Consumption licked her blood, and drank
Her marrow up; her breath smelled mortally;
And in her bowels plague and fever lurked;
And in her very heart, and reins, and life,
Corruption's worm gnawed greedily unseen.

Many her haunts. Thou mightst have seen her now
With Indolence, lolling on the mid-day couch,
And whispering drowsy words; and now at dawn,
Loudly and rough, joining the sylvan horn;
Or sauntering in the park, and to the tale
Of slander giving ear; or sitting fierce,
Rude, blasphemous, malicious, raving, mad,
Where fortune to the fickle die was bound.

But chief she loved the scene of deep debauch,
Where revelry, and dance, and frantic song,
Disturbed the sleep of honest men; and where
The drunkard sat, she entered in, well pleased,
With eye brimful of wanton mirthfulness,
And urged him still to fill another cup.

And at the shadowy twilight, in the dark
And gloomy night, I looked, and saw her come
Abroad, arrayed in harlot's soft attire;
And walk without in every street, and lie
In wait at every corner, full of guile:
And as the unwary youth of simple heart,
And void of understanding, passed, she caught
And kissed him, and with lips of lying said,
I have peace-offerings with me; I have paid
My vows this day; and therefore came I forth
To meet thee, and to seek thee diligently,
To seek thy face, and I have found thee here.
My bed is decked with robes of tapestry,
With carved work and sheets of linen fine;
Perfumed with aloes, myrrh, and cinnamon.
Sweet are stolen waters! pleasant is the bread
In secret eaten! the goodman is from home.
Come, let us take our fill of love till morn
Awake; let us delight ourselves with loves.
With much fair speech, she caused the youth to yield
And forced him with the flattering of her tongue.
I looked, and saw him follow to her house,
As goes the ox to slaughter; as the fool
To the correction of the stocks; or bird
That hastes into the subtle fowler's snare,
And knows not, simple thing, 'tis for its life.
I saw him enter in, and heard the door
Behind them shut; and in the dark, still night,
When God's unsleeping eye alone can see,
He went to her adulterous bed. At morn
I looked, and saw him not among the youths.
I heard his father mourn, his mother weep,
For none returned that went with her. The dead
Were in her house, her guests in depths of hell.
She wove the winding-sheet of souls, and laid
Them in the urn of everlasting death.

Such was the Shadow fools pursued on earth,
Under the name of Pleasure; fair outside,
Within corrupted, and corrupting still.
Ruined and ruinous, her sure reward,
Her total recompense, was still, as he,
The bard, recorder of Earth's Seasons, sung,
"Vexation, disappointment, and remorse."
Yet at her door the young and old, and some
Who held high character among the wise,
Together stood, and strove among themselves,
Who first should enter, and be ruined first.

Strange competition of immortal souls!
To sweat for death! to strive for misery!
But think not Pleasure told her end was death.
Even human folly then had paused at least,
And given some signs of hesitation; nor
Arrived so hot, and out of breath, at wo.
Though contradicted every day by facts
That sophistry itself would stumble o'er,
And to the very teeth a liar proved,
Ten thousand times, as if unconscious still
Of inward blame, she stood and waved her hand,
And pointed to her bower, and said to all
Who passed, Take yonder flowery path, my steps
Attend; I lead the smoothest way to heaven;
This world receive as surety for the next:
And many simple men, most simple, though
Renowned for learning much, and wary skill,
Believed, and turned aside, and were undone.

Another leaf of finished Time we turn,
And read of fame, terrestrial fame which died,
And rose not at the resurection morn;
Not that by virtue earned, the true renown,
Begun on earth, and lasting in the skies,

Worthy the lofty wish of seraphim,—
The approbation of the Eye that sees
The end from the beginning, sees from cause
To most remote effect. Of it we read
In book of God's remembrance, in the book
Of life, from which the quick and dead were judged;
The book that lies upon the Throne, and tells
Of glorious acts by saints and angels done;
The record of the holy, just, and good.

Of all the phantoms fleeting in the mist
Of Time, though meagre all, and ghostly thin,
Most unsubstantial, unessential shade
Was earthly Fame. She was a voice alone,
And dwelt upon the noisy tongues of men.
She never thought, but gabbled ever on,
Applauding most what least deserved applause.
The motive, the result, was naught to her.
The deed alone, though dyed in human gore,
And steeped in widow's tears, if it stood out
To prominent display, she talked of much,
And roared around it with a thousand tongues.
As changed the wind her organ, so she changed
Perpetually; and whom she praised to-day,
Vexing his ear with acclamations loud,
To-morrow blamed, and hissed him out of sight.

Such was her nature, and her practice such.
But, O! her voice was sweet to mortal ears,
And touched so pleasantly the strings of pride
And vanity, which in the heart of man
Were ever strung harmonious to her note,
That many thought, to live without her song
Was rather death than life. To live unknown,
Unnoticed, unrenowned! to die unpraised,
Unepitaphed! to go down to the pit,

And moulder into dust among vile worms,
And leave no whispering of a name on earth !—
Such thought was cold about the heart and chilled
The blood. Who could endure it ? who could choose,
Without a struggle, to be swept away
From all remembrance, and have part no more
With living men ? Philosophy failed here,
And self-approving pride. Hence it became
The aim of most, and main pursuit, to win
A name, to leave some vestige as they passed,
That following ages might discern, they once
Had been on earth, and acted something there.

Many the roads they took, the plans they tried.
The man of science to the shade retired,
And laid his head upon his hand, in mood
Of awful thoughtfulness, and dived, and dived
Again, deeper and deeper still, to sound
The cause remote ; resolved, before he died,
To make some grand discovery, by which
He should be known to all posterity.

And in the silent vigils of the night,
When uninspired men reposed, the bard,
Ghastly of countenance, and from his eye
Oft streaming wild unearthly fire, sat up,
And sent imagination forth, and searched
The far and near, heaven, earth, and gloomy hell,
For fiction new, for thought, unthought before ;
And when some curious, rare idea peered
Upon his mind, he dipped his hasty pen,
And by the glimmering lamp, or moonlight beam
That through his lattice peeped, wrote fondly down,
What seemed in truth imperishable song.

And sometimes too, the reverend divine,
In meditation deep of holy things
And vanities of Time, heard Fame's sweet voice
Approach his ear; and hung another flower,
Of earthly sort, about the sacred truth;
And ventured whiles to mix the bitter text,
With relish suited to the sinner's taste.

And oft-times too, the simple hind, who seemed
Ambitionless, arrayed in humble garb,
While round him, spreading, fed his harmless flock,
Sitting was seen, by some wild warbling brook,
Carving his name upon his favorite staff;
Or, in ill-favored letters, tracing it
Upon the aged thorn, or on the face
Of some conspicuous, oft-frequented stone,
With persevering, wondrous industry;
And hoping as he toiled amain, and saw
The characters take form, some other wight,
Long after he was dead and in the grave,
Should loiter there at noon, and read his name.

In purple some, and some in rags, stood forth
For reputation. Some displayed a limb
Well-fashioned; some, of lowlier mind, a cane
Of curious workmanship and marvellous twist.
In strength some sought it, and in beauty more.
Long, long, the fair one labored at the glass,
And, being tired, called in auxiliar skill,
To have her sails, before she went abroad,
Full spread and nicely set, to catch the gale
Of praise; and much she caught, and much deserved,
When outward loveliness was index fair
Of purity within: but oft, alas!
The bloom was on the skin alone; and when
She saw, sad sight! the roses on her cheek

Wither, and heard the voice of Fame retire
And die away, she heaved most piteous sighs,
And wept most lamentable tears; and whiles,
In wild delirium, made rash attempt,
Unholy mimicry of Nature's work!
To re-create, with frail and mortal things,
Her withered face. Attempt how fond and vain!
Her frame itself soon mouldered down to dust;
And, in the land of deep forgetfulness,
Her beauty and her name were laid beside
Eternal silence and the loathsome worm;
Into whose darkness flattery ventured not;
Where none had ears to hear the voice of Fame.

Many the roads they took, the plans they tried,
And awful oft the wickedness they wrought.
To be observed, some scrambled up to thrones,
And sat in vestures dripping wet with gore.
The warrior dipped his sword in blood, and wrote
His name on lands and cities desolate.
The rich bought fields, and houses built, and raised
The monumental piles up to the clouds,
And called them by their names: and, strange to tell!
Rather than be unknown, and pass away
Obscurely to the grave, some, small of soul,
That else had perished unobserved, acquired
Considerable renown by oaths profane;
By jesting boldly with all sacred things;
And uttering fearlessly whate'er occurred;
Wild, blasphemous, perditionable thoughts,
That Satan in them moved; by wiser men
Suppressed, and quickly banished from the mind.

Many the roads they took, the plans they tried.
But all in vain. Who grasped at earthly fame,
Grasped wind; nay worse, a serpent grasped, that thro'

His hand slid smoothly, and was gone; but left
A sting behind which wrought him endless pain.
For oft her voice was old Abaddon's lure,
By which he charmed the foolish soul to death.

So happiness was sought in pleasure, gold,
Renown, by many sought. But should I sing
Of all the trifling race, my time, thy faith
Would fail, of things erectly organized,
And having rational articulate voice,
And claiming outward brotherhood with man,
Of him that labored sorely, in his sweat
Smoking afar, then hurried to the wine,
Deliberately resolving to be mad;
Of him who taught the ravenous bird to fly
This way or that, thereby supremely blest;
Or rode in fury with the howling pack,
Affronting much the noble animal,
He spurred into such company; of him
Who down into the bowels of the earth
Descended deeply, to bring up the wreck
Of some old earthen ware, which having stowed,
With every proper care, he home returned
O'er many a sea, and many a league of land,
Triumphantly to show the marvellous prize;
And him that vexed his brain and theories built
Of gossamer upon the brittle winds,
Perplexed exceedingly why shells were found
Upon the mountain tops, but wondering not
Why shells were found at all, more wondrous still!
Of him who strange enjoyment took in tales
Of fairy folk, and sleepless ghosts, and sounds
Unearthly, whispering in the ear of night
Disastrous things; and him who still foretold
Calamity which never came, and lived
In terror all his days of comets rude,

That should unmannerly and lawless drive
Athwart the path of earth, and burn mankind;
As if the appointed hour of doom, by God
Appointed, ere its time should come! as if
Too small the number of substantial ills,
And real fears, to vex the sons of men.
These, had they not possessed immortal souls,
And been accountable, might have been passed
With laughter, and forgot; but, as it was,
And is, their folly asks a serious tear.

Keen was the search, and various, and wide,
For happiness. Take one example more,
So strange, that common fools looked on amazed;
And wise and sober men together drew,
And trembling stood; and angels in the heavens
Grew pale, and talked of vengeance as at hand;—
The sceptic's route, the unbeliever's, who,
Despising reason, revelation, God,
And kicking 'gainst the pricks of conscience, rushed
Deliriously upon the bossy shield
Of the Omnipotent; and in his heart
Purposed to deify the idol Chance;
And labored hard,—oh, labor worse than naught!—
And toiled with dark and crooked reasoning,
To make the fair and lovely earth, which dwelt
In sight of Heaven, a cold and fatherless,
Forsaken thing, that wandered on, forlorn,
Undestined, uncompassioned, unupheld;
A vapor eddying in the whirl of chance,
And soon to vanish everlastingly.
He travailed sorely, and made many a tack,
His sails oft shifting, to arrive,—dread thought!—
Arrive at utter nothingness; and have
Being no more, no feeling, memory,
No lingering consciousness that e'er he was.

Guilt's midnight wish! last, most abhorred thought,
Most desperate effort of extremest sin!
Others, pre-occupied, ne'er saw true Hope:
He, seeing, aimed to stab her to the heart,
And with infernal chymistry to wring
The last sweet drop from Sorrow's cup of gall;
To quench the only ray that cheered the earth,
And leave mankind in night which had no star.
Others the stream of Pleasure troubled; he
Toiled much to dry her very fountain head.
Unpardonable man! sold under sin!
He was the devil's pioneer, who cut
The fences down of Virtue, sapped her walls,
And opened a smooth and easy way to death.
Traitor to all existence, to all life!
Soul-suicide! determined foe of being,
Intended murderer of God, Most High!
Strange road, most strange! to seek for happiness!
Hell's mad houses are full of such, too fierce,
Too furiously insane, and desperate,
To rage unbound 'mong evil spirits damned.

Fertile was earth in many things, not least
In fools, who mercy both and judgment scorned,
Scorned love, experience scorned, and onward rushed
To swift destruction, giving all reproof,
And all instructions, to the winds; and much
Of both they had, and much despised of both.

Wisdom took up her harp, and stood in place
Of frequent concourse, stood in every gate,
By every way, aud walked in every street;
And, lifting up her voice, proclaimed: "Be wise,
Ye fools! be of an understanding heart;
Forsake the wicked, come not near his house,
Pass by, make haste, depart and turn away.

Me follow, me, whose ways are pleasantness,
Whose paths are peace, whose end is perfect joy."
The Seasons came and went, and went and came,
To teach men gratitude; and as they passed,
Gave warning of the lapse of Time, that else
Had stolen unheeded by. The gentle Flowers
Retired, and, stooping o'er the wilderness,
Talked of humility, and peace, and love.
The Dews came down unseen at evening-tide,
And silently their bounties shed, to teach
Mankind unostentatious charity.
With arm in arm the forest rose on high,
And lesson gave of brotherly regard.
And, on the rugged mountain-brow exposed,
Bearing the blast alone, the ancient oak
Stood, lifting high his mighty arm, and still
To courage in distress exhorted loud.
The flocks, the herds, the birds, the streams, the breeze,
Attuned the heart to melody and love.
Mercy stood in the cloud, with eye that wept
Essential love; and, from her glorious bow,
Bending to kiss the earth in token of peace,
With her own lips, her gracious lips, which God
Of sweetest accent made, she whispered still,
She whispered to Revenge, Forgive, forgive.
The Sun, rejoicing round the earth, announced
Daily the wisdom, power, and love of God.
The Moon awoke, and from her maiden face,
Shedding her cloudy locks, looked meekly forth,
And with her virgin Stars walked in the heavens,
Walked nightly there, conversing as she walked,
Of purity, and holiness, and God.
In dreams and visions, sleep instructed much.
Day uttered speech to day, and night to night
Taught knowledge. Silence had a tongue; the grave,
The darkness, and the lonely waste, had each

A tongue, that ever said, Man! think of God!
Think of thyself! think of eternity!
Fear God, the thunders said; Fear God, the waves.
Fear God, the lightning of the storm replied.
Fear God, deep loudly answered back to deep:
And, in the temples of the Holy One,
Messiah's messengers, the faithful few,
Faithful 'mong many false, the Bible opened,
And cried, Repent! repent, ye sons of men!
Believe, be saved; and reasoned awfully
Of temperance, righteousness, and judgment soon
To come, of ever-during life and death:
And chosen bards from age to age awoke
The sacred lyre, and full on Folly's ear,
Numbers of righteous indignation poured:
And God, omnipotent, when mercy failed,
Made bare his holy arm, and with the stroke
Of vengeance smote; the fountains of the deep
Broke up, heaven's windows opened, and sent on men
A flood of wrath, sent plague and famine forth;
With earthquake rocked the world beneath, with storms
Above laid cities waste, and turned fat lands
To barrenness, and with the sword of war
In fury marched, and gave them blood to drink.
Angels remonstrated, Mercy beseeched,
Heaven smiled and frowned, Hell groaned, Time fled, Death shook
His dart, and threatened to make repentance vain,—
Incredible assertion! men rushed on
Determinedly to ruin; shut their ears,
Their eyes, to all advice, to all reproof;
O'er mercy and o'er judgment, downward rushed
To misery; and,—most incredible
Of all!—to misery rushed, along the way
Of disappointment and remorse, where still,

At every step, adders, in pleasure's form,
Stung mortally; and Joys,—whose bloomy cheeks
Seemed glowing high with immortality.
Whose bosoms prophesied superfluous bliss,—
While in the arms received, and locked in close
And riotous embrace, turned pale, and cold,
And died, and smelled of putrefaction rank;
Turned, in the very moment of delight,
A loathsome, heavy corpse, that with the clear
And hollow eyes of death, stared horribly.

All tribes, all generations of the earth,
Thus wantonly to ruin drove alike.
We heard indeed of golden and silver days,
And of primeval innocence unstained:
A pagan tale! but by baptized bards,
Philosophers, and statesmen, who were still
Held wise and cunning men, talked of so much,
That most believed it so, and asked not why.

The pair, the family first made, were ill;
And for their great peculiar sin, incurred
The Curse, and left it due to all their race;
And bold example gave of every crime,
Hate, murder, unbelief, reproach, revenge.
A time, 'tis true, there came, of which thou soon
Shalt hear, the Sabbath Day, the Jubilee
Of earth, when righteousness and peace prevailed.
This time except, who writes the history
Of men, and writes it true, must write them bad;
Who reads, must read of violence and blood.
The man, who could the story of one day
Peruse, the wrongs, oppressions, cruelties,
Deceits, and perjuries, and vanities,
Rewarded worthlessness, rejected worth,
Assassinations, robberies, thefts, and wars,

Disastrous accidents, life thrown away,
Divinity insulted, Heaven despised,
Religion scorned,—and not been sick at night,
And sad,—had gathered greater store of mirth,
Than ever wise man in the world could find.

One cause of folly, one especial cause,
Was this : Few knew what wisdom was, though well
Defined in God's own words, and printed large,
On heaven and earth in characters of light,
And sounded in the ear by every wind.

Wisdom is humble, said the voice of God.
'Tis proud, the world replied. Wisdom, said God,
Forgives, forbears, and suffers, not for fear
Of man, but God. Wisdom revenges, said
The world; is quick and deadly of resentment,
Thrusts at the very shadow of affront,
And hastes, by death, to wipe its honor clean.
Wisdom, said God, loves enemies, entreats,
Solicits, begs for peace. Wisdom, replied
The world, hates enemies, will not ask peace,
Conditions spurns, and triumphs in their fall.
Wisdom mistrusts itself, and leans on Heaven,
Said God. It trusts and leans upon itself,
The world replied. Wisdom retires, said God,
And counts it bravery to bear reproach,
And shame, and lowly poverty, upright;
And weeps with all who have just cause to weep.
Wisdom, replied the world, struts forth to gaze,
Treads the broad stage of life with clamorous foot,
Attracts all praises, counts it bravery
Alone to wield the sword, and rush on death;
And never weeps but for his own disgrace.
Wisdom, said God, is highest, when it stoops
Lowest before the Holy Throne; throws down

Its crown, abased; forgets itself, admires,
And breathes adoring praise. There Wisdom stoops,
Indeed, the world replied, there stoops, because
It must, but stoops with dignity; and thinks
And meditates the while of inward worth.

Thus did Almighty God, and thus the world,
Wisdom define: and most the world believed,
And boldly called the truth of God a lie.
Hence, he that to the worldly wisdom shaped
His character, became the favorite
Of men, was honorable termed, a man
Of spirit, noble, glorious, lofty soul!
And as he crossed the earth in chase of dreams,
Received prodigious shouts of warm applause.
Hence, who to godly wisdom framed his life
Was counted mean, and spiritless, and vile;
And as he walked obscurely in the path
Which led to heaven, fools hissed with serpent tongue,
And poured contempt upon his holy head,
And poured contempt on all who praised his name.

But false as this account of wisdom was,
The world's I mean, it was its best, the creed
Of sober, grave, and philosophic men,
With much research and cogitation framed,
Of men who with the vulgar scorned to sit.

The popular belief seemed rather worse,
When heard replying to the voice of truth.

The wise man, said the Bible, walks with God;
Surveys, far on, the endless line of life;
Values his soul, thinks of eternity,
Both worlds considers, and provides for both;
With Reason's eye his passions guards; abstains

From evil; lives on hope, on hope, the fruit
Of faith; looks upward, purifies his soul,
Expands his wings, and mounts into the sky;
Passes the sun, and gains his father's house,
And drinks with angels from the fount of bliss.

The multitude aloud replied,—replied
By practice, for they were not bookish men
Nor apt to form their principles in words,—
The wise man, first of all, eradicates,
As much as possible, from out his mind,
All thought of death, God, and eternity;
Admires the world, and thinks of Time alone;
Avoids the Bible, all reproof avoids;
Rocks Conscience, if he can, asleep; puts out
The eye of Reason, prisons, tortures, binds,
And makes her thus, by violence and force,
Give wicked evidence against herself;
Lets passion loose, the substance leaves, pursues
The shadow vehemently, but ne'er o'ertakes;
Puts by the cup of holiness and joy;
And drinks, carouses deeply, in the bowl
Of death; grovels in dust, pollutes, destroys,
His soul; is miserable to acquire
More misery; deceives to be deceived;
Strives, labors to the last, to shun the truth;
Strives, labors to the last, to damn himself;
Turns desperate, shudders, groans, blasphemes, and dies,
And sinks—where could he else?—to endless woe!
And drinks the wine of God's eternal wrath.

The learned thus, and thus the unlearned world,
Wisdom defined. In sound they disagreed;
In substance, in effect, in end, the same;
And equally to God and truth opposed,

Opposed as darkness to the light of heaven.
Yet were there some, that seemed well-meaning men,
Who systems planned, expressed in supple words,
Which praised the man as wisest, that in one
United both; pleased God, and pleased the world;
And with the saint, and with the sinner, had,
Changing his garb, unseen, a good report.
And many thought their definition best;
And in their wisdom grew exceeding wise.

Union abhorred! dissimulation vain!
Could Holiness embrace the harlot Sin?
Could life wed death? Could God with Mammon dwell?
Oh, foolish men! oh, men for ever lost!
In spite of mercy lost, in spite of wrath!
In spite of Disappointment and Remorse,
Which made the way to ruin, ruinous!

Hear what they were: The progeny of Sin,
Alike, and oft combined; but differing much
In mode of giving pain. As felt the gross,
Material part, when in the furnace cast,
So felt the soul, the victim of Remorse.
It was a fire which on the verge of God's
Commandments burned, and on the vitals fed
Of all who passed. Who passed, there met Remorse,
A violent fever seized his soul; the heavens
Above, the earth beneath, seemed glowing brass,
Heated seven times; he heard dread voices speak,
And mutter horrid prophecies of pain,
Severer and severer yet to come;
And as he writhed and quivered, scorched within,
The Fury round his torrid temples flapped
Her fiery wings, and breathed upon his lips
And parched tongue the withered blast of hell.

It was the suffering begun, thou sawst
In symbol of the Worm that never dies.

The other, Disappointment, rather seemed
Negation of delight. It was a thing
Sluggish and torpid, tending towards death.
Its breath was cold, and made the sportive blood
Stagnant, and dull, and heavy, round the wheels
Of life. The roots of that whereon it blew,
Decayed, and with the genial soil no more
Held sympathy; the leaves, the branches drooped,
And mouldered slowly down to formless dust;
Not tossed and driven by violence of winds,
But withering where they sprung, and rotting there
Long disappointed, disappointed still,
The hopeless man, hopeless in his main wish,
As if returning back to nothing, felt;
In strange vacuity of being hung,
And rolled and rolled his eye on emptiness,
That seemed to grow more empty every hour.

One of this mood I do remember well,
We name him not,—what now are earthly names?
In humble dwelling born, retired, remote
In rural quietude, 'mong hills, and streams,
And melancholy deserts, where the Sun
Saw, as he passed, a shepherd only, here
And there, watching his little flock, or heard
The ploughman talking to his steers; his hopes,
His morning hopes, awoke before him, smiling,
Among the dews and holy mountain airs;
And fancy colored them with every hue
Of heavenly loveliness. But soon his dreams
Of childhood fled away, those rainbow dreams,
So innocent and fair, that withered Age,
Even at the grave, cleared up his dusty eye,

And, passing all between, looked fondly back
To see them once again, ere he departed:
These fled away, and anxious thought, that wished
To go, yet whither knew not well to go,
Possessed his soul, and held it still awhile.
He listened, and heard from far the voice of fame,
Heard and was charmed; and deep and sudden vow
Of resolution, made to be renowned;
And deeper vowed again to keep his vow.
His parents saw, his parents, whom God made
Of kindest heart, saw, and indulged his hope.
The ancient page he turned, read much, thought much,
And with old bards of honorable name
Measured his soul severely; and looked up
To fame, ambitious of no second place.
Hope grew from inward faith, and promised fair.
And out before him opened many a path
Ascending, where the laurel highest waved
Her branch of endless green. He stood admiring,
But stood, admired, not long. The harp he seized,
The harp he loved, loved better than his life,
The harp which uttered deepest notes, and held
The ear of thought a captive to its song.
He searched and meditated much, and whiles,
With rapturous hand, in secret, touched the lyre,
Aiming at glorious strains; and searched again
For theme deserving of immortal verse;
Chose now, and now refused, unsatisfied;
Pleased, then displeased, and hesitating still.

Thus stood his mind, when round him came a cloud;
Slowly and heavily it came, a cloud
Of ills, we mention not. Enough to say,
'Twas cold, and dead, impenetrable gloom.
He saw its dark approach, and saw his hopes,
One after one, put out, as nearer still

It drew his soul; but fainted not at first,
Fainted not soon. He knew the lot of man
Was troubled, and prepared to bear the worst;
Endure what'er should come, without a sigh
Endure, and drink, even to the very dregs,
The bitterest cup that Time could measure out;
And, having done, look up, and ask for more.

He called philosophy, and with his heart
Reasoned. He called religion too, but called
Reluctantly, and therefore was not heard.
Ashamed to be o'ermatched by earthly woes,
He sought, and sought, with eye that dimmed apace,
To find some avenue to light, some place
On which to rest a hope; but sought in vain.
Darker and darker and darker still the darkness grew,
At length he sunk, and Disappointment stood
His only comforter, and mournfully
Told all was passed. His interest in life,
In being, ceased: and now he seemed to feel,
And shuddered as he felt, his powers of mind
Decaying in the spring-time of his day.
The vigorous, weak became; the clear, obscure.
Memory gave up her charge, Decision reeled,
And from her flight, Fancy returned, returned
Because she found no nourishment abroad.
The blue heavens withered, and the moon, and sun,
And all the stars, and the green earth, and morn
And evening, withered; and the eyes, and smiles,
And faces, of all men and women, withered;
Withered to him; and all the universe,
Like something which had been, appeared; but now
Was dead and mouldering fast away. He tried
No more to hope, wished to forget his vow,
Wished to forget his harp; then ceased to wish.
That was his last. Enjoyment now was done.

He had no hope, no wish, and scarce a fear.
Of being sensible, and sensible
Of loss, he as some atom seemed, which God
Had made superfluously, and needed not
To build creation with; but back again
To nothing threw, and left it in the void,
With everlasting sense that once it was.

Oh! who can tell what days, what nights, he spent,
Of tideless, waveless, sailless, shoreless woe!
And who can tell how many, glorious once,
To others and themselves of promise full,
Conducted to this pass of human thought,
This wilderness of intellectual death,
Wasted and pined, and vanished from the earth,
Leaving no vestige of memorial there!

It was not so with him. When thus he lay,
Forlorn of heart, withered and desolate,
As leaf of Autumn, which the wolfish winds,
Selecting from its falling sisters, chase,
Far from its native grove, to lifeless wastes,
And leave it there alone, to be forgotten
Eternally, God passed in mercy by,—
His praise be ever new!—and on him breathed,
And bade him live, and put into his hands
A holy harp, into his lips a song,
That rolled its numbers down the tide of Time:
Ambitious now but little, to be praised
Of men alone; ambitious most, to be
Approved of God, the Judge of all; and have
His name recorded in the book of life.

Such things were Disappointment and Remorse,
And oft united both, as friends severe,
To teach men wisdom; but the fool, untaught,

Was foolish still. His ear he stopped, his eyes
He shut, and blindly, deafly obstinate,
Forced desperately his way from wo to wo.

One place, one only place, there was on earth,
Where no man e'er was fool, however mad.
"Men may live fools, but fools they cannot die."
Ah! 'twas a truth most true; and sung in Time,
And to the sons of men, by one well known
On earth for lofty verse and lofty sense.
Much hast thou seen, fair youth, much heard; but thou
Hast never seen a death bed, never heard
A dying groan. Men saw it often. 'Twas sad,
To all most sorrowful and sad; to guilt,
'Twas anguish, terror, darkness, without bow.
But, oh! it had a most convincing tongue,
A potent oratory, that secured
Most mute attention; and it spoke the truth
So boldly, plainly, perfectly distinct,
That none the meaning could mistake or doubt;
And had withal a disenchanting power,
A most omnipotent and wondrous power,
Which in a moment broke, for ever broke,
And utterly dissolved, the charms, and spells,
And cunning sorceries of earth and hell.
And thus it spoke to him who ghastly lay,
And struggled for another breath: Earth's cup
Is poisoned; her renown, most infamous;
Her gold, seem as it may, is really dust;
Her titles, slanderous names; her praise, reproach;
Her strength, an idiot's boast; her wisdom, blind;
Her gain, eternal loss; her hope, a dream;
Her love, her friendship, enmity with God;
Her promises, a lie; her smile, a harlot's;
Her beauty, paint, and rotten within; her pleasures,

Deadly assassins masked; her laughter, grief;
Her breasts, the sting of Death; her total sum,
Her all! most utter vanity; and all
Her lovers mad, insane most grievously,
And most insane because they know it not.

Thus did the mighty reasoner, Death, declare,
And volumes more; and in one word confirmed
The Bible whole, Eternity is all.
But few spectators, few believed, of those
Who staid behind. The wisest, best of men,
Believed not to the letter full; but turned,
And on the world looked forth, as if they thought
The well-trimmed hypocrite had something still
Of inward worth. The dying man alone,
Gave faithful audience, and the words of Death,
To the last jot, believed, believed and felt;
But oft, alas! believed and felt too late.

And had Earth, then, no joys, no native sweets,
No happiness, that one, who spoke the truth,
Might call her own? She had; true, native sweets,
Indigenous delights, which up the tree
Of holiness, embracing as they grew,
Ascended, and bore fruit of heavenly taste;
In pleasant memory held, and talked of oft,
By yonder Saints, who walk the golden streets
Of New Jerusalem, and compass round
The Throne, with nearest vision blessed. Of these,
Hereafter, thou shalt hear, delighted hear;—
One page of beauty in the life of man.

THE

COURSE OF TIME.

BOOK IV.

ANALYSIS OF BOOK IV.

Sketches are given by the Bard of several features in the history and affairs of men, which appeared wonderful.

One singular feature was the universal love of independence united with lust for power, so that the essence of "earth's liberty" was, after all its praises, nothing but this: "each sought to make all subject to his will;" but REAL liberty was the freedom from sin and passion, effected by the truth and spirit of God.

A wonderful phenomenon appeared in the Christian heart. This exhibited a scene of strangest conflicts between opposite principles, and inconsistent emotions. But the final victory was found on the side of holiness; and the Christian, after all his internal struggles, and all the abuse and slander of Earth, was brought in triumph to the world of glory.

The Books composed in time presented also an occasion of wonder. They were numerous as the swarms of locusts sent on rebellious Egypt, but, like their authors, went to oblivion under the curse that returns dust to kindred dust.

Various things in the government and providence of God, furnished ground of wonder among men. The origin of evil, the predetermination of accountable actions, the mystery of the Trinity and Incarnation, were subjects which Theology and Philosophy and Fancy toiled in vain to comprehend.

There seemed something wondrous in the unequal distribution of worldly possession and intellectual gifts. But the Providence of God plainly taught that He did not estimate men by their outward circumstances or their mere talents, but by their MORAL WORTH. A pertinent and affecting illustration is found in the history of the gifted, wretched Byron.

THE

COURSE OF TIME

BOOK IV.

THE world had much of strange and wonderful,
In passion much, in action, reason, will,
And much in Providence, which still retired
From human eye, and led Philosophy,
That ill her ignorance liked to own, through dark
And dangerous paths of speculation wild.
Some striking features, as we pass, we mark,
In order such as memory suggests.

One passion prominent appears, the lust
Of power, which oft-times took the fairer name
Of liberty, and hung the popular flag
Of freedom out. Many, indeed, its names.
When on the throne it sat, and round the neck
Of millions riveted its iron chain,
And on the shoulders of the people laid
Burdens unmerciful, it title took
Of tyranny, oppression, despotism;
And every tongue was weary cursing it.
When in the multitude it gathered strength,
And, like an ocean bursting from its bounds,
Long beat in vain, went forth resistlessly,
It bore the stamp and designation, then,
Of popular fury, anarchy, rebellion;
And honest men bewailed all order void;

All laws annulled; all property destroyed;
The venerable, murdered in the streets;
The wise, despised; streams red with human blood;
Harvests, beneath the frantic foot trod down;
Lands, desolate; and famine at the door.

These are a part; but other names it had,
Innumerous as the shapes and robes it wore.
But under every name, in nature still
Invariably the same, and always bad.
We own, indeed, that oft against itself
It fought, and sceptre both and people gave
An equal aid; as long exemplified
In Albion's isle, Albion, queen of the seas;
And in the struggle, something like a kind
Of civil liberty grew up, the best
Of mere terrestrial root; but, sickly, too,
And living only, strange to tell! in strife
Of factions equally contending; dead,
That very moment dead, that one prevailed.

Conflicting cruelly against itself,
By its own hand it fell; part slaying part.
And men who noticed not the suicide,
Stood wondering much, why earth, from age to age,
Was still enslaved; and erring causes gave.

This was earth's liberty, its nature this,
However named, in whomsoever found,—
And found it was in all of woman born,—
Each man to make all subject to his will;
To make them do, undo, eat, drink, stand, move,
Talk, think, and feel, exactly as he chose.
Hence the eternal strife of brotherhoods,
Of individuals, families, commonwealths.
The root from which it grew was pride; bad root,

And bad the fruit it bore. Then wonder not,
That long the nations from it richly reaped
Oppression, slavery, tyranny, and war;
Confusion, desolation, trouble, shame.
And marvellous though it seem, this monster, when
It took the name of slavery, as oft
It did, had advocates to plead its cause;
Beings that walked erect, and spoke like men;
Of Christian parentage descended, too,
And dipped in the baptismal font, as sign
Of dedication to the Prince who bowed
To death, to set the sin-bound prisoner free,

Unchristian thought! on what pretence soe'er
Of right, inherited, or else acquired;
Of loss, or profit, or what plea you name,
To buy and sell, to barter, whip, and hold
In chains, a being of celestial make;
Of kindred form, of kindred faculties,
Of kindred feelings, passions, thoughts, desires;
Born free, and heir of an immortal hope;
Thought villanous, absurd, detestable!
Unworthy to be harbored in a fiend!
And only overreached in wickedness
By that, birth, too, of earthly liberty,
Which aimed to make a reasonable man
By legislation think, and by the sword
Believe. This was that liberty renowned,
Those equal rights of Greece and Rome, where men,
All, but a few, were bought, and sold, and scourged,
And killed, as interest or caprice enjoined;
In after times talked of, written of, so much,
That most, by sound and custom led away,
Believed the essence answered to the name.
Historians on this theme were long and warm.
Statesmen, drunk with the fumes of vain debate,

In lofty swelling phrase, called it perfection.
Philosophers its rise, advance, and fall,
Traced carefully : and poets kindled still,
As memory brought it up ; their lips were touched
With fire, and uttered words that men adored.
Even he, true bard of Zion, holy man !
To whom the Bible taught this precious verse,
"He is the freeman whom the truth makes free,"
By fashion, though by fashion little swayed,
Scarce kept his harp from pagan freedom's praise.

The captive prophet, whom Jehovah gave
The future years, described it best, when he
Beheld it rise in vision of the night :
A dreadful beast, and terrible, and strong
Exceedingly, with mighty iron teeth ;
And, lo, it brake in pieces, and devoured,
And stamped the residue beneath its feet !

True liberty was Christian, sanctified,
Baptized, and found in Christian hearts alone ;
First-born of Virtue, daughter of the skies,
Nursling of truth divine, sister of all
The graces, meekness, holiness, and love ;
Giving to God, and man, and all below,
That symptom showed of sensible existence,
Their due, unasked ; fear to whom fear was due ;
To all, respect, benevolence, and love ;
Companion of religion, where she came,
There freedom came ; where dwelt, there freedom dwelt,
Ruled where she ruled, expired where she expired.

"He was the freeman whom the truth made free,"
Who, first of all, the bands of Satan broke ;
Who broke the bands of sin ; and for his soul,

In spite of fools, consulted seriously;
In spite of fashion, persevered in good;
In spite of wealth or poverty, upright;
Who did as reason, not as fancy, bade;
Who heard temptation sing, and yet turned not
Aside; saw Sin bedeck her flowery bed,
And yet would not go up; felt at his heart
The sword unsheathed, yet would not sell the truth;
Who, having power, had not the will to hurt;
Who blushed alike to be, or have a slave;
Who blushed at naught but sin, feared naught but
God;
Who, finally, in strong integrity
Of soul, 'midst want, or riches, or disgrace,
Uplifted, calmly sat, and heard the waves
Of stormy folly breaking at his feet,
Now shrill with praise, now hoarse with foul reproach,
And both despised sincerely; seeking this
Alone, The approbation of his God,
Which still with conscience witnessed to his peace.

This, this is freedom, such as angels use,
And kindred to the liberty of God.
First-born of Virtue, daughter of the skies!
The man, the state, in whom she ruled, was free;
All else were slaves of Satan, Sin, and Death.

Already thou hast something heard of good
And ill, of vice and virtue, perfect each;
Of those redeemed, or else abandoned quite;
And more shalt hear, when, at the judgment-day,
The characters of mankind we review.
Seems aught which thou hast heard astonishing?
A greater wonder now thy audience asks;
Phenomena in all the universe,
Of moral being most anomalous,

Inexplicable most, and wonderful.
I'll introduce thee to a single heart,
A human heart. We enter not the worst,
But one by God's renewing Spirit touched,
A Christian heart, awaked from sleep of sin.
What seest thou here? what markst? Observe it well.
Will, passion, reason, hopes, fears, joy, distress,
Peace, turbulence, simplicity, deceit,
Good, ill, corruption, immortality,
A temple of the Holy Ghost, and yet
Oft lodging fiends; the dwelling-place of all
The heavenly virtues, charity and truth,
Humility, and holiness, and love;
And yet the common haunt of anger, pride,
Hatred, revenge, and passions foul with lust;
Allied to heaven, yet parleying oft with hell;
A soldier listed in Messiah's band,
Yet giving quarter to Abaddon's troops;
With seraphs drinking from the well of life,
And yet carousing in the cup of death;
An heir of heaven, and walking thitherward,
Yet casting back a covetous eye on earth:
Emblem of strength, and weakness; loving now,
And now abhorring sin; indulging now,
And now repenting sore; rejoicing now,
With joy unspeakable, and full of glory;
Now weeping bitterly, and clothed in dust;
A man willing to do, and doing not;
Doing, and willing not; embracing what
He hates, what most he loves abandoning;
Half saint, and sinner half; half life, half death;
Commixture strange of heaven, and earth, and hell.

What seest thou here? what mark'st? A battle-field,
Two banners spread, two dreadful fronts of war

In shock of opposition fierce, engaged.
God, angels, saw whole empires rise in arms,
Saw kings exalted, heard them tumble down,
And others raised,—and heeded not; but here
God, angels, looked; God, angels, fought; and Hell,
With all his legions, fought: here, error fought
With truth, with darkness light, and life with death;
And here, not kingdoms, reputations, worlds,
Were won; the strife was for eternity,
The victory was never-ending bliss,
The badge, a chaplet from the tree of life.

While thus, within, contending armies strove
Without, the Christian had his troubles too.
For, as by God's unalterable laws,
And ceremonial of the Heaven of Heavens,
Virtue takes place of all, and worthiest deeds
Sit highest at the feast of bliss; on earth,
The opposite was fashion's rule polite.
Virtue the lowest place at table took,
Or served, or was shut out; the Christian still
Was mocked, derided, persecuted, slain;
And Slander, worse than mockery, or sword,
Or death, stood nightly by her horrid forge,
And fabricated lies to stain his name,
And wound his peace; but still he had a source
Of happiness, that men could neither give
Nor take away. The avenues that led
To immortality before him lay.
He saw, with faith's far-reaching eye, the fount
Of life, his Father's house, his Saviour God,
And borrowed thence to help his present want.

Encountered thus with enemies, without,
Within, like bark that meets opposing winds
And floods, this way, now that, she steers athwart,

Tossed by the wave, and driven by the storm;
But still the pilot, ancient at the helm,
The harbor keeps in eye; and after much
Of danger passed, and many a prayer rude,
He runs her safely in: so was the man
Of God beset, so tossed by adverse winds;
And so his eye upon the land of life
He kept. Virtue grew daily stronger, sin
Decayed; his enemies, repulsed, retired;
Till, at the stature of a perfect man
In Christ arrived, and with the Spirit filled,
He gained the harbor of eternal rest.

But think not virtue, else than dwells in God
Essentially, was perfect, without spot.
Examine yonder suns. At distance seen,
How bright they burn; how gloriously they shine,
Mantling the worlds around in beamy light!
But nearer viewed, we through their lustre see
Some dark behind; so virtue was on earth,
So is in heaven, and so shall always be.
Though good it seem, immaculate, and fair
Exceedingly, to saint or angel's gaze,
The uncreated Eye, that searches all,
Sees it imperfect; sees, but blames not; sees,
Well pleased, and best with those who deepest dive
Into themselves, and know themselves the most;
Taught thence in humbler reverence to bow
Before the Holy One; and oftener view
His excellence, that in them still may rise,
And grow his likeness, growing evermore.

Nor think that any, born of Adam's race,
In his own proper virtue, entered heaven.
Once fallen from God and perfect holiness,
No being, unassisted, e'er could rise,

Or sanctify the sin-polluted soul.
Oft was the trial made, but vainly made.
So oft as men, in earth's best livery clad,
However fair, approached the gates of heaven.
And stood presented to the eye of God,
Their impious pride so oft his soul abhorred.
Vain hope! in patch-work of terrestrial grain,
To be received into the courts above!
As vain as towards yonder suns to soar,
On wing of waxen plumage, melting soon.

Look round, and see those numbers infinite,
That stand before the Throne, and in their hands
Palms waving high, as token of victory
For battles won. These are the sons of men
Redeemed, the ransomed of the Lamb of God
All these, and millions more of kindred blood,
Who now are out on messages of love.
All these, their virtue, beauty, excellence,
And joy, are purchase of redeeming blood;
Their glory, bounty of redeeming love.

O Love divine!—Harp, lift thy voice on high!
Shout, angels! shout aloud, ye sons of men!
And burn, my heart, with the eternal flame!
My lyre, be eloquent with endless praise!—
O Love divine! immeasurable Love!
Stooping from heaven to earth, from earth to hell,
Without beginning, endless, boundless Love!
Above all asking, giving far, to those
Who naught deserved, who naught deserved but death,
Saving the vilest! saving me! O Love
Divine! O Saviour God! O Lamb, once slain!
At thought of thee, thy love, thy flowing blood,
All thoughts decay; all things remembered fade;
All hopes return; all actions done by men

Or angels, disappear, absorbed and lost;
All fly, as from the great white Throne, which he,
The prophet, saw, in vision wrapped, the heavens
And earth, and sun, and moon, and starry host,
Confounded, fled, and found a place no more.

One glance of wonder, as we pass, deserve
The books of Time. Productive was the world
In many things, but most in books. Like swarms
Of locusts, which God sent to vex a land
Rebellious long, admonished long in vain,
Their numbers they poured annually on man,
From heads conceiving still. Perpetual birth!
Thou wonderest how the world contained them all?
Thy wonder stay. Like men, this was their doom,
"That dust they were, and should to dust return."
And oft their fathers, childless and bereaved,
Wept o'er their graves, when they themselves were green;
And on them fell, as fell on every age,
As on their authors fell, oblivious Night,
Which o'er the past lay, darkling, heavy, still,
Impenetrable, motionless, and sad,
Having his dismal, leaden plumage stirred
By no remembrancer, to show the men
Who after came what was concealed beneath.

The story-telling tribe, alone, outran
All calculation far, and left behind,
Lagging, the swiftest numbers. Dreadful, even
To fancy, was their never-ceasing birth;
And room had lacked, had not their life been short.
Excepting some, their definition take
Thou thus, expressed in gentle phrase, which leaves
Some truth behind; A Novel was a book
Three-volumed, and once read, and oft crammed full

Of poisonous error, blackening every page,
And oftener still, of trifling, second-hand
Remark, and old, diseased, putrid thought,
And miserable incident, at war
With nature, with itself and truth at war;
Yet charming still the greedy reader on,
Till done, he tried to recollect his thoughts,
And nothing found, but dreaming emptiness.
These, like ephemera, sprung, in a day,
From lean and shallow-soiled brains of sand,
And in a day expired; yet, while they lived,
Tremendous oft-times was the popular roar;
And cries of—Live for ever! struck the skies.

One kind alone remained, seen through the gloom
And sullen shadow of the past: as lights
At intervals they shone, and brought the eye,
That backward travelled, upward, till arrived
At him, who, on the hills of Midian, sang
The patient man of Uz; and from the lyre
Of angels, learned the early dawn of Time.
Not light and momentary labor these,
But discipline and self-denial long,
And purpose stanch, and perseverance, asked,
And energy that inspiration seemed.
Composed of many thoughts, possessing each
Innate and underived vitality;
Which, having fitly shaped, and well arranged
In brotherly accord, they builded up;
A stately superstructure, that, nor wind,
Nor wave, nor shock of falling years, could move;
Majestic and indissolubly firm;
As ranks of veteran warriors in the field,
Each by himself alone and singly seen,
A tower of strength; in massy phalanx knit,

And in embattled squadron rushing on,
A sea of valor, dread, invincible.

Books of this sort, or sacred, or profane,
Which virtue helped, were titled, not amiss,
"The medicine of the mind:" who read them, read
Wisdom, and was refreshed; and on his path
Of pilgrimage, with healthier step advanced.

In mind, in matter, much was difficulty
To understand. But, what in deepest night
Retired, inscrutable, mysterious, dark,—
Was evil, God's decrees, and deeds decreed,
Responsible: why God, the just and good,
Omnipotent and wise, should suffer sin
To rise: why man was free, accountable;
Yet God foreseeing, overruling all.
Where'er the eye could turn, whatever tract
Of moral thought it took, by reason's torch,
Or Scripture's led, before it still this mount
Sprung up, impervious, insurmountable,
Above the human stature rising far;
Horizon of the mind, surrounding still
The vision of the soul with clouds and gloom.
Yet did they oft attempt to scale its sides,
And gain its top. Philosophy, to climb,
With all her vigor, toiled from age to age;
From age to age, Theology, with all
Her vigor, toiled; and vagrant Fancy toiled.
Not weak and foolish only, but the wise,
Patient, courageous, stout, sound-headed man,
Of proper discipline, of excellent wind,
And strong of intellectual limb, toiled hard;
And oft above the reach of common eye
Ascended far, and seemed well nigh the top,
But only seemed; for still another top

Above them rose, till, giddy grown and mad,
With gazing at these dangerous heights of God,
They tumbled down, and in their raving said,
They o'er the summit saw. And some believed,
Believed a lie; for never man on earth,
That mountain crossed, or saw its farther side.
Around it lay the wreck of many a Sage,
Divine, Philosopher; and many more
Fell daily, undeterred by millions fallen;
Each wondering why he failed to comprehend
God, and with finite measure infinite.
To pass it, was no doubt desirable;
And few of any intellectual size,
That did not, sometime in their day, attempt;
But all in vain; for as the distant hill,
Which, on the right or left, the traveller's eye
Bounds, seems advancing as he walks, and oft
He looks, and looks, and thinks to pass; but still
It forward moves, and mocks his baffled sight,
Till night descends, and wraps the scene in gloom;
So did this moral height the vision mock;
So lifted up its dark and cloudy head,
Before the eye, and met it evermore;
And some, provoked, accused the righteous God.
Accused of what? hear human boldness now!
Hear guilt, hear folly, madness, all extreme!
Accused of what? the God of truth accused
Of cruelty, injustice, wickedness.
Abundant sin! because a mortal man,
A worm, at best, of small capacity,
With scarce an atom of Jehovah's works
Before him, and with scarce an hour to look
Upon them, should presume to censure God,
The infinite and uncreated God!
To sit, in judgment, on Himself, his works,
His providence! and try, accuse, condemn!

If there is aught, thought or to think, absurd,
Irrational and wicked, this is more,
This most; the sin of devils, or of those
To devils growing fast. Wise men and good
Accused themselves, not God; and put their hands
Upon their mouths, and in the dust adored.

The Christian's faith had many mysteries too;
The uncreated holy Three in One,
Divine incarnate, human in divine;
The inward call; the Sanctifying Dew
Coming unseen, unseen departing thence;
Anew creating all, and yet not heard;
Compelling, yet not felt. Mysterious these,
Not that Jehovah to conceal them wished,
Not that religion wished. The Christian faith,
Unlike the timorous creeds of pagan priests,
Was frank, stood forth to view, invited all
To prove, examine, search, investigate,
And gave herself a light to see her by.
Mysterious these, because too large for eye
Of man, too long for human arm to mete.

Go to yon mount, which on the north side stands
Of New Jerusalem, and lifts its head
Serene in glory bright, except the hill,
The Sacred Hill of God, whereon no foot
Must tread, highest of all creation's walks,
And overlooking all, in prospect vast,
From out the ethereal blue. That cliff ascend,
Gaze thence, around thee look; naught now impedes
Thy view; yet still thy vision, purified
And strong although it be, a boundary meets;
Or rather, thou wilt say, thy vision fails
To gaze throughout illimitable space,
And find the end of infinite: and so

It was with all the mysteries of faith.
God set them forth unveiled to the full gaze
Of man, and asked him to investigate;
But Reason's eye, however purified,
And on whatever tall and goodly height
Of observation placed, to comprehend
Them fully, sought in vain: in vain seeks still;
But, wiser now and humbler, she concludes,
From what she knows already of his love
All gracious, that she cannot understand;
And gives him credit, reverence, praise for all.

Another feature in the ways of God,
That wondrous seemed, and made some men complain,
Was the unequal gift of worldly things.
Great was the difference, indeed, of men
Externally, from beggar to the prince.
The highest take and lowest, and conceive
The scale between. A noble of the earth,
One of its great, in splendid mansion dwelt;
Was robed in silk and gold; and every day
Fared sumptuously; was titled, honored, served.
Thousands his nod awaited, and his will
For law received. Whole provinces his march
Attended, and his chariot drew, or on
Their shoulders bore aloft the precious man.
Millions, abased, fell prostrate at his feet:
And millions more thundered adoring praise.
As far as eye could reach, he called the land
His own, and added yearly to his fields.
Like tree that of the soil took healthy root,
He grew on every side, and towered on high,
And over half a nation shadowing wide,
He spread his ample boughs. Air, earth, and sea,
Nature entire, the brute, and rational,
To please him ministered, and vied among

Themselves, who most should his desires prevent,
Watching the moving of his rising thoughts,
Attentively, and hasting to fulfil.
His palace rose and kissed the gorgeous clouds:
Streams bent their music to his will, trees sprung,
The native waste put on luxuriant robes;
And plans of happy cottages cast out
Their tenants, and became a hunting-field.
Before him bowed the distant isles, with fruits
And spices rare; the South her treasures brought;
The East and West sent; and the frigid North
Came with her offering of glossy furs.
Musicians soothed his ear with airs select;
Beauty held out her arms; and every man
Of cunning skill, and curious device,
And endless multitudes of liveried wights,
His pleasure waited with obsequious look.
And when the wants of nature were supplied
And common-place extravagances filled,
Beyond their asking; and caprice itself,
In all its zig-zag appetites, gorged full,
The man new wants and new expenses planned;
Nor planned alone. Wise, learned, sober men,
Of cogitation deep, took up his case,
And planned for him new modes of folly wild;
Contrived new wishes, wants, and wondrous means
Of spending with despatch; yet, after all,
His fields extended still, his riches grew,
And what seemed splendor infinite, increased.
So lavishly upon a single man
Did Providence his bounties daily shower.

Turn now thy eye, and look on Poverty;
Look on the lowest of her ragged sons.
We find him by the way, sitting in dust;
He has no bread to eat, no tongue to ask,

No limbs to walk, no home, no house, no friend.
Observe his goblin cheek, his wretched eye;
See how his hand, if any hand he has,
Involuntary opens, and trembles forth,
As comes the traveller's foot; and hear his groan,
His long and lamentable groan, announce
The want that gnaws within. Severely now
The sun scorches and burns his old bald head;
The frost now glues him to the chilly earth.
On him hail, rain, and tempest, rudely beat;
And all the winds of heaven, in jocular mood,
Sport with his withered rags, that, tossed about,
Display his nakedness to passers by,
And grievously burlesque the human form.
Observe him yet more narrowly. His limbs,
With palsy shaken, about him, blasted lie;
And all his flesh is full of putrid sores
And noisome wounds, his bones, of racking pains.
Strange vesture this for an immortal soul!
Strange retinue to wait a lord of earth!
It seems as Nature, in some surly mood,
After debate and musing long, had tried
How vile and miserable thing her hand
Could fabricate, then made this meagre man,
A sight so full of perfect misery,
That passengers their faces turned away,
And hasted to be gone; and delicate
And tender women took another path.

This great disparity of outward things
Taught many lessons; but this taught in chief,
Though learned by few: That God no value set,
That man should none, on goods of worldly kind!
On transitory, frail, external things,
Of migratory, ever-changing sort:
And further taught, that in the soul alone,

The thinking, reasonable, willing soul,
God placed the total excellence of man;
And meant him evermore to seek it there.

But stranger still the distribution seemed
Of intellect, though fewer here complained,
Each with his share, upon the whole, content.
One man there was—and many such you might
Have met—who never had a dozen thoughts
In all his life, and never changed their course;
But told them o'er, each in its customed place,
From morn till night, from youth to hoary age.
Little above the ox that grazed the field,
His reason rose; so weak his memory,
The name his mother called him by, he scarce
Remembered; and his judgment so untaught,
That what at evening played along the swamp,
Fantastic, clad in robe of fiery hue,
He thought the devil in disguise, and fled
With quivering heart and winged footsteps home.
The word philosophy he never heard,
Or science; never heard of liberty,
Necessity, or laws of gravitation;
And never had an unbelieving doubt.
Beyond his native vale he never looked;
But thought the visual line, that girt him round,
The world's extreme; and thought the silver Moon,
That nightly o'er him led her virgin host,
No broader than his father's shield. He lived,—
Lived where his father lived, died where he died,
Lived happy, and died happy, and was saved.
Be not surprised. He loved and served his God.

There was another, large of understanding,
Of memory infinite, of judgment deep,
Who knew all learning, and all science knew;

And all phenomena, in heaven and earth,
Traced to their causes; traced the labyrinths
Of thought, association, passion, will;
And all the subtle, nice affinities
Of matter traced, its virtues, motions, laws;
And most familiarly and deeply talked
Of mental, moral, natural, divine.
Leaving the earth at will, he soared to heaven,
And read the glorious visions of the skies;
And to the music of the rolling spheres
Intelligently listened; and gazed far back
Into the awful depths of Deity;
Did all that mind assisted most could do;
And yet in misery lived, in misery died,
Because he wanted holiness of heart.

A deeper lesson this to mortals taught,
And nearer cut the branches of their pride,
That not in mental, but in moral worth,
God excellence placed; and only to the good,
To virtue, granted happiness, alone.

Admire the goodness of Almighty God!
He riches gave, he intellectual strength,
To few, and therefore none commands to be
Or rich, or learned; nor promises reward
Of peace to these. On all, He moral worth
Bestowed, and moral tribute asked from all.
And who that could not pay? who born so poor,
Of intellect so mean, as not to know
What seemed the best; and, knowing, might not do,
As not to know what God and conscience bade,
And what they bade not able to obey;
And he, who acted thus, fulfilled the law
Eternal, and promise reaped of peace;
Found peace this way alone: who sought it else,

Sought mellow grapes beneath the icy Pole,
Sought blooming roses on the cheek of death,
Sought substance in a world of fleeting shades.

Take one example, to our purpóse quite.
A man of rank, and of capacious soul,
Who riches had and fame, beyond desire;
An heir of flattery, to titles born,
And reputation and luxurious life:
Yet not content with ancestorial name,
Or to be known because his fathers were,
He on this height hereditary stood,
And, gazing higher, purposed in his heart
To take another step. Above him seemed,
Alone, the mount of song, the lofty seat
Of canonized bards; and thitherward,
By nature taught, and inward melody,
In prime of youth, he bent his eagle eye.
No cost was spared. What books he wished, he read;
What sage to hear he heard; what scenes to see,
He saw. And first in rambling school-boy days
Britannia's mountain walks, and heath-girt lakes,
And story-telling glens, and founts, and brooks,
And maids, as dew-drops pure and fair, his soul
With grandeur filled, and melody, and love.
Then travel came, and took him where he wished.
He cities saw, and courts, and princely pomp;
And mused alone on ancient mountain-brows:
And mused on battle-fields, where valor fought
In other days; and mused on ruins gray
With years; and drank from old and fabulous wells,
And plucked the vine that first-born prophets plucked:
And mused on famous tombs, and on the wave
Of Ocean mused, and on the desert waste;
The heavens and earth of every country saw.
Where'er the old inspiring Genii dwelt,

Aught that could rouse, expand, refine the soul,
Thither he went, and meditated there.

He touched his harp, and nations heard, entranced.
As some vast river of unfailing source,
Rapid, exhaustless, deep, his numbers flowed,
And opened new fountains in the human heart.
Where Fancy halted, weary in her flight,
In other men, his, fresh as morning, rose,
And soared untrodden heights, and seemed at home,
Where angels bashful looked. Others, though great,
Beneath their arguments seemed struggling whiles;
He, from above descending, stooped to touch
The loftiest thought; and proudly stooped, as though
It scarce deserved his verse. With Nature's self
He seemed an old acquaintance, free to jest
At will with all her glorious majesty.
He laid his hand upon "the Ocean's mane,"
And played familiar with his hoary locks;
Stood on the Alps, stood on the Appenines,
And with the thunder talked, as friend to friend;
And wove his garland of the lightning's wing,
In sportive twist—the lightning's fiery wing,
Which, as the footsteps of the dreadful God,
Marching upon the storm in vengeance, seemed;
Then turned, and with the grasshopper, who sung
His evening song beneath his feet, conversed.
Suns, moons, and stars, and clouds, his sisters were;
Rocks, mountains, meteors, seas, and winds, and storms,
His brothers, younger brothers, whom he scarce
As equals deemed. All passions of all men,
The wild and tame, the gentle and severe;
All thoughts, all maxims, sacred and profane;
All creeds, all seasons, Time, Eternity;
All that was hated, and all that was dear;

All that was hoped, all that was feared, by man;
He tossed about, as tempest, withered leaves;
Then, smiling, looked upon the wreck he made.
With terror now he froze the cowering blood,
And now dissolved the heart in tenderness;
Yet would not tremble, would not weep himself;
But back into his soul retired, alone,
Dark, sullen, proud, gazing contemptuously
On hearts and passions prostrate at his feet.
So Ocean, from the plains his waves had late
To desolation swept, retired in pride,
Exulting in the glory of his might,
And seemed to mock the ruin he had wrought.

As some fierce comet of tremendous size,
To which the stars did reverence, as it passed,
So he through learning and through fancy took
His flight sublime, and on the loftiest top
Of Fame's dread mountain sat; not soiled and worn,
As if he from the earth had labored up;
But as some bird of heavenly plumage fair,
He looked, which down from higher regions came,
And perched it there, to see what lay beneath.

The nations gazed, and wondered much, and praised.
Critics before him fell in humble plight,
Confounded fell, and made debasing signs
To catch his eye, and stretched, and swelled themselves
To bursting nigh, to utter bulky words
Of admiration vast: and many, too,
Many that aimed to imitate his flight,
With weaker wing, unearthly fluttering made,
And gave abundant sport to after days.

Great man! the nations gazed, and wondered much,
And praised; and many called his evil good.

Wits wrote in favor of his wickedness,
And kings to do him honor took delight.
Thus, full of titles, flattery, honor, fame,
Beyond desire, beyond ambition, full,
He died. He died of what? Of wretchedness;—
Drank every cup of joy, heard every trump
Of fame, drank early, deeply drank, drank draughts
That common millions might have quenched; then died
Of thirst, because there was no more to drink.
His goddess, Nature, wooed, embraced, enjoyed,
Fell from his arms, abhorred; his passions died,
Died, all but dreary, solitary Pride;
And all his sympathies in being died.
As some ill-guided bark, well built and tall,
Which angry tides cast out on desert shore,
And then, retiring, left it there to rot
And moulder in the winds and rains of heaven;
So he, cut from the sympathies of life,
And cast ashore from pleasure's boisterous surge,
A wandering, weary, worn, and wretched thing,
Scorched, and desolate, and blasted soul,
A gloomy wilderness of dying thought,—
Repined, and groaned, and withered from the earth.
His groanings filled the land, his numbers filled;
And yet he seemed ashamed to groan;—Poor man—
Ashamed to ask, and yet he needed help.

Proof this, beyond all lingering of doubt,
That not with natural or mental wealth,
Was God delighted, or his peace secured;
That not in natural or mental wealth,
Was human happiness or grandeur found.
Attempt how monstrous, and how surely vain!
With things of earthly sort, with aught but God,
With aught but moral excellence, truth and love,

To satisfy and fill the immortal soul!
Attempt, vain inconceivably! attempt
To satisfy the Ocean with a drop,
To marry Immortality to Death,
And with the unsubstantial Shade of Time,
To fill the embrace of all eternity!

THE

COURSE OF TIME.

BOOK V.

ANALYSIS OF BOOK V.

In this Book the Bard sketches the "Joys of Time." Whether happiness or misery preponderated, and where happiness might be found, were subjects of debate among men. True happiness had no exclusive locality, but was within the reach of all. She always went in company with duty.

Among the numerous contributions to this happiness were the joys of childhood, the joys of maternal affection, the joys of youthful love, the joys of friendship The study of nature, and contemplation of earth's scenery, also afforded their joys. Joys were felt in anticipations of the future; in recollections of the past; in repose after labor; even in grief.

From these sources all men experienced joy; but the pious man shared the highest degree.

And finally, in earth's history, there came a period when general joy pervaded it. This was the "thousand years" of Messiah's reign, foretold by the prophets, preceded by a terrible contest between the opposing powers of Truth and Error.

THE

COURSE OF TIME.

BOOK V.

Praise God, ye servants of the Lord! praise God,
Ye angels strong! praise God, ye sons of men!
Praise him who made, and who redeemed your souls,
Who gave you hope, reflection, reason, will;
Minds that can pierce eternity remote,
And live at once on future, present, past;
Can speculate on systems yet to make,
And back recoil on ancient days of Time,
Of Time, soon past, soon lost among the shades
Of buried years. Not so the actions done
In Time, the deeds of reasonable men.
As if engraven with pen of iron grain,
And laid in flinty rock, they stand, unchanged,
Written on the various pages of the past;
If good, in rosy characters of love;
If bad, in letters of vindictive fire.

God may forgive, but cannot blot them out.
Systems begin and end, Eternity
Rolls on his endless years, and men, absolved
By mercy from the consequence, forget
The evil deed, and God imputes it not;
But neither systems ending nor begun,
Eternity that rolls his endless years,

Nor men absolved, and sanctified, and washed
By mercy from the consequence, nor yet
Forgetfulness, nor God imputing not,
Can wash the guilty deed, once done, from out
The faithful annals of the past: who reads,
And many read, there finds it, as it was,
And is, and shall for ever be,—a dark,
Unnatural, and loathly moral spot.

The span of Time was short, indeed; and now
Three-fourths were past, the last begun, and on
Careering to its close, which soon we sing.
But first our promise we redeem, to tell
The joys of Time, her joys of native growth;
And briefly must, what longer tale deserves.

Wake, dear remembrances! wake, childhood-days!
Loves, friendships, wake! and wake, thou morn and even!
Sun! with thy orient locks; night, moon, and stars!
And thou, celestial bow! and all ye woods,
And hills, and vales, first trod in dawning life,
And hours of holy musing, wake! wake, earth
And, smiling to remembrance, come, and bring,
For thou canst bring, meet argument for song
Of heavenly harp, meet hearing for the ear
Of heavenly auditor, exalted high.

God gave much peace on earth, much holy joy;
Oped fountains of perennial spring, whence flowed
Abundant happiness to all who wished
To drink; not perfect bliss;—that dwells with us,
Beneath the eyelids of the Eternal One,
And sits at his right hand alone;—but such
As well deserved the name, abundant joy;

Pleasures, on which the memory of saints
Of highest glory, still delights to dwell.

It was, we own, subject of much debate,
And worthy men stood on opposing sides,
Whether the cup of mortal life had more
Of sour or sweet. Vain question this, when asked
In general terms, and worthy to be left
Unsolved. If most was sour, the drinker, not
The cup, we blame. Each in himself the means
Possessed to turn the bitter sweet, the sweet
To bitter. Hence, from out the self-same fount,
One nectar drank, another draughts of gall.
Hence, from the self-same quarter of the sky,
One saw ten thousand angels look and smile;
Another saw as many demons frown.
One discord heard, where harmony inclined
Another's ear. The sweet was in the taste,
The beauty in the eye, and in the ear
The melody; and in the man,—for God
Necessity of sinning laid on none,—
To form the taste, to purify the eye,
And tune the ear, that all he tasted, saw,
Or heard, might be harmonious, sweet, and fair.
Who would, might groan; who would, might sing
for joy.

Nature lamented little. Undevoured
By spurious appetites, she found enough,
Where least was found; with gleanings satisfied,
Or crumbs, that from the hand of luxury fell;
Yet seldom these she ate, but ate the bread
Of her own industry, made sweet by toil;
And walked in robes that her own hand had spun;
And slept on down her early rising bought.
Frugal and diligent in business, chaste

And abstinent, she stored for helpless age,
And, keeping in reserve her spring-day health,
And dawning relishes of life, she drank
Her evening cup with excellent appetite;
And saw her eldest sun decline, as fair
As rose her earliest morn, and pleased as well.

Whether in crowds or solitudes, in streets
Or shady groves, dwelt Happiness, it seems
In vain to ask; her nature makes it vain;
Though poets much, and hermits talked, and sung
Of brooks, and crystal founts, and weeping dews,
And myrtle bowers, and solitary vales,
And with the nymph made assignations there,
And wooed her with the love-sick oaten reed;
And sages too, although less positive,
Advised their sons to court her in the shade.
Delirious babble all! Was happiness,
Was self-approving, God-approving joy,
In drops of dew, however pure? in gales,
However sweet? in wells, however clear?
Or groves, however thick with verdant shade?

True, these were of themselves exceeding fair:
How fair at morn and even! worthy the walk
Of loftiest mind, and gave, when all within
Was right, a feast of overflowing bliss;
But were the occasion, not the cause of joy.
They waked the native fountains of the soul,
Which slept before; and stirred the holy tides
Of feeling up, giving the heart to drink
From its own treasures draughts of perfect sweet.

The Christian faith, which better knew the heart
Of man, him thither sent for peace, and thus
Declared: Who finds it, let him find it there;

Who finds it not, for ever let him seek
In vain; 'tis God's most holy, changeless will.

True Happiness had no localities,
No tones provincial, no peculiar garb.
Where Duty went, she went, with Justice went,
And went with Meekness, Charity, and Love.
Where'er a tear was dried, a wounded heart
Bound up, a bruised spirit with the dew
Of sympathy anointed, or a pang
Of honest suffering soothed, or injury
Repeated oft, as oft by love forgiven;
Where'er an evil passion was subdued,
Or Virtue's feeble embers fanned; where'er
A sin was heartily abjured, and left;
Where'er a pious act was done, or breathed
A pious prayer, or wished a pious wish;
There was a high and holy place, a spot
Of sacred light, a most religious fane,
Where Happiness, descending, sat and smiled.

But these apart, in sacred memory lives
The morn of life, first morn of endless days,
Most joyful morn! nor yet for nought the joy.
A being of eternal date commenced,
A young immortal then was born! and who
Shall tell what strange variety of bliss
Burst on the infant soul, when first it looked
Abroad on God's creation fair, and saw
The glorious earth and glorious heaven, and face
Of man sublime, and saw all new, and felt
All new! when thought awoke, though never more
To sleep! when first it saw, heard, reasoned, willed,
And triumphed in the warmth of conscious life!

Nor happy only, but the cause of joy,
Which those who never tasted always mourned.
What tongue!—no tongue shall tell what bliss
o'erflowed
The mother's tender heart, while round her hung
The offspring of her love, and lisped her name,
As living jewels dropped unstained from heaven,
That made her fairer far, and sweeter seem,
Than every ornament of costliest hue!
And who hath not been ravished, as she passed
With all her playful band of little ones,
Like Luna, with her daughters of the sky,
Walking in matron majesty and grace?
All who had hearts here pleasure found: and oft
Have I, when tired with heavy task,—for tasks
Were heavy in the world below,—relaxed
My weary thoughts among their guiltless sports,
And led them by their little hands a-field,
And watched them run and crop the tempting flower,
Which oft, unasked, they brought me, and bestowed
With smiling face, that waited for a look
Of praise,—and answered curious questions, put
In much simplicity, but ill to solve;
And heard their observations strange and new,
And settled whiles their little quarrels, soon
Ending in peace, and soon forgot in love.
And still I looked upon their loveliness,
And sought through nature for similitudes
Of perfect beauty, innocence, and bliss,
And fairest imagery around me thronged;
Dew-drops at day-spring on a seraph's locks,
Roses that bathe about the well of life,
Young Loves, young Hopes, dancing on Morning's
cheek,
Gems leaping in the coronet of Love!
So beautiful, so full of life, they seemed

As made entire of beams of angels' eyes.
Gay, guileless, sportive, lovely, little things!
Playing around the den of Sorrow, clad
In smiles, believing in their fairy hopes,
And thinking man and woman true! all joy,
Happy all day, and happy all the night!

Hail, holy Love! thou word that sums all bliss,
Gives and receives all bliss, fullest when most
Thou givest! spring-head of all felicity,
Deepest when most is drawn! emblem of God!
O'erflowing most when greatest numbers drink!
Essence that binds the uncreated Three,
Chain that unites creation to its Lord,
Centre to which all being gravitates,
Eternal, ever-growing, happy Love!
Enduring all, hoping, forgiving all;
Instead of law, fulfilling every law;
Entirely blest, because thou seek'st no more,
Hopest not, nor fear'st; but on the present livest,
And hold'st perfection smiling in thy arms.
Mysterious, infinite, exhaustless Love!
On earth mysterious, and mysterious still
In heaven! sweet chord that harmonizes all
The harps of Paradise! the spring, the well,
That fills the bowl and banquet of the sky!

But why should I to thee of Love divine?
Who happy, and not eloquent of Love?
Who holy, and, as thou art, pure, and not
A temple where her glory ever dwells,
Where burn her fires, and beams her perfect eye?

Kindred to this, part of this holy flame,
Was youthful love—the sweetest boon of Earth.
Hail, Love! first Love, thou word that sums all bliss,

The sparkling cream of all Time's blessedness,
The silken down of happiness complete!
Discerner of the ripest grapes of joy,
She gathered, and selected with her hand,
All finest relishes, all fairest sights,
All rarest odors, all divinest sounds,
All thoughts, all feelings dearest to the soul;
And brought the holy mixture home, and filled
The heart with all superlatives of bliss!
But, who would that expound, which words transcends,
Must talk in vain. Behold a meeting scene
Of early love, and thence infer its worth.

It was an eve of Autumn's holiest mood.
The corn fields bathed in Cynthia's silver light,
Stood ready for the reaper's gathering hand;
And all the Winds slept soundly. Nature seemed,
In silent contemplation, to adore
Its Maker. Now and then, the aged leaf
Fell from its fellows, rustling to the ground;
And, as it fell, bade man think on his end.
On vale and lake, on wood and mountain high,
With pensive wing outspread, sat heavenly Thought,
Conversing with itself. Vesper looked forth,
From out her western hermitage, and smiled;
And up the east, unclouded, rode the Moon
With all her Stars, gazing on earth intense,
As if she saw some wonder walking there.

Such was the night, so lovely, still, serene,
When, by a hermit thorn that on the hill
Had seen a hundred flowery ages pass,
A damsel kneeled to offer up her prayer,
Her prayer nightly offered, nightly heard.
This ancient thorn had been the meeting place
Of love, before his country's voice had called

The ardent youth to fields of honor far
Beyond the wave: and hither now repaired,
Nightly, the maid, by God's all-seeing eye
Seen only, while she sought this boon alone,
"Her lover's safety, and his quick return."
In holy, humble attitude she kneeled,
And to her bosom, fair as moonbeam, pressed
One hand, the other lifted up to heaven.
Her eye, upturned, bright as the star of morn,
As violet meek, excessive ardor streamed,
Wafting away her earnest heart to God.
Her voice, scarce uttered, soft as Zephyr sighs
On morning lily's cheek, though soft and low,
Yet heard in heaven, heard at the mercy-seat.
A tear-drop wandered on her lovely face;
It was a tear of faith and holy fear,
Pure as the drops that hang at dawning-time,
On yonder willows by the stream of life.
On her the Moon looked steadfastly: the Stars,
That circle nightly round the eternal Throne,
Glanced down, well pleased; and Everlasting Love
Gave gracious audience to her prayer sincere.

Oh, had her lover seen her thus alone,
Thus holy, wrestling thus, and all for him!
Nor did he not: for oft-times Providence,
With unexpected joy the fervent prayer
Of faith surprised. Returned from long delay,
With glory crowned of righteous actions won,
The sacred thorn, to memory dear, first sought
The youth, and found it at the happy hour,
Just when the damsel kneeled herself to pray.
Wrapped in devotion, pleading with her God,
She saw him not, heard not his foot approach.
All holy images seemed too impure
To emblem her he saw. A seraph kneeled,

Beseeching for his ward, before the Throne,
Seemed fittest, pleased him best. Sweet was the
thought!
But sweeter still the kind remembrance came,
That she was flesh and blood, formed for himself,
The plighted partner of his future life.
And as they met, embraced, and sat, embowered,
In woody chambers of the starry night,
Spirits of love about them ministered,
And God, approving, blest the holy joy!

Nor unremembered in the hour when friends
Met. Friends, but few on earth, and therefore dear,
Sought oft, and sought almost as oft in vain;
Yet always sought, so native to the heart,
So much desired, and coveted by all.
Nor wonder thou—thou wonderest not nor need'st.
Much beautiful, and excellent, and fair,
Was seen beneath the sun; but naught was seen
More beautiful, or excellent, or fair,
Than face of faithful friend, fairest when seen
In darkest day: and many sounds were sweet,
Most ravishing and pleasant to the ear;
But sweeter none than voice of faithful friend,
Sweet always, sweetest, heard in loudest storm.
Some I remember, and will ne'er forget;
My early friends, friends of my evil day;
Friends in my mirth, friends in my misery too;
Friends given by God in mercy and in love;
My counsellors, my comforters, and guides;
My joy in grief, my second bliss in joy;
Companions of my young desires; in doubt,
My oracles, my wings in high pursuit.
Oh, I remember, and will ne'er forget,
Our meeting spots, our chosen, sacred hours,
Our burning words that uttered all the soul,

Our faces beaming with unearthly love;
Sorrow with sorrow sighing, hope with hope
Exulting, heart embracing heart entire.
As birds of social feather helping each
His fellow's flight, we soared into the skies,
And cast the clouds beneath our feet, and Earth
With all her tardy, leaden-footed Cares,
And talked the speech and ate the food of heaven!
These I remember, these selectest men,
And would their names record; but what avails
My mention of their name? Before the Throne
They stand illustrious 'mong the loudest harps,
And will receive thee glad, my friend and theirs.
For all are friends in heaven, all faithful friends!
And many friendships, in the days of Time
Begun, are lasting here, and growing still;
So grows ours evermore, both theirs and mine.

Nor is the hour of lonely walk forgot,
In the wide desert, where the view was large.
Pleasant were many scenes, but most to me
The solitude of vast extent, untouched
By hand of art, where Nature sowed, herself,
And reaped her crops; whose garments were the clouds,
Whose minstrels, brooks; whose lamps, the moon and stars;
Whose organ-choir, the voice of many waters;
Whose banquets, morning dews; whose heroes, storms;
Whose warriors, mighty winds; whose lovers, flowers;
Whose orators, the thunderbolts of God;
Whose palaces, the everlasting hills;
Whose ceiling, heaven's unfathomable blue:
And from whose rocky turrets, battled high,
Prospect immense spread out on all sides round,

Lost now between the welkin and the main,
Now walled with hills that slept above the storm.

Most fit was such a place for musing men,
Happiest sometimes, when musing without aim.
It was, indeed, a wondrous sort of bliss
The lonely bard enjoyed, when forth he walked,
Unpurposed; stood, and knew not why; sat down,
And knew not where; arose, and knew not when;
Had eyes, and saw not; ears, and nothing heard;
And sought—sought neither heaven nor earth—sought naught,
Nor meant to think; but ran, meantime, through vast
Of visionary things, fairer than aught
That was; and saw the distant tops of thoughts,
Which men of common stature never saw,
Greater than aught that largest words could hold,
Or give idea of, to those who read.
He entered in to Nature's holy place,
Her inner chamber, and beheld her face
Unveiled; and heard unutterable things,
And incommunicable visions saw;
Things then unutterable, and visions then
Of incommunicable glory bright;
But by the lips of after ages formed
To words, or by their pencil pictured forth;
Who, entering farther in, beheld again,
And heard unspeakable and marvelous things,
Which other ages in their turn revealed,
And left to others, greater wonders still.

The earth abounded much in silent wastes;
Nor yet is heaven without its solitudes,
Else incomplete in bliss, whither who will
May oft retire, and meditate alone,
Of God, redemption, holiness, and love;

Nor needs to fear a setting sun, or haste
Him home from rainy tempest unforseen,
Or, sighing, leave his thoughts for want of time.

But whatsoever was both good and fair,
And highest relish of enjoyment gave,
In intellectual exercise was found,
When, gazing through the future, present, past,
Inspired, thought linked to thought, harmonious flowed
In poetry—the loftiest mood of mind;
Or when philosophy the reason led
Deep through the outward circumstance of things;
And saw the master-wheels of Nature move;
And travelled far along the endless line
Of certain and of probable; and made,
At every step, a new discovery,
That gave the soul sweet sense of larger room
High these pursuits, and sooner to be named,
Deserved; at present, only named, again
To be resumed, and praised in longer verse.

Abundant and diversified above
All number, were the sources of delight;
As infinite as were the lips that drank;
And to the pure, all innocent and pure;
The simplest still to wisest men the best.
One made acquaintanceship with plants and flowers,
And happy grew in telling all their names;
One classed the quadrupeds; a third, the fowls;
Another found in minerals his joy:
And I have seen a man, a worthy man,
In happy mood conversing with a fly;
And as he, through his glass, made by himself,
Beheld its wondrous eye and plumage fine,
From leaping scarce he kept, for perfect joy.

And from my path I with my friend have turned,
A man of excellent mind and excellent heart,
And climbed the neighboring hill, with arduous step,
Fetching from distant cairn, or from the earth
Digging, with labor sure, the ponderous stone,
Which, having carried to the highest top,
We downward rolled; and as it strove, at first,
With obstacles that seemed to match its force,
With feeble, crooked motion to and fro
Wavering, he looked with interest most intense,
And prayed almost; and as it gathered strength,
And straightened the current of its furious flow,
Exulting in the swiftness of its course,
And, rising now with rainbow-bound immense,
Leaped down careering o'er the subject plain,
He clapped his hands in sign of boundless bliss,
And laughed and talked, well paid for all his toil:
And when at night the story was rehearsed,
Uncommon glory kindled in his eye.

And there were, too,—Harp! lift thy voice on high,
And run in rapid numbers o'er the face
Of Nature's scenery,—and there were day
And night, and rising suns and setting suns,
And clouds that seemed like chariots of saints,
By fiery coursers drawn, as brightly hued
As if the glorious, bushy, golden locks
Of thousand cherubim had been shorn off,
And on the temples hung of Morn and Even.
And there were moons, and stars, and darkness streaked
With light; and voice and tempest heard secure,
And there were seasons coming evermore,
And going still, all fair, and always new,
With bloom, and fruit, and fields of hoary grain.
And there were hills of flock, and groves of song,

And flowery streams, and garden walks embowered,
Where, side by side, the rose and lily bloomed;
And sacred founts, wild harps, and moonlight glens,
And forests vast, fair lawns, and lonely oaks,
And little willows, sipping at the brook;
Old wizard haunts, and dancing seats of mirth;
Gay festive bowers, and palaces in dust;
Dark owlet nooks, and caves, and battled rocks;
And winding valleys, roofed with pendent shade;
And tall and perilous cliffs, that overlooked
The breadth of Ocean, sleeping on his waves;
Sounds, sights, smells, tastes, the heaven and earth, profuse
In endless sweets, above all praise of song:
For not to use alone did Providence
Abound; but large example gave to man
Of grace, and ornament, and splendor rich,
Suited abundantly to every taste,
In bird, beast, fish, winged and creeping thing,
In herb and flower, and in the restless change,
Which, on the many-colored seasons, made
The annual circuit of the fruitful earth.

Nor do I aught of earthly sort remember,—
If partial feeling to my native place
Lead not my lyre astray,—of fairer view,
And comelier walk, than the blue mountain-paths,
And snowy cliffs of Albion renowned;
Albion, an isle long blessed with gracious laws,
And gracious kings, and favored much of Heaven,
Though yielding oft penurious gratitude.
Nor do I of that isle remember aught
Of prospect more sublime and beautiful,
Than Scotia's northern battlement of hills,
Which first I from my father's house beheld,
At dawn of life; beloved in memory still,

And standard still of rural imagery.
What most resembles them, the fairest seems,
And stirs the eldest sentiments of bliss;
And, pictured on the tablet of my heart,
Their distant shapes eternally remain,
And in my dreams their cloudy tops arise.

Much of my native scenery appears,
And presses forward to be in my song;
But must not now, for much behind awaits
Of higher note. Four trees I pass not by,
Which o'er our house their evening shadow threw;
Three ash, and one of elm. Tall trees they were,
And old, and had been old a century
Before my day. None living could say aught
About their youth; but they were goodly trees
And oft I wondered,—as I sat and thought
Beneath their summer shade, or, in the night
Of winter, heard the spirits of the wind
Growling among their boughs,—how they had grown
So high, in such a rough tempestuous place;
And when a hapless branch, torn by the blast,
Fell down, I mourned, as if a friend had fallen.

These I distinctly hold in memory still,
And all the desert scenery around.
Nor strange, that recollection there shonld dwell,
Where first I heard of God's redeeming love;
First felt and reasoned, loved and was beloved;
And first awoke the harp to holy song.

To hoar and green there was enough of joy.
Hopes, friendships, charities, and warm pursuit,
Gave comfortable flow to youthful blood.
And there were old remembrances of days,
When, on the glittering dews of orient life,

Shone sunshine hopes, unfailed, unperjured, then;
And there were childish sports, and school-boy feats,
And school-boy spots, and earnest vows of love,
Uttered, when passion's boisterous tide ran high,
Sincerely uttered, though but seldom kept:
And there were angel looks, and sacred hours
Of rapture, hours that in a moment passed,
And yet were wished to last for evermore;
And venturous exploits, and hardy deeds,
And bargains shrewd, achieved in manhood's prime;
And thousand recollections, gay and sweet,
Which, as the old and venerable man
Approached the grave, around him, smiling, flocked,
And breathed new ardor through his ebbing veins,
And touched his lips with endless eloquence,
And cheered and much refreshed his withered heart.

Indeed, each thing remembered, all but guilt,
Was pleasant, and a constant source of joy.
Nor lived the old on memory alone.
He in his children lived a second life,
With them again took root, sprang with their hopes,
Entered into their schemes, partook their fears,
Laughed in their mirth, and in their gain grew rich.
And sometimes on the eldest cheek was seen
A smile as hearty as on face of youth,
That saw in prospect sunny hopes invite,
Hope's pleasures, sung to harp of sweetest note,
Harp, heard with rapture on Britannia's hills,
With rapture heard by me, in morn of life.

Nor small the joy of rest to mortal men,
Rest after labor, sleep approaching soft,
And wrapping all the weary faculties
In sweet repose. Then Fancy, unrestrained
By sense or judgment, strange confusion made

Of future, present, past, combining things
Unseemly, things unsociable in nature,
In most absurd communion, laughable,
Though sometimes vexing sore the slumbering soul.
Sporting at will, she, through her airy halls,
With moonbeams paved, and canopied with stars,
And tapestried with marvelous imagery,
And shapes of glory, infinitely fair,
Moving and mixing in most wondrous dance,—
Fantastically walked, but pleased so well,
That ill she liked the judgment's voice severe,
Which called her home when noisy morn awoke.
And oft she sprang beyond the bounds of Time,
On her swift pinion lifting up the souls
Of righteous men, on high to God and heaven,
Where they beheld unutterable things;
And heard the glorious music of the blessed,
Circling the throne of the Eternal Three;
And, with the spirits unincarnate, took
Celestial pastime, on the hills of God,
Forgetful of the gloomy pass between.

Some dreams were useless, moved by turbid course
Of animal disorder; not so all.
Deep moral lessons some impressed, that naught
Could afterwards deface: and oft in dreams,
The master passion of the soul displayed
His huge deformity, concealed by day,
Warning the sleeper to beware, awake:
And oft in dreams, the reprobate and vile,
Unpardonable sinner,—as he seemed
Toppling upon the perilous edge of hell,—
In dreadful apparition, saw before
His visions pass the shadows of the damned;
And saw the glare of hollow, cursed eyes
Spring from the skirts of the infernal night;

And saw the souls of wicked men, new dead,
By devils hearsed into the fiery gulf;
And heard the burning of the endless flames;
And heard the weltering of the waves of wrath;
And sometimes, too, before his fancy, passed
The Worm that never dies, writhing its folds
In hideous sort, and with eternal Death
Held horrid colloquy, giving the wretch
Unwelcome earnest of the wo to come.
But these we leave, as unbefitting song,
That promised happy narrative of joy.

But what, of all the joys of earth, was most
Of native growth, most proper to the soil,
Not elsewhere known, in worlds that never fell,
Was joy that sprung from disappointed wo.
The joy in grief, the pleasure after pain,
Fears turned to hopes, meetings expected not,
Deliverances from dangerous attitudes,
Better for worse, and best sometimes for worst,
And all the seeming ill ending in good,—
A sort of happiness composed, which none
Has had experience of, but mortal man;
Yet not to be despised. Look back, and one
Behold, who would not give her tear for all
The smiles that dance about the cheek of Mirth.

Among the tombs she walks at noon of night,
In miserable garb of widowhood.
Observe her yonder, sickly, pale, and sad,
Bending her wasted body o'er the grave
Of him who was the husband of her youth.
The moonbeams, trembling through these ancient
yews,
That stand like ranks of mourners round the bed
Of death, fall dismally upon her face,

Her little, hollow, withered face, almost
Invisible, so worn away with wo.
The tread of hasty foot, passing so late,
Disturbs her not; nor yet the roar of mirth,
From neighboring revelry ascending loud.
She hears, sees naught, fears naught. One thought alone
Fills all her heart and soul, half hoping, half
Remembering, sad, unutterable thought!
Uttered by silence and by tears alone.
Sweet tears! the awful language, eloquent
Of infinite affection, far too big
For words. She sheds not many now. That grass,
Which springs so rankly o'er the dead, has drunk
Already many showers of grief; a drop
Or two are all that now remain behind,
And, from her eye that darts strange fiery beams,
At dreary intervals, drip down her cheek,
Falling most mournfully from bone to bone.
But yet she wants not tears. That babe, that hangs
Upon her breast, that babe that never saw
Its father—he was dead before its birth—
Helps her to weep, weeping before its time,
Taught sorrow by the mother's melting voice,
Repeating oft the father's sacred name.
Be not surprised at this expense of wo!
The man she mourns was all she called her own,
The music of her ear, light of her eye,
Desire of all her heart, her hope, her fear,
The element in which her passions lived,
Dead now, or dying all: nor long shall she
Visit that place of skulls. Night after night,
She wears herself away. The moonbeam, now,
That falls upon her unsubstantial frame,
Scarce finds obstruction; and upon her bones,
Barren as leafless boughs in winter-time,

Her infant fastens his little hands, as oft,
Forgetful, she leaves him a while unheld.
But, look, she passes not away in gloom.
A light from far illumes her face, a light
That comes beyond the moon, beyond the sun—
The light of truth divine, the glorious hope
Of resurrection at the promised morn,
And meetings then which ne'er shall part again.

Indulge another note of kindred tone,
Where grief was mixed with melancholy joy.

Our sighs were numerous, and profuse our tears,
For she, we lost, was lovely, and we loved
Her much. Fresh in our memory, as fresh
As yesterday, is yet the day she died.
It was an April day; and blithely all
The youth of nature leaped beneath the sun,
And promised glorious manhood; and our hearts
Were glad, and round them danced the lightsome blood,
In healthy merriment, when tidings came,
A child was born: and tidings came again,
That she who gave it birth was sick to death.
So swift trode sorrow on the heels of joy!
We gathered round her bed, and bent our knees
In fervent supplication to the Throne
Of Mercy, and perfumed our prayers with sighs
Sincere, and penitential tears, and looks
Of self-abasement; but we sought to stay
An angel on the earth, a spirit ripe
For heaven; and Mercy, in her love, refused,
Most merciful, as oft, when seeming least!
Most gracious when she seemed the most to frown!
The room I well remember, and the bed
On which she lay, and all the faces, too,

That crowded dark and mournfully around.
Her father there and mother, bending, stood;
And down their aged cheeks fell many drops
Of bitterness. Her husband, too, was there,
And brothers, and they wept; her sisters, too,
Did weep and sorrow, comfortless; and I,
Too, wept, though not to weeping given; and all
Within the house was dolorous and sad.
This I remember well; but better still,
I do remember, and will ne'er forget,
The dying eye! That eye alone was bright,
And brighter grew, as nearer death approached.
As I have seen the gentle little flower
Look fairest in the silver beam which fell,
Reflected from the thunder-cloud that soon
Came down, and o'er the desert scattered far
And wide its loveliness. She made a sign
To bring her babe—'t was brought, and by her placed.
She looked upon its face that neither smiled
Nor wept, nor knew who gazed upon 't; and laid
Her hand upon its little breast, and sought
For it, with look that seemed to penetrate
The heavens, unutterable blessings, such
As God to dying parents only granted,
For infants left behind them in the world.
"God keep my child!" we heard her say, and heard
No more. The Angel of the Covenant
Was come, and, faithful to his promise, stood
Prepared to walk with her through death's dark vale.
And now her eyes grew bright, and brighter still,
Too bright for ours to look upon, suffused
With many tears, and closed without a cloud.
They set as sets the morning star, which goes
Not down behind the darkened west, nor hides
Obscured among the tempests of the sky,
But melts away into the light of heaven.

Loves, friendships, hopes, and dear remembrances,
The kind embracings of the heart, and hours
Of happy thought, and smiles coming to tears,
And glories of the heaven and starry cope
Above, and glories of the earth beneath,—
These were the rays that wandered through the gloom
Of mortal life; wells of the wilderness,
Redeeming features in the face of Time,
Sweet drops, that made the mixed cup of Earth
A palatable draught—too bitter else.

About the joys and pleasures of the world,
This question was not seldom in debate:
Whether the righteous man, or sinner, had
The greatest share, and relished them the most?
Truth gives the answer thus, gives it distinct,
Nor needs to reason long: The righteous man.
For what was he denied of earthly growth,
Worthy the name of good? Truth answers, Naught.
Had he not appetites, and sense, and will?
Might he not eat, if Providence allowed,
The finest of the wheat? Might he not drink
The choicest wine? True, he was temperate;
But, then, was temperance a foe to peace?
Might he not rise and clothe himself in gold?
Ascend, and stand in palaces of kings?
True, he was honest still, and charitable:
Were, then, these virtues foes to human peace?
Might he not do exploits, and gain a name?
Most true, he trode not down a fellow's right,
Nor walked up to a throne on skulls of men:
Were justice, then, and mercy, foes to peace?
Had he not friendships, loves, and smiles, and hopes?
Sat not around his table sons and daughters?
Was not his ear with music pleased? his eye
With light? his nostrils with perfumes? his lips

With pleasant relishes? Grew not his herds?
Fell not the rain upon his meadows? reaped
He not his harvests? and did not his heart
Revel, at will, through all the charities
And sympathies of nature, unconfined?
And were not these all sweetened and sanctified
By dews of holiness, shed from above?
Might he not walk through Fancy's airy halls?
Might he not History's ample page survey?
Might he not, finally, explore the depths
Of mental, moral, natural, divine?
But why enumerate thus? One word enough.
There was no joy in all created things,
No drop of sweet, that turned not in the end
To sour, of which the righteous man did not
Partake; partake, invited by the voice
Of God, his Father's voice, who gave him all
His heart's desire: and o'er the sinner still,
The Christian had this one advantage more,
That when his earthly pleasures failed—and fail
They always did to every soul of man,—
He sent his hopes on high, looked up and reached
His sickle forth, and reaped the fields of heaven,
And plucked the clusters from the vines of God.

Nor was the general aspect of the world
Always a moral waste. A time there came,
Though few believed it e'er should come; a time,
Typed by the Sabbath day recurring once
In seven, and by the year of rest indulged
Septennial to the lands on Jordan's banks;
A time foretold by Judah's bards in words
Of fire; a time, seventh part of time, and set
Before the eighth and last, the Sabbath day
Of all the earth, when all had rest and peace.
Before its coming many to and fro

Ran, ran from various cause; by many sent
From various cause, upright and crooked both.
Some sent and ran for love of souls, sincere
And more, at instance of a holy name.
With godly zeal much vanity was mixed;
And circumstance of gaudy civil pomp;
And speeches buying praise for praise; and lists,
And endless scrolls, surcharged with modest names
That sought the public eye; and stories, told
In quackish phrase, that hurt their credit, even
When true; combined with wise and prudent means,
Much wheat, much chaff, much gold, and much alloy;
But God wrought with the whole, wrought most with
    what
To man seemed weakest means, and brought result
Of good, from good and evil both; and breathed
Into the withered nations breath of life,
The breath of life, of liberty and truth,
By means of knowledge, breathed into the soul.

  Then was the evil day of tyranny,
Of kingly and of priestly tyranny,
That bruised the nations long. As yet, no state
Beneath the heavens had tasted freedom's wine,
Though loud of freedom was the talk of all.
Some groaned more deeply, being heavier tasked;
Some wrought with straw, and some without; but all
Were slaves, or meant to be; for rulers, still,
Had been of equal mind, excepting few,
Cruel, rapacious, tyrannous, and vile,
And had with equal shoulder propped the Beast.
As yet, the Church, the holy spouse of God,
In members few, had wandered in her weeds
Of mourning, persecuted, scorned, reproached,
And buffeted, and killed; in members few,
Though seeming many whiles; then fewest, oft,

When seeming most. She still had hung her harp
Upon the willow-tree, and sighed, and wept
From age to age. Satan began the war,
And all his angels, and all wicked men,
Against her fought by while, or fierce attack,
Six thousand years; but fought in vain. She stood
Troubled on every side, but not distressed;
Weeping, but yet despairing not; cast down,
But not destroyed: for she upon the palms
Of God was graven, and precious in his sight,
As apple of his eye; and, like the bush
On Midia's mountain seen, burned unconsumed;
But to the wilderness retiring, dwelt,
Debased in sackcloth, and forlorn in tears.

As yet had sung the scarlet-colored Whore,
Who on the breast of civil power reposed
Her harlot head, (the Church a harlot then,
When first she wedded civil power,) and drank
The blood of martyred saints,—whose priests were lords,
Whose coffers held the gold of every land,
Who held a cup of all pollutions full,
Who with a double horn the people pushed,
And raised her forehead, full of blasphemy,
Above the holy God, usurping oft
Jehovah's incommunicable names.
The nations had been dark; the Jews had pined,
Scattered, without a name, beneath the Curse;
War had abounded, Satan raged, unchained;
And earth had still been black with moral gloom.

But now the cry of men oppressed went up
Before the Lord, and to remembrance came
The tears of all his saints, their tears, and groans.
Wise men had read the number of the name;

The prophet-years had rolled; the time, and times,
And half a time, were now fulfilled complete;
The seven fierce vials of the wrath of God,
Poured by seven angels strong, were shed abroad
Upon the earth and emptied to the dregs;
The prophecy for confirmation stood;
And all was ready for the sword of God.

The righteous saw, and fled without delay
Into the chambers of Omnipotence.
The wicked mocked, and sought for erring cause,
To satisfy the dismal state of things;
The public credit gone, the fear in time
Of peace, the starving want in time of wealth,
The insurrection muttering in the streets,
And pallid consternation spreading wide;
And leagues, though holy termed, first ratified
In hell, on purpose made to under-prop
Iniquity, and crush the sacred truth.

Meantime, a mighty angel stood in heaven,
And cried aloud, "Associate now yourselves,
Ye princes, potentates, and men of war,
And mitred heads, associate now yourselves,
And be dispersed; embattle, and be broken.
Gird on your armor, and be dashed to dust.
Take counsel, and it shall be brought to naught.
Speak, and it shall not stand." And suddenly
The armies of the saints, imbannered, stood
On Zion hill; and with them angels stood
In squadron bright, and chariots of fire;
And with them stood the Lord, clad like a man
Of war, and, to the sound of thunder, led
The battle on. Earth shook, the kingdoms shook;
The Beast, the lying Seer, dominions, fell;
Thrones, tyrants fell, confounded in the dust,

Scattered and driven before the breath of God,
As chaff of summer threshing floor, before
The wind. Three days the battle wasting slew.
The sword was full, the arrow drunk with blood;
And to the supper of Almighty God,
Spread in Hamonah's vale, the fowls of heaven,
And every beast, invited, came, and fed
On captains' flesh, and drank the blood of kings.

And, lo! another angel stood in heaven,
Crying aloud with mighty voice, "Fallen, fallen,
Is Babylon the Great, to rise no more.
Rejoice, ye prophets! over her rejoice,
Apostles! holy men, all saints, rejoice!
And glory give to God and to the Lamb."
And all the armies of disburdened earth,
As voice of many waters, and as voice
Of thunderings, and voice of multitudes,
Answered, Amen. And every hill and rock,
And sea, and every beast, answered, Amen.
Europa answered, and the farthest bounds
Of woody Chili, Asia's fertile coasts,
And Afric's burning wastes, answered, Amen.
And Heaven, rejoicing, answered back, Amen.

Not so the wicked. They afar were heard
Lamenting. Kings, who drank her cup of whoredoms,
Captains, and admirals, and mighty men,
Who lived deliciously; and merchants, rich
With merchandise of gold, and wine, and oil;
And those who traded in the souls of men,
Known by their gaudy robes of priestly pomp;—
All these afar off stood, crying, Alas!
Alas! and wept, and gnashed their teeth, and groaned,
And with the owl that on her ruins sat,
Made dolorous concert in the ear of Night.

And over her again the Heavens rejoiced,
And Earth returned again the loud response.

Thrice happy days! thrice blessed the man who saw
Their dawn! The Church and State, that long had held
Unholy intercourse, were now divorced;
Princes were righteous men, judges upright;
And first, in general, now—for in the worst
Of times there were some honest seers—the priest
Sought other than the fleece among his flocks,
Best paid when God was honored most; and, like
A cedar, naurished well, Jerusalem grew,
And towered on high, and spread, and flourished fair;
And underneath her boughs the nations lodged,
All nations lodged, and sung the song of peace.
From the four winds, the Jews, eased of the Curse
Returned, and dwelt with God in Jacob's land,
And drank of Sharon and of Carmel's vine.
Satan was bound, though bound, not banished quite,
But lurked about the timorous skirts of things,
Ill lodged, and thinking whiles to leave the earth,
And with the wicked,—for some wicked were,—
Held midnight meetings, as the saints were wont,
Fearful of day, who once was as the sun,
And worshiped more. The bad, but few, became
A taunt and hissing now, as heretofore
The good; and, blushing, hasted out of sight.
Disease was none; the voice of war forgot;
The sword, a share; a pruning-hook the spear.
Men grew and multiplied upon the earth,
And filled the city and the waste; and Death
Stood waiting for the lapse of tardy Age,
That mocked him long. Men grew and multiplied,
But lacked not bread; for God his promise brought
To mind, and blessed the land with plenteous rain,

And made it blessed for dews and precious things
Of heaven, and blessings of the deep beneath,
And blessings of the sun and moon, and fruits
Of day and night, and blessings of the vale,
And precious things of the eternal hills,
And all the fulness of perpetual spring.

The prison-house, where chained felons pined,
Threw open his ponderous doors, let in the light
Of heaven, and grew into a church, where God
Was worshipped. None were ignorant, selfish none;
Love took the place of law; where'er you met
A man, you met a friend, sincere and true.
Kind looks foretold as kind a heart within;
Words as they sounded, meant; and promises
Were made to be performed. Thrice happy days!
Philosophy was sanctified, and saw
Perfections that she thought a fable, long.
Revenge his dagger dropped, and kissed the hand
Of Mercy; Anger cleared his cloudy brow,
And sat with Peace; Envy grew red, and smiled
On Worth; Pride stooped, and kissed Humility;
Lust washed his miry hands, and wedded, leaned
On chaste Desire; and Falsehood laid aside
His many-folded cloak, and bowed to Truth;
And Treachery up from his mining came,
And walked above the ground with righteous Faith:
And Covetousness unclenched his sinewy hand,
And opened his door to Charity, the fair;
Hatred was lost in Love; and Vanity,
With a good conscience pleased, her feathers cropped;
Sloth in the morning rose with Industry;
To Wisdom Folly turned; and Fashion turned
Deception off, in act as good as word.
The hand that held a whip was lifted up
To bless; slave was a word in ancient books

Met only; every man was free; and all
Feared God, and served him day and night in love.

How fair the daughter of Jerusalem then!
How gloriously from Zion Hill she looked!
Clothed with the sun, and in her train the moon,
And on her head a coronet of stars,
And girdling round her waist, with heavenly grace,
The bow of Mercy bright; and in her hand
Immanuel's cross, her sceptre and her hope.

Desire of every land! the nations came,
And worshipped at her feet; all nations came,
Flocking like doves: Columba's painted tribes,
That from the Magellan to the Frozen Bay,
Beneath the Arctic, dwelt; and drank the tides
Of Amazona, prince of earthly streams;
Or slept at noon beneath the giant shade
Of Andes' mount; or, roving northward, heard
Nigara sing, from Erie's billow down
To Frontenac, and hunted thence the fur
To Labrador: and Afric's dusky swarms,
That from Morocco to Angola dwelt,
And drank the Niger from his native wells,
Or roused the lion in Numidia's groves;
The tribes that sat among the fabled cliffs
Of Atlas, looking to Atlanta's wave;
With joy and melody, arose and came.
Zara awoke and came, and Egypt came,
Casting her idol gods into the Nile.
Black Ethiopia, that shadowless,
Beneath the Torrid burned, arose and came.
Dauma and Medra, and the pirate tribes
Of Algeri, with incense came, and pure
Offerings, annoying now the seas no more.
The silken tribes of Asia, flocking, came,

Innumerous: Ishmael's wandering race, that rode
On camels o'er the spicy tract that lay
From Persia to the Red Sea coast; the king
Of broad Cathay, with numbers infinite,
Of many lettered casts; and all the tribes
That dwelt from Tigris, to the Ganges' wave,
And worshipped fire, or Brahma, fabled god;
Cashmeres, Circassians, Banyans, tender race!
That swept the insect from their path, and lived
On herbs and fruits; and those who peaceful dwelt
Along the shady avenue that stretched
From Agra to Lahore; and all the hosts
That owned the Crescent late, deluded long;
The Tartar hordes, that roamed from Oby's bank,
Ungoverned, southward to the wondrous Wall.
The tribes of Europe came; the Greek, redeemed
From Turkish thrall, the Spaniard came, and Gaul,
And Britain with her ships, and, on his sledge,
The Laplander, that nightly watched the bear
Circling the Pole; and those who saw the flames
Of Hecla burn the drifted snow; the Russ,
Long-whiskered, and equestrian Pole; and those
Who drank the Rhine, or lost the evening sun
Behind the Alpine towers; and she that sat
By Arno, classic stream; Venice; or Rome,
Head quarters long of sin! first guileless now,
And meaning as she seemed, stretched forth her hands;
And all the Isles of ocean rose and came,
Whether they heard the roll of banished tides,
Antipodes to Albion's wave, or watched
The Moon ascending chalky Teneriffe,
And with Atlanta holding nightly love.
The Sun, the Moon, the Constellations, came:
Thrice twelve and ten that watched the Antarctic
sleep,
Twice six that near the Ecliptic dwelt, thrice twelve

And one, that with the Streamers danced, and saw
The Hyperborean Ice guarding the Pole.
The East, the West, the South, and snowy North,
Rejoicing met, and worshipped reverently
Before the Lord, in Zion's holy hill;
And all the places round about were blessed.

The animals, as once in Eden, lived
In peace. The wolf dwelt with the lamb, the bear
And leopard with the ox. With looks of love,
The tiger and the scaly crocodile
Together met, at Gumbia's palmy wave.
Perched on the eagle's wing, the bird of song,
Singing, arose, and visited the sun;
And with the falcon sat the gentle lark.
The little child leapt from its mother's arms,
And stroked the crested snake, and rolled unhurt
Among his speckled waves, and wished him home;
And sauntering school-boys, slow returning, played
At eve about the lion's den, and wove,
Into his shaggy mane, fantastic flowers.
To meet the husbandman, early abroad,
Hasted the deer, and waved its woody head,
And round his dewy steps, the hare, unscared,
Sported; and toyed familiar with his dog.
The flocks and herds, o'er hill and valley spread,
Exulting, cropped the ever-budding herb.
The desert blossomed, and the barren sung.
Justice and Mercy, Holiness and Love,
Among the people walked, Messiah reigned,
And Earth kept Jubilee a thousand years.

THE

COURSE OF TIME.

BOOK VI.

ANALYSIS OF BOOK VI.

At the opening of the Book, the Bard glances at the final destruction of the Earth, as if the astonishing change were actually again taking place under his eye. But, checking himself, he proceeds to describe the years which followed the millennial rest.

Ungodliness again abounded. Ambition and love of ease, principles which had always struggled for the mastery of man, regained their ascendancy. Every form of sin, which had existed before the reign of Messiah, was renewed, and new forms were invented. The age was, however, enlightened and polished, and the universal contempt of God was wholly wilful.

In the meantime, strange phenomena and disasters gave presage of Earth's approaching dissolution. Men disturbed, not reformed, inquired the meaning in alarm; but soon forgot the whole, in their guilty pleasures; and Earth hasted to fill up the measure of her wickedness.

Here the Bard pauses in his narrative, as the numerous occupants of heaven suspend their various employments, to join in an evening hymn of praise. All are represented as turning towards the unveiled Godhead, while the sainted Isaiah takes the harp, and, standing before the throne, utters the holy song. At its close, the thousands infinite, who "circling stand, bowing afar," devoutly respond their assent.

THE

COURSE OF TIME.

BOOK VI.

Resume thy tone of wo, immortal Harp!
The song of mirth is past, the Jubilee
Is ended, and the sun begins to fade!
Soon passed, for Happiness counts not the hours:
To her a thousand years seem as a day;
A day—a thousand years to Misery.
Satan is loose, and Violence is heard,
And Riot in the street, and Revelry
Intoxicate, and Murder, and Revenge.
Put on your armor now, ye righteous! put
The helmet of salvation on, and gird
Your loins about with truth; add righteousness,
And add the shield of faith, and take the sword
Of God—awake and watch!—the day is near,
Great day of God Almighty and the Lamb!
The harvest of the earth is fully ripe;
Vengeance begins to tread the great wine-press
Of fierceness and of wrath; and Mercy pleads,
Mercy that pleaded long, she pleads—no more!
Whence comes that darkness? whence those yells of wo?
What thunderings are these that shake the world?
Why fall the lamps from heaven as blasted figs?
Why tremble righteous men? why angels pale?
Why is all fear? what has become of hope?

God comes! — God, in his car of vengeance, comes! —
Hark! louder on the blast, come hollow shrieks
Of dissolution! in the fitful scowl
Of night, near and more near, angels of death
Incessant flap their deadly wings, and roar
Through all the fevered air! the mountains rock,
The moon is sick, and all the stars of heaven
Burn feebly! oft and sudden gleams the fire,
Revealing awfully the brow of Wrath!
The Thunder, long and loud, utters his voice,
Responsive to the Ocean's troubled growl!
Night comes, last night, the long, dark, dark, dark, night,
That has no morn beyond it, and no star!
No eye of man hath seen a night like this!
Heaven's trampled Justice girds itself for fight!
Earth, to thy knees, and cry for mercy! cry
With earnest heart, for thou art growing old
And hoary, unrepented, unforgiven!
And all thy glory mourns! The vintage mourns!
Bashan and Carmel, mourn and weep; and mourn.
Thou Lebanon! with all thy cedars, mourn.
Sun! glorying in thy strength from age to age,
So long observant of thy hour, put on
Thy weeds of wo, and tell the Moon to weep;
Utter thy grief at mid-day, morn, and even;
Tell all the nations, tell the Clouds that sit
About the portals of the east and west,
And wanton with thy golden locks, to wait
Thee not to-morrow, for no morrow comes!
Tell men and women, tell the new-born child,
And every eye that sees, to come, and see
Thee set behind Eternity, for thou
Shalt go to bed to-night, and ne'er awake!
Stars! walking on the pavement of the sky,

Out-sentinels of heaven, watching the earth,
Cease dancing now ; your lamps are growing dim,
Your graves are dug among the dismal clouds,
And angels are assembling round your bier!
Orion, mourn! and Mazzaroth, and thou,
Arcturus! mourn, with all thy northern sons,
Daughters of Pleiades! that nightly shed
Sweet influence, and thou, fairest of stars!
Eye of the morning, weep! and weep at eve!
Weep setting, now to rise no more, "and flame
On forehead of the dawn,"—as sung the bard,
Great bard! who used on earth a seraph's lyre,
Whose numbers wandered through eternity,
And gave sweet foretaste of the heavenly harps!
Minstrel of sorrow! native of the dark,
Shrub-loving Philomel, that wooed the Dews,
At midnight from their starry beds, and, charmed,
Held them around thy song till dawn awoke,
Sad bird! pour through the gloom thy weeping song,
Pour all thy dying melody of grief,
And with the turtle spread the wave of wo!
Spare not thy reed, for thou shalt sing no more!

Ye holy bards!—if yet a holy bard
Remain—what chord shall serve you now! what harp!
What harp shall sing the dying Sun asleep,
And mourn behind the funeral of the Moon!
What harp of boundless, deep, exhaustless wo,
Shall utter forth the groanings of the damned!
And sing the obsequies of wicked souls!
And wail their plunge in the eternal fire!—
Hold, hold your hands! hold, angels!—God laments,
And draws a cloud of mourning round his throne!
The Organ of Eternity is mute!
And there is silence in the Heaven of Heavens!

Daughters of beauty! choice of beings made!
Much praised, much blamed, much loved; but fairer far
Than aught beheld, than aught imagined else
Fairest, and dearer than all else most dear;
Light of the darksome wilderness! to Time
As stars to night, whose eyes were spells that held
The passenger forgetful of his way,
Whose steps were majesty, whose words were song,
Whose smiles were hope, whose actions, perfect grace,
Whose love, the solace, glory, and delight
Of man, his boast, his riches, his renown;
When found, sufficient bliss! when lost, despair!—
Stars of creation! images of love!
Break up the fountains of your tears, your tears,
More eloquent than learned tongue, or lyre
Of purest note! your sunny raiment stain,
Put dust upon your heads, lament and weep,
And utter all your minstrelsy of wo!

Go to, ye wicked, weep and howl; for all
That God hath written against you is at hand.
The cry of Violence hath reached his ear,
Hell is prepared, and Justice whets his sword.
Weep all of every name! Begin the wo,
Ye woods, and tell it to the doleful winds;
And doleful winds, wail to the howling hills;
And howling hills, mourn to the dismal vales;
And dismal vales, sigh to the sorrowing brooks;
And sorrowing brooks, weep to the weeping stream
And weeping stream, awake the groaning deep;
And let the instrument take up the song,
Responsive to the voice, harmonious wo!
Ye Heavens, great arch-way of the universe,
Put sackcloth on; and Ocean, clothe thyself
In garb of widowhood, and gather all

Thy waves into a groan, and utter it,
Long, loud, deep, piercing, dolorous, immense:
The occasion asks it !—Nature dies, and God
And angels come to lay her in the grave!

But we have overleaped our theme; behind,
A little season waits a verse or two,
The years that followed the millennial rest.
Bad years they were; and first, as signal sure,
That at the core religion was diseased,
The sons of Levi strove again for place,
And eminence, and names of swelling pomp;
Setting their feet upon the people's neck,
And slumbering in the lap of civil power,
Of civil power again tyrannical:
And second sign, sure sign, whenever seen,
That holiness was dying in a land,
The Sabbath was profaned and set at naught;
The honest seer, who spoke the truth of God
Plainly, was left with empty walls; and round*
The frothy orator, who busked his tales
In quackish pomp of noisy word, the ear
Tickling, but leaving still the heart unprobed,
The judgment uninformed,—numbers immense
Flocked, gaping wide, with passions high inflamed;
And on the way returning, heated, home,
Of eloquence, and not of truth, conversed—
Mean eloquence that wanted sacred truth.

Two principles from the beginning strove
In human nature, still dividing man,—
Sloth and activity; the lust of praise,
And indolence that rather wished to sleep.
And not unfrequently in the same mind
They dubious contest held; one gaining now,
And now the other crowned, and both again

Keeping the field, with equal combat fought.
Much different was their voice. Ambition called
To action, sloth invited to repose.
Ambition early rose, and, being up,
Toiled ardently, and late retired to rest;
Sloth lay till mid-day, turning on his couch,
Like ponderous door upon its weary hinge,
And, having rolled him out with much ado,
And many a dismal sigh, and vain attempt,
He sauntered out, accoutred carelessly,—
With half-oped, misty, unobservant eye,
Somniferous, that weighed the object down
On which its burden fell,—an hour or two,
Then with a groan retired to rest again.
The one, whatever deed had been achieved,
Thought it too little, and too small the praise;
The other tried to think—for thinking so
Answered his purpose best—that what of great
Mankind could do had been already done;
And therefore laid him calmly down to sleep.

Different in mode, destructive both alike.
Destructive always indolence; and love
Of fame destructive always too, if less
Than praise of God it sought, content with less:
Even then not current, if it sought his praise
From other motive than resistless love;
Though base, main-spring of action in the world;
And, under name of vanity and pride,
Was greatly practised on by cunning men.
It opened the niggard's purse, clothed nakedness,
Gave beggars food, and threw the Pharisee
Upon his knees, and kept him long in act
Of prayer; it spread the lace upon the fop,
His language trimmed, and planned his curious gait;
It stuck the feather on the gay coquette,

And on her finger laid the heavy load
Of jewelry; it did—what did it not?
The gospel preached, the gospel paid, and sent
The gospel; conquered nations, cities built,
Measured the furrow of the field with nice
Directed share, shaped bulls, and cows, and rams,
And threw the ponderous stone; and, pitiful,
Indeed, and much against the grain, it dragged
The stagnant, dull, predestinated fool
Through learning's halls, and made him labor much
Abortively; though sometimes not unpraised
He left the sage's chair, and home returned,
Making his simple mother think that she
Had borne a man. In schools designed to root
Sin up, and plant the seeds of holiness
In youthful minds, it held a signal place.
The little infant man, by nature proud,
Was taught the Scriptures by the love of praise,
And grew religious as he grew in fame.
And thus the principle, which out of heaven
The devil threw, and threw him down to hell,
And keeps him there, was made an instrument
To moralize and sanctify mankind,
And in their hearts beget humility;
With what success it needs not now to say.

Destructive both we said, activity
And sloth: behold the last exemplified,
In literary man. Not all at once,
He yielded to the soothing voice of sleep;
But, having seen a bough of laurel wave,
He effort made to climb; and friends, and even
Himself, talked of his greatness, as at hand,
And, prophesying, drew his future life.
Vain prophecy! his fancy, taught by sloth,
Saw, in the very threshold of pursuit,

A thousand obstacles; he halted first,
And while he halted, saw his burning hopes
Grow dim and dimmer still; ambition's self,
The advocate of loudest tongue, decayed;
His purposes, made daily, daily broken,
Like plant uprooted oft, and set again,
More sickly grew, and daily wavered more;
Till at the last, decision, quite worn out,
Decision, fulcrum of the mental powers,
Resigned the blasted soul to staggering chance;
Sleep gathered fast, and weighed him downward still;
His eye fell heavy from the mount of fame;
His young resolves to benefit the world
Perished and were forgotten; he shut his ear
Against the painful news of rising worth;
And drank with desperate thirst the poppy's juice;
A deep and mortal slumber settled down
Upon his weary faculties oppressed;
He rolled from side to side, and rolled again;
And snored, and groaned, and withered and expired,
And rotted on the spot, leaving no name.

The hero best example gives of toil
Unsanctified. One word his history writes,
"He was a murderer above the laws,
And greatly praised for doing murderous deeds."
And now he grew, and reached his perfect growth;
And also now the sluggard soundest slept,
And by him lay the uninterred corpse.

Of every order, sin and wickedness,
Deliberate, cool, malicious villany,
This age, attained maturity, unknown
Before; and seemed in travail to bring forth
Some last, enormous, monstrous deed of guilt,
Original, unprecedented guilt,

That might obliterate the memory
Of what had hitherto been done most vile.
Inventive men were paid, at public cost,
To plan new modes of sin; the holy Word
Of God was burned, with acclamations loud;
New tortures were invented for the good;—
For still some good remained, as whiles through sky
Of thickest clouds, a wandering star appeared;—
New oaths of blasphemy were framed and sworn;
And men in reputation grew, as grew
The stature of their crimes. Faith was not found.
Truth was not found, truth always scarce, so scarce
That half the misery which groaned on earth,
In ordinary times, was progeny
Of disappointment, daily coming forth
From broken promises, that might have ne'er
Been made, or, being made, might have been kept;
Justice and mercy, too, were rare, obscured
In cottage garb: before the palace door,
The beggar rotted, starving in his rags;
And on the threshold of luxurious domes,
The orphan child laid down his head, and died;
Nor unamusing was his piteous cry
To women, who had now laid tenderness
Aside, best pleased with sights of cruelty;
Flocking, when fouler lusts would give them time,
To horrid spectacles of blood, where men,
Or guiltless beasts, that seemed to look to heaven,
With eye imploring vengeance on the earth,
Were tortured for the merriment of kings.
The advocate for him who offered most
Pleaded; the scribe, according to the hire,
Worded the lie, adding, for every piece,
An oath of confirmation; judges raised
One hand to intimate the sentence, death,
Imprisonment, or fine, or loss of goods,

And in the other held a lusty bribe,
Which they had taken to give the sentence wrong,
So managing the scale of justice still,
That he was wanting found who poorest seemed.

But laymen most renowned for devilish deeds,
Labored at distance still behind the priest;
He shore his sheep, and, having packed the wool,
Sent them unguarded to the hill of wolves;
And to the bowl deliberately sat down,
And with his mistress mocked at sacred things.

The theatre was, from the very first,
The favorite haunt of Sin, though honest men,
Some very honest, wise, and worthy men,
Maintained it might be turned to good account,
And so perhaps it might, but never was.
From first to last, it was an evil place:
And now such things were acted there, as made
The devils blush; and from the neighborhood,
Angels and holy men, trembling, retired:
And what with dreadful aggravation crowned
This dreary time, was sin against the light.
All men knew God, and, knowing, disobeyed;
And gloried to insult him to his face.

Another feature only we shall mark.
It was withal a highly polished age,
And scrupulous in ceremonious rite.
When stranger stranger met upon the way,
First, each to each bowed most respectfully,
And large profession made of humble service,
And then the stronger took the other's purse,
And he that stabbed his neighbor to the heart,
Stabbed him politely, and returned the blade
Reeking into its sheath with graceful air.

Meantime the earth gave symptoms of her end,
And all the scenery above proclaimed,
That the great last catastrophe was near.
The Sun at rising staggered and fell back,
As one too early up, after a night
Of late debauch; then rose, and shone again,
Brighter than wont; and sickened again, and paused
In zenith altitude, as one fatigued;
And shed a feeble twilight ray at noon,
Rousing the wolf before his time to chase
The shepherd and his sheep, that sought for light,
And darkness found, astonished, terrified;
Then, out of course, rolled furious down the west,
As chariot reined by awkward charioteer;
And, waiting at the gate, he on the earth
Gazed, as he thought he ne'er might see't again.
The bow of mercy, heretofore so fair,
Ribbed with the native hues of heavenly love,
Disastrous colors showed, unseen till now;
Changing upon the watery gulf, from pale
To fiery red, and back again to pale;
And o'er it hovered wings of wrath. The Moon
Swaggered in midst of heaven, grew black, and dark,
Unclouded, uneclipsed. The Stars fell down,
Tumbling from off their towers like drunken men,
Or seemed to fall; and glimmered now, and now
Sprang out in sudden blaze and dimmed again,
As lamp of foolish virgin lacking oil.
The heavens, this moment, looked serene; the next,
Glowed like an oven with God's displeasure hot.

Nor less, below, was intimation given,
Of some disaster great and ultimate.
The tree that bloomed, or hung with clustering fruit,
Untouched by visible calamity
Of frost or tempest, died and came again.

The flower and herb fell down as sick; then rose
And fell again. The fowls of every hue,
Crowding together, sailed on weary wing;
And, hovering, oft they seemed about to light;
Then soared, as if they thought the earth unsafe.
The cattle looked with meaning face on man.
Dogs howled, and seemed to see more than their masters.
And there were sights that none had seen before;
And hollow, strange, unprecedented sounds,
And earnest whisperings ran along the hills
At dead of night; and long, deep, endless sighs,
Came from the dreary vale; and from the waste
Came horrid shrieks, and fierce unearthly groans,
The wail of evil spirits, that now felt
The hour of utter vengeance near at hand.
The winds from every quarter blew at once,
With desperate violence, and, whirling, took
The traveller up, and threw him down again,
At distance from his path, confounded, pale;
And shapes, strange shapes! in winding sheets were seen,
Gliding through night, and singing funeral songs,
And imitating sad, sepulchral rites;
And voices talked among the clouds, and still
The words that men could catch were spoken of them,
And seemed to be the words of wonder great,
And expectation of some vast event.
Earth shook, and swam, and reeled, and opened her jaws,
By earthquake tossed, and tumbled to and fro;
And, louder than the ear of man had heard,
The Thunder bellowed, and the Ocean groaned.

The race of men, perplexed, but not reformed,
Flocking together, stood in earnest crowds,

Conversing of the awful state of things.
Some curious explanations gave, unlearned;
Some tried affectedly to laugh, and some
Gazed stupidly; but all were sad and pale,
And wished the comment of the wise. Nor less
These prodigies, occurring night and day,
Perplexed philosophy. The magi tried,—
Magi, a name not seldom given to fools,
In the vocabulary of earthly speech,—
They tried to trace them still to second cause,
But scarcely satisfied themselves; though round
Their deep deliberations, crowding came,
And, wondering at their wisdom, went away,
Much quieted and very much deceived,
The people, always glad to be deceived.

These warnings passed, they, unregarded, passed,
And all in wonted order calmly moved.
The pulse of Nature regularly beat,
And on her cheek the bloom of perfect health
Again appeared. Deceitful pulse! and bloom
Deceitful! and deceitful calm! The Earth
Was old, and worn within; but, like the man
Who noticed not his mid-day strength decline,
Sliding so gently round the curvature
Of life, from youth to age,—she knew it not.
The calm was like the calm, which oft the man,
Dying, experienced before his death;
The bloom was but a hectic flush, before
The eternal paleness. But all these were taken,
By this last race of men, for tokens of good;
And blustering public News aloud proclaimed—
News always gabbling ere they well had thought—
Prosperity, and joy, and peace; and mocked
The man who, kneeling, prayed, and trembled still;
And all in earnest to their sins returned.

It was not so in heaven. The elders round
The Throne conversed about the state of man,
Conjecturing—for none of certain knew—
That Time was at an end. They gazed intense
Upon the Dial's face, which yonder stands
In gold, before the Sun of Righteousness,
Jehovah, and computes time, seasons, years,
And destinies, and slowly numbers o'er
The mighty cycles of eternity;
By God alone completely understood,
But read by all, revealing much to all.
And now, to saints of eldest skill, the ray,
Which on the gnomon fell of Time, seemed sent
From level west, and hasting quickly down.
The holy Virtues, watching, saw, besides,
Great preparation going on in heaven,
Betokening great event, greater than aught
That first-created seraphim had seen.
The faithful messengers, who have for wing
The lightning, waiting, day and night, on God,
Before his face, beyond their usual speed,
On pinion of celestial light were seen,
Coming and going, and their road was still
From heaven to earth, and back again to heaven:
The angel of Mercy, bent before the Throne,
By earnest pleading, seemed to hold the hand
Of Vengeance back, and win a moment more
Of late repentance for some sinful world
In jeopardy: and now, the hill of God,
The mountain of his majesty, rolled flames
Of fire, now smiled with momentary love,
And now again with fiery fierceness burned;
And from behind the darkness of his Throne,
Through which created vision never saw,
The living Thunders, in their native caves,
Muttered the terrors of Omnipotence,

And ready seemed, impatient to fulfil
Some errand of exterminating wrath.

Meanwhile the Earth increased in wickedness,
And hasted daily to fill up her cup.
Satan raged loose, Sin had her will, and Death
Enough. Blood trode upon the heels of Blood,
Revenge, in desperate mood, at midnight met
Revenge, War brayed to War, Deceit deceived
Deceit, Lie cheated Lie, and Treachery
Mined under Treachery, and Perjury
Swore back on Perjury, and Blasphemy
Arose with hideous Blasphemy, and Curse
Loud answered Curse; and drunkard, stumbling, fell
O'er drunkard fallen; and husband husband met,
Returning each from other's bed defiled;
Thief stole from thief, and robber on the way
Knocked robber down, and Lewdness, Violence,
And Hate, met Lewdness, Violence, and Hate.
Oh, Earth! thy hour was come! the last elect
Was born, complete the number of the good,
And the last sand fell from the glass of Time.
The cup of guilt was full up to the brim;
And Mercy, weary with beseeching, had
Retired behind the sword of Justice, red
With ultimate and unrepenting wrath;
But man knew not: he o'er his bowl laughed loud,
And, prophesying, said, "To-morrow shall
As this day be, and more abundant still!"
As thou shalt hear—But, hark! the trumpet sounds,
And calls to evening song; for, though with hymn
Eternal, course succeeding course extol
In presence of the incarnate, holy God,
And celebrate his never-ending praise,—
Duly at morn and night, the multitudes
Of men redeemed, and angels, all the hosts

Of glory, join in universal song,
And pour celestial harmony, from harps
Above all number, eloquent and sweet,
Above all thought of melody conceived.
And now behold the fair inhabitants,
Delightful sight! from numerous business turn,
And round and round through all the extent of bliss
Towards the temple of Jehovah bow,
And worship reverently before his face!

Pursuits are various here, suiting all tastes,
Though holy all, and glorifying God.
Observe yon band pursue the sylvan stream:
Mounting among the cliffs, they pull the flower,
Springing as soon as pulled, and, marvelling, pry
Into its veins, and circulating blood,
And wondrous mimicry of higher life;
Admire its colors, fragrance, gentle shape;
And thence admire the God who made it so—
So simple, complex, and so beautiful.

Behold yon other band, in airy robes
Of bliss. They weave the sacred bower of rose
And myrtle shade, and shadowy verdant bay,
And laurel, towering high; and round their song,
The pink and lily bring, and amaranth,
Narcissus sweet, and jassamine; and bring
The clustering vine, stooping with flower and fruit,
The peach and orange, and the sparkling stream,
Warbling with nectar to their lips unasked;
And talk the while of everlasting love.

On yonder hill, behold another band,
Of piercing, steady, intellectual eye,
And spacious forehead of sublimest thought.
They reason deep of present, future, past;

And trace effect to cause; and meditate
On the eternal laws of God, which bind
Circumference to centre; and survey,
With optic tubes, that fetch remotest stars
Near them, the systems circling round immense
Innumerous. See how,—as he, the sage,
Among the most renowned in days of Time,
Renowned for large, capacious holy soul,
Demonstrates clearly motion, gravity,
Attraction and repulsion, still opposed;
And dips into the deep, original,
Unknown, mysterious elements of things,—
See how the face of every auditor
Expands with admiration of the skill,
Omnipotence, and boundless love of God!

These other, sitting near the tree of life,
In robes of linen flowing white and clean,
Of holiest aspect, of divinest soul,
Angels and men,—into the glory look
Of the Redeeming Love, and turn the leaves
Of man's redemption o'er, the secret leaves,
Which none on earth were found worthy to open;
And, as they read the mysteries divine,
The endless mysteries of salvation, wrought
By God's incarnate Son, they humbler bow
Before the Lamb, and glow with warmer love.

These other, there relaxed beneath the shade
Of yon embowering palms, with friendship smile,
And talk of ancient days, and young pursuits,
Of dangers passed, of godly triumphs won
And sing the legends of their native land,
Less pleasing far than this their Father's house.

Behold that other band, half lifted up
Between the hill and dale, reclined beneath

The shadow of impending rocks, 'mong streams,
And thundering waterfalls, and waving boughs;
That band of countenance sublime and sweet,
Whose eye, with piercing, intellectual ray,
Now beams severe, or now bewildered seems,
Left rolling wild, or fixed in idle gaze,
While Fancy and the Soul are far from home;
These hold the pencil, art divine! and throw
Before the eye remembered scenes of love;
Each picturing to each the hills, and skies,
And treasured stories of the world he left;
Or, gazing on the scenery of heaven,
They dip their hand in color's native well,
And, on the everlasting canvass, dash
Figures of glory, imagery divine,
With grace and grandeur in perfection knit.

But, whatso'er the spirits blessed pursue,
Where'er they go, whatever sights they see
Of glory and bliss through all the tracts of heaven,—
The centre, still, the figure eminent,
Whither they ever turn, on whom all eyes
Repose with infinite delight, is God
And his incarnate Son, the Lamb once slain
On Calvary, to ransom ruined men.

None idle here. Look where thou wilt, they all
Are active, all engaged in meet pursuit;
Not happy else. Hence is it that the song
Of heaven is ever new; for daily thus,
And nightly new discoveries are made
Of God's unbounded wisdom, power, and love,
Which give the understanding larger room,
And swell the hymn with ever-growing praise.

Behold they cease! and every face to God
Turns; and we pause from high poetic theme,

Not worthy least of being sung in heaven;
And on unveiled Godhead look from this,
Our oft frequented hill. He takes the harp,
Nor needs to seek befitting phrase: unsought,
Numbers harmonious roll along the lyre;
As river in its native bed, they flow
Spontaneous, flowing with the tide of thought.
He takes the harp—a bard of Judah leads,
This night, the boundless song, the bard that once,
When Israel's king was sad and sick to death,
A message brought of fifteen added years.
Before the Throne he stands sublime, in robes
Of glory; and now his fingers wake the chords
To praise, which we and all in heaven repeat.

Harps of Eternity! begin the song,
Redeemed and angel harps! begin to God,
Begin the anthem ever sweet and new,
While I extol Him, holy, just, and good.
Life, beauty, light, intelligence, and love
Eternal, uncreated, infinite!
Unsearchable Jehovah! God of truth!
Maker, upholder, governor of all!
Thyself unmade, ungoverned, unupheld!
Omnipotent, unchangeable, Great God!
Exhaustless fulness! giving unimpaired!
Bounding immensity, unspread, unbound!
Highest and best! beginning, middle, end!
All-seeing Eye! all-seeing, and unseen!
Hearing, unheard! all-knowing, and unknown!
Above all praise! above all height of thought!
Proprietor of immortality!
Glory ineffable! bliss underived!
Of old thou buildst thy throne on righteousness,
Before the morning Stars their song began,

Or silence heard the voice of praise. Thou laidst
Eternity's foundation stone, and sawst
Life and existence out of Thee begin.
Mysterious more, the more displayed, where still
Upon thy glorious Throne thou sitst alone,
Hast sat alone, and shalt for ever sit
Alone, Invisible, Immortal One!
Behind essential brightness unbeheld.
Incomprehensible! what weight shall weigh,
What measure measure Thee! What know we more
Of Thee, what need to know, than Thou hast taught,
And bidst us still repeat, at morn and even?—
God! Everlasting Father! Holy One!
Our God, our Father, our Eternal All!
Source whence we came, and whither we return;
Who made our spirits, who our bodies made,
Who made the heaven, who made the flowery land,
Who made all made, who orders, governs all,
Who walks upon the wind, who holds the wave
In hollow of thy hand, whom thunders wait,
Whom tempests serve, whom flaming fires obey,
Who guides the circuit of the endless years,
And sitst on high, and makest creation's top
Thy footstool, and beholdst, below Thee, all—
All naught, all less than naught, and vanity.
Like transient dust that hovers on the scale,
Ten thousand worlds are scattered in thy breath.
Thou sitst on high, and measurest destinies,
And days, and months, and wide-revolving years,
And dost according to thy holy will;
And none can stay thy hand, and none withhold
Thy glory; for in judgment, Thou, as well
As mercy, art exalted, day and night.
Past, present, future, magnify thy name.
Thy works all praise Thee, all thy angels praise,
Thy saints adore, and on thv altars burn

The fragrant incense of perpetual love.
They praise Thee now, their hearts, their voices
praise,
And swell the rapture of the glorious song.
Harp ! lift thy voice on high ! shout, angels, shout !
And loudest, ye redeemed ! glory to God,
And to the Lamb who bought us with his blood,
From every kindred, nation, people, tongue ;
And washed, and sanctified, and saved our souls ;
And gave us robes of linen pure, and crowns
Of life, and made us kings and priests to God.
Shout back to ancient Time ! Sing loud, and wave
Your palms of triumph ! sing, Where is thy sting,
O Death ! where is thy victory, O Grave !
Thanks be to God, eternal thanks, who gave
Us victory through Jesus Christ, Our Lord.
Harp ! lift thy voice on high ! shout, angels, shout !
And loudest, ye redeemed ! glory to God,
And to the Lamb, all glory and all praise,
All glory and all praise, at morn and even,
That come and go eternally, and find
Us happy still, and Thee for ever blessed !
Glory to God and to the Lamb. Amen.
For ever, and for evermore. Amen.

And those who stood upon the sea of glass,
And those who stood upon the battlements
And lofty towers of New Jerusalem,
And those who circling stood, bowing afar,
Exalted on the everlasting hills,
Thousands of thousands, thousands infinite,
With voice of boundless love, answered, Amen.
And through Eternity, near and remote,
The worlds, adoring, echoed back, Amen ;
And God the Father, Son, and Holy Ghost,
The One Eternal, smiled superior bliss !

And every eye, and every face in heaven,
Reflecting and reflected, beamed with love.

Nor did he not, the Virtue new arrived,
From Godhead gain an individual smile,
Of high acceptance, and of welcome high,
And confirmation evermore in good.
Meantime the landscape glowed with holy joy.
Zephyr, with wing dipped from the well of life,
Sporting through Paradise, shed living dews;
The flowers, the spicy shrubs, the lawns, refreshed,
Breathed their selectest balm, breathed odors, such
As angels love; and all the trees of heaven,
The cedar, pine, and everlasting oak,
Rejoicing on the mountains, clapped their hands.

THE

COURSE OF TIME.

BOOK VII.

ANALYSIS OF BOOK VII.

After the Hymn of praise, the Bard resumes his story. He relates the destruction of the Earth, the Resurrection of the dead, and the Transformation of the living.

On the morn of the final day every appearance of Nature was as usual; but at mid-day universal darkness prevailed, and every action and motion ceased; an Angel from Heaven proclaimed the end of Time, and another blew the Trump of God, at which the dead awoke and the living were changed.

The remainder of the Book is occupied with a description of circumstances connected with the momentous scene; the living surprised in the midst of their thousand various occupations of study, labor, pleasure, crime; the dead of every age and nation springing to life, in the wilderness, the cultivated field, amid ancient ruins, in the streets of populous cities, from the depths of the mighty waters.

THE

COURSE OF TIME.

BOOK VII.

As one who meditates at evening tide,
Wandering alone by voiceless solitudes,
And flies, in fancy, far beyond the bounds
Of visible and vulgar things, and things
Discovered hitherto, pursuing tracts
As yet untravelled and unknown, through vast
Of new and sweet imaginings; if chance
Some airy harp, waked by the gentle sprites
Of twilight, or light touch of sylvan maid,
In soft succession fall upon his ear,
And fill the desert with its heavenly tones;
He listens intense, and pleased exceedingly,
And wishes it may never stop; yet when
It stops, grieves not; but to his former thoughts
With fondest haste returns: so did the Seer,
So did his audience, after worship passed,
And praise in heaven, return to sing, to hear
Of man, not worthy less the sacred lyre,
Or the attentive ear; and thus the bard,
Not unbesought, again resumed his song.

In customed glory bright, that morn, the Sun
Rose, visiting the earth with light and heat,
And joy; and seemed as full of youth and strong
To mount the steep of heaven, as when the Stars

Of morning sung to his first dawn, and night
Fled from his face; the spacious sky received
Him, blushing as a bride, when on her looked
The bridegroom; and, spread out beneath his eye,
Earth smiled. Up to his warm embrace, the Dews,
That all night long had wept his absence, flew;
The herbs and flowers their fragrant stores unlocked,
And gave the wanton breeze, that, newly woke,
Revelled in sweets, and from its wings shook health,
A thousand grateful smells; the joyous woods
Dried in his beams their locks, wet with the drops
Of night; and all the sons of music sung
Their matin song—from arbored bower, the thrush,
Concerting with the lark that hymned on high.
On the green hill the flocks, and in the vale
The herds, rejoiced; and, light of heart, the hind
Eyed amorously the milk-maid as she passed,
Not heedless, though she looked another way.

No sign was there of change. All nature moved
In wonted harmony. Men, as they met,
In morning salutation, praised the day,
And talked of common things. The husbandman
Prepared the soil, and silver-tongued Hope
Promised another harvest. In the streets,
Each wishing to make profit of his neighbor,
Merchants, assembling, spoke of trying times,
Of bankruptcies, and markets glutted full,
Or, crowding to the beach,—where, to their ear,
The oath of foreign accent, and the noise
Uncouth of trade's rough sons, made music sweet,
Elate with certain gain,—beheld the bark,
Expected long, enriched with other climes,
Into the harbor safely steer; or saw,
Parting with many a weeping farewell sad,
And blessing uttered rude, and sacred pledge,

The rich-laden carack, bound to distant shore,
And hopefully talked of her coming back,
With richer freight; or sitting at the desk,
In calculation deep and intricate
Of loss and profit balancing, relieved,
At intervals, the irksome task, with thought
Of future ease, retired in villa snug.

With subtle look, amid his parchments, sat
The lawyer, weaving his sophistries for court
To meet at mid-day. On his weary couch,
Fat Luxury, sick of the night's debauch,
Lay groaning, fretful at the obtrusive beam,
That through his lattice peeped derisively.
The restless miser had begun again
To count his heaps. Before her toilet stood
The fair, and, as with guileful skill she decked
Her loveliness, thought of the coming ball,
New lovers, or the sweeter nuptial night.
And evil men, of desperate, lawless life,
By oath of deep damnation leagued to ill,
Remorselessly, fled from the face of day,
Against the innocent their counsel held,
Plotting unpardonable deeds of blood,
And villanies of fearful magnitude.
Despots, secured behind a thousand bolts,
The workmanship of fear, forged chains for man.
Senates were meeting, statesmen loudly talked
Of national resources, war and peace,
And sagely balanced empires soon to end;
And faction's jaded minions, by the page
Paid for abuse and oft-repeated lies,
In daily prints, the thoroughfare of news,
For party schemes, made interest, under cloak
Of liberty, and right, and public weal.
In holy conclave, bishops spoke of tithes,

And of the awful wickedness of men.
Intoxicate with sceptres, diadems,
And universal rule, and panting hard
For fame, heroes were leading on the brave
To battle. Men, in science deeply read,
And academic theory, foretold
Improvements vast; and learned sceptics proved
That earth should with eternity endure—
Concluding madly, that there was no God.

No sign of change appeared: to every man
That day seemed as the past. From noontide path
The sun looked gloriously on earth, and all
Her scenes of giddy folly smiled secure,
When suddenly, alas, fair earth! the sun
Was wrapped in darkness, and his beams returned
Up to the throne of God, and over all
The earth came night, moonless and starless night.
Nature stood still. The seas and rivers stood,
And all the winds and every living thing.
The cataract, that, like a giant wroth,
Rushed down impetuously, as seized at once,
By sudden frost, with all his hoary locks,
Stood still; and beasts of every kind stood still.
A deep and dreadful silence reigned alone!
Hope died in every breast, and on all men
Came fear and trembling. None to his neighbor spoke.
Husband thought not of wife, nor of her child
The mother, nor friend of friend, nor foe of foe.
In horrible suspense all mortals stood;
And, as they stood and listened, chariots were heard
Rolling in heaven. Revealed in flaming fire,
The angel of God appeared in stature vast,
Blazing, and, lifting up his hand on high,
By Him that lives for ever, swore, that Time
Should be no more. Throughout, creation heard

And sighed; all rivers, lakes, and seas, and woods,
Desponding waste, and cultivated vale,
Wild cave, and ancient hill, and every rock,
Sighed. Earth, arrested in her wonted path,
As ox struck by the lifted axe, when naught
Was feared, in all her entrails deeply groaned.
A universal crash was heard, as if
The ribs of Nature broke, and all her dark
Foundations failed; and deadly paleness sat
On every face of man, and every heart
Grew chill, and every knee his fellow smote.
None spoke, none stirred, none wept; for horror held
All motionless, and fettered every tongue.
Again, o'er all the nations silence fell:
And, in the heavens, robed in excessive light,
That drove the thick of darkness far aside,
And walked with penetration keen, through all
The abodes of men, another angel stood,
And blew the trump of God: Awake, ye dead,
Be changed, ye living, and put on the garb
Of immortality. Awake, arise!—
The God of judgment comes! This said the voice,
And Silence, from eternity that slept
Beyond the sphere of the creating Word,
And all the noise of Time, awakened, heard.
Heaven heard, and earth, and farthest hell, through all
Her regions of despair; the ear of Death
Heard, and the sleep that for so long a night
Pressed on his leaden eyelids, fled; and all
The dead awoke, and all the living changed.

Old men, that on their staff, bending, had leaned,
Crazy and frail, or sat, benumbed with age,
In weary listlessness, ripe for the grave,
Felt through their sluggish veins and withered limbs,

New vigor flow; the wrinkled face grew smooth;
Upon the head, that Time had razored bare,
Rose bushy locks; and as his son in prime
Of strength and youth, the aged father stood.
Changing herself, the mother saw her son
Grow up, and suddenly put on the form
Of manhood; and the wretch that begging sat,
Limbless, deformed, at corner of the way,
Unmindful of his crutch, in joint and limb,
Arose complete; and he, that on the bed
Of mortal sickness, worn with sore distress,
Lay breathing forth his soul to death, felt now
The tide of life and vigor rushing back;
And, looking up, beheld his weeping wife,
And daughter fond, that o'er him, bending, stooped
To close his eyes. The frantic madman, too,
In whose confused brain reason had lost
Her way, long driven at random to and fro,
Grew sober, and his manacles fell off.
The newly-sheeted corpse arose, and stared
On those who dressed it; and the coffined dead,
That men were bearing to the tomb, awoke,
And mingled with their friends; and armies, which
The trump surprised, met in the furious shock
Of battle, saw the bleeding ranks, new fallen,
Rise up at once, and to their ghastly cheeks
Return the stream of life in healthy flow;
And as the anatomist, with all his band
Of rude disciples, o'er the subject hung,
And impolitely hewed his way, through bones
And muscles of the sacred human form,
Exposing barbarously to wanton gaze,
The mysteries of nature, joint embraced
His kindred joint, the wounded flesh grew up,
And suddenly the injured man awoke,
Among their hands, and stood arrayed complete

In immortality—forgiving scarce
The insult offered to his clay in death.

That was the hour, long wished for by the good,
Of universal jubilee to all
The sons of bondage; from the oppressor's hand
The scourge of violence fell, and from his back,
Healed of its stripes, the burden of the slave.

The youth of great religious soul, who sat
Retired in voluntary loneliness,
In reverie extravagant now wrapped,
Or poring now on book of ancient date,
With filial awe, and dipping oft his pen
To write immortal things; to pleasure deaf,
And joys of common men, working his way
With mighty energy, not uninspired,
Through all the mines of thought; reckless of pain,
And weariness, and wasted health, the scoff
Of Pride, or growl of Envy's hellish brood;
While Fancy, voyaged far beyond the bounds
Of years revealed, heard many a future age,
With commendation loud, repeat his name,—
False prophetess! the day of change was come,—
Behind the shadow of eternity,
He saw his visions set of earthly fame,
For ever set; nor sighed, while through his veins,
In lighter current, ran immortal life;
His form renewed to undecaying health;
To undecaying health his soul, erewhile
Not tuned amiss to God's eternal praise.

All men, in field and city, by the way,
On land or sea, lolling in gorgeous hall,
Or plying at the oar; crawling in rags
Obscure, or dazzling in embroidered gold;

Alone, in companies, at home, abroad;
In wanton merriment surprised and taken,
Or kneeling reverently in act of prayer;
Or cursing recklessly, or uttering lies;
Or lapping greedily, from slander's cup,
The blood of reputation; or between
Friendships and brotherhoods devising strife;
Or plotting to defile a neighbor's bed;
In duel met with dagger of revenge;
Or casting on the widow's heritage
The eye of covetousness; or, with full hand,
On mercy's noiseless errands, unobserved,
Administering; or meditating fraud
And deeds of horrid barbarous intent;
In full pursuit of unexperienced hope,
Fluttering along the flowery path of youth;
Or steeped in disappointment's bitterness,
The fevered cup that guilt must ever drink,
When parched and fainting on the road of ill;
Beggar and king, the clown and haughty lord;
The venerable sage, and empty fop;
The ancient matron, and the rosy bride;
The virgin chaste, and shrivelled harlot vile;
The savage fierce, and man of science mild;
The good and evil, in a moment, all
Were changed, corruptible to incorrupt,
And mortal to immortal, ne'er to change.

And now, descending from the bowers of heaven,
Soft airs o'er all the earth, spreading, were heard,
And Hallelujahs sweet, the harmony
Of righteous souls that came to repossess
Their long neglected bodies: and anon
Upon the ear fell horribly the sound
Of cursing, and the yells of damned despair,
Uttered by felon spirits, that the trump

Had summoned from the burning glooms of hell
To put their bodies on, reserved for wo.

Now, starting up among the living changed,
Appeared innumerous the risen dead.
Each particle of dust was claimed: the turf,
For ages trod beneath the careless foot
Of men, rose, organized in human form;
The monumental stones were rolled away;
The doors of death were opened; and in the dark
And loathsome vault, and silent charnel house,
Moving, were heard the mouldered bones, that sought
Their proper place. Instinctive, every soul
Flew to its clayey part; from grass-grown mould,
The nameless spirit took its ashes up,
Reanimate; and, merging from beneath
The flattered marble, undistinguished rose
The great, nor heeded once the lavish rhyme,
And costly pomp of sculptured garnish vain.
The Memphian mummy, that, from age to age
Descending, bought and sold a thousand times,
In hall of curious antiquary stowed,
Wrapped in mysterious weeds, the wondrous theme
Of many an erring tale, shook off its rags;
And the brown son of Egypt stood beside
The European, his last purchaser.
In vale remote, the hermit rose, surprised
At crowds that rose around him, where he thought
His slumbers had been single; and the bard,
Who fondly covenanted with his friend,
To lay his bones beneath the sighing bough
Of some old lonely tree, rising, was pressed
By multitudes that claimed their proper dust
From the same spot; and he, that, richly hearsed,
With gloomy garniture of purchased wo,
Embalmed, in princely sepulchre was laid,

Apart from vulgar men, built nicely round
And round by the proud heir, who blushed to think
His father's lordly clay should ever mix
With peasant dust,—saw by his side awake
The clown that long had slumbered in his arms.

The family tomb, to whose devouring mouth
Descended sire and son, age after age,
In long, unbroken, hereditary line,
Poured forth at once, the ancient father rude,
And all his offspring of a thousand years.
Refreshed from sweet repose, awoke the man
Of charitable life—awoke and sung:
And from his prison house, slowly and sad,
As if unsatisfied with holding near
Communion with the earth, the miser drew
His carcass forth, and gnashed his teeth, and howled,
Unsolaced by his gold and silver then.
From simple stone in lonely wilderness,
That hoary lay, o'er-lettered by the hand
Of oft-frequenting pilgrim, who had taught
The willow tree to weep, at morn and even,
Over the sacred spot,—the martyr saint,
To song of seraph harp, triumphant, rose,
Well pleased that he had suffered to the death.
"The cloud-capped towers, the gorgeous palaces,"
As sung the bard by Nature's hand anointed,
In whose capacious giant numbers rolled
The passions of old Time, fell lumbering down.
All cities fell, and every work of man,
And gave their portion forth of human dust,
Touched by the mortal finger of decay.
Tree, herb, and flower, and every fowl of heaven,
And fish, and animal, the wild and tame,
Forthwith dissolving, crumbled into dust.

Alas! ye sons of strength, ye ancient oaks,
Ye holy pines, ye elms, and cedars tall,
Like towers of God, far seen on Carmel mount,
Or Lebanon, that waved your boughs on high,
And laughed at all the winds,—your hour was come!
Ye laurels, ever green, and bays, that wont
To wreath the patriot's and the poet's brow,
Ye myrtle bowers, and groves of sacred shade,
Where Music ever sung, and Zephyr fanned
His airy wing, wet with the dews of life,
And Spring forever smiled, the fragrant haunt
Of Love, and Health, and ever-dancing Mirth,—
Alas! how suddenly your verdure died,
And ceased your minstrelsy, to sing no more!
Ye flowers of beauty, penciled by the hand
Of God, who annually renewed your birth,
To gem the virgin robes of Nature chaste,
Ye smiling-featured daughters of the Sun!
Fairer than queenly bride, by Jordan's stream
Leading your gentle lives, retired, unseen;
Or on the sainted cliffs on Zion hill
Wandering, and holding with the heavenly dews,
In holy revelry, your nightly loves,
Watched by the stars, and offering, every morn,
Your incense, grateful both to God and man;—
Ye lovely, gentle things, alas! no spring
Shall ever wake you now! ye withered all!
All in a moment drooped, and on your roots
The grasp of everlasting winter seized!
Children of song, ye birds that dwelt in air,
And stole your notes from angel's lyres, and first
In levee of the morn, with eulogy
Ascending, hailed the advent of the dawn;
Or, roosted on the pensive evening bough,
In melancholy numbers, sung the day
To rest;—your little wings, failing, dissolved,

In middle air, and on your harmony
Perpetual silence fell! Nor did his wing,
That sailed in track of gods sublime, and fanned
The sun, avail the eagle then; quick smitten,
His plumage withered in meridian height,
And, in the valley, sunk the lordly bird,
A clod of clay. Before the ploughman fell
His steers, and in midway the furrow left.
The shepherd saw his flocks around him turn
To dust. Beneath his rider fell the steed
To ruins; and the lion in his den
Grew cold and stiff, or in the furious chase,
With timid fawn, that scarcely missed his paws.
On earth no living thing was seen but men,
New-changed, or rising from the opening tomb.

Athens, and Rome, and Babylon, and Tyre,
And she that sat on Thames, queen of the seas,
Cities once famed on earth, convulsed through all
Their mighty ruins, threw their millions forth.
Palmyra's dead, where Desolation sat,
From age to age, well pleased, in solitude,
And silence, save when traveller's foot, or owl
Of night, or fragment mouldering down to dust,
Broke faintly on his desert ear,—awoke.
And Salem, holy city! where the Prince
Of Life, by death, a second life secured
To man, and with him, from the grave, redeemed,
A chosen number brought, to retinue
His great ascent on high, and give sure pledge,
That death was foiled,—her generations, now,
Gave up, of kings and priests, and Pharisees;
Nor even the Sadducee, who fondly said,
No morn of resurrection e'er should come,
Could sit the summons; to his ear did reach
The trumpet's voice, and, ill prepared for what

He oft had proved should never be, he rose
Reluctantly, and on his face began
To burn eternal shame. The cities, too,
Of old, ensepulchred beneath the flood,
Or deeply slumbering under mountains huge,
That Earthquake, servant of the wrath of God,
Had on her wicked population thrown;
And marts of busy trade, long ploughed and sown,
By history unrecorded, or the song
Of bard, yet not forgotten their wickedness,
In heaven;—poured forth their ancient multitudes,
That vainly wished their sleep had never broke.
From battle-fields, where men by millions met
To murder each his fellow, and make sport
To kings and heroes, things long since forgot,
Innumerous armies rose, unbannered all,
Unpanoplied, unpraised; nor found a prince,
Or general, then, to answer for their crimes.
The hero's slaves, and all the scarlet troops
Of antichrist, and all that fought for rule,—
Many high-sounding names, familiar once
On earth, and praised exceedingly, but now
Familiar most in hell, their dungeon fit,
Where they may war eternally with God's
Almighty thunderbolts, and win them pangs
Of keener wo,—saw, as they sprung to life,
The widow and the orphan ready stand,
And helpless virgin, ravished in their sport,
To plead against them at the coming doom.
The Roman legions, boasting once, how loud!
Of liberty, and fighting bravely o'er
The torrid and the frigid zone, the sands
Of burning Egypt, and the frozen hills
Of snowy Albion, to make mankind
Their thralls, untaught that he who made or kept
A slave could ne'er himself be truly free,—

That morning, gathered up their dust, which lay
Wide-scattered over half the globe; nor saw
Their eagled banners then. Sennacherib's hosts,
Embattled once against the sons of God,
With insult bold, quick as the noise of mirth
And revelry, sunk in their drunken camp,
When death's dark angel, at the dead of night,
Their vitals touched, and made each pulse stand still:
Awoke in sorrow; and the multitudes
Of Gog, and all the fated crew that warred
Against the chosen saints, in the last days,
At Armageddon, when the Lord came down,
Mustering his host on Israel's holy hills,
And, from the treasures of his snow and hail,
Rained terror, and confusion rained, and death,
And gave to all the beasts, and fowls of heaven,
Of captains' flesh, and blood of men of war,
A feast of many days,—revived, and, doomed
To second death, stood in Hamonah's vale.

Nor yet did all that fell in battle rise,
That day, to wailing. Here and there were seen
The patriot bands that from his guilty throne
The despot tore, unshackled nations, made
The prince respect the people's laws, drove back
The wave of proud invasion, and rebuked
The frantic fury of the multitude,
Rebelled, and fought and fell for liberty
Right understood, true heroes in the speech
Of heaven, where words express the thoughts of him
Who speaks; not undistinguished, these, though few,
That morn, arose, with joy and melody.

All woke—the north and south gave up their dead.
The caravan, that in mid-journey sunk,
With all its merchandise, expected long,

And long forgot, ingulfed beneath the tide
Of death, that the wild Spirit of the winds
Swept, in his wrath, along the wilderness,
In the wide desert,—woke, and saw all calm
Around, and populous with risen men;
Nor of his relics thought the pilgrim then,
Nor merchant of his silks and spiceries.

And he, far voyaging from home and friends,
Too curious, with a mortal eye to peep
Into the secrets of the Pole, forbid
By nature, whom fierce Winter seized, and froze
To death, and wrapped in winding sheet of ice,
And sung the requiem of his shivering ghost,
With the loud organ of his mighty winds,
And on his memory threw the snow of ages,—
Felt the long-absent warmth of life return,
And shook the frozen mountain from his bed.

All rose, of every age, of every clime.
Adam and Eve, the great progenitors
Of all mankind, fair as they seemed, that morn,
When first they met in Paradise, unfallen,
Uncursed,—from ancient slumber broke, where once,
Euphrates rolled his stream; and by them stood,
In stature equal, and in soul as large,
Their last posterity, though poets sung,
And sages proved them far degenerate.

Blessed sight! not unobserved by angels, nor
Unpraised,—that day, 'mong men of every tribe
And hue, from those who drank of Tenglio's stream
To those who nightly saw the Hermit Cross,
In utmost south retired,—rising, were seen
The fair and ruddy sons of Albion's land,
How glad!—not those who travelled far, and sailed,

To purchase human flesh, or wreath the yoke
Of vassalage on savage liberty,
Or suck large fortune from the sweat of slaves;
Or, with refined knavery, to cheat,
Politely villanous, untutored men
Out of their property; or gather shells,
Intaglios rude, old pottery, and store
Of mutilated gods of stone, and scraps
Of barbarous epitaphs defaced, to be
Among the learned the theme of warm debate,
And infinite conjecture, sagely wrong!—
But those, denied to self, to earthly fame
Denied, and earthly wealth; who kindred left,
And home, and ease, and all the cultured joys,
Conveniences, and delicate delights,
Of ripe society; in the great cause
Of man's salvation greatly valorous,—
The warriors of Messiah, messengers
Of peace, and light, and life, whose eye, unscaled,
Saw up the path of immortality,
Far into bliss, saw men, immortal men,
Wide wandering from the way: eclipsed in night,
Dark, moonless, moral night; living like beasts,
Like beasts descending to the grave, untaught
Of life to come, unsanctified, unsaved;
Who, strong, though seeming weak; who, warlike though
Unarmed with bow and sword; appearing mad,
Though sounder than the schools alone e'er made
The doctor's head; devote to God and truth,
And sworn to man's eternal weal, beyond
Repentance sworn, or thought of turning back;
And casting far behind all earthly care,
All countryships, all national regards,
And enmities, all narrow bourns of state
And selfish policy; beneath their feet

Treading all fear of opposition down,
All fear of danger, of reproach all fear,
And evil tongues; went forth, from Britain went,
A noiseless band of heavenly soldiery,
From out the armory of God equipped
Invincible, to conquer sin, to blow
The trump of freedom in the despot's ear,
To tell the bruted slave his manhood high,
His birthright liberty, and in his hand
To put the writ of manumission, signed
By God's own signature; to drive away
From earth the dark, infernal legionry
Of superstition, ignorance, and hell;
High on the pagan hills, where Satan sat,
Encamped, and o'er the subject kingdoms threw
Perpetual night, to plant Immanuel's cross,
The ensign of the Gospel blazing round
Immortal truth; and, in the wilderness
Of human waste, to sow eternal life;
And from the rock, were Sin, with horrid yell,
Devoured its victims unredeemed, to raise
The melody of grateful hearts to Heaven:
To falsehood, truth; to pride, humility;
To insult, meekness; pardon to revenge;
To stubborn prejudice, unwearied zeal;
To censure, unaccusing minds; to stripes,
Long suffering; to want of all things, hope;
To death, assured faith of life to come;—
Opposing. These great worthies, rising, shone
Through all the tribes and nations of mankind,
Like Hesper, glorious once among the stars
Of twilight, and around them, flocking, stood,
Arrayed in white, the people they had saved.

Great Ocean! too, that morning, thou the call
Of restitution heardst, and reverently

To the last trumpet's voice, in silence, listened.
Great Ocean! strongest of creation's sons!
Unconquerable, unreposed, untired,
That rolled the wild, profound, eternal bass,
In Nature's anthem, and made music, such
As pleased the ear of God! original,
Unmarred, unfaded work of Deity,
And unburlesqued by mortal's puny skill,
From age to age enduring and unchanged,
Majestical, inimitable, vast;
Loud uttering satire, day and night, on each
Succeeding race, and little pompous work
Of man!—unfallen, religious, holy Sea!
Thou bowedst thy glorious head to none, fearedst none,
Heardst none, to none didst honor, but to God
Thy Maker, only worthy to receive
Thy great obeisance! Undiscovered Sea!
Into thy dark, unknown, mysterious caves,
And secret haunts, unfathomably deep
Beneath all visible retired, none went,
And came again, to tell the wonders there.
Tremendous Sea! what time thou lifted up
Thy waves on high, and with thy winds and storms
Strange pastime took, and shook thy mighty sides
Indignantly,—the pride of navies fell;
Beyond the arm of help, unheard, unseen,
Sunk friend and foe, with all their wealth and war;
And on thy shores, men of a thousand tribes,
Polite and barbarous, trembling stood, amazed,
Confounded, terrified, and thought vast thoughts
Of ruin, boundlessness, omnipotence,
Infinitude, eternity; and thought

And wondered still, and grasped, and grasped, and grasped
Again; beyond her reach, exerting all
The soul, to take thy great idea in,
To comprehend incomprehensible;
And wondered more, and felt their littleness,
Self-purifying, unpolluted Sea!
Lover unchangeable, thy faithful breast
For ever heaving to the lovely Moon,
That, like a shy and holy virgin, robed
In saintly white, walked nightly in the heavens,
And to the everlasting serenade
Gave gracious audience; nor was wooed in vain.
That morning, thou, that slumbered not before,
Nor slept, great Ocean! laid thy waves to rest,
And hushed thy mighty minstrelsy. No breath
Thy deep composure stirred, no fin, no oar;
Like beauty newly dead, so calm, so still,
So lovely, thou, beneath the light that fell
From angel-chariots, sentinelled on high,
Reposed, and listened, and saw thy living change,
Thy dead arise. Charybdis listened, and Scylla;
And savage Euxine, on the Thracian beach,
Lay motionless: and every battle-ship
Stood still, and every ship of merchandise,
And all that sailed, of every name, stood still.
Even as the ship of war, full fledged, and swift,
Like some fierce bird of prey, bore on her foe,
Opposing with as fell intent, the wind
Fell withered from her wings that idly hung;
The stormy bullet, by the cannon thrown
Uncivilly against the heavenly face
Of men, half sped, sunk harmlessly, and all
Her loud, uncircumcised, tempestuous crew,
How ill prepared to meet their God! — were changed,

Unchangeable—the pilot at the helm
Was changed, and the rough captain, while he
mouthed
The huge, enormous oath. The fisherman,
That in his boat, expectant, watched his lines,
Or mended on the shore his net, and sung,
Happy in thoughtlessness, some careless air,
Heard Time depart, and felt the sudden change.
In solitary deep, far out from land,
Or steering from the port with many a cheer,
Or while returning from long voyage, fraught
With lusty wealth, rejoicing to have escaped
The dangerous main, and plagues of foreign
climes,—
The merchant quaffed his native air, refreshed;
And saw his native hills in the sun's light,
Serenely rise; and thought of meetings glad,
And many days of ease and honor, spent
Among his friends—unwarned man! even then,
The knell of Time broke on his reverie,
And, in the twinkling of an eye, his hopes,
All earthly, perished all. As sudden rose,
From out their watery beds, the Ocean's dead,
Renewed; and, on the unstirring billows, stood
From pole to pole, thick covering all the sea—
Of every nation blent, and every age.

Wherever slept one grain of human dust,
Essential organ of a human soul,
Wherever tossed, obedient to the call
Of God's omnipotence, it hurried on
To meet its fellow particles, revived,
Rebuilt, in union indestructible.
No atom of his spoils remained to Death.
From his strong arm, by stronger arm released,
Immortal now in soul and body both,

Beyond his reach, stood all the sons of men,
And saw, behind, his valley lie, unfeared.

O Death! with what an eye of desperate lust,
From out thy emptied vaults, thou then didst look
After the risen multitudes of all
Mankind! Ah! thou hadst been the terror long,
And murderer, of all of woman born.
None could escape thee! In thy dungeon house,
Where darkness dwelt, and putrid loathsomeness,
And fearful silence, villanously still,
And all of horrible and deadly name,—
Thou satst, from age to age, insatiate,
And drank the blood of men, and gorged their flesh,
And with thy iron teeth didst grind their bones
To powder, treading out, beneath thy feet,
Their very names and memories. The blood
Of nations could not slake thy parched throat.
No bribe could buy thy favor for an hour,
Or mitigate thy ever-cruel rage
For human prey. Gold, beauty, virtue, youth,
Even helpless, swaddled innocency, failed
To soften thy heart of stone! the infant's blood
Pleased well thy taste, and while the mother wept,
Bereaved by thee, lonely and waste in wo,
Thy ever-grinding jaws devoured her too.

Each son of Adam's family beheld,
Where'er he turned, whatever path of life
He trode, thy goblin form before him stand,
Like trusty old assassin, in his aim
Steady and sure as eye of destiny,
With scythe, and dart, and strength invincible,
Equipped, and ever menacing his life.

He turned aside, he drowned himself in sleep,
In wine, in pleasure; travelled, voyaged, sought
Receipts for health from all he met; betook
To business, speculate, retired; returned
Again to active life, again retired;
Returned, retired again; prepared to die,
Talked of thy nothingness, conversed of life
To come, laughed at his fears, filled up the cup,
Drank deep, refrained; filled up, refrained again;
Planned, built him round with splendor, won ap-
plause,
Made large alliances with men and things,
Read deep in science and philosophy,
To fortify his soul; heard lectures prove
The present ill, and future good; observed
His pulse beat regular, extended hope;
Thought, dissipated thought, and thought again;
Indulged, abstained, and tried a thousand schemes,
To ward thy blow, or hide thee from his eye;
But still thy gloomy terrors, dipped in sin,
Before him frowned, and withered all his joy.
Still, feared and hated thing! thy ghostly shape
Stood in his avenues of fairest hope;
Unmannerly and uninvited, crept
Into his haunts of most select delight.
Still, on his halls of mirth, and banqueting,
And revelry, thy shadowy hand was seen
Writing thy name of—Death. Vile worm, that gnawed
The root of all his happiness terrene, the gall
Of all his sweet, the thorn of every rose
Of earthly bloom, cloud of his noon-day sky,
Frost of his spring, sigh of his loudest laugh,
Dark spot on every form of loveliness,
Rank smell amidst his rarest spiceries,
Harsh dissonance of all his harmony,
Reserve of every promise, and the if

Of all to-morrows!—now, beyond thy vale,
Stood all the ransomed multitude of men,
Immortal all: and, in their visions, saw
Thy visage grim no more. Great payment day!
Of all thou ever conquered, none was left
In thy unpeopled realms, so populous once.
He, at whose girdle hang the keys of death,
And life, not bought but with the blood of Him
Who wears, the eternal Son of God, that morn,
Dispelled the cloud that sat so long, so thick,
So heavy o'er thy vale; opened all thy doors,
Unopened before; and set thy prisoners free.
Vain was resistance, and to follow vain.
In thy unveiled caves, and solitudes
Of dark and dismal emptiness, thou satst,
Rolling thy hollow eyes, disabled thing!
Helpless, despised, unpitied, and unfeared,
Like some fallen tyrant, chained in sight of all
The people; from thee dropped thy pointless dart,
Thy terrors withered all, thy ministers,
Annihilated, fell before thy face,
And on thy maw eternal Hunger seized.

Nor yet, sad monster! wast thou left alone.
In thy dark dens some phantoms still remained,—
Ambition, Vanity, and earthly Fame,
Swollen Ostentation, meagre Avarice,
Mad Superstition, smooth Hypocrisy,
And Bigotry intolerant, and Fraud,
And wilful Ignorance, and sullen Pride,
Hot Controversy, and the subtle ghost
Of vain Philosophy, and worldly Hope,
And sweet-lipped, hollow-hearted Flattery.
All these, great personages once on earth,
And not unfollowed, nor unpraised, were left,
Thy ever-unredeemed, and with thee driven

To Erebus, through whose uncheered wastes,
Thou mayest chase them, with thy broken scythe
Fetching vain strokes, to all eternity,
Unsatisfied, as men who, in the days
Of Time, their unsubstantial forms pursued.

THE

COURSE OF TIME.

BOOK VIII.

ANALYSIS OF BOOK VIII.

The Bard describes the appearance of the vast Assembly of men gathered for the Final Judgment.

All were divested of the extraneous circumstances by which they were distinguished in life, each retaining simply his moral character. Various classes in the Assembly are particularized; the lover of fame, the logician, the recluse, the bigot, the indolent, the sceptic, the dupe of fashion, the unforgiving parent, the seducer, the dishonest judge and advocate, the liar, duellist, suicide, hypocrite, the slanderer, the ungodly minister, the man of envy.

When the Bard has named these classes, and presented their character, and their feelings in the awful Assembly, the Spirit whose inquiries had given occasion for the Bard's communications, asks whether any of the several classes of the unholy ever actually believed themselves advancing to a future Bar of Judgment. The answer is given that they did not. The word of God was properly and perfectly believed by none of them; the necessary and certain fruit of faith being obedience and holiness.

THE

COURSE OF TIME.

BOOK VIII.

Reanimated, now, and dressed in robes
Of everlasting wear, in the last pause
Of expectation, stood the human race,
Buoyant in air, or covering shore and sea,
From east to west, thick as the eared grain,
In golden autumn waved, from field to field,
Profuse, by Nilus' fertile wave, while yet
Earth was, and men were in her valleys seen.

Still, all was calm in heaven. Nor yet appeared
The Judge, nor aught appeared, save here and there,
On wing of golden plumage borne at will,
A curious angel, that from out the skies
Now glanced a look on man, and then retired.
As calm was all on earth. The ministers
Of God's unsparing vengeance, waited, still
Unbid. No sun, no moon, no star, gave light.
A blessed and holy radiance, travelled far
From day original, fell on the face
Of men, and every countenance revealed;
Unpleasant to the bad, whose visages
Had lost all guise of seeming happiness,
With which on earth such pains they took to hide
Their misery in. On their grim features, now
The plain, unvisored index of the soul,

The true, untampered witness of the heart,
No smile of hope, no look of vanity
Beseeching for applause, was seen; no scowl
Of self-important, all-despising pride,
That once upon the poor and needy fell,
Like winter on the unprotected flower,
Withering their very being to decay.
No jesting mirth, no wanton leer, was seen,
No sullen lower of braggart fortitude
Defying pain, nor anger, nor revenge;
But fear instead, and terror, and remorse;
And chief, one passion, to its answering, shaped
The features, of the damned, and in itself
Summed all the rest,—unutterable despair.

What on the righteous shone of foreign light,
Was all redundant day, they needed not.
For as, by nature, Sin is dark, and loves
The dark, still hiding from itself in gloom,
And in the darkest hell is still itself
The darkest hell, and the severest wo,
Where all is wo; so Virtue, ever fair!
Doth by a sympathy as strong as binds
Two equal hearts, well pleased in wedded love,
For ever seek the light, for ever seek
All fair and lovely things, all beauteous forms,
All images of excellence and truth;
And from her own essential being, pure
As flows the fount of life that spirits drink,
Doth to herself give light, nor from her beams,
As native to her as her own existence,
Can be divorced, nor of her glory shorn,—
Which now, from every feature of the just,
Divinely rayed, yet not from all alike;
In measure, equal to the soul's advance
In virtue, was the lustre of the face.

It was a strange assembly: none, of all
That congregation vast, could recollect
Aught like it in the history of man.
No badge of outward state was seen, no mark
Of age, or rank, or national attire,
Or robe professional, or air of trade.
Untitled, stood the man that once was called
My lord, unserved, unfollowed; and the man
Of tithes, right reverend in the dialect
Of Time addressed, ungowned, unbeneficed,
Uncorpulent; nor now, from him who bore,
With ceremonious gravity of step,
And face of borrowed holiness o'erlaid,
The ponderous book before the awful priest,
And opened and shut the pulpit's sacred gates
In style of wonderful observancy
And reverence excessive, in the beams
Of sacerdotal splendor lost, or if
Observed, comparison ridiculous scarce
Could save the little, pompous, humble man
From laughter of the people,—not from him
Could be distinguished then the priest untithed.
None levees held, those marts where princely smiles
Were sold for flattery, and obeisance mean,
Unfit from man to man; none came or went,
None wished to draw attention, none was poor,
None rich, none young, none old, deformed none;
None sought for place or favor, none had aught
To give, none could receive, none ruled, none served;
No king, no subject was; unscutcheoned all,
Uncrowned, unplumed, unhelmed, unpedigreed,
Unlaced, uncoroneted, unbestarred.
Nor countryman was seen, nor citizen;
Republican, nor humble advocate
Of monarchy; nor idle worshipper,
Nor beaded papist, nor Mahometan;

Episcopalian none, nor presbyter;
Nor Lutheran, nor Calvanist, nor Jew,
Nor Greek, nor sectary of any name.
Nor, of those persons, that loud title bore,
Most high and mighty, most magnificent,
Most potent, most august, most worshipful,
Most eminent, words of great pomp, that pleased
The ear of vanity, and made the worms
Of earth mistake themselves for gods,—could one
Be seen, to claim these phrases obsolete.

It was a congregation vast of men,
Of unappendaged and unvarnished men,
Of plain, unceremonious human beings,
Of all but moral character bereaved.
His vice, or virtue, now, to each remained,
Alone. All else, with their grave-clothes, men had
Put off, as badges worn by mortal, not
Immortal man; alloy that could not pass
The scrutiny of Death's refining fires;
Dust of Time's wheels, by multitudes pursued
Of fools that shouted—Gold! fair painted fruit,
At which the ambitious idiot jumped, while men
Of wiser mood immortal harvest reaped;
Weeds of the human garden, sprung from earth's
Adulterate soil, unfit to be transplanted,
Though by the mortal botanist, too oft,
For plants of heavenly seed mistaken and nursed,
Mere chaff, that Virtue, when she rose from earth,
And waved her wings to gain her native heights,
Drove from the verge of being, leaving Vice
No mask to hide her in; base-born of Time,
In which God claimed no property, nor had
Prepared for them a place in heaven or hell.
Yet did these vain distinctions, now forgot,
Bulk largely in the filmy eye of Time,

And were exceeding fair, and lured to death
Immortal souls. But they were passed, for all
Ideal now was passed; reality
Alone remained; and good and bad, redeemed
And unredeemed, distinguished sole the sons
Of men. Each, to his proper self reduced,
And undisguised, was what his seeming showed.

The man of earthly fame, whom common men
Made boast of having seen, who scarce could pass
The ways of Time, for eager crowds that pressed
To do him homage, and pursued his ear
With endless praise, for deeds unpraised above,
And yoked their brutal natures, honored much
To drag his chariot on,—unnoticed stood,
With none to praise him, none to flatter there.

Blushing and dumb, that morning, too, was seen
The mighty reasoner, he who deeply searched
The origin of things, and talked of good
And evil, much, of causes and effects,
Of mind and matter, contradicting all
That went before him, and himself, the while,
The laughing-stock of angels; diving far
Below his depth, to fetch reluctant proof,
That he himself was mad and wicked too,
When, proud and ignorant man, he meant to prove
That God had made the universe amiss,
And sketched a better plan. Ah! foolish sage!
He could not trust the word of Heaven, nor see
The light which from the Bible blazed,—that lamp
Which God threw from his palace down to earth,
To guide his wandering children home,—yet leaned
His cautious faith on speculations wild,
And visionary theories absurd,
Prodigiously, deliriously absurd,

Compared with which, the most erroneous flight
That poet ever took when warm with wine,
Was moderate conjecturing: he saw,
Weighed in the balance of eternity,
His lore how light, and wished, too late, that he
Had staid at home, and learned to know himself,
And done, what peasants did, disputed less,
And more obeyed. Nor less he grieved his time
Misspent, the man of curious research,
Who travelled far through lands of hostile clime
And dangerous inhabitant, to fix
The bounds of empires passed, and ascertain
The burial-place of heroes, never born;
Despising present things, and future too,
And groping in the dark unsearchable
Of finished years,—by dreary ruins seen,
And dungeons damp, and vaults of ancient waste,
With spade and mattock, delving deep to raise
Old vases and dismembered idols rude;
With matchless perseverance, spelling out
Words without sense. Poor man! he clapped his hands
Enraptured, when he found a manuscript
That spoke of pagan gods; and yet forgot
The God who made the sea and sky, alas!
Forgot that trifling was a sin; stored much
Of dubious stuff, but laid no treasure up
In heaven; on mouldered columns scratched his name,
But ne'er inscribed it in the book of life.

Unprofitable seemed, and unapproved,
That day, the sullen, self-vindictive life
Of the recluse. With crucifixes hung,
And spells, and rosaries, and wooden saints,
Like one of reason reft, he journeyed forth,

In show of miserable poverty,
And chose to beg,—as if to live on sweat
Of other men, had promised great reward;
On his own flesh inflicted cruel wounds,
With naked foot embraced the ice, by the hour
Said mass, and did most grievous penance vile;
And then retired to drink the filthy cup
Of secret wickedness, and fabricate
All lying wonders, by the untaught received
For revelations new. Deluded wretch!
Did he no know, that the most Holy One
Required a cheerful life and holy heart?

Most disappointed in that crowd of men,
The man of subtle controversy stood,
The bigot theologian, in minute
Distinctions skilled, and doctrines unreduced
To practice; in debate how loud! how long!
How dexterous! in Christian love how cold!
His vain conceits were orthodox alone.
The immutable and heavenly truth, revealed
By God, was naught to him. He had an art,
A kind of hellish charm, that made the lips
Of truth speak falsehood, to his liking turned
The meaning of the text, made trifles seem
The marrow of salvation; to a word,
A name, a sect, that sounded in the ear,
And to the eye so many letters showed,
But did no more,—gave value infinite;
Proved still his reasoning best, and his belief,
Though propped on fancies wild as madmen's dreams,
Most rational, most scriptural, most sound;
With mortal heresy denouncing all
Who in his arguments could see no force.
On points of faith, too fine for human sight,
And never understood in heaven, he placed

His everlasting hope, undoubting placed,
And died; and, when he opened his ear, prepared
To hear, beyond the grave, the minstrelsy
Of bliss, he heard, alas! the wail of wo.
He proved all creeds false but his own, and found,
At last, his own most false—most false, because
He spent his time to prove all others so.

O, love-destroying, cursed Bigotry!
Cursed in heaven, but cursed more in hell,
Where millions curse thee, and must ever curse!
Religion's most abhorred! perdition's most
Forlorn! God's most abandoned! hell's most damned!
The infidel, who turned his impious war
Against the walls of Zion, on the rock
Of ages built, and higher than the clouds,
Sinned, and received his due reward; but she
Within her walls sinned more. Of Ignorance
Begot, her daughter, Persecution, walked
The earth, from age to age, and drank the blood
Of God's peculiar children, and was drunk,
And in her drunkenness dreamed of doing good.
The supplicating hand of innocence,
That made the tiger mild, and in his wrath
The lion pause, the groans of suffering most
Severe, were naught to her; she laughed at groans;
No music pleased her more, and no repast
So sweet to her, as blood of men redeemed
By blood of Christ. Ambition's self, though mad,
And nursed on human gore, with her compared,
Was merciful. Nor did she always rage.
She had some hours of meditation, set
Apart, wherein she to her study went,
The Inquisition, model most complete
Of perfect wickedness, where deeds were done,—
Deeds! let them ne'er be named,—and sat and planned

Deliberately, and with most musing pains,
How, to extremest thrill of agony,
The flesh, and blood, and souls of holy men,
Her victims, might be wrought; and when she saw
New tortures of her laboring fancy born,
She leaped for joy, and made great haste to try
Their force—well pleased to hear a deeper groan.

But now her day of mirth was passed, and come
Her day to weep, her day of bitter groans,
And sorrow unbemoaned, the day of grief
And wrath retributory poured in full
On all that took her part. The man of sin,
The mystery of iniquity, her friend
Sincere, who pardoned sin, unpardoned still,
And in the name of God blasphemed, and did
All wicked, all abominable things,
Most abject stood, that day, by devils hissed,
And by the looks of those he murdered, scorched:
And plagued with inward shame, that on his cheek
Burned, while his votaries, who left the earth,
Secure of bliss, around him, undeceived,
Stood, undeceivable till then; and knew,
Too late, him fallible, themselves accursed,
And all their passports and certificates,
A lie: nor disappointed more, nor more
Ashamed, the Mussulman, when he saw, gnash
His teeth and wail, whom he expected judge.
All these were damned for bigotry, were damned,
Because they thought that they alone served God,
And served him most, when most they disobeyed.

Of those forlorn and sad, thou mightst have marked,
In number most innumerable, stand
The indolent; too lazy these to make
Inquiry for themselves, they stuck their faith

To some well-fatted priest, with offerings bribed
To bring them oracles of peace, and take
Into his management all the concerns
Of their eternity; managed how well
They knew, that day, and might have sooner known,
That the commandment was, Search, and believe
In Me, and not in man; who leans on him
Leans on a broken reed, that will impierce
The trusted side. I am the way, the truth,
The life, alone, and there is none besides.

This did they read, and yet refused to search,
To search what easily was found, and, found,
Of price uncountable. Most foolish, they
Thought God with ignorance pleased, and blinded faith,
That took not root in reason, purified
With holy influence of his Spirit pure;
So, on they walked, and stumbled in the light
Of noon, because they would not open their eyes;
Effect how sad of sloth! that made them risk
Their piloting to the eternal shore,
To one who could mistake the lurid flash
Of hell for heaven's true star, rather than bow
The knee, and by one fervent word obtain
His guidance sure, who calls the stars by name.
They prayed by proxy, and at second hand
Believed, and slept, and put repentance off,
Until the knock of death awoke them, when
They saw their ignorance both, and him they paid
To bargain of their souls 'twixt them and God,
Fled, and began repentance without end.
How did they wish, that morning, as they stood
With blushing covered, they had for themselves
The Scripture searched, had for themselves believed,
And made acquaintance with the Judge ere then.

Great day of termination to the joys
Of sin! to joys that grew on mortal boughs,
On trees whose seed fell not from heaven, whose top
Reached not above the clouds. From such, alone,
The epicure took all his meals. In choice
Of morsels for the body, nice he was,
And scrupulous, and knew all wines by smell
Or taste, and every composition knew
Of cookery; but grossly drank, unskilled,
The cup of spiritual pollution up,
That sickened his soul to death, while yet his eyes
Stood out with fat. His feelings were his guide.
He ate, and drank, and slept, and took all joys,
Forbid and unforbid, as impulse urged
Or appetite, nor asked his reason why.
He said, he followed Nature still, but lied;
For she was temperate and chaste, he full
Of wine and all adultery; her face
Was holy, most unholy his; her eye
Was pure, his shot unhallowed fire; her lips
Sang praise to God, his uttered oaths profane;
Her breath was sweet, his rank with foul debauch
Yet pleaded he a kind and feeling heart,
Even when he left a neighbor's bed defiled.
Like migratory fowls, that flocking sailed
From isle to isle, steering by sense alone,
Whither the clime their liking best beseemed;
So he was guided, so he moved through good
And evil, right and wrong, but, ah! to fate
All different; they slept in dust, unpained;
He rose, that day, to suffer endless pain.

Cured of his unbelief, the skeptic stood,
Who doubted of his being while he breathed,
Than whom glossography itself, that spoke
Huge folios of nonsense every hour,

And left, surrounding every page, its marks
Of prodigal stupidity, scarce more
Of folly raved. The tyrant, too, who sat
In grisly council, like a spider couched,
With ministers of locust countenance,
And made alliances to rob mankind,
And holy termed,—for still, beneath a name
Of pious sound, the wicked sought to veil
Their crimes,—forgetful of his right divine,
Trembled, and owned oppression was of hell;
Nor did the uncivil robber, who unpursed
The traveller on the highway, and cut
His throat, anticipate severer doom.

In that assembly there was one, who, while
Beneath the sun, aspired to be a fool;
In different ages known by different names,
Not worth repeating here. Be this enough:
With scrupulous care exact, he walked the rounds
Of fashionable duty, laughed when sad;
When merry, wept; deceiving, was deceived;
And flattering, flattered. Fashion was his god.
Obsequiously he fell before its shrine,
In slavish plight, and trembled to offend.
If graveness suited, he was grave; if else,
He travailed sorely, and made brief repose,
To work the proper quantity of sin.
In all submissive, to his changing shape,
Still changing, girded he his vexed frame,
And laughter made to men of sounder head.
Most circumspect he was of bows, and nods,
And salutations; and most seriously
And deeply meditated he of dress;
And in his dreams saw lace and ribbons fly.
His soul was naught; he damned it, every day,
Unceremoniously. Oh! fool of fools!

Pleased with a painted smile, he fluttered on,
Like fly of gaudy plume, by fashion driven,
As faded leaves by Autumn's wind, till Death
Put forth his hand, and drew him out of sight.
Oh ! fool of fools ! polite to man ; to God
Most rude ; yet had he many rivals, who,
Age after age, great striving made to be
Ridiculous, and to forget they had
Immortal souls, that day remembered well.

As rueful stood his other half, as wan
Of cheek. Small her ambition was, but strange.
The distaff, needle, all domestic cares,
Religion, children, husband, home, were things
She could not bear the thought of, bitter drugs,
That sickened her soul. The house of wanton mirth
And revelry, the mask, the dance, she loved,
And in their service soul and body spent
Most cheerfully. A little admiration,
Or true or false, no matter which, pleased her,
And o'er the wreck of fortune lost, and health
And peace, and an eternity of bliss
Lost, made her sweetly smile. She was convinced,
That God had made her greatly out of taste ;
And took much pains to make herself anew.
Bedaubed with paint, and hung with ornaments
Of curious selection, gaudy toy !
A show unpaid for, paying to be seen !
As beggar by the way, most humbly asking
The alms of public gaze,—she went abroad.
Folly admired, and indication gave
Of envy, cold Civility made bows
And smoothly flattered, Wisdom shook his head,
And Laughter shaped his lip into a smile ;
Sobriety did stare, Forethought grew pale,
And Modesty hung down the head and blushed,

And Pity wept, as, on the frothy surge
Of fashion tossed, she passed them by, like sail
Before some devilish blast, and got no time
To think, and never thought, till on the rock
She dashed, of ruin, anguish, and despair.

O how unlike this giddy thing in Time!
And at the day of judgment how unlike,
The modest, meek, retiring dame! Her house
Was ordered well, her children taught the way
Of life, who, rising up in honor, called
Her blessed. Best pleased to be admired at home,
And hear, reflected from her husband's praise,
Her own, she sought no gaze of foreign eye;
His praise alone, and faithful love, and trust
Reposed, was happiness enough for her.
Yet who, that saw her pass, and heard the poor
With earnest benedictions on her steps
Attend, could from obeisance keep his eye,
Or tongue from due applause? In virtue fair,
Adorned with modesty, and matron grace
Unspeakable, and love, her face was like
The light, most welcome to the eye of man,
Refreshing most, most honored, most desired,
Of all he saw in the dim world below.
As morning when she shed her golden locks,
And on the dewy top of Hermon walked,
Or Zion hill; so glorious was her path.
Old men beheld, and did her reverence,
And bade their daughters look, and take from her
Example of their future life; the young
Admired, and new resolve of virtue made.
And none who was her husband asked; his air
Serene, and countenance of joy, the sign
Of inward satisfaction, as he passed
The crowd, or sat among the elders, told.

In holiness complete, and in the robes
Of saving righteousness, arrayed for heaven,
How fair, that day, among the fair, she stood!
How lovely on the eternal hills her steps!

Restored to reason, on that morn, appeared
The lunatic, who raved in chains, and asked
No mercy when he died. Of lunacy,
Innumerous were the causes; humbled pride,
Ambition disappointed, riches lost,
And bodily disease, and sorrow, oft
By man inflicted on his brother man;
Sorrow that made the reason drunk, and yet
Left much untasted--so the cup was filled;
Sorrow that, like an ocean, dark, deep, rough,
And shoreless, rolled its billows o'er the soul
Perpetually, and without hope of end.

Take one example, one of female wo.
Loved by a father and a mother's love,
In rural peace she lived, so fair, so light
Of heart, so good, and young, that reason, scarce,
The eye could credit, but would doubt, as she
Did stoop to pull the lily or the rose
From morning's dew, if it reality
Of flesh and blood, or holy vision, saw,
In imagery of perfect womanhood.
But short her bloom, her happiness was short.
One saw her loveliness, and, with desire
Unhallowed, burning, to her ear addressed
Dishonest words: "Her favor was his life,
His heaven; her frown his wo, his night, his death.
With turgid phrase, thus wove in flattery's loom,
He on her womanish nature won, and age
Suspicionless, and ruined, and forsook.
For he a chosen villain was at heart,

And capable of deeds that durst not seek
Repentance. Soon her father saw her shame,
His heart grew stone, he drove her forth to want
And wintry winds, and with a horrid curse
Pursued her ear, forbidding all return.

Upon a hoary cliff, that watched the sea,
Her babe was found—dead. On its little cheek,
The tear that nature bade it weep, had turned
An ice-drop, sparkling in the morning beam;
And to the turf its helpless hands were frozen.
For she, the woful mother, had gone mad,
And laid it down, regardless of its fate,
And of her own. Yet had she many days
Of sorrow in the world, but never wept.
She lived on alms, and carried in her hand
Some withered stalks she gathered in the spring.
When any asked the cause, she smiled and said,
They were her sisters, and would come and watch
Her grave when she was dead. She never spoke
Of her deceiver, father, mother, home,
Or child, or heaven, or hell, or God, but still
In lonely places walked, and ever gazed
Upon the withered stalks, and talked to them;
Till, wasted to the shadow of her youth,
With wo too wide to see beyond, she died—
Not unatoned for by imputed blood,
Nor by the Spirit that mysterious works,
Unsanctified. Aloud, her father cursed,
That day, his guilty pride, which would not own
A daughter, whom the God of heaven and earth
Was not ashamed to call his own; and he,
Who ruined her, read from her holy look,
That pierced him with perdition manifold,
His sentence, burning with vindictive fire.

The judge that took a bribe; he who amiss
Pleaded the widow's cause, and by delay
Delaying ever, made the law at night
More intricate than at the dawn, and on
The morrow farther from a close, than when
The sun last set, till he who in the suit
Was poorest, by his emptied coffers, proved
His cause the worst; and he that had the bag
Of weights deceitful, and the balance false;
And he that with a fraudful lip deceived
In buying or in selling;—these, that morn,
Found custom no excuse for sin, and knew
Plain dealing was a virtue, but too late.
And he that was supposed to do nor good
Nor ill, surprised, could find no neutral ground,
And learned, that to do nothing was to serve
The devil, and transgress the laws of God.
The noisy quack, that by profession lied,
And uttered falsehoods of enormous size,
With countenance as grave as truth beseemed;
And he that lied for pleasure, whom a lust
Of being heard and making people stare,
And a most steadfast hate of silence, drove
Far wide of sacred truth, who never took
The pains to think of what he was to say,
But still made haste to speak, with weary tongue,
Like copious stream for ever flowing on;—
Read clearly in the lettered heavens, what, long
Before, they might have read, For every word
Of folly, you, this day, shall give account;
And every liar shall his portion have
Among the cursed, without the gates of life.

With groans that made no pause, lamenting there
Were seen the duellist and suicide.

This thought, but thought amiss, that of himself
He was entire proprietor; and so,
When he was tired of Time, with his own hand,
He opened the portals of Eternity,
And sooner than the devils hoped, arrived
In hell. The other, of resentment quick,
And for a word, a look, a gesture, deemed
Not scrupulously exact in all respect,
Prompt to revenge, went to the cited field,
For double murder armed, his own, and his
That as himself he was ordained to love.
The first, in pagan books of early times,
Was heroism pronounced, and greatly praised.
In fashion's glossary of later days,
The last was honor called, and spirit high.
Alas! 'twas mortal spirit, honor which
Forgot to wake at the last trumpet's voice,
Bearing the signature of Time alone,
Uncurrent in Eternity, and base.
Wise men suspected this before; for they
Could never understand what honor meant,
Or why that should be honor termed, which made
Man murder man, and broke the laws of God
Most wantonly. Sometimes, indeed, the grave,
And those of Christian creed imagined, spoke
Admiringly of honor, lauding much
The noble youth, who, after many rounds
Of boxing, died; or, to the pistol shot
His breast exposed, his soul to endless pain.
But they who most admired, and understood
This honor best, and on its altar laid
Their lives, most obviously were fools; and, what
Fools only, and the wicked, understood,
The wise agreed was some delusive Shade,
That with the mist of time should disappear.

Great day of revelation! in the grave
The hypocrite had left his mask, and stood
In naked ugliness. He was a man
Who stole the livery of the court of heaven,
To serve the devil in; in virtue's guise,
Devoured the widow's house and orphan's bread;
In holy phrase transacted villanies
That common sinners durst not meddle with.
At sacred feast, he sat among the saints,
And with his guilty hands touched holiest things,
And none of sin lamented more, or sighed
More deeply, or with graver countenance,
Or longer prayer, wept o'er the dying man,
Whose infant children, at the moment, he
Planned how to rob. In sermon style he bought,
And sold, and lied; and salutations made
In scripture terms. He prayed by quantity,
And with his repetitions long and loud,
All knees were weary. With one hand he put
A penny in the urn of poverty,
And with the other took a shilling out.
On charitable lists,—those trumps which told
The public ear, who had in secret done
The poor a benefit, and half the alms
They told of, took themselves to keep them sounding:
He blazed his name, more pleased to have it there
Than in the book of life. Seest thou the man!
A serpent with an angel's voice! a grave
With flowers bestrewed! and yet few were deceived.
His virtues being over-done, his face
Too grave, his prayers too long, his charities
Too pompously attended, and his speech
Larded too frequently and out of time
With serious phraseology,—were rents
That in his garments opened in spite of him,
Through which the well-accustomed eye could see

The rottenness of his heart. None deeper blushed,
As in the all-piercing light he stood, exposed,
No longer herding with the holy ones.
Yet still he tried to bring his countenance
To sanctimonious seeming; but, meanwhile,
The shame within, now visible to all,
His purpose balked. The righteous smiled, and even
Despair itself some signs of laughter gave,
As ineffectually he strove to wipe
His brow, that inward guiltiness defiled.
Detected wretch! of all the reprobate,
None seemed maturer for the flames of hell,
Where still his face from ancient custom, wears
A holy air, which says to all that pass
Him by, "I was a hypocrite on earth."

That was the hour which measured out to each,
Impartially his share of reputation,
Correcting all mistakes, and from the name
Of the good man all slanders wiping off.
Good name was dear to all. Without it, none
Could soundly sleep, even on a royal bed,
Or drink with relish from a cup of gold;
And with it, on his borrowed straw, or by
The leafless hedge, beneath the open heavens,
The weary beggar took untroubled rest.
It was a music of most heavenly tone,
To which the heart leaped joyfully, and all
The spirits danced. For honest fame, men laid
Their heads upon the block, and, while the axe
Descended, looked and smiled. It was of price
Invaluable. Riches, health, repose,
Whole kingdoms, life, were given for it, and he
Who got it was the winner still; and he
Who sold it durst not open his ear, nor look
On human face, he knew himself so vile.

Yet it, with all its preciousness, was due
To Virtue, and around her should have shed,
Unasked, its savory smell; but Vice, deformed
Itself, and ugly, and of flavor rank,
To rob fair Virtue of so sweet an incense,
And with it to anoint and salve its own
Rotten ulcers, and perfume the path that led
To death,—strove daily by a thousand means:
And oft succeeded to make Virtue sour
In the world's nostrils, and its loathly self
Smell sweetly. Rumor was the messenger
Of defamation, and so swift that none
Could be the first to tell an evil tale;
And was, withal, so infamous for lies,
That he who of her sayings, on his creed,
The fewest entered, was deemed wisest man.
The fool, and many who had credit, too,
For wisdom, grossly swallowed all she said,
Unsifted; and although, at every word,
They heard her contradict herself, and saw,
Hourly, they were imposed upon and mocked,
Yet still they ran to hear her speak, and stared,
And wondered much, and stood aghast, and said
It could not be; and, while they blushed for shame
At their own faith, and seemed to doubt, believed,
And whom they met, with many sanctions, told.
So did experience fail to teach;—so hard
It was to learn this simple truth,—confirmed
At every corner by a thousand proofs,
That common Fame most impudently lied.

'Twas Slander filled her mouth with lying words—
Slander, the foulest whelp of Sin. The man
In whom this spirit entered was undone.
His tongue was set on fire of hell, his heart
Was black as death, his legs were faint with haste

To propagate the lie his soul had framed,
His pillow was the peace of families
Destroyed, the sigh of innocence reproached,
Broken friendships, and the strife of brotherhoods;
Yet did he spare his sleep, and hear the clock
Number the midnight watches, on his bed,
Devising mischief more; and early rose,
And made most hellish meals of good men's names.

From door to door you might have seen him speed,
Or placed amidst a group of gaping fools,
And whispering in their ears, with his foul lips.
Peace fled the neighborhood in which he made
His haunts; and, like a moral pestilence,
Before his breath, the healthy shoots and blooms
Of social joy and happiness decayed.
Fools only in his company were seen,
And those forsaken of God, and to themselves
Given up. The prudent shunned him and his house
As one who had a deadly moral plague.
And fain would all have shunned him at the day
Of judgment; but in vain. All who gave ear
With greediness, or wittingly their tongues
Made herald to his lies, around him wailed;
While on his face, thrown back by injured men,
In characters of ever-blushing shame,
Appeared ten thousand slanders, all his own.

Among the accursed, who sought a hiding place
In vain, from fierceness of Jehovah's rage,
And from the hot displeasure of the Lamb,
Most wretched, most contemptible, most vile,—
Stood the false priest, and in his conscience felt
The fellest gnaw of the Undying Worm.
And so he might, for he had on his hands
The blood of souls, that would not wipe away.

Hear what he was. He swore in sight of God
And man, to preach his master, Jesus Christ;
Yet preached himself: he swore that love of souls,
Alone, had drawn him to the church; yet strewed
The path that led to hell with tempting flowers,
And in the ear of sinners, as they took
The way of death, he whispered peace: he swore
Away all love of lucre, all desire
Of earthly pomp; and yet a princely seat
He liked, and to the clink of Mammon's box
Gave most rapacious ear. His prophecies,
He swore, were from the Lord; and yet, taught lies
For gain: with quackish ointment, healed the wounds
And bruises of the soul outside, but left,
Within, the pestilent matter unobserved,
To sap the moral constitution quite,
And soon to burst again, incurable.
He with untempered mortar daubed the walls
Of Zion, saying, Peace, when there was none.
The man who came with thirsty soul to hear
Of Jesus, went away unsatisfied;
For he another gospel preached than Paul,
And one that had no Saviour in't; and yet,
His life was worse. Faith, charity, and love,
Humility, forgiveness, holiness,
Were words well lettered in his sabbath creed;
But with his life he wrote as plain, Revenge,
Pride, tyranny, and lust of wealth and power
Inordinate, and lewdness unashamed.
He was a wolf in clothing of the lamb,
That stole into the fold of God, and on
The blood of souls, which he did sell to death,
Grew fat; and yet, when any would have turned
Him out, he cried, "Touch not the priest of God."
And that he was anointed, fools believed;
But knew, that day, he was the devil's priest,

Anointed by the hands of Sin and Death,
And set peculiarly apart to ill,—
While on him smoked the vials of perdition,
Poured measureless. Ah me! what cursing then
Was heaped upon his head by ruined souls,
That charged him with their murder, as he stood,
With eye of all the unredeemed most sad,
Waiting the coming of the Son of Man!
But let me pause, for thou hast seen his place
And punishment, beyond the sphere of love.

Much was removed that tempted once to sin.
Avarice no gold, no wine the drunkard, saw.
But Envy had enough, as heretofore,
To fill his heart with gall and bitterness.
What made the man of envy what he was,
Was worth in others, vileness in himself.
A lust of praise, with undeserving deeds,
And conscious poverty of soul: and still
It was his earnest work and daily toil,
With lying tongue, to make the noble seem
Mean as himself. On fame's high hill he saw
The laurel spread its everlasting green,
And wished to climb; but felt his knees too weak,
And stood, below, unhappy, laying hands
Upon the strong, ascending gloriously
The steps of honor, bent to draw them back,
Involving oft the brightness of their path,
In mists his breath had raised. Whene'er he heard,
As oft he did, of joy and happiness,
And great prosperity, and rising worth,
'Twas like a wave of wormwood o'er his soul
Rolling its bitterness. His joy was wo,
The wo of others. When, from wealth to want,
From praises to reproach, from peace to strife,
From mirth to tears, he saw a brother fall,

Or Virtue make a slip,—his dreams were sweet.
But chief with Slander, daughter of his own,
He took unhallowed pleasure. When she talked,
And with her filthy lips defiled the best,
His ear drew near; with wide attention gaped
His mouth; his eye, well pleased, as eager gazed
As glutton, when the dish he most desired
Was placed before him; and a horrid mirth,
At intervals, with laughter shook his sides.
The critic, too, who, for a bit of bread,
In book that fell aside before the ink
Was dry, poured forth excessive nonsense, gave
Him much delight. The critics,—some, but few,—
Were worthy men, and earned renown which had
Immortal roots; but most were weak and vile.
And, as a cloudy swarm of summer flies,
With angry hum and slender lance, beset
The sides of some huge animal; so did
They buzz about the illustrious man, and fain,
With his immortal honor, down the stream
Of fame would have descended; but, alas!
The hand of Time drove them away. They were,
Indeed, a simple race of men, who had
One only art, which taught them still to say,
Whate'er was done might have been better done;
And with this art, not ill to learn, they made
A shift to live. But, sometimes too, beneath
The dust they raised, was worth a while obscured;
And then did Envy prophesy and laugh.
O Envy! hide thy bosom, hide it deep.
A thousand snakes, with black, envenomed mouths,
Nest there, and hiss, and feed through all thy heart.

Such one I saw, here interposing, said
The new arrived in that dark den of shame,
Whom who hath seen shall never wish to see

Again. Before him, in the infernal gloom,
That omnipresent shape of Virtue stood
On which he ever threw his eye; and, like
A cinder that had life and feeling, seemed
His face, with inward pining, to be what
He could not be. As being that had burned
Continually, in slow-consuming fire,—
Half an eternity, and was to burn
For evermore, he looked. Oh! sight to be
Forgotten! thought too horrible to think!

But say, believing in such wo to come,
Such dreadful certainty of endless pain,
Could beings of forecasting mould, as thou
Entitlest men, deliberately walk on,
Unscared, and overleap their own belief
Into the lake of ever-burning fire?

Thy tone of asking seems to make reply,
And rightly seems: They did not so believe.
Not one of all thou sawst lament and wail
In Tophit, perfectly believed the word
Of God, else none had thither gone. Absurd,
To think that beings, made with reason, formed
To calculate, compare, choose, and reject,
By nature taught, and self, and every sense,
To choose the good, and pass the evil by,
Could, with full credence of a time to come,
When all the wicked should be really damned,
And cast beyond the sphere of light and love,
Have persevered in sin! Too foolish this
For folly in its prime. Can aught that thinks
And wills choose certain evil, and reject
Good, in his heart believing he does so?
Could man choose pain, instead of endless joy?
Mad supposition, though maintained by some

Of honest mind. Behold a man condemned!
Either he ne'er inquired, and therefore he
Could not believe; or, else, he carelessly
Inquired, and something other than the word
Of God received into his cheated faith;
And therefore he did not believe, but down
To hell descended, leaning on a lie.

Faith was bewildered much by men who meant
To make it clear, so simple in itself,
A thought so rudimental and so plain,
That none by comment could it plainer make.
All faith was one. In object, not in kind,
The difference lay. The faith that saved a soul,
And that which in the common truth believed,
In essence, were the same. Hear, then, what faith,
True, Christian faith, which brought salvation, was:
Belief in all that God revealed to men;
Observe, in all that God revealed to men,
In all he promised, threatened, commanded, said,
Without exception, and without a doubt.
Who thus believed, being by the Spirit touched,
As naturally the fruits of faith produced,
Truth, temperance, meekness, holiness, and love,
As human eye from darkness sought the light.
How could he else? If he, who had firm faith
The morrow's sun should rise, ordered affairs
Accordingly; if he, who had firm faith
That spring, and summer, and autumnal days,
Should pass away, and winter really come,
Prepared accordingly; if he, who saw
A bolt of death approaching, turned aside
And let it pass;—as surely did the man,
Who verily believed the word of God,
Though erring whiles, its general laws obey,
Turn back from hell, and take the way to heaven.

That faith was necessary, some alleged,
Unreined and uncontrollable by will.
Invention savoring much of hell! Indeed,
It was the master-stroke of wickedness,
Last effort of Abaddon's council dark,
To make man think himself a slave to fate,
And, worst of all, a slave to fate in faith,
For thus 'twas reasoned then: From faith alone,
And from opinion, springs all action; hence,
If faith's compelled, so is all action too:
But deeds compelled are not accountable;
So man is not amenable to God.

Arguing that brought such monstrous birth, though good
It seemed, must have been false. Most false it was,
And by the book of God condemned, throughout.
We freely own, that truth, when set before
The mind, with perfect evidence, compelled
Belief; but error lacked such witness, still:
And none, who now lament in moral night,
The word of God refused on evidence
That might not have been set aside as false.
To reason, try, choose, and reject, was free.
Hence God, by faith, acquitted, or condemned;
Hence righteous men, with liberty of will,
Believed; and hence thou sawst in Erebus
The wicked, who as freely disbelieved
What else had led them to the land of life.

THE

COURSE OF TIME.

BOOK IX.

ANALYSIS OF BOOK IX.

The Book opens with an apostrophe to Religion. The Bard resumes his narrative, and, continuing the description of the Assembly collected for Judgment, particularizes several classes of the Redeemed. While he mentions the classes, he points them out as they appear on the heavenly summits rejoicing.

First among the holy shone the faithful minister of God. The religious philosopher appeared in uncommon glory. The righteous governor and uncorrupted statesman, the man of active benevolence, and the Christian poet, were each conspicuous. None of the Redeemed were obscure, and multitudes were illustrious that had no name on earth.

The Bard mentions the effect produced on the minds of the assembled multitudes by the absolute certainties of their situation, by the correct judgments they now formed, the just impressions they had of themselves, and the predictions they saw fulfilled.

Suddenly a host of Angels appear, and the vast multitude of good and bad are separated to right and left in the final parting; the righteous being gathered with joy beneath a canopy of golden beams; the wicked bound under a dark and thundering cloud of wrath, where stood also Satan and his host, waiting for Judgment and the vengeance due to his rebellion in heaven, and his stratagems on earth. Thus separated, the Redeemed and the Reprobate stand expecting the Judge, and reading, upon either side of a bright arch bending high between them, a thrilling inscription.

THE

COURSE OF TIME.

BOOK IX.

Fairest of those that left the calm of heaven,
And ventured down to man, with words of peace,
Daughter of Grace! known by whatever name,
Religion, Virtue, Piety, or Love
Of Holiness, the day of thy reward
Was come. Ah! thou wast long despised, despised
By those thou wooedst from death to endless life.
Modest and meek, in garments white as those
That seraphs wear, and countenance as mild
As Mercy looking on Repentance' tear;
With eye of purity, now darted up
To God's eternal throne, now humbly bent
Upon thyself, and, weeping down thy cheek,
That glowed with universal love immense,
A tear, pure as the dews that fall in heaven;
In thy left hand, the olive branch, and in
Thy right, the crown of immortality;—
With noiseless foot, thou walkedst the vales of earth,
Beseeching men, from age to age, to turn
From utter death, to turn from wo to bliss;
Beseeching evermore, and evermore
Despised—not evermore despised, not now,
Not at the day of doom; most lovely then,
Most honorable, thou appeared, and most
To be desired. The guilty heard the song

Of thy redeemed, how loud! and saw thy face,
How fair! Alas! it was too late! the hour
Of making friends was passed, thy favor then
Might not be sought; but recollection, sad
And accurate, as miser counting o'er
And o'er again the sum he must lay out,
Distinctly in the wicked's ear rehearsed
Each opportunity despised and lost,
While on them gleamed thy holy look, that like
A fiery torrent went into their souls.
The day of thy reward was come, the day
Of great remuneration to thy friends,
To those, known by whatever name, who sought,
In every place, in every time, to do
Unfeignedly their Maker's will, revealed,
Or gathered else from nature's school; well pleased
With God's applause alone, that, like a stream
Of sweetest melody, at still of night
By wanderer heard, in their most secret ear
For ever whispered, Peace; and, as a string
Of kindred tone awoke, their inmost soul
Responsive answered, Peace; inquiring still
And searching, night and day, to know their duty,
When known, with undisputing trust, with love
Unquenchable, with zeal, by reason's lamp
Inflamed,—performing; and to Him, by whose
Profound, all-calculating skill alone,
Results—results even of the slightest act,
Are fully grasped, with unsuspicious faith,
All consequences leaving; to abound,
Or want, alike prepared; who knew to be
Exalted how, and how to be abased;
How best to live, and how to die when asked.
Their prayers sincere, their alms in secret done,
Their fightings with themselves, their abstinence
From pleasure, though by mortal eye unseen,

Their hearts of resignation to the will
Of Heaven, their patient bearing of reproach
And shame, their charity, and faith, and hope,—
Thou didst remember, and in full repaid.
No bankrupt thou, who at the bargained hour
Of payment due, sent to his creditors
A tale of losses and mischances, long.
Ensured by God himself, and from the stores
And treasures of his wealth, at will supplied,—
Religion, thou alone, of all that men,
On earth, gave credit, to be reimbursed
On the other side the grave, didst keep thy word,
Thy day, and all thy promises fulfilled.

As in the mind, rich with unborrowed wealth,
Where multitudes of thoughts for utterance strive,
And all so fair, that each seems worthy first
To enter on the tongue, and from the lips
Have passage forth,—selection hesitates
Perplexed, and loses time, anxious, since all
Cannot be taken, to take the best; and yet
Afraid, lest what he left be worthier still;
And grieving much, where all so goodly look,
To leave rejected one, or in the rear
Let any be obscured: so did the bard,
Though not unskilled, as on that multitude
Of men who once awoke to judgment, he
Threw back reflection, hesitating pause.
For as his harp, in tone severe, had sung
What figure the most famous sinners made,
When from the grave they rose unmasked; so did
He wish to character the good; but yet,
Among so many, glorious all, all worth
Immortal fame, with whom begin, with whom
To end, was difficult to choose; and long
His auditors, upon the tiptoe raised

Of expectation, might have kept, had not
His eye—for so it is in heaven, that what
Is needed always is at hand—beheld
That moment, on a mountain near the throne
Of God, the most renowned of the redeemed,
Rejoicing : nor who first, who most, to praise,
Debated more ; but thus, with sweeter note,
Well pleased to sing, with highest eulogy,
And first, whom God applauded most,—began.

With patient ear, thou now hast heard,—though whiles,
Aside digressing, ancient feeling turned
My lyre,—what shame the wicked had, that day,
What wailing, what remorse ; so hear, in brief,
How bold the righteous stood, the men redeemed,
How fair in virtue, and in hope how glad !
And first among the holy shone, as best
Became, the faithful minister of God.

See where he walks on yonder mount that lifts
Its summit high, on the right hand of bliss,
Sublime in glory, talking with his peers
Of the incarnate Saviour's love, and passed
Affliction lost in present joy ! See how
His face with heavenly ardor glows, and how
His hand, enraptured, strikes the golden lyre !
As now, conversing of the Lamb, once slain,
He speaks ; and now, from vines that never hear
Of winter, but in monthly harvest yield
Their fruit abundantly, he plucks the grapes
Of life ! But what he was on earth it most
Behoves to say. Elect by God himself,
Anointed by the Holy Ghost, and set
Apart to the great work of saving men ;
Instructed fully in the will divine,

Supplied with grace in store, as need might ask,
And with the stamp and signature of heaven,
Truth, mercy, patience, holiness, and love.
Accredited ;—he was a man, by God,
The Lord, commissioned to make known to men
The eternal counsels ; in his Master's name,
To treat with them of everlasting things,
Of life, death, bliss, and wo ; to offer terms
Of pardon, grace, and peace, to the rebelled ;
To teach the ignorant soul, to cheer the sad ;
To bind, to loose, with all authority,
To give the feeble strength, the hopeless hope.
To help the halting, and to lead the blind;
To warn the careless, heal the sick of heart,
Arouse the indolent, and on the proud
And obstinate offender to denounce
The wrath of God. All other men, what name
Soe'er they bore, whatever office held,
If lawful held,—the magistrate supreme,
Or else subordinate, were chosen by men,
Their fellows, and from men derived their power,
And were accountable for all they did,
To men; but he, alone, his office held
Immediately from God, from God received
Authority, and was to none but God
Amenable. The elders of the church,
Indeed, upon him laid their hands, and set
Him visibly apart to preach the word
Of life; but this was merely outward rite,
And decent ceremonial, performed
On all alike, and oft, as thou hast heard,
Performed on those God never sent ; his call,
His consecration, his anointing, all
Were inward, in the conscience heard and felt.
Thus, by Jehovah chosen, and ordained
To take into his charge the souls of men,

And for his trust to answer at the day
Of judgment,—great plenipotent of heaven,
And representative of God on earth,—
Fearless of men and devils; unabashed
By sin enthroned, or mockery of a prince,
Unawed by armed legions, unseduced
By offered bribes, burning with love to souls
Unquenchable, and mindful still of his
Great charge and vast responsibility;—
High in the temple of the living God,
He stood, amidst the people, and declared
Aloud the truth, the whole revealed truth,
Ready to seal it with his blood. Divine
Resemblance most complete! with mercy now
And love, his face, illumed, shone gloriously;
And frowning now indignantly, it seemed
As if offended Justice, from his eye,
Streamed forth vindictive wrath! Men heard, alarmed;
The uncircumcised infidel believed;
Light-thoughted Mirth grew serious, and wept;
The laugh profane sunk in a sigh of deep
Repentance; the blasphemer, kneeling, prayed,
And, prostrate in the dust, for mercy called;
And cursed, old, forsaken sinners gnashed
Their teeth, as if their hour had been arrived.
Such was his calling, his commission such.
Yet he was humble, kind, forgiving, meek,
Easy to be entreated, gracious, mild;
And, with all patience and affection, taught,
Rebuked, persuaded, solaced, counselled, warned,
In fervent style and manner. Needy, poor,
And dying men, like music, heard his feet
Approach their beds; and guilty wretches took
New hope, and in his prayers wept and smiled,
And blessed him, as they died forgiven; and all

Saw in his face contentment, in his life,
The path to glory and perpetual joy.
Deep-learned in the philosophy of heaven,
He searched the causes out of good and ill,
Profoundly calculating their effects
Far past the bounds of Time; and balancing,
In the arithmetic of future things,
The loss and profit of the soul to all
Eternity. A skilful workman he
In God's great moral vineyard: what to prune
With cautious hand he knew, what to uproot;
What were mere weeds, and what celestial plants,
Which had unfading vigor in them, knew;
Nor knew alone, but watched them night and day,
And reared and nourished them, till fit to be
Transplanted to the paradise below.

Oh! who can speak his praise? great, humble man!
He in the current of destruction stood,
And warned the sinner of his wo; led on
Immanuel's members in the evil day;
And, with the everlasting arms embraced
Himself around, stood in the dreadful front
Of battle, high, and warred victoriously
With death and hell. And now was come his rest,
His triumph day. Illustrious like a sun,
In that assembly, he, shining from far,
Most excellent in glory, stood assured,
Waiting the promised crown, the promised throne,
The welcome and approval of his Lord.
Nor one alone, but many—prophets, priests,
Apostles, great reformers, all that served
Messiah faithfully, like stars appeared
Of fairest beam; and round them gathered, clad
In white, the vouchers of their ministry—
The flock their care had nourished, fed, and saved.

Nor yet in common glory blazing, stood
The true philosopher, decided friend
Of truth and man. Determined foe of all
Deception, calm, collected, patient, wise.
And humble, undeceived by outward shape
Of things, by fashion's revelry uncharmed,
By honor unbewitched,—he left the chase
Of vanity, and all the quackeries
Of life, to fools and heroes, or whoe'er
Desired them; and with reason, much despised,
Traduced, yet heavenly reason, to the shade
Retired—retired, but not to dream, or build
Of ghostly fancies, seen in the deep noon
Of sleep, ill-balanced theories; retired,
But did not leave mankind; in pity, not
In wrath, retired; and still, though distant, kept
His eye on men; at proper angle took
His stand to see them better, and, beyond
The clamor which the bells of folly made,
That most had hung about them, to consult
With nature, how their madness might be cured,
And how their true substantial comforts might
Be multiplied. Religious man! what God
By prophets, priests, evangelists, revealed
Of sacred truth, he thankfully received,
And, by its light directed, went in search
Of more. Before him, darkness fled; and all
The goblin tribe, that hung upon the breasts
Of Night, and haunted still the moral gloom
With shapeless forms, and blue, infernal lights,
And indistinct, and devilish whisperings,
That the miseducated fancies vexed
Of superstitious men,—at his approach,
Dispersed, invisible. Where'er he went,
This lesson still he taught, To fear no ill
But sin, no being but Almighty God.

All-comprehending sage! too hard alone
For him was man's salvation; all besides,
Of use or comfort, that distinction made
Between the desperate savage, scarcely raised
Above the beast whose flesh he ate, undressed,
And the most polished of the human race,
Was product of his persevering search.
Religion owed him much, as from the false
She suffered much; for still his main design,
In all his contemplations, was to trace
The wisdom, providence, and love of God,
And to his fellows, less observant, show
Them forth. From prejudice redeemed, with all
His passions still, above the common world,
Sublime in reason and in aim sublime,
He sat, and on the marvellous works of God
Sedately thought; now glancing up his eye,
Intelligent, through all the starry dance,
And penetrating now the deep remote
Of central causes in the womb opaque
Of matter hid; now with inspection nice,
Entering the mystic labyrinths of the mind,
Where thought, of notice ever shy, behind
Thought, disappearing, still retired; and still,
Thought meeting thought, and thought awakening thought,
And mingling still with thought in endless maze,—
Bewildered observation; now, with eye
Yet more severely purged, looking far down
Into the heart, where passion wove a web
Of thousand thousand threads, in grain and hue
All different; then, upward venturing whiles,
But reverently, and in his hand, the light
Revealed, near the eternal Throne, he gazed,
Philosophizing less than worshipping.
Most truly great! his intellectual strength

And knowledge vast, to men of lesser mind,
Seemed infinite; yet, from his high pursuits,
And reasonings most profound, he still returned
Home, with an humbler and a warmer heart:
And none so lowly bowed before his God,
As none so well His awful majesty
And goodness comprehended; or so well
His own dependency and weakness knew.

How glorious now, with vision purified
At the Essential Truth, entirely free
From error, he, investigating still,—
For knowledge is not found, unsought, in heaven,—
From world to world, at pleasure, roves, on wing
Of golden ray upborne; or, at the feet
Of heaven's most ancient sages, sitting, hears
New wonders of the wondrous works of God!

Illustrious, too, that morning, stood the man
Exalted by the people, to the throne
Of government, established on the base
Of justice, liberty, and equal right;
Who, in his countenance sublime, expressed
A nation's majesty, and yet was meek
And humble; and in royal palace gave
Example to the meanest, of the fear
Of God, and all integrity of life
And manners; who, august, yet lowly; who,
Severe, yet gracious; in his very heart,
Detesting all oppression, all intent
Of private aggrandizement; and, the first
In every public duty, held the scales
Of justice, and as the law, which reigned in him,
Commanded, gave rewards; or, with the edge
Vindictive, smote, now light, now heavily,
According to the stature of the crime.

Conspicuous like an oak of healthiest bough,
Deep-rooted in his country's love, he stood,
And gave his hand to virtue, helping up
The honest man to honor and renown;
And, with the look which goodness wears in wrath,
Withering the very blood of Knavery,
And from his presence driving far, ashamed.

Nor less remarkable, among the blessed,
Appeared the man, who, in the senate-house,
Watchful, unhired, unbribed, and uncorrupt,
And party only to the common weal,
In virtue's awful rage, pleaded for right,
With truth so clear, with argument so strong,
With action so sincere, and tone so loud
And deep, as made the despot quake behind
His adamantine gates, and every joint,
In terror, smite his fellow-joint relaxed;
Or, marching to the field, in burnished steel,
While, frowning on his brow, tremendous hung
The wrath of a whole people, long provoked,—
Mustered the stormy wings of war, in day
Of dreadful deeds; and led the battle on,
When Liberty, swift as the fires of heaven,
In fury rode, with all her hosts, and threw
The tyrant down, or drove invasion back.
Illustrious he—illustrious all appeared,
Who ruled supreme in righteousness; or held
Inferior place, in steadfast rectitude
Of soul. Peculiarly severe had been
The nurture of their youth, their knowledge great,
Great was their wisdom, great their cares, and great
Their self-denial, and their service done
To God and man; and great was their reward,
At hand, proportioned to their worthy deeds.

Breathe all thy minstrelsy, immortal Harp !
Breathe numbers warm with love, while I rehearse—
Delighted theme, resembling most the songs
Which, day and night, are sung before the Lamb !—
Thy praise, O Charity ! thy labors most
Divine ; thy sympathy with sighs, and tears,
And groans ; thy great, thy god-like wish, to heal
All misery, all fortune's wounds, and make
The soul of every living thing rejoice.
O thou wast needed much in days of Time !
No virtue, half so much !—None half so fair !
To all the rest, however fine, thou gavest
A finishing and polish, without which
No man e'er entered heaven. Let me record
His praise, the man of great benevolence,
Who pressed thee closely to his glowing heart,
And to thy gentle bidding made his feet
Swift minister. Of all mankind, his soul
Was most in harmony with heaven ; as one
Sole family of brothers, sisters, friends,
One in their origin, one in their rights
To all the common gifts of providence,
And in their hopes, their joys, and sorrows one,
He viewed the universal human race.
He needed not a law of state, to force
Grudging submission to the law of God.
The law of love was in his heart, alive ;
What he possessed, he counted not his own ;
But, like a faithful steward in a house
Of public alms, what freely he received
He freely gave, distributing to all
The helpless the last mite beyond his own
Temperate support, and reckoning still the gift
But justice, due to want ; and so it was,
Although the world, with compliment not ill
Applied, adorned it with a fairer name.

Nor did he wait till to his door the voice
Of supplication came, but went abroad,
With foot as silent as the starry dews,
In search of misery that pined unseen,
And would not ask. And who can tell what sights
He saw! what groans he heard, in that cold world
Below! where Sin, in league with gloomy Death,
Marched daily through the length and breadth of all
The land, wasting at will, and making earth,
Fair earth! a lazar-house, a dungeon dark,
Where Disappointment fed on ruined Hope;
Where Guilt, worn out, leaned on the triple edge
Of want, remorse, despair; where Cruelty
Reached forth a cup of wormwood to the lips
Of Sorrow, that to deeper Sorrow wailed;
Where Mockery, and Disease, and Poverty
Met miserable Age, erewhile sore bent
With his own burden; where the arrowy winds
Of winter pierced the naked orphan babe,
And chilled the mother's heart, who had no home;
And where, alas! in mid-time of his day,
The honest man, robbed by some villain's hand,
Or with long sickness pale, and paler yet
With want and hunger, oft drank bitter draughts
Of his own tears, and had no bread to eat.
Oh! who can tell what sights he saw, what shapes
Of wretchedness! or who describe what smiles
Of gratitude illumined the face of wo,
While from his hand he gave the bounty forth!
As when the Sun, to Cancer wheeling back,
Returned from Capricorn, and showed the north,
That long had lain in cold and cheerless night,
His beamy countenance; all nature then
Rejoiced together glad; the flower looked up
And smiled; the forest, from his locks, shook off
The hoary frosts, and clapped his hands; the birds

Awoke, and, singing, rose to meet the day;
And from his hollow den, where many months
He slumbered sad in darkness, blithe and light
Of heart the savage sprung, and saw again
His mountains shine, and with new songs of love
Allured the virgin's ear: so did the house,
The prison-house of guilt, and all the abodes
Of unprovided helplessness, revive,
As on them looked the sunny messenger
Of Charity. By angels tended still,
That marked his deeds, and wrote them in a book
Of God's remembrance; careless he to be
Observed of men, or have each mite bestowed
Recorded punctually, with name and place,
In every bill of news. Pleased to do good,
He gave, and sought no more, nor questioned much,
Nor reasoned, who deserved; for well he knew
The face of need. Ah me! who could mistake?
The shame to ask, the want that urged within,
Composed a look so perfectly distinct
From all else human, and withal so full
Of misery, that none could pass, untouched,
And be a Christian, or thereafter claim,
In any form, the name or rights of man,
Or, at the day of judgment, lift his eye;
While he, in name of Christ, who gave the poor
A cup of water, or a bit of bread,
Impatient for his advent, waiting stood,
Glowing in robes of love and holiness,
Heaven's fairest dress! and round him ranged, in white,
A thousand witnesses appeared, prepared
To tell his gracious deeds before the Throne.

Nor unrenowned among the most renowned,
Nor 'mong the fairest unadmired, that morn,

When highest fame was proof of highest worth,
Distinguished stood the bard; not he, who sold
The incommunicable, heavenly gift,
To Folly, and with lyre of perfect tone,
Prepared by God himself, for holiest praise,—
Vilest of traitors! most dishonest man!—
Sat by the door of Ruin, and made there
A melody so sweet, and in the mouth
Of drunkenness and debauch, that else had croaked
In natural discordance jarring harsh,
Put so divine a song, that many turned
Aside, and entered in undone, and thought,
Meanwhile, it was the gate of heaven, so like
An angel's voice the music seemed; nor he,
Who, whining grievously of damsel coy,
Or blaming fortune, that would nothing give
For doing naught, in indolent lament
Unprofitable, passed his piteous days,
Making himself the hero of his tale,
Deserving ill the poet's name: but he,
The bard, by God's own hand anointed, who,
To Virtue's all-delighting harmony,
His numbers tuned: who, from the fount of truth,
Poured melody, and beauty poured, and love,
In holy stream, into the human heart;
And, from the height of lofty argument,
Who "justified the ways of God to man,"
And sung what still he sings, approved in heaven;
Though now with bolder note, above the damp
Terrestrial, which the pure celestial fire
Cooled, and restrained in part his flaming wing.

Philosophy was deemed of deeper thought,
And judgment more severe, than Poetry;
To fable, she, and fancy, more inclined.
And yet, if Fancy, as was understood,

Was of creative nature, or of power,
With self-wrought stuff, to build a fabric up,
To mortal vision wonderful and strange,
Philosophy, the theoretic, claimed,
Undoubtedly, the first and highest place
In Fancy's favor. Her material souls,
Her chance, her atoms shaped alike, her white
Proved black, her universal nothing, all;
And all her wondrous systems, how the mind
With matter met; how man was free, and yet
All pre-ordained; how evil first began;
And chief her speculations, soaring how,
Of the eternal, uncreated Mind,
Which left all reason infinitely far
Behind—surprising feat of theory!—
Were pure creation of her own, webs wove
Of gossamer in Fancy's lightest loom.
And nowhere, on the list of being made
By God recorded: but her look, meanwhile,
Was grave and studious; and many thought
She reasoned deeply, when she wildly raved.

The true, legitimate, anointed bard,
Whose song through ages poured its melody,
Was most severely thoughtful, most minute
And accurate of observation, most
Familiarly acquainted with all modes
And phases of existence. True, no doubt,
He had originally drunk, from out
The fount of life and love, a double draught,
That gave whate'er he touched a double life:
But this was mere desire at first, and power
Devoid of means to work by; need was still
Of persevering, quick, inspective mood
Of mind, of faithful memory, vastly stored,
From universal being's ample field,

With knowledge; and a judgment, sound and clear,
Well disciplined in nature's rules of taste;
Discerning to select, arrange, combine,
From infinite variety, and still
To nature true; and guide withal, hard task,
The sacred, living impetus divine,
Discreetly through the harmony of song.
Completed thus, the poet sung; and age
To age, enraptured, heard his measures flow;
Enraptured, for he poured the very fat
And marrow of existence, through his verse,
And gave the soul, that else, in selfish cold,
Unwarmed by kindred interest, had lain,
A roomy life, a glowing relish high,
A sweet, expansive brotherhood of being—
Joy answering joy, and sigh responding sigh,
Through all the fibres of the social heart.
Observant, sympathetic, sound of head,
Upon the ocean vast of human thought,
With passion rough and stormy, venturing out
Even as the living billows rolled, he threw
His numbers over them, seized as they were,
And to perpetual ages left them fixed,
To each, a mirror of itself displayed;
Despair for ever lowering dark on Sin,
And Happiness on Virtue smiling fair.

He was a minister of fame, and gave
To whom he would renown; nor missed himself—
Although despising much the idiot roar
Of popular applause, that sudden, oft,
Unnaturally turning, whom it nursed
Itself devoured—the lasting fame, the praise
Of God and holy men, to excellence given.
Yet less he sought his own renown, than wished
To have the eternal images of truth

And beauty, pictured in his verse, admired.
'Twas these, taking immortal shape and form
Beneath his eye, that charmed his midnight watch,
And oft his soul with awful transports shook
Of happiness, unfelt by other men.
This was that spell, that sorcery, which bound
The poet to the lyre, and would not let
Him go ; that hidden mystery of joy,
Which made him sing in spite of fortune's worst,
And was, at once, both motive and reward.

Nor now among the choral harps, in this
The native clime of song, are those unknown,
With higher note ascending, who, below,
In holy ardor, aimed at lofty strains.
True fame is never lost: many, whose names
Were honored much on earth, are famous here
For poetry, and, with archangel harps,
Hold no unequal rivalry in song ;
Leading the choirs of heaven, in numbers high,
In numbers ever sweet and ever new.

Behold them yonder, where the river pure
Flows warbling down before the throne of God ;
And, shading on each side, the tree of life
Spreads its unfading boughs !—See how they shine,
In garments white, quaffing deep draughts of love,
And harping on their harps, new harmonies
Preparing for the ear of God, Most High !

But why should I, of individual worth,
Of individual glory, longer sing ?
No true believer was, that day, obscure ;
No holy soul but had enough of joy ;
No pious wish without its full reward.
Who in the Father and the Son believed,

With faith that wrought by love to holy deeds,
And purified the heart, none trembled there,
Nor had by earthly guise his rank concealed;
Whether, unknown, he tilled the ground remote,
Observant of the seasons, and adored
God in the promise, yearly verified,
Of seed-time, harvest, summer, winter, day
And night, returning duly at the time
Appointed; or, on the shadowy mountain side,
Worshipped at dewy eve, watching his flocks;
Or, trading, saw the wonders of the deep,
And as the needle to the starry Pole
Turned constantly, so he his heart to God;
Or else, in servitude severe, was taught
To break the bonds of sin; or, begging, learned
To trust the Providence that fed the raven,
And clothed the lily with her annual gown.

Most numerous, indeed, among the saved,
And many, too, not least illustrious, shone
The men who had no name on earth. Eclipsed
By lowly circumstance, they lived unknown,
Like stream that in the desert warbles clear,
Still nursing, as it goes, the herb and flower,
Though never seen; or like the star, retired
In solitudes of ether, far beyond
All sight, not of essential splendor less,
Though shining unobserved. None saw their pure
Devotion, none their tears, their faith, and love,
Which burned within them, both to God and man,—
None saw but God. He, in his bottle, all
Their tears preserved, and every holy wish
Wrote in his book; and, not as they had done,
But as they wished with all their heart to do,
Arrayed them now in glory, and displayed,—

No longer hid by coarse, uncourtly garb,—
In lustre equal to their inward worth.

Man's time was passed, and his eternity
Begun. No fear remained of change. The youth,
Who, in the glowing morn of vigorous life,
High-reaching after great religious deeds,
Was suddenly cut off, with all his hopes
In sunny bloom, and unaccomplished left
His withered aims,—saw everlasting days,
Before him, dawning, rise, in which to achieve
All glorious things, and get himself the name
That jealous Death too soon forbade on earth.

Old things had passed away, and all was new;
And yet, of all the new-begun, naught so
Prodigious difference made, in the affairs
And thoughts of every man, as certainty.
For doubt, all doubt, was gone, of every kind;
Doubt that erewhile, beneath the lowest base
Of mortal reasonings, deepest laid, crept in,
And made the strongest, best cemented towers
Of human workmanship, so weakly shake,
And to their lofty tops so waver still,
That those who built them, feared their sudden fall.
But doubt, all doubt, was passed; and, in its place,
To every thought that in the heart of man
Was present, now had come an absolute,
Unquestionable certainty, which gave
To each decision of the mind immense
Importance, raising to its proper height
The sequent tide of passion, whether joy
Or grief. The good man knew, in very truth,
That he was saved to all eternity,
And feared no more; the bad had proof complete,
That he was damned for ever; and believed

Entirely, that on every wicked soul
Anguish should come, and wrath, and utter wo.

Knowledge was much increased, but wisdom more.
The film of Time, that still before the sight
Of mortal vision danced, and led the best
Astray, pursuing unsubstantial dreams,
Had dropped from every eye. Men saw that they
Had vexed themselves in vain, to understand
What now no hope to understand remained;
That they had often counted evil good,
And good for ill; laughed when they should have
wept,
And wept, forlorn, when God intended mirth.
But what, of all their follies passed, surprised
Them most, and seemed most totally insane
And unaccountable, was value set
On objects of a day, was serious grief
Or joy for loss or gain of mortal things.
So utterly impossible it seemed,
When men their proper interests saw, that aught
Of terminable kind, that aught, which e'er
Could die, or cease to be, however named,
Should make a human soul—a legal heir
Of everlasting years—rejoice or weep,
In earnest mood; for nothing now seemed worth
A thought, but had eternal bearing in't.

Much truth had been assented to in Time,
Which never, till this day, had made a due
Impression on the heart. Take one example.
Early from heaven it was revealed, and oft
Repeated in the world, from pulpits preached,
And penned and read in holy books, that God
Respected not the persons of mankind.
Had this been truly credited and felt,

The king, in purple robe, had owned, indeed,
The beggar for his brother; pride of rank
And office thawed into paternal love;
Oppression feared the day of equal rights,
Predicted; covetous extortion kept
In mind the hour of reckoning, soon to come;
And bribed injustice thought of being judged,
When he should stand, on equal foot, beside
The man he wronged, and surely—nay, 'tis true,
Most true, beyond all whispering of doubt,
That he, who lifted up the reeking scourge,
Dripping with gore from the slave's back, before
He struck again, had paused, and seriously
Of that tribunal thought, where God himself
Should look him in the face, and ask in wrath,
"Why didst thou this? Man! was he not thy brother,
Bone of thy bone, and flesh and blood of thine?"
But, ah! this truth, by heaven and reason taught,
Was never fully credited on earth.
The titled, flattered, lofty men of power,
Whose wealth bought verdicts of applause for deeds
Of wickedness, could ne'er believe the time
Should truly come when judgment should proceed
Impartially against them, and they, too,
Have no good speaker at the Judge's ear,
No witnesses to bring them off for gold,
No power to turn the sentence from its course;
And they of low estate, who saw themselves,
Day after day, despised, and wronged, and mocked,
Without redress, could scarcely think the day
Should e'er arrive, when they, in truth, should stand
On perfect level with the potentates
And princes of the earth, and have their cause
Examined fairly, and their rights allowed.
But now this truth was felt, believed and felt,

That men were really of a common stock,
That no man ever had been more than man.

Much prophecy—revealed by holy bards,
Who sung the will of heaven by Judah's streams—
Much prophecy, that waited long the scoff
Of lips uncircumcised, was then fulfilled;
To the last tittle scrupulously fulfilled.
It was foretold by those of ancient days,
A time should come, when wickedness should weep
Abased; when every lofty look of man
Should be bowed down, and all his haughtiness
Made low; when righteousness alone should lift
The head in glory, and rejoice at heart;
When many, first in splendor and renown,
Should be most vile; and many, lowest once,
And last in Poverty's obscurest nook,
Highest and first in honor, should be seen,
Exalted; and when some, when all the good,
Should rise to glory and eternal life;
And all the bad, lamenting, wake, condemned
To shame, contempt, and everlasting grief.

These prophecies had tarried long, so long
That many wagged the head, and, taunting, asked,
"When shall they come?" but asked no more, nor mocked;
For the reproach of prophecy was wiped
Away, and every word of God found true.

And, oh! what change of state, what change of rank,
In that assembly everywhere was seen!
The humble-hearted laughed, the lofty mourned,
And every man, according to his works
Wrought in the body, there took character.

Thus stood they mixed, all generations stood!
Of all mankind, innumerable throng!
Great harvest of the grave!—waiting the will
Of heaven, attentively, and silent all,
As forest spreading out beneath the calm
Of evening skies, when even the single leaf
Is heard distinctly rustle down and fall;
So silent they, when from above, the sound
Of rapid wheels approached, and suddenly
In heaven appeared a host of angels strong,
With chariots and with steeds of burning fire:
Cherub, and Seraph, Thrones, Dominions, Powers,
Bright in celestial armor, dazzling, rode.
And, leading in the front, illustrious shone
Michael and Gabriel, servants long approved
In high commission,—girt that day with power,
Which naught created, man or devil, might
Resist. Nor waited, gazing, long; but, quick
Descending, silently and without song,
As servants bend to do their master's work,
To middle air they raised the human race,
Above the path long travelled by the sun;
And as a shepherd from the sheep divides
The goats; or husbandman, with reaping bands,
In harvest, separates the precious wheat,
Selected from the tares; so did they part
Mankind, the good and bad, to right and left,
To meet no more; these ne'er again to smile,
Nor those to weep; these never more to share
Society of mercy with the saints,
Nor, henceforth, those to suffer with the vile.
Strange parting! not for hours, nor days, nor months,
Nor for ten thousand times ten thousand years;
But for a whole eternity!—though fit,
And pleasant to the righteous, yet to all
Strange, and most strangely felt! The sire, to right

Retiring, saw the son—sprung from his loins,
Beloved how dearly once; but who forgot,
Too soon, in sin's intoxicating cup,
The father's warnings and the mother's tears—
Fall to the left among the reprobate;
And sons, redeemed, beheld the fathers, whom
They loved and honored once, gathered among
The wicked. Brothers, sisters, kinsmen, friends;
Husband and wife, who ate at the same board,
And under the same roof, united, dwelt,
From youth to hoary age, bearing the chance
And change of Time together, parted then
For evermore. But none, whose friendship grew
From virtue's pure and everlasting root,
Took different roads; these, knit in stricter bonds
Of amity, embracing, saw no more
Death, with his scythe, stand by; nor heard the word,
The bitter word, which closed all earthly friendships,
And finished every feast of love—Farewell.
To all, strange parting! to the wicked, sad
And terrible! New horror seized them, while
They saw the saints withdrawing, and with them
All hope of safety, all delay of wrath.

Beneath a crown of rosy light,—like that
Which once, in Goshen, on the flocks, and herds,
And dwellings, smiled, of Jacob, while the land
Of Nile was dark; or like the pillar bright
Of sacred fire, that stood above the sons
Of Israel, when they camped at midnight by
The foot of Horeb, or the desert side
Of Sinai;—now, the righteous took their place,
All took their place, who ever wished to go
To heaven, for heaven's own sake. Not one remained
Among the accursed, that e'er desired with all
The heart to be redeemed, that ever sought

Submissively to do the will of God,
Howe'er it crossed his own; or to escape
Hell, for aught other than its penal fires.
All took their place, rejoicing, and beheld,
In centre of the crown of golden beams
That canopied them o'er, these gracious words,
Blushing with tints of love: "Fear not, my saints."

To other sight of horrible dismay,
Jehovah's ministers the wicked drove,
And left them bound immovable in chains
Of Justice. O'er their heads a bowless cloud
Of indignation hung; a cloud it was
Of thick and utter darkness, rolling, like
An ocean, tides of livid, pitchy flame;
With thunders charged, and lightnings ruinous,
And red with forked vengeance, such as wounds
The soul; and full of angry shapes of wrath,
And eddies whirling with tumultuous fire,
And forms of terror raving to and fro,
And monsters unimagined heretofore,
By guilty men in dreams before their death,
From horrid to more horrid changing still,
In hideous movement through that stormy gulf;
And evermore the Thunders, murmuring, spoke
From out the darkness, uttering loud these words,
Which every guilty conscience echoed back:
"Ye knew your duty, but ye did it not."
Dread words! that barred excuse, and threw the weight
Of every man's perdition on himself,
Directly home. Dread words! heard then, and heard
For ever through the wastes of Erebus.
"Ye knew your duty, but ye did it not!"
These were the words which glowed upon the sword,
Whose wrath burned fearfully behind the cursed,

As they were driven away from God to Tophet.
"Ye knew your duty, but ye did it not!"
These are the words to which the harps of grief
Are strung; and, to the chorus of the damned,
The rocks of hell repeat them, evermore;
Loud echoed through the caverns of despair,
And poured in thunder on the ear of Wo.

Nor ruined men alone, beneath that cloud,
Trembled. There, Satan and his legions stood,
Satan, the first and eldest sinner,—bound
For judgment. He, by other name, held once
Conspicuous rank in heaven among the sons
Of happiness, rejoicing, day and night.
But pride, that was ashamed to bow to God,
Most High, his bosom filled with hate, his face
Made black with envy, and in his soul begot
Thoughts guilty of rebellion 'gainst the throne
Of the Eternal Father and the Son,—
From everlasting built on righteousness.

Ask not how pride, in one created pure,
Could grow; or sin without example spring,
Where holiness alone was sown: esteem't
Enough, that he, as every being made
By God, was made entirely holy, had
The will of God before him set for law
And regulation of his life, and power
To do as bid; but was, meantime, left free,
To prove his worth, his gratitude, his love;
How proved besides? for how could service done
That might not else have been withheld, evince
The will to serve, which, rather than the deed,
God doth require, and virtue counts alone?
To stand or fall, to do or leave undone,
Is reason's lofty privilege, denied

To all below, by instinct bound to fate,
Unmeriting, alike, reward or blame.

Thus free, the Devil chose to disobey
The will of God, and was thrown out from heaven,
And with him all his bad example stained:
Yet not to utter punishment decreed,
But left to fill the measure of his sin,
In tempting and seducing man—too soon,
Too easily seduced! And, from the day
He first set foot on earth,—of rancor full,
And pride, and hate, and malice, and revenge,—
He set himself, with most felonious aim
And hellish perseverance, to root out
All good, and in its place to plant all ill;
To rub and raze, from all created things,
The fair and holy portraiture divine,
And on them to enstamp his features grim,
To draw all creatures off from loyalty
To their Creator, and to make them bow
The knee to him. Nor failed of great success,
As populous hell, this day, can testify.
He held, indeed, large empire in the world,
Contending proudly with the King of heaven.
To him temples were built, and sacrifice
Of costly blood upon his altars flowed;
And—what best pleased him, for in show he seemed
Then likest God—whole nations, bowing, fell
Before him, worshipping, and from his lips
Entreated oracles, which he, by priests,
For many were his priests in every age,—
Answered, though guessing but at future things,
And erring oft, yet still believed; so well
His ignorance, in ambiguous phrase, he veiled.

Nor needs it wonder, that with man once fallen,
His tempting should succeed. Large was his mind

And understanding; though impaired by sin,
Still large; and constant practice, day and night,
In cunning, guile, and all hypocrisy,
From age to age, gave him experience vast
In sin's dark tactics, such as boyish man,
Unarmed by strength divine, could ill withstand.
And well he knew his weaker side; and still,
His lures, with baits that pleased the senses, busked
To his impatient passions offering terms
Of present joy, and bribing reason's eye
With earthly wealth, and honors near at hand.
Nor failed to misadvise his future hope
And faith, by false, unkerneled promises
Of heavens of sensual gluttony and love,
That suited best their grosser appetites.
Into the sinner's heart, who lived secure,
And feared him least, he entered at his will.
But chief, he chose his residence in courts
And conclaves, stirring princes up to acts
Of blood and tyranny; and moving priests
To barter truth, and swap the souls of men
For lusty benefices, and address
Of lofty sounding. Nor the saints elect,
Who walked with God, in virtue's path sublime,
Did he not sometimes venture to molest;
In dreams and moments of unguarded thought,
Suggesting guilty doubts and fears, that God
Would disappoint their hope; and in their way
Bestrewing pleasures, tongued so sweet, and so
In holy garb arrayed, that many stooped,
Believing them of heavenly sort, and fell;
And to their high professions, brought disgrace
And scandal; to themselves, thereafter, long
And bitter nights of sore repentance, vexed
With shame, unwonted sorrow, and remorse.

And more they should have fallen, and more have wept,
Had not their guardian angels, who, by God
Commissioned, stood beside them in the hour
Of danger, whether craft, or fierce attack,
To Satan's deepest skill opposing skill
More deep, and to his strongest arm, an arm
More strong,—upborne them in their hands, and filled
Their souls with all discernment, quick, to pierce
His stratagems and fairest shows of sin.

Now, like a roaring lion, up and down
The world, destroying, though unseen, he raged;
And now, retiring back to Tartarus,
Far back, beneath the thick of guiltiest dark,
Where night ne'er heard of day, in council grim,
He sat with ministers whose thoughts were damned,
And there such plans devised, as, had not God
Checked and restrained, had added earth entire
To hell, and uninhabited left heaven,
Jehovah unadored. Nor unsevere,
Even then, his punishment deserved. The Worm
That never dies, coiled in his bosom, gnawed
Perpetually; sin after sin brought pang
Succeeding pang; and, now and then, the bolts
Of Zion's King, vindictive, smote his soul
With fiery wo to blast his proud designs;
And gave him earnest of the wrath to come.
And chief, when, on the cross, Messiah said,
"'Tis finished," did the edge of vengeance smite
Him through, and all his gloomy legions touch
With new despair. But yet, to be the first
In mischief, to have armies at his call,
To hold dispute with God, in days of Time,
His pride and malice fed, and bore him up

Above the worst of ruin. Still, to plan
And act great deeds, though wicked, brought at least
The recompense which nature hath attached
To all activity, and aim pursued
With perseverance, good or bad; for as,
By nature's laws, immutable and just,
Enjoyment stops where indolence begins;
And purposeless, to-morrow borrowing sloth,
Itself, heaps on its shoulders loads of wo,
Too heavy to be borne; so industry—
To mediate, to plan, resolve, perform,
Which in itself is good—as surely brings
Reward of good, no matter what be done:
And such reward the Devil had, as long
As the decrees eternal gave him space
To work. But now, all action ceased; his hope
Of doing evil perished quite; his pride,
His courage, failed him; and beneath that cloud
Which hung its central terrors o'er his head,
With all his angels, he, for sentence, stood,
And rolled his eyes around, that uttered guilt
And wo, in horrible perfection joined.
As he had been the chief and leader, long,
Of the apostate crew that warred with God
And holiness; so now, among the bad,
Lowest, and most forlorn, and trembling most,
With all iniquity deformed and foul,
With all perdition ruinous and dark,
He stood,—example awful of the wrath
Of God! and mark, to which all sin must fall!—
And made, on every side, so black a hell,
That spirits, used to night and misery,
To distance drew, and looked another way;
And from their golden cloud, far off, the saints
Saw round him darkness grow more dark, and heard
The impatient thunderbolts, with deadliest crash

And frequentest, break o'er his head,—the sign
That Satan, there, the vilest sinner, stood.

Ah me! what eyes were there beneath that cloud!
Eyes of despair, final and certain! eyes
That looked, and looked, and saw, where'er they looked,
Interminable darkness! utter wo!

'Twas pitiful to see the early flower
Nipped by the unfeeling frost, just when it rose,
Lovely in youth, and put its beauties on.
'Twas pitiful to see the hopes of all
The year, the yellow harvest, made a heap,
By rains of judgment; or by torrents swept
With flocks and cattle, down the raging flood;
Or scattered by the winnowing winds, that bore
Upon their angry wings, the wrath of heaven.
Sad was the field, where, yesterday, was heard
The roar of war; and sad the sight of maid,
Of mother, widow, sister, daughter, wife,
Stooping and weeping over senseless, cold,
Defaced, and mangled lumps of breathless earth,
Which had been husbands, fathers, brothers, sons
And lovers, when that morning's sun arose.
'Twas sad to see the wonted seat of friend
Removed by death; and sad to visit scenes,
When old, where, in the smiling morn of life,
Lived many, who both knew and loved us much,
And they all gone, dead, or dispersed abroad;
And stranger faces seen among their hills.
'Twas sad to see the little orphan babe
Weeping and sobbing on its mother's grave.
'Twas pitiful to see an old, forlorn,
Decrepit, withered wretch, unhoused, unclad,

Starving to death with poverty and cold.
'Twas pitiful to see a blooming bride,
That promise gave of many a happy year,
Touched by decay, turn pale, and waste, and die.
'Twas pitiful to hear the murderous thrust
Of ruffian's blade that sought the life entire.
'Twas sad to hear the blood come gurgling forth
From out the throat of the wild suicide.
Sad was the sight of widowed, childless age
Weeping.—I saw it once. Wrinkled with time,
And hoary with the dust of years, an old
And worthy man came to his humble roof,
Tottering and slow, and on the threshold stood.
No foot, no voice, was heard within. None came
To meet him, where he had oft met a wife,
And sons, and daughters, glad at his return;
None came to meet him; for that day had seen
The old man lay, within the narrow house,
The last of all his family; and now
He stood in solitude, in solitude
Wide as the world; for all, that made to him
Society, had fled beyond its bound.
Wherever strayed his aimless eye, there lay
The wreck of some fond hope, that touched his soul
With bitter thoughts, and told him all was passed.
His lonely cot was silent, and he looked
As if he could not enter. On his staff,
Bending, he leaned; and from his weary eye,
Distressing sight! a single tear-drop wept.
None followed, for the fount of tears was dry.
Alone and last, it fell from wrinkle down
To wrinkle, till it lost itself, drunk by
The withered cheek, on which again no smile
Should come, or drop of tenderness be seen.
This sight was very pitiful; but one
Was sadder still, the saddest seen in Time.

A man, to-day, the glory of his kind,
In reason clear, in understanding large,
In judgment sound, in fancy quick, in hope
Abundant, and in promise, like a field
Well cultured, and refreshed with dews from God;
To-morrow, chained, and raving mad, and whipped
By servile hands; sitting on dismal straw,
And gnashing with his teeth against the chain,
The iron chain, that bound him hand and foot;
And trying whiles to send his glaring eye
Beyond the wide circumference of his wo;
Or, humbling more, more miserable still,
Giving an idiot laugh that served to show
The blasted scenery of his horrid face;
Calling the straw his sceptre, and the stone,
On which he, pinioned, sat, his royal throne.
Poor, poor, poor man! fallen far below the brute!
His reason strove in vain to find her way,
Lost in the stormy desert of his brain;
And, being active still, she wrought all strange,
Fantastic, execrable, monstrous things.

All these were sad, and thousands more, that sleep
Forgotten beneath the funeral pall of Time;
And bards, as well became, bewailed them much,
With doleful instruments of weeping song.
But what were these? What might be worse had in't,
However small, some grains of happiness;
And man ne'er drank a cup of earthly sort,
That might not held another drop of gall;
Or, in his deepest sorrow, laid his head
Upon a pillow, set so close with thorns,
That might not held another prickle still.
Accordingly, the saddest human look
Had hope in't; faint, indeed, but still 'twas hope.
But why excuse the misery of earth?

Say it was dismal, cold, and dark, and deep,
Beyond the utterance of strongest words;
But say that none remembered it, who saw
The eye of beings damned for evermore,
Rolling, and rolling, rolling still in vain,
To find some ray, to see beyond the gulf
Of an unavenued, fierce, fiery, hot,
Interminable, dark Futurity!
And rolling still, and rolling still in vain!

Thus stood the reprobate beneath the shade
Of terror, and beneath the crown of love,
The good; and there was silence in the vault
Of heaven; and, as they stood and listened, they heard
Afar to left, among the utter dark,
Hell rolling o'er his waves of burning fire,
And thundering through his caverns, empty then,
As if he preparation made, to act
The final vengeance of the fiery Lamb.
And there was heard, coming from out the Pit,
The hollow wailing of Eternal Death,
And horrid cry of the Undying Worm.

The wicked paler turned, and scarce the good
Their color kept; but were not long dismayed.
That moment, in the heavens, how wondrous fair!
The angel Mercy stood, and, on the bad
Turning his back, over the ransomed threw
His bow, bedropped with imagery of love,
And promises on which their faith reclined.
Throughout, deep, breathless silence reigned again,
And on the circuit of the upper spheres,
A glorious seraph stood, and cried aloud,
That every ear of man and devil heard,
"Him that is filthy, let be filthy still;
Him that is holy, let be holy still."

And, suddenly, another squadron bright,
Of high, archangel glory, stooping, brought
A marvellous bow,—one base upon the Cross,
The other on the shoulder of the Bear,
They placed,—from south to north, spanning the heavens,
And on each hand dividing good and bad,—
Who read, on either side, these burning words,
Which ran along the arch in living fire,
And wanted not to be believed in full:
"As ye have sown, so shall ye reap this day."

THE

COURSE OF TIME.

BOOK X.

ANALYSIS OF BOOK X.

In the beginning the Author invokes the presence and aid of the Holy Spirit, while he interprets the notes of the ancient Bard describing the Day of Judgment.

The Bard proceeds Soon millions infinite of holy spirits are heard and seen gathering before the Eternal Throne, from heaven and from countless worlds around. Silence ensues, and from a radiant cloud the voice of God comes forth, announces to the assembled millions the object of calling them to his presence, and states that the destiny of Man is concluded, the Day of Retribution come, and the generations of Earth collected at the place of Judgment. The voice then addresses the Son Messiah, assigning to him the covenanted office of Judge. The Son, taking the Book of God's Remembrance, the Crowns of life, and the Sword of justice, and attended by the summoned millions, move forth in glory, becomes visible to the assembled sons of men, and ascends the Throne between the good and bad. An angel unfolds the book. In awful silence, the Judge waits, while every conscience attests the record. He rises to pronounce the sentence. No creature breathes; the spheres and stars, with every particle of matter, stand still.—Those trembling on the left hear a dread decree of burning words; the Sword of justice gleams and plunges in their midst; they sink in utter darkness, returning one groan of boundless wo, as Hell closes round, and the Undying Worm and Second Death begin their endless repast.—The last Fire then consumes the Earth.—Finally, the righteous hear a joyous welcome, receive their crowns, and ascend with the Judge, singing with the angels, "Glory to God and to the Lamb"

THE

COURSE OF TIME.

BOOK X.

God of my fathers! holy, just, and good!
My God! my Father! my unfailing Hope!
Jehovah! let the incense of my praise,
Accepted, burn before thy mercy-seat,
And in thy presence burn, both day and night.
Maker! Preserver! my Redeemer! God!
Whom have I in the heavens but Thee alone?
On earth, but Thee, whom should I praise, whom love?
For Thou hast brought me hitherto, upheld
By thy omnipotence; and from thy grace,
Unbought, unmerited, though not unsought—
The wells of thy salvation, hast refreshed
My spirit, watering it, at morn and even;
And, by thy Spirit, which thou freely givest
To whom thou wilt, hast led my venturous song,
Over the vale and mountain tract, the light
And shade of man; into the burning deep
Descending now, and now circling the mount,
Where highest sits Divinity enthroned;
Rolling along the tide of fluent thought,
The tide of moral, natural, divine;
Gazing on past and present, and again,
On rapid pinion borne, outstripping Time,
In long excursion, wandering through the groves

Unfading, and the endless avenues,
That shade the landscape of Eternity;
And talking there with holy angels met,
And future men, in glorious vision seen!
Nor unrewarded have I watched at night,
And heard the drowsy sound of neighboring sleep.
New thought, new imagery, new scenes of bliss
And glory, unrehearsed by mortal tongue,
Which, unrevealed, I trembling, turned and left,
Bursting at once upon my ravished eye,—
With joy unspeakable have filled my soul,
And made my cup run over with delight:
Though in my face the blasts of adverse winds,
While boldly circumnavigating man,
Winds seeming adverse, though perhaps not so,
Have beat severely; disregarded beat,
When I, behind me, heard the voice of God,
And his propitious Spirit say, Fear not!

God of my fathers! ever present God!
This offering, more, inspire, sustain, accept;
Highest, if numbers answer to the theme;
Best answering, if thy Spirit dictate most.
Jehovah! breathe upon my soul; my heart
Enlarge; my faith increase; increase my hope;
My thoughts exalt; my fancy sanctify,
And all my passions, that I near thy throne
May venture, unreproved; and sing the day,
Which none unholy ought to name, the Day
Of Judgment! greatest day, passed or to come!
Day! which,—deny me what thou wilt, deny
Me home, or friend, or honorable name,—
Thy mercy grant, I thoroughly prepared,
With comely garment of redeeming love,
May meet, and have my Judge for Advocate.

Come, Gracious Influence, Breath of the Lord,
And touch me trembling, as thou touched the man,
Greatly beloved, when he in vision saw,
By Ulai's stream, the Ancient sit; and talked
With Gabriel, to his prayer swiftly sent,
At evening sacrifice. Hold my right hand,
Almighty! hear me, for I ask through Him,
Whom thou hast heard, whom thou wilt always hear,
Thy Son, our interceding Great High Priest!
Reveal the future, let the years to come
Pass by, and open my ear to hear the harp,
The prophet harp, whose wisdom I repeat,
Interpreting the voice of distant song;—
Which thus again resumes the lofty verse,
Loftiest, if I interpret faithfully
The holy numbers which my spirit hears.

Thus came the day, the Harp again began,
The day that many thought should never come,
That all the wicked wished should never come,
That all the righteous had expected long;
Day greatly feared, and yet too little feared,
By him who feared it most; day laughed at much
By the profane, the trembling day of all
Who laughed; day when all shadows passed, all dreams;
When substance, when reality commenced;
Last day of lying, final day of all
Deceit, all knavery, all quackish phrase;
Ender of all disputing, of all mirth
Ungodly, of all loud and boasting speech;
Judge of all judgments, Judge of every judge,
Adjuster of all causes, rights and wrongs;
Day oft appealed to, and appealed to oft
By those who saw its dawn with saddest heart;
Day most magnificent in Fancy's range,

Whence she returned, confounded, trembling, pale,
With overmuch of glory faint and blind;
Day most important held, prepared for most,
By every rational, wise, and holy man;
Day of eternal gain, for worldly loss;
Day of eternal loss for worldly gain;
Great day of terror, vengeance, wo, despair;
Revealer of all secrets, thoughts, desires;
Rein-trying, heart-investigating day,
That stood between Eternity and Time,
Reviewed all past, determined all to come,
And bound all destinies for evermore;
Believing day of unbelief; great day,
That set in proper light the affairs of earth,
And justified the Government Divine;
Great day!—what can we more? what should we
more?
Great triumph day of God's incarnate Son!
Great day of glory to the Almighty God!
Day! whence the everlasting years begin
Their date, new era in eternity,
And oft referred to in the song of heaven!

Thus stood the apostate, thus the ransomed stood,
Those held by justice fast, and these by love,
Reading the fiery scutcheonry, that blazed
On high, upon the great celestial bow:
"As ye have sown, so shall ye reap this day."
All read, all understood, and all believed,
Convinced of judgment, righteousness, and sin.

Meantime the universe throughout was still.
The cope, above and round about, was calm;
And motionless, beneath them, lay the Earth,
Silent and sad, as one that sentence waits,
For flagrant crime;—when suddenly was heard,

Behind the azure vaulting of the sky,
Above, and far remote from reach of sight,
The sound of trumpets, and the sound of crowds,
And prancing steeds, and rapid chariot wheels,
That from four quarters rolled, and seemed in haste,
Assembling at some place of rendezvous;
And so they seemed to roll, with furious speed,
As if none meant to be behind the first.
Nor seemed alone; that day, the golden trump,
Whose voice, from centre to circumference
Of all created things, is heard distinct,
God had bid Michael sound, to summon all
The hosts of bliss to presence of their King;
And, all the morning, millions infinite,
That millions governed each, Dominions, Powers,
Thrones, Principalities, with all their hosts,
Had been arriving near the capital,
And royal city, New Jerusalem,
From heaven's remotest bounds. Nor yet from heaven
Alone came they, that day. The worlds around,
Or neighboring nearest on the verge of night,
Emptied, sent forth their whole inhabitants.
All tribes of being came, of every name,
From every coast, filling Jehovah's courts.
From morn till mid-day, in the squadrons poured
Immense, along the bright celestial roads.
Swiftly they rode, for love unspeakable,
To God, and to Messiah, Prince of Peace,
Drew them, and made obedience haste to be
Approved. And now, before the Eternal Throne,—
Brighter, that day, than when the Son prepared
To overthrow the seraphim rebelled,—
And circling round the mount of Deity,
Upon the sea of glass all round about,
And down the borders of the stream of life,
And over all the plains of Paradise,

For many a league of heavenly measurement,—
Assembled, stood the immortal multitudes,
Millions, above all number infinite,
The nations of the blessed. Distinguished each,
By chief of goodly stature blazing far;
By various garb, and flag of various hue
Streaming through heaven from standard lifted high—
The arms and imagery of thousand worlds.
Distinguished each, but all arrayed complete,
In armor bright, of helmet, shield, and sword;
And mounted all in chariots of fire.
A military throng, blent, not confused;
As soldiers on some day of great review
Burning in splendor of refulgent gold,
And ornament, on purpose, long devised
For this expected day. Distinguished each,
But all accoutred as became their Lord,
And high occasion; all in holiness,
The livery of the soldiery of God,
Vested; and shining all with perfect bliss,
The wages that his faithful servants win.

Thus stood they numberless around the mount
Of presence; and, adoring, waited, hushed
In deepest silence, for the voice of God.
That moment, all the Sacred Hill on high
Burned, terrible with glory, and, behind
The uncreated lustre, hid the Lamb,
Invisible; when, from the radiant cloud,
This voice, addressing all the hosts of heaven,
Proceeded, not in words as we converse,
Each with his fellow, but in language such
As God doth use, imparting, without phrase
Successive, what, in speech of creatures, seems
Long narrative, though long, yet losing much
In feeble symbols of the thought Divine.

My servants long approved, my faithful sons,
Angels of glory, Thrones, Dominions, Powers,
Well pleased, this morning, I have seen the speed
Of your obedience, gathering round my throne,
In order due, and well-becoming garb;
Illustrious, as I see, beyond your wont,
As was my wish, to glorify this day:
And now, what your assembling means, attend.

This day concludes the destiny of man.
The hour appointed from eternity,
To judge the earth, in righteousness, is come;
To end the war of Sin, that long has fought,
Permitted, against the sword of Holiness;
To give to men and devils, as their works,
Recorded in my all-remembering book,
I find; good to the good, and great reward
Of everlasting honor, joy, and peace,
Before my presence here for evermore;
And to the evil, as their sins provoke,
Eternal recompense of shame and wo,
Cast out beyond the bounds of light and love.

Long have I stood, as ye, my sons, well know,
Between the cherubim, and stretched my arms
Of mercy out, inviting all to come
To me and live; my bowels long have moved
With great compassion; and my justice passed
Trangression by, and not imputed sin.
Long here, upon my everlasting throne,
I have beheld my love and mercy scorned;
Have seen my laws despised, my name blasphemed,
My providence accused, my gracious plans
Opposed; and long, too long, have I beheld
The wicked triumph, and my saints reproached
Maliciously, while on my altars lie,

Unanswered still, their prayers and their tears,
That seek my coming, wearied with delay;
And long, Disorder in my moral reign
Has walked rebelliously, disturbed the peace
Of my eternal government, and wrought
Confusion, spreading far and wide, among
My works inferior, which groan to be
Released. Nor long shall groan. The hour of grace,
The final hour of grace, is fully passed;
The time accepted for repentance, faith,
And pardon, is irrevocably passed;
And Justice, unaccompanied, as wont,
With Mercy, now goes forth, to give to all
According to their deeds. Justice alone,—
For why should Mercy any more be joined?
What hath not mercy, mixed with judgment, done,
That mercy, mixed with judgment and reproof,
Could do? Did I not revelation make,
Plainly and clearly, of my will entire?
Before them set my holy law, and gave
Them knowledge, wisdom, prowess to obey,
And win, by self-wrought works, eternal life?
Rebelled, did I not send them terms of peace,
Which, not my justice, but my mercy asked?—
Terms, costly to my well-beloved Son;
To them, gratuitous, exacting faith
Alone for pardon, works evincing faith?
Have I not early risen, and sent my seers,
Prophets, apostles, teachers, ministers,
With signs and wonders, working in my name?
Have I not still, from age to age, raised up,
As I saw needful, great, religious men,
Gifted by me with large capacity,
And by my arm omnipotent upheld,
To pour the numbers of my mercy forth,
And roll my judgments on the ear of man?

And lastly, when the promised hour was come,—
What more could most abundant mercy do?—
Did I not send Immanuel forth, my Son,
Only begotten, to purchase, by his blood,
As many as believed upon his name?
Did he not die to give repentance, such
As I accept, and pardon of all sins?
Has he not taught, beseeched, and shed abroad
The Spirit unconfined, and given at times
Example fierce of wrath and judgment, poured
Vindictively on nations guilty long?
What means of reformation, that my Son
Has left behind, untried? what plainer words,
What arguments more strong, as yet remain?
Did he not tell them, with his lips of truth,
The righteous should be saved, the wicked damned?
And has he not, awake both day and night,
Here interceded with prevailing voice,
At my right hand, pleading his precious blood,
Which magnified my holy law, and bought
For all who wished, perpetual righteousness!
And have not you, my faithful servants, all
Been frequent forth, obedient to my will,
With messages of mercy and of love,
Administering my gifts to sinful man?
And have not all my mercy, all my love,
Been sealed and stamped with signature of heaven?
By proof of wonders, miracles, and signs
Attested, and attested more by truth
Divine, inherent in the tidings sent?
This day declares the consequence of all.
Some have believed, are sanctified, and saved,
Prepared for dwelling in this holy place,
In these their mansions, built before my face;
And now, beneath a crown of golden light,
Beyond our wall, at place of judgment, they,

Expecting, wait the promised, due reward.
The others stand with Satan, bound in chains,
The others, who refused to be redeemed:
They stand, unsanctified, unpardoned, sad,
Waiting the sentence that shall fix their wo.
The others, who refused to be redeemed;
For all had grace sufficient to believe,
All who my gospel heard; and none who heard
It not, shall by its law, this day, be tried.
Necessity of sinning, my decrees
Imposed on none; but rather, all inclined
To holiness; and grace was bountiful,
Abundant, overflowing with my word;
My word of life and peace, which to all men,
Who shall or stand or fall, by law revealed,
Was offered freely, as 'twas freely sent,
Without all money, and without all price.
Thus they have all, by willing act, despised
Me, and my Son, and sanctifying Spirit.
But now, no longer shall they mock or scorn.
The day of grace and mercy is complete,
And Godhead from their misery absolved.

So saying, He, the Father infinite,
Turning, addressed Messiah, where he sat,
Exalted gloriously, at his right hand.
This day belongs to justice and to thee,
Eternal Son, thy right for service done,
Abundantly fulfilling all my will;
By promise thine, from all eternity,
Made in the ancient Covenant of Grace;
And thine, as most befitting, since in thee
Divine and human meet, impartial Judge,
Consulting thus the interest of both.
Go then, my Son, divine similitude,
Image express of Deity unseen,

The book of my remembrance take; and take
The golden crowns of life, due to the saints;
And take the seven last thunders ruinous;
Thy armor take; gird on thy sword, thy sword
Of justice ultimate, reserved, till now,
Unsheathed, in the eternal armory;
And mount the living chariot of God.
Thou goest not now, as once, to Calvary,
To be insulted, buffeted, and slain;
Thou goest not now, with battle and the voice
Of war, as once against the rebel hosts.
Thou goest a Judge, and findst the guilty bound;
Thou goest to prove, condemn, acquit, reward.
Not unaccompanied; all these, my saints,
Go with thee, glorious retinue, to sing
Thy triumph, and participate thy joy;
And I, the Omnipresent, with thee go;
And with thee all the glory of my throne.

Thus said the Father; and the Son beloved,
Omnipotent, Omniscient, Fellow God,
Arose, resplendent with Divinity;
And He the book of God's remembrance took;
And took the seven last thunders ruinous;
And took the crowns of life, due to the saints;
His armor took; girt on his sword, his sword
Of justice ultimate, reserved, till now,
Unsheathed, in the eternal armory;
And up the living chariot of God
Ascended, signifying all complete.

And now the Trump of wondrous melody,
By man or angel never heard before,
Sounded with thunder, and the march began,
Not swift, as cavalcade, on battle bent,
But, as became procession of a judge,

Solemn, magnificent, majestic, slow;
Moving sublime with glory infinite,
And numbers infinite, and awful song,
They passed the gate of heaven, which many a league,
Opened either way, to let the glory forth
Of this great march. And now, the sons of men
Beheld their coming, which, before, they heard;
Beheld the glorious countenance of God!
All light was swallowed up, all objects seen
Faded; and the Incarnate, visible
Alone, held every eye upon him fixed;
The wicked saw his majesty severe;
And those who pierced Him saw his face with clouds
Of glory circled round, essential bright!
And to the rocks and mountains called in vain,
To hide them from the fierceness of his wrath;
Almighty power their flight restrained, and held
Them bound immovable before the bar.

The righteous, undismayed and bold,—best proof,
This day, of fortitude sincere, -sustained
By inward faith, with acclamations loud,
Received the coming of the Son of Man?
And, drawn by love, inclined to his approach,
Moving to meet the brightness of his face.

Meantime, 'tween good and bad, the Judge his wheels
Stayed, and, ascending, sat upon the great
White Throne, that morning founded there by power
Omnipotent, and built on righteousness
And truth. Behind, before, on every side,
In native and reflected blaze of bright,
Celestial equipage, the myriads stood,
That with his marching came; rank above rank,
Rank above rank, with shield and flaming sword.

'Twas silence all! and quick, on right and left,
A mighty angel spread the book of God's
Remembrance; and, with conscience now sincere
All men compared the record, written there
By finger of Omniscience; and received
Their sentence, in themselves, of joy or wo;
Condemned or justified, while yet the Judge
Waited, as if to let them prove themselves.
The righteous, in the book of life displayed,
Rejoicing, read their names; rejoicing, read
Their faith for righteousness received, and deeds
Of holiness, as proof of faith complete.
The wicked, in the book of endless death,
Spread out to left, bewailing, read their names;
And read beneath them, Unbelief, and fruit
Of unbelief, vile, unrepented deeds,
Now unrepentable for evermore;
And gave approval of the wo affixed.

This done, the Omnipotent, Omniscient Judge
Rose infinite, the sentence to pronounce,
The sentence of eternal wo or bliss!
All glory heretofore seen or conceived,
All majesty, annihilated, dropped,
That moment, from remembrance, and was lost;
And silence, deepest hitherto esteemed,
Seemed noisy to the stillness of this hour.
Comparisons I seek not, nor should find,
If sought. That silence, which all being held,
When God's Almighty Son, from off the walls
Of heaven the rebel angels threw, accursed,
So still, that all creation heard their fall
Distinctly, in the lake of burning fire,—
Was now forgotten, and every silence else.
All being rational, created then,
Around the judgment seat, intensely listened.

No creature breathed. Man, angel, devil, stood
And listened; the spheres stood still, and every
star
Stood still, and listened; and every particle,
Remotest in the womb of matter, stood,
Bending to hear, devotional and still.
And thus upon the wicked, first, the Judge
Pronounced the sentence, written before of old:
"Depart from me, ye cursed, into the fire,
Prepared eternal in the Gulf of Hell,
Where ye shall weep and wail for evermore,
Reaping the harvest which your sins have sown."

So saying, God grew dark with utter wrath;
And, drawing now the sword, undrawn before,
Which through the range of infinite, all around,
A gleam of fiery indignation threw,
He lifted up his hand omnipotent,
And down among the damned the burning edge
Plunged; and from forth his arrowy quiver sent,
Emptied, the seven last thunders ruinous,
Which, entering, withered all their souls with fire.
Then first was vengeance, first was ruin seen!
Red, unrestrained, vindictive, final, fierce!
They, howling, fled to west among the dark;
But fled not these the terrors of the Lord.
Pursued, and driven beyond the Gulf, which frowns
Impassable, between the good and bad,
And downward far remote to left, oppressed
And scorched with the avenging fires, begun
Burning within them,—they upon the verge
Of Erebus, a moment, pausing stood,
And saw, below, the unfathomable lake,
Tossing with tides of dark, tempestuous wrath;
And would have looked behind; but greater wrath,
Behind, forbade, which now no respite gave

To final misery. God, in the grasp
Of his Almighty strength, took them upraised,
And threw them down, into the yawning pit
Of bottomless perdition, ruined, damned,
Fast bound in chains of darkness evermore;
And Second Death, and the Undying Worm,
Opening their horrid jaws, with hideous yell,
Falling, received their everlasting prey.
A groan returned, as down they sunk, and sunk,
And ever sunk, among the utter dark!
A groan returned! the righteous heard the groan,
The groan of all the reprobate, when first
They felt damnation sure! and heard Hell close!
And heard Jehovah and his love retire!
A groan returned! the righteous heard the groan,
As if all misery, all sorrow, grief,
All pain, all anguish, all despair, which all
Have suffered, or shall feel, from first to last
Eternity, had gathered to one pang,
And issued in one groan of boundless wo!

And now the wall of hell, the outer wall,
First gateless then, closed round them; that which thou
Hast seen, of fiery adamant, emblazed
With hideous imagery, above all hope,
Above all flight of fancy, burning high,
And guarded evermore, by Justice, turned
To Wrath, that hears, unmoved, the endless groan
Of those wasting within; and sees, unmoved,
The endless tear of vain repentance fall.

Nor ask if these shall ever be redeemed.
They never shall! Not God, but their own sin,
Condemns them. What could be done, as thou hast heard,

Has been already done; all has been tried,
That wisdom infinite, and boundless grace,
Working together, could devise; and all
Has failed. Why now succeed? Though God should
stoop,
Inviting still, and send his Only Son
To offer grace in hell, the pride, that first
Refused, would still refuse; the unbelief,
Still unbelieving, would deride and mock;
Nay more, refuse, deride, and mock; for sin
Increasing still, and growing, day and night,
Into the essence of the soul, become
All sin, makes what in time seemed probable,—
Seemed probable, since God invited them,—
For ever now impossible. Thus they,
According to the eternal laws which bind
All creatures, bind the Uncreated One,
Though we name not the sentence of the Judge,—
Must daily grow in sin and punishment,
Made by themselves their necessary lot,
Unchangeable to all eternity.

What lot! what choice! I sing not, cannot sing.
Here, highest seraphs tremble on the lyre,
And make a sudden pause!—but thou hast seen.
And here, the bard, a moment, held his hand,
As one who saw more of that horrid wo
Than words could utter; and again resumed.

Nor yet had vengeance done. The guilty Earth,
Inanimate, debased, and stained by sin,
Seat of rebellion, of corruption long,
And tainted with mortality throughout,—
God sentenced next; and sent the final fires
Of ruin forth, to burn and to destroy.
The saints its burning saw, and thou mayest see.

Look yonder, round the lofty golden walls
And galleries of New Jerusalem,
Among the imagery of wonders passed;
Look near the southern gate; look, and behold—
On spacious canvass, touched with living hues—
The Conflagration of the ancient earth,
The handiwork of high archangel, drawn
From memory of what he saw, that day.
See! how the mountains, how the valleys burn,
The Andes burn, the Alps, the Apennines,
Taurus and Atlas; all the islands burn;
The Ocean burns, and rolls his waves of flame.
See how the lightnings, barbed, red with wrath,
Sent from the quiver of Omnipotence,
Cross and recross the fiery gloom, and burn
Into the centre!—burn without, within,
And help the native fires, which God awoke,
And kindled with the fury of his wrath.
As inly troubled, now she seems to shake;
The flames, dividing, now, a moment, fall;
And now, in one conglomerated mass,
Rising, they glow on high, prodigious blaze!
Then fall and sink again, as if, within,
The fuel, burned to ashes, was consumed.
So burned the Earth upon that dreadful day,
Yet not to full annihilation burned.
The essential particles of dust remained,
Purged, by the final, sanctifying fires,
From all corruption; from all stain of sin,
Done there by man or devil, purified.
The essential particles remained, of which
God built the world again, renewed, improved,
With fertile vale, and wood of fertile bough;
And streams of milk and honey, flowing song;
And mountains cinctured with perpetual green;
In clime and season fruitful, as at first,

When Adam woke, unfallen, in Paradise.
And God, from out the fount of native light,
A handful took of beams, and clad the sun
Again in glory; and sent forth the moon
To borrow thence her wonted rays, and lead
Her stars, the virgin daughters of the sky.
And God revived the winds, revived the tides;
And, touching her from his Almighty hand,
With force centrifugal, she onward ran,
Coursing her wonted path, to stop no more.
Delightful scene of new inhabitants!
As thou, this morn, in passing hither, sawst.

Thus done, the glorious Judge, turning to right,
With countenance of love unspeakable,
Beheld the righteous, and approved them thus:
"Ye blessed of my Father, come, ye just,
Enter the joy eternal of your Lord;
Receive your crowns, ascend, and sit with me,
At God's right hand, in glory evermore!"

Thus said the Omnipotent, Incarnate God;
And waited not the homage of the crowns,
Already thrown before him; nor the loud
Amen of universal, holy praise;
But turned the living chariot of fire,
And swifter now,—as joyful to declare
This day's proceedings in his Father's court,
And to present the number of his sons
Before the Throne,—ascended up to heaven,
And all his saints, and all his angel bands,
As, glorious, they on high ascended, sung
Glory to God and to the Lamb!—they sung
Messiah, fairer than the sons of men,
And altogether lovely. Grace is poured
Into thy lips, above all measure poured;

And therefore God hath blessed thee evermore.
Gird, gird thy sword upon thy thigh, O thou
Most Mighty! with thy glory ride; with all
Thy majesty, ride prosperously, because
Of meekness, truth, and righteousness. Thy throne,
O God, for ever and for ever stands;
The sceptre of thy kingdom still is right;
Therefore hath God, thy God, anointed thee
With oil of gladness and perfumes of myrrh,
Out of the ivory palaces, above
Thy fellows, crowned the Prince of endless peace!

Thus sung they God, their Saviour: and themselves
Prepared complete to enter now, with Christ,
Their living Head, into the Holy Place.
Behold! the daughter of the King, the bride,
All glorious within, the bride adorned,
Comely in broidery of gold! behold,
She comes, apparelled royally, in robes
Of perfect righteousness, fair as the sun,
With all her virgins, her companions fair,—
Into the Palace of the King she comes,
She comes to dwell for evermore! Awake,
Eternal harps! awake, awake, and sing!—
The Lord, the Lord, our God Almighty, reigns!

Thus the Messiah, with the hosts of bliss,
Entered the gates of heaven, unquestioned now,
Which closed behind them, to go out no more;
And stood, accepted, in his Father's sight;
Before the glorious, everlasting Throne,
Presenting all his saints; not one was lost,
Of all that he in Covenant received.
And, having given the kingdom up, he sat,
Where now he sits and reigns, on the right hand
Of glory; and our God is all in all!

Thus have I sung beyond thy first request,
Rolling my numbers o'er the track of man,
The world at dawn, at mid-day, and decline;
Time gone, the righteous saved, the wicked damned
And God's eternal government approved.

THE END.

www.ingramcontent.com/pod-product-compliance
Lightning Source LLC
LaVergne TN
LVHW021140110826
845150LV00005B/1078

* 9 7 8 1 4 2 5 5 4 8 5 6 8 *